The Social Transcript

The Social Transcript

Uncovering Library Philosophy

CHARLES B. OSBURN

Beta Phi Mu Monograph Series

LIBRARIES
UNLIMITED
A Member of the Greenwood Publishing Group
Westport, Connecticut • London

Library of Congress Cataloging-in-Publication Data

Osburn, Charles B.
The social transcript : uncovering library philosophy / Charles B. Osburn.
p. cm.—(Beta Phi Mu monograph series)
Includes bibliographical references and index.
ISBN 978-1-59158-758-3 (alk. paper)
1. Library science—Philosophy. 2. Libraries and society. I. Title.
Z665.O83 2009
020.1—dc22 2008031213

British Library Cataloguing in Publication Data is available.

Library of Congress Catalog Card Number: 2008031213
ISBN: 978-1-59158-758-3
ISSN: 1041-2751

First published in 2009

Libraries Unlimited, 88 Post Road West, Westport, CT 06881
A Member of the Greenwood Publishing Group, Inc.
www.lu.com

Printed in the United States of America

The paper used in this book complies with the Permanent Paper Standard issued by the National Information Standards Organization (Z39.48-1984).

10 9 8 7 6 5 4 3 2 1

IN MEMORIAM

Ross Atkinson, 1945–2006
The consummate scholar librarian

Contents

Prologue

> A good explanation should be more basic than the phenomena it explains and should not contain important aspects of those phenomena.
>
> —Herbert A. Simon, 1989

This book introduces a philosophy for the library in cultural evolution, specifically for its role in the integration of mind and society. Consideration of the library within the processes of cultural evolution offers a context for understanding *why* this particular social institution functions, rather than *how* it functions, and in doing so identifies the basis for an explanatory and guiding philosophy. While many fleeting glimpses into a potential library philosophy are scattered throughout the literatures of library history and library and information science, there is no comprehensive description of the library function in concept adequate to the explanation of that institution's long life. Concept of and practice in the library are confused in the mind of both the public and the scholar so often that misleading conceptions and fundamental misunderstandings about what the library is and why it exists arise quite easily. This situation emanates primarily from the strong image of practice, which is what the public sees and what most of the professional and scholarly literature addresses; in so far as the library is concerned, image of practice almost invariably overshadows concept of function.

In concept rather than in concrete, the library is a matter of rational social process, a process far more fundamental to humanity than isolated procedures and transactions would suggest. Survival of the library concept through the millennia poses a curious mystery, for the library has always existed as an institution that only expends the financial resources of its host organization or individual, never recovering enough to maintain even minimal solvency. The library neither directly saves lives nor eases physical suffering, and it offers nothing obvious to personal security within the community; yet these would seem to be the most fundamental of human needs. Therefore, I came to surmise, a philosophy that transcends individual libraries must be buried deep within an aspect of the library social phenomenon itself that would explain the tenacious existence of that institution and, consequently, the ultimate purpose behind the labor and equipment intensity of its operations, whose cost is borne by society. And indeed there is.

Library philosophy can be derived from an understanding of that institution's place in cultural evolution, where it has met a very human need since the beginnings of recorded communication. Examination of studies in cultural evolution and related sciences confirms the validity of this cultural approach, which sets into relief the library as a concept of process profoundly integral in fascinating ways to the uniquely human condition. Yet it is equally true that one can read with great profit many of the excellent, seemingly thorough and comprehensive, books and articles on cultural evolution without ever encountering reference to the word library, or even very much about literacy, books, or reading. One is left to presume that the library function is there, although only implied ever so tacitly in the most general of considerations, because it simply is understood to be there. As a librarian with a decided humanist inclination, I have been drawn into a more intensive study of this anomaly in scholarship. Because of the very broad spectrum of scholarly and scientific interest in cultural evolution, library philosophy is framed in this book by experts in their respective fields of evolution, culture, psychology, sociology, philosophy, anthropology, archeology, theory of history, biology, genetics, chemistry, physics, linguistics, communication, literacy, environmental science, library history and theory, psychiatry, neuroscience, literary theory, and others. Having drawn so heavily on research and theory in fields outside librarianship, which is my background, I use what may be considered an unusual number of direct quotations and have adopted the less customary measure of identifying the profession of each scholar cited. From the resulting synthesis of this spectrum of relevant studies emerges a pattern that leads to an enhanced understanding of the library function in society. Rather than in form, it is within function that library philosophy is embedded. The title of this book refers to the social transcript, which is not a term in common use even though the phenomenon it designates may be readily recognizable. For present purposes, it may suffice to know that social transcript first was suggested in a variance of this specific linguistic construction by economic philosopher Kenneth Boulding. It refers to the handing-down process of culture, whereby generations pass on to subsequent generations their knowledge and skills, their experience, beliefs, customs, and values. It is as elementary to the human condition as the fact that we do not start life and begin each day as a *tabula rasa*, having constantly to re-invent the wheel and wonder whether the sun will rise in the morning and set in the evening; at the same time, it also is as sophisticated as the acceleration of mental processes. As its fuller definition in Chapter 5 will make evident, the social transcript is the explanation of why we are never truly alone and is both the result and the consequence of our being social, sentient, learning, cooperating, and communicating creatures. For the phenomenon referred to in this book as the social transcript constitutes the way humanity builds upon the past, thus helping to construct the present and productively contemplate a future.

This essay is also an explanation of why the library is not about books and computers, but rather about people and ideas, and why the library has continued and even flourished throughout the trials and errors of civilization.

For the past quarter century the former notion is one I have tried to instill in the mind of students in preparation for a library career and of junior members of the library staff, while much too often sensing little evidence of successful communication. One reason for this uninspired result stems from the fact that, pressed by the business of library and the academy, I had never taken proper time to think through my impression of library function carefully and comprehensively; the conclusion that the library is about people and ideas above anything else always had been more a visceral response to a nagging notion than a reasoned conclusion to sustained thought. Also, to my knowledge, no single comprehensive rationale for such a concept had ever been advanced. What has been lacking is a full description of the library's social purpose and of its context through the course of civilization, not in terms of history, but rather in terms of the human needs and opportunities that flow through the mind. To locate library philosophy, I conjectured, there must first be an interlacing of purpose and context. More specifically, it became evident to me that library philosophy can be extracted from its function as a social institution within cultural evolution, which is a conclusion that becomes still more evident with the development of an understanding of the peculiarly human cultural needs the library has met for the individual and society throughout its long existence. I have found that this can be achieved most effectively through the study of pertinent research and theory in many fields.

Theories relative to the operation of libraries, rather than relative to why its operations are necessary in the first place, are indeed abundant. But they do not, alone, define the library function in such a way as to suggest a philosophy. There is no single statement of philosophy that presents a coherent explanation of why the library function has flourished and what it accomplishes for humanity. The many theories and partial philosophies that do exist tend to be highly prescriptive because they are directed at the operations themselves as a means of improving them. The iteration of such theories does not constitute a philosophy.

Nonetheless, the philosophy is there, having been deeply embedded in the social function of the library throughout the millennia, continuing still today and every day. My contention is that, as valuable as these and many other attempts at philosophy are, they have not been successful in the sense of being generally applicable and widely accepted because they have been focused, for the most part, on the internal procedures and transactions of library and information science, rather than on the library as a conceptual institution in culture. They have not focused on library purpose in its full context. The subtitle of the present book indicates that there really is a library philosophy to be uncovered from deep within the age-old layers of library function as a uniquely human creation. But that philosophy remains to be uncovered, rather than created or invented or even discovered, because it has managed to cloak itself in both the daily detail of life's urgency and the timeless evolution of culture of which it is so integral a part.

The library maintains its essential dimension in cultural evolution in three ways: through the ongoing selection from an ever-expanding corpus of recorded thought to be entered into the social transcript; through the organization of its services for consultation; and through the assurance it instills in society for the transcript's security. In fulfilling its function in society, the library enables the transcript to transcend the otherwise limiting dimensions of communication associated with time and space. Society expects and depends upon the social transcript, and is perpetually reassured by its presence, whether consciously or subconsciously. When examined in the general context of cultural evolution, the paramount dominance of the library within this intellectual phenomenon of the social transcript, which Arthur O. Lovejoy illustrates as the great chain of being in his book of that title, becomes quite evident. But the utility of this cultural technology for humanity extends beyond communication of the most fundamental of ideas that have advanced humanity. For the library fosters mental integration of the rich spectrum of ideas, questions, sensations, experiences, along with their nuanced meanings and possibilities that have been and continue to be subsumed in the force of cultural evolution in the individual and society. Considered in its full potential, the cultural technology called library produces both a capacity and an environment that, together, enable and stimulate the intellectual powers of humanity, stir imagination and creativity, and afford intellectual comfort. Its function is the stewardship of the social transcript.

The notion that we stand on the shoulders of those who have preceded us has become, unfortunately, almost a platitude and much too pedestrian a truism. But that should not be permitted to obscure the fact that some of those who have preceded us in assessing the nature, magnitude, and significance of cultural evolution are, indeed, giants. They are intellectual giants of both the distant past and the immediate present, working in many disciplines. I have enjoyed assembling this story, mostly because doing so has brought me into contact, remote as it is, with many of those excellent minds that have been staunchly committed to a more profound understanding of concepts that often are referred to casually as human, not least among which is the human condition. The carefully reasoned expression of those minds in the many works I have had the pleasure to contemplate in the process of preparing this synthesis has been in every way inspiring. I suffer no delusions that this book will solve what seems to have become the library philosophy enigma. Perhaps it is an enigma that can not and should not be solved, anyway; instead, the idea of a library philosophy should be pondered and discussed and its implications entered into the consciousness of those who realize the philosophy in practice, teaching, and research. I do reserve the hope, however, that the findings presented in this investigation will stir such activity.

I should like to thank Dr. Elizabeth Aversa, Director of the School of Library and Information Studies at The University of Alabama, for providing me, during retirement, the office space and peripheral academic amenities necessary to thinking and writing in an efficient manner. Also, I should like to acknowledge the staff of the Circulation and Interlibrary Loan departments of the University Libraries, who proved to be steadfast partners in this endeavor by accommodating both ongoing and occasional needs.

Sharon Osburn, a truly magnificent woman and my wonderful better half, has been an unfailing source of encouragement, support, and insightful critique throughout the research and writing of this book. Her very extraordinary understanding of why I needed to engage in this activity and of what it would mean for my presence, both in body and spirit, made the project possible and ultimately enabled it to be an effort of full commitment. Because of her understanding, encouragement, and attention to critical reading, this is a much better book than it would otherwise have been.

PART I

Siting the Philosophy

CHAPTER 1

Echoes of a Philosophy

The wrong view of science betrays itself in the craving to be right; for it is not his possession of knowledge, of irrefutable truth, that makes the man of science, but his persistent and recklessly critical *quest* for truth.

—Karl Popper, 1959

Introduction

Concept of and practice in the library so often are confused in the mind of both the public and the scholar that fundamental misunderstandings easily arise about what the library is and why it exists. This situation emanates primarily from the strong image of practice, which is what the public sees and what most of the professional and scholarly literature addresses. As a consequence, image of practice almost invariably overshadows concept of function. In concept rather than in concrete, however, the library is a matter of rational social process, a process far more fundamental to humanity than isolated procedures and transactions could possibly suggest.

What frequently is taken in the most negative sense as ambivalence toward the purpose of the library is valid to some extent, for a holistic understanding of the library purpose has not been developed within the profession and certainly not within society. Such an understanding is camouflaged by an apparent duality that is characterized on the one hand by daily service and on the other by very long-term maintenance of cultural record. This has proved to be particularly unfortunate for the profession because, to the extent that it reflects an attitude, the word "ambivalence" carries connotations that are strongly disparaging. In a harsh critique of the profession from outside its ranks in the mid-twentieth century, sociologist William J. Goode (1961, pp. 311–312) recalled in support of his argument that social philosopher Talcott Parsons had spoken of "the 'anomie' of librarians, meaning that they have no clear-cut conception of what they should be doing." As a consequence, Goode explained, "they experience considerable cognitive bafflement and also react defensively." Whether or not this criticism remains valid today to the same extent or for all the same reasons, the fact continues to be that the LIS profession has not yet come to grips with an understanding of the nature of the library's dual purpose, or more correctly its total purpose, and the full range of implications contained therein. Which is not to say that this condition has escaped attention entirely. Far from it. As sociologist Lloyd Vernor Ballard (1936, p. 231) aptly put it three-quarters of a century ago, "Expressed metaphorically 'the newspaper is the library of the moment: the library is the newspaper of all time'. That is, it is both the memory of the race and concrete basis of its personality." But such a perspective has been exceptional. What may appear at first to be simply the ambivalence of library purpose surely has hindered the design of a library philosophy satisfactory to a majority of those interested and, as will be demonstrated, continues to do so.

This situation has been of quite long duration, incurring consequences detrimental to the profession and very likely to society. More than seventy years ago, library educator J. Periam Danton (1934) surveyed the literature of librarianship and found an unfortunate dearth of guiding principles, the great preponderance of writings, he observed, being concerned instead with process, achievement, and the immediate objective.

The conclusion of Danton's survey (1934, p. 529), that "There has certainly been no single, comprehensive philosophy of librarianship, and the isolated articles and addresses of a philosophical nature have been in the first place too few, in the second place either too limited or far too general, and, finally totally incapable of being co-ordinated into a unified whole" continues to be valid.[1] Given that premise, Danton (p. 545) saw fit to denigrate library activity as "bewildered groping," and wisely added that "we can scarcely expect society to think of the library in terms of its own constituent elements until we have made some progress in defining what the library's ends are or should be." Gathering his own thoughts about the need for a philosophy and matching them with those of others, Danton (p. 539) produced a list of six advantages to librarianship to be found in the formulation of a philosophy. They are abstracted here as follows: 1) the achievement of a definite and recognized place for the library in the social order; 2) the validation of librarianship; 3) the assignment of meaning to technical and mechanical processes; 4) added precision and sureness in action resulting from clear knowledge of purpose; 5) distinction between several types of library workers; 6) recognition of a definite principle of unified organization within the profession. In other words, Danton advised that a contextual purpose was needed both to guide and explain the internal procedures and transactions of the library.

Within the year following Danton's carefully reasoned "plea," library theorist Henry Evelyn Bliss (1935, pp. 234–235) offered a rejoinder. His argument was that many other fields are either not far ahead of librarianship in establishing a philosophy, or are far behind. What he did find missing in the guidance of librarianship are "Principles, we answer; librarianship lacks the adequate statement, or restatement, of valid principles of belief, of purpose, of method, and of conduct... clarification and illumination of thought are reciprocating mental developments tending to attain to self-consistent and logical verity." Considerably later, library theorist Maurice B. Line (1965, p. 272) concluded in substance and tone similar to Danton's that "Our lack of practice in looking at our ends has led to a certain unrealism in determining our means. We have tended to assume we know what we are doing, and therefore that we need only perfect our methods of doing it. This has led to an unhealthy preoccupation with methodology and techniques." And still, at the close of the twentieth century, library theorist Jim Zwadlo's (1997, p. 104) examination of the literature yielded results comparable to those of Bliss, observing that a philosophy for the field is unnecessary. He concluded that a single philosophy cannot adequately accommodate the many ideas, often conflicting, contained in the concepts of library and librarianship, but that if there were one it would have to be an amalgamation (a "con-fusion," he says) of the many. For Zwadlo, more important than achieving an end product is the *process* of discussing, understanding and reconciling these ideas. In matters of a philosophy, process surely is the key to a meaningful product and essential to a shared understanding and commitment.

In the evident absence of a guiding philosophy it is no wonder that a clear schism between theory and practice would develop, as is noted in sociologist William J. Goode's (1961, p. 317) evaluation of librarianship as a profession: "There is a wide discrepancy between values and practices... in which the practitioner must risk unpopularity by serving the larger interests of the society." And it is above all in this context that the supposed ambivalence of the profession falls most clearly and heavily on the public library among the various types of libraries, because the potential diversity of its community is far greater than that served by any other type of library. Its activities and mission are much more broadly defined by the varied purposes of its community than are the respective purposes of the other types of libraries (school, special, and academic). Policy matters stemming directly from mission are the most immediately affected by the diverse and ever-changing community demand, which includes political pressure, both real and perceived. For example, in his sweeping perspective on the public library in England, library historian Paul Sykes (1979, p. 97) finds that "the attempt to popularize libraries by providing light fiction has been a resounding failure, since the inducement was not sufficiently attractive to the majority of the population. Herein lies the heart of the problem; the nature of the library service has long been contaminated as a result of a failure to identify priorities. The inevitable struggle to operate the treadmill created by insatiable demand from the majority has depleted scarce resources concurrently with the erosion of credibility of the library service as a national institution of real merit." A philosophical basis from which to perceive and determine mission, goals, objectives, and priorities would be essential in addressing these issues rationally.

To the extent to which the library operates, develops theory, and formally prepares its personnel in the absence of a fundamental philosophy, its focus is narrowed to individual, isolated functions, and its policies succumb without much struggle to what may be extraneous forces. Hence, it is with good reason that the library as a social institution seems to operate with ambivalent purpose and with little direction except that offered by the challenges and opportunities of the moment and the accomplishment of daily routines, along with their improvement in efficiency and supposedly in effectiveness. "The simple fact is that no measurement, no experiment or observation, is possible without a relevant theoretical framework," writes library educator D. S. Kothari, (1975, p. 5). This apparent condition does not instill confidence either within the profession, the local community, or the greater society.

Offering a larger frame for the picture, however, physicist John Ziman (1968, p. 38) argues that society does tend to believe scientific knowledge, for example, "even if we do not believe that it is necessarily, in a logically rigorous manner true," because "a theory provides a logical ordering, a pattern, for observations." So, the fundamental problems that stem from serving what seem to be dual purposes—those of having at once a purpose in immediate service as well as a purpose in cultural evolution—has left the library in somewhat of a quandary about where to seek guidance, and in a state of poor understanding of its purpose on the part of the local community and the greater society being served. This situation has not been discussed widely either within the profession or in any kind of ongoing dialogue with society. But the single most troubling aspect of the situation is that, although balancing and reconciling the perceived duality of the library's function may prove to be the essential intellectual problem of librarianship, the profession nonetheless tends not to address it directly in a forum that could result in a more comprehensive understanding.[2]

In his assessment of the general application of functional analysis, librarian John M. Christ (1969, p. 245) describes the potential value of that research methodology to librarianship as well, but also observes that functional analysis encounters primary obstacles in the library application. He concludes that the solution to such problems cannot be found in the absence of an understanding of the purpose of the library, which he stresses is a requirement of the methodology: "Such a question is basically a philosophical consideration. Library science, however, has not developed a clear, well-defined philosophical base. As a result, explanations of the library tend to be forced into a causal orbit where cause-effect relationships exhaust the scope of the research." And, as is to be expected, this impediment harkens back to other related complications stemming from the lack of a clear purpose, to which allusion has already been made in this chapter. "It is the part of philosophy to breathe a cosmic and unifying spirit over multitudes of loosely related facts," writes library educator Arnold K. Borden (1931, p. 175). "Without it there is a failure to see relationships and the field as a whole. The results are stagnation, atrophy, and inability to progress." But the lack of a guiding philosophy against which to test practice also has been identified as a particular problem for all research into operations, for, as library philosopher Pierce Butler (1933, p. 110) observes quite fundamentally, "There can be no search until the searcher has decided what he shall look for," having already summarized (p. 108) with "Before there can be scientific observation there must be intellectual consideration. Chronologically experiment comes after hypothesis, not before it."

It is logical that the failure of librarianship to establish the purpose of the library, thereby revealing the common ground of all libraries, would result in a strongly negative effect on the formal preparation of its emerging practitioners. In that regard, cultural historian Raymond Irwin (1949, p. 16) has argued that "in academic circles there is an uncomfortable suspicion that the existing curriculum is insecurely based, and requires underpinning by the addition of more scholarly foundations. Hence the search for some indisputable mark of scholarship such as might be conveyed by a philosophy of librarianship." And slightly more than a decade later, sociologist William J. Goode (1961, p. 312) saw a definite dichotomy of theory separating the classroom from practice in the library. Noting that he understood the value of subjects such as communications theory, sociology, psychology, and learning for library education, he also saw that "most day-to-day professional work utilizes rather concrete, rule-of-thumb, local regulations and rules, and a major cataloging system." Most likely that is what he saw because that had become, in fact, the only object of emphasis identifiable in the absence of reasons why the activities of day-to-day professional work are important at all, except to accomplish them efficiently and, from the immediate clientele perspective, effectively. Another decade later, Jesse Shera (1972, p. 496) found that library education continued to suffer the consequences of its neglect of theoretical foundations. "Thus library education is today paying the price of its failure to be concerned with the theoretical foundations of the profession. It has not sought for, much less developed, a viable theory of librarianship out of which education and research could have emerged. As a result ends have often been confused with means, and means with ends," and furthermore that (p. 348) "one could go on and on with all the 'landmark' contributions and discussions of library education [listing a substantial number of them], all of them repeating the same tired old criticisms that have fallen largely upon deaf, or at least unresponsive ears." In summary, if it is true, as library theorist D. J. Foskett (1962, p. 5) advises, that "It is in the formation of an attitude of mind that we can distinguish between education and mere training," then the role of a philosophy for librarianship clearly moves to an even higher level of importance. To repeat, it is the contention of this essay that the philosophy of librarianship is located within the function and philosophy of library.

During the twentieth century it had become clear, yet evidently not clear enough, that the absence of a library philosophy thus had become an obstacle to the general health of the library as a social institution in its most fundamental dimensions: Guidance at all levels of the service and its evaluation; explanation of purpose; social nature of the library; unity of the profession; research to strengthen fulfillment of purpose; and the ongoing preparation of professionals to carry the mission forward. But that is not to suggest that a great deal of thinking had not been taking place before, during, and following the twentieth century. Pieces of philosophy had indeed been developing for a very long time, but have remained only in the form of echoes reminding that the philosophy behind the library still needs to be pursued, but with a more significant focus.

Stages of Philosophy Development

Models for the function of the library had been established at least by the early third century B.C. in the Alexandrian Library of ancient Egypt, where one Callimachus, a poet and the earliest known bio-bibliographer and library cataloger, created pioneering principles for organizing the library's intellectual content. History does not record the philosophy that guided him in this enterprise, but it can be inferred from his actions that he must have been guided by one. Callimachus established a catalog, the *Pinakes*, which also was intended to be a complete inventory of Greek literature up to that time. Owing to the usual devastation by war and the normal effects of time, little beyond the most germinal evidence and inference remain to inform us about the social concerns and the thinking of the library leaders that led to the institution of these early libraries, but it is obvious that every effort possible at the time had been made to facilitate use of the collections. Even from those early moments in civilization, the library clearly had a social purpose related to preservation and communication, closely linked to each other in mutual dependence and in support of the most human of concerns.

Throughout subsequent generations, a number of librarians, as well as other scholars, have defined significant perspectives on the library purpose and philosophy, but only a few have done so in an attempt to be comprehensive in the sense of formulating and recording a philosophy. With the intention of demonstrating that a rich, but scattered, basis for library philosophy already is in place, the following paragraphs recall a few of those individuals who have been of greatest influence.

One of the earliest to write comprehensively about the purpose of the library and the ways to develop it accordingly was the Frenchman Gabriel Naudé (1600–1653). In his 1627 book, *Advis pour dresser une bibliothèque* (Naudé, 1950), which library historian James Thompson (1977, p. 15) regards as "the first important treatise on library science," Naudé was explicit about the importance of the representation of multiple sides of an issue in the collection, as well as about the importance of its organization so that its use by contemporary middle-class citizens would be facilitated. Library historian Jack A. Clarke (1970, p. 21) concludes that Naudé's "system, quite naturally, reflected the 'logical' order of knowledge, as he perceived it, and the intellectual preoccupations of his day." Of considerable significance, Naudé advised that books should be selected on the basis of their content rather than their artifactual value, and that they should be arranged by subject. To inform his advice as fully as possible beyond his first-hand experience in establishing and administering the Bibliothèque Mazarine, Naudé had conducted research, gathering bits and pieces about library management from published sources and from the experience of others. Naudé's manual, revised for a second edition seventeen years later, became quite influential and was a source for much subsequent Western thinking about the library. According to Clarke (p. 142), he had written the "first treatise on library economy that consistently treated libraries as instruments for the dissemination of scholarship rather than as the playthings for rich men," and cultural historian Raymond Irwin (1964, p. 41) has credited him as "the first to propound a theory of library economy."

Those who write about library operations, transactions, and responsibilities must have in mind a contextual purpose or theory, but not all refer to those ideas per se, and fewer still advance them in a broad context. Among the few who do is Gottfried Wilhelm von Leibniz (1646–1716), German librarian, philosopher, and developer of the calculus widely in use today, who believed that the library should also exert an ethical influence on society by making freely available and thoroughly catalogued the works of the best minds. Having spent the greater part of his adult life as a librarian, Leibniz is best known in that field for his classification theory, whose "unifying element throughout is the principle of utility for man," according to cultural historian Hans Georg Schulte-Albert (1971, p. 148). He was familiar with the work of Gabriel Naudé (p. 142), and advocated a classified catalogue supplemented by an author catalogue, arranged alphabetically and supported by syndetic devices. Moreover, through his directorship of the Ducal Library at Wolfenbüttel he realized his principles in practice and pursued adoption of the concept of a universal library that would contain all the recorded ideas of mankind, even in the wake of more than two hundred years' production by the printing press. The library theory propounded by Leibniz was significant because of his personal and professional authority during a critical time in intellectual history.

During the decades following Leibniz, debate about the purpose of the library grew in intensity, especially with the advent of the public library movement toward the middle of the nineteenth century. This movement was in part the result of an accumulation of ideas about reading and learning that owed its origin to the ancient Greek philosophers, especially Plato and Aristotle, who, according to library historian Barbara McCrimmon (1994, p. 496), saw the library as "the memory of **civilization and a repository of intellectual energy that could teach, inform, broaden,** and enhance life." Plato's thought very generally had envisioned the purpose of life as achievement of the ideal to be translated into continuous personal improvement that would lead through ever more lofty intellectual development toward an elusive perfection. In the context of the many implications for education that accompanied a growing rate of literacy, the Industrial Revolution, and a library workforce that was beginning to professionalize, these ancient thoughts found an especially welcome reception. Thus, the purpose of a library for the public, in particular, was raised to a level of interest not experienced before and perhaps not since that time. Public librarian Clarence E. Sherman (1939, pp. 44–45) identifies three theories that in his view guided public libraries prior to World War II: the censorship theory, which advocates providing what people *should* read; the sponsorship theory, which advocates providing material believed to be dependable; and the leadership theory, which combines the sponsorship theory with a new thrust of bold leadership for the library in informal education. The latter theory clearly argued to turn the library away from engaging in what theretofore had been well understood as insular library responsibilities toward an extension of those responsibilities.

Sheyali Ramamrita Ranganathan (1892-1972)

Moving to the twentieth century, few would disagree with Douglas J. Foskett's assessment (1962, p. 8) that "The most sustained attempt to work out a philosophy of librarianship is that of Dr. Ranganathan," or with that of information scientist Kenneth G. B. Bakewell (1980, p. 467) that Ranganathan "stands as one of the immortals of library science."

He is best known for his work on colon classification and for his general library philosophy, as expressed primarily in his seminal book *The Five Laws of Library Science* (1931) and elsewhere throughout his prolific career. In the matter of library philosophy, writes Ronald C. Benge (1970, p. 246), "The pioneer work has been done by Ranganathan, and his 'five laws' can be applied to all library studies." The first law, Books are for Use, embodies what Ranganathan (1931, p. 1) saw as an elemental truth, one that is fundamental to matters of administration. In fact, he says, "it is so self-evident that one may be inclined to say that it is trivial. But, that is an invariable characteristic of all first laws." The second law, Every Person His or Her Book, recognizes that there are varied and ever-changing needs, and that maturity has its educational aptitudes, aspirations, and urgencies. Belief to the contrary, he says (p. 147), can be traced to "'the Camel theory' of education—that before we start on the journey of life we can be given all the mental food necessary to carry us through the whole way." The third law, Every Book Its Reader, addresses the principle of intellectual freedom, by which is meant (p. 300) "the opportunity to see and examine the book collection with as much freedom as in ones own private library." The fourth law, Save The Time Of The Reader, refers to principles of efficiency in specific library operations. And the fifth law, A Library Is A Growing Organism, embraces the idea that the library, as an institution, has all the attributes of a growing organism; that it takes in new matter, casts off old matter, changes in size and takes new shapes and forms.

In that regard, Ranganathan (1931, pp. 382-383) writes that "Apart from sudden and apparently discontinuous changes involved in metamorphosis, it is also subject to a slow continuous change which leads to what is known as a 'variation', in biological parlance, and to the evolution of new forms." He also writes (p. 415) that the vital principle of the library, which is common to all its different forms and will continue to be its distinguishing feature, is that it is an instrument of universal education, and assembles together and freely distributes all the tools of education and disseminates knowledge with their aid. He calls this principle "the spirit of the library," emphasizing that it "persists through all its forms like the inner man." Ranganathan's reference to the spirit of the library seems to be very close to what is referred to in the present essay as the concept of library; a concept or spirit that inhabits humanity, not a practice, is the composition of library philosophy.

Library educator and theorist Mohinder Pratap Satija (1986, p. 90) recounts that Ranganathan once said about his Five Laws that "in appearance, the laws are like a meek cow, but when the laws leap, they turn out like a ferocious tiger," meaning that when one first reads the laws they are deceptive in their simplicity, if not in their apparent naïveté; but upon closer analysis they present a deep and broad interlacing of implications, both theoretical and practical. Included in information scientist M. A. Gopinath's (2003) slender biographical narrative of Ranganathan is an informative personal account of how he came to formulate his Five Laws, and it is emphasized (p. 2424) that in the philosopher's mind all of his four dozen books and his large number of articles and presentations form a single unit analyzing the laws: "Indeed, they are like chapters of one huge book."

Gopinath provides insight into Ranganathan's reasoning in his account of how the library leader visited more than one hundred libraries in various stages of development, finding "no common point of emergence of the new trends in different library practices. All development appeared to be a matter of trial and error, and severely empirical. Ranganathan's scientific approach could not be reconciled to this state of affairs, and it led him to think deeply and search for a common root. The result was the formulation of the five laws of library science." Gopinath (p. 2424) quotes Ranganathan's expression of the logic that guided him, in an almost uncanny way that parallels closely, as will be seen in Chapter 3, the intrinsic function of the library in culture:

> Prior experience in scientific study and pursuit induced in me a sense of revolt against having to hold in memory and deal with myriads of unrelated pieces of information and practices. Cannot all these empirical aggregates of information and practices be reduced to a handful of basic principles? Cannot the process of induction be applied in this case? Cannot all the known practices be got by the process of deduction from the basic principles? Do not the basic principles contain, as necessary implications, many other practices not current or known at present? Will they not become necessary as and when the boundary conditions set by society change?

Pierce Butler (1886-1953)

While the writings of S. R. Ranganathan are voluminous in their embracing presentation of a library philosophy, those of library educator and philosopher Pierce Butler are considerably less so and, indeed, are for the most part incorporated in one slim volume that is still in print, *An Introduction to Library Science* (1933). Jesse Shera (1980a, p. 105) has said about this particular work that "In the literature of librarianship, which is characterized mainly by its ephemera, Butler's little volume stands out as a true landmark in the development of library thought." Butler (1933, p. 29) judged the rational side, or the scientific aspect, of the fundamental phenomenon of librarianship to be "the transmission of the accumulated experience of society to its individual members through the instrumentality of the book. This transmission has other aspects which can never be apprehended by science." In his *Introduction* he wrote that "What memory is to man, "the graphic record is, in part, to modern society" (p. 32), and that in the pages of each book "remain the knowledge that is distilled from human experience" (p. 60). Underscoring the integrated relation of the library and cultural evolution, Butler (pp. 79-80) observed that "Every major change in the social ideal has produced an alteration in the constitution of the library." Elsewhere (p. 26) he continues this line of thought, noting that if he had but one message for librarians it might well be summarized in his hopes about their understanding of the library, particularly that it "will always be regarded as essentially but one aspect of the whole compound of human activity . . . They will transfer their attention from process to function. They will come to strive for accurate understanding just as ardently as they now do for practical efficiency." The synthesis developed in the present essay can be taken as an elaboration on this idea.

Jesse H. Shera (1903-1982)

Throughout the present study, there is frequent reference to information scientist and philosopher Jesse Hauk Shera for, as one of the most learned and reasoned voices in the library profession, he also has been one of the most vociferous exponents of the need for a library philosophy to stir thinking in some depth about the library's purpose. The thrust of his undertaking was to advance librarianship as a concept, rather than as a place or a thing; it would be a concept that embodies many elements and aspects all united in one, and we are told by colleague and biographer Margaret Kaltenbach (1980, p. 524) that he considered this his single most significant contribution to the profession. In developing persuasive arguments for the library as concept, Shera placed the library within a very large social frame, analyzing and identifying philosophically and in depth the library's role in society. He explains (1975, p. 169) this concept:

> The library as a social invention is concerned with the improvement of the individual, but through the improvement of the individual it seeks the advancement of society. Individuals not only make the society, society continually reshapes the individual; this is perhaps the most important key to dynamics of the library. The basic bond through which individuals achieve unity in a culture is through the communication of information. Thus information is the cement with which the structure of society is held together.

Using so broad a brush in his depiction of the social role of the library, it is no wonder that Jesse Shera saw all of librarianship—in all its types and sizes—as a totality, and that he consistently upheld the position that documentation and information science are integral parts of librarianship, with information science contributing a theoretical underpinning. Relatively early in his career, Shera was recognized by British library leader James H. Wellard (1940, p. 107) as having introduced a fundamental principle for the profession; "it is the principle of shaping library policy according to changing social conditions and current social needs."

Jesse Shera found in an approach he called social epistemology the basis for a cohesive, productive engagement in librarianship. He may not have coined the term,[3] but he was present at the coining and preached the concept widely, defining it (1972, p. 112) as a discipline which

> should provide a framework for the investigation of the complex problem of the nature of the intellectual process in society—a study of the ways in which society as a whole achieves a perceptive relation to its total environment. It should lift the study of intellectual life from that of a scrutiny of the

> individual to an inquiry into the means by which a society, nation, or culture achieves understanding of the totality of stimuli which act upon it. The focus of this new discipline should be upon the production, flow, integration, and consumption of communicated thought throughout the social fabric.

As the conceptual and normative study of the social relevance of knowledge to social relations, interests, and institutions, this approach accommodated the considerations he found of greatest significance for the application of his philosophy to learning, research, and practice. Social epistemology places the focus on society, rather than on the individual or even the library, and advocates a macroscopic examination of the cognitive processes that lead to understanding in its total environment in order to communicate knowledge from age to age, from individual to society, and from society to individual. "What is the function of the library in society," he asks (1973, pp. 196-197). He answers: "I believe we will all agree that it is to maximize the social utility of graphic records for the benefit of the individual, and through the individual the improvement of society." Jesse Shera's thoughts about the place of the library are scattered through many publications, an assortment of which are cited throughout this text and included in the appended list of references.

A. Broadfield

Shortly after World War II, an English public librarian named A. Broadfield published *A Philosophy of Librarianship* (1949), which reflects a personal ideal almost to the extreme and with little or no regard—other than contempt—for the basic fact that, by far, the majority of libraries are not independent, but are part of a host institution, part of a larger bureaucracy. In that regard he writes (p. 11) that "One of the main causes of the misery of man in society is the inability of human beings to do without a government." Broadfield expresses his philosophy strictly from the perspective of the individual reader, for whom he advocates total intellectual freedom, no matter the prevailing social conditions. "The library exists for the sake of freedom of thought" (1949, p. 11), he writes. The librarian's sole duty is to the individual, so judgment plays little or no part. Clearly, his faith in the judgment and intentions of the individual is extended with little reservation.

Raymond Irwin (1950, p. 62) describes the *Philosophy* as "a reasoned and mildly impassioned attack on positivism." Broadfield's book includes a chapter on what he considers the unfortunate influence of nineteenth-century social philosopher Auguste Comte on librarianship, for he says (p. 108) Comte's "philosophy of the sciences was an authoritarian dogma," which is perhaps the most derogatory assessment possible from this particular public librarian.

It is easy to see in Broadfield's book the strongest advocacy of the intellectual freedoms championed by most Western librarians today, at least in formal positions adopted by the professional associations. Broadfield offers a number of axioms, among which is the non sequitur (p. 108) that "There is no use in upholding freedom of thought if we are not prepared to think ourselves." Perhaps the single idea of Broadfield that comes closest to fully capturing his philosophy is his statement (p. 35) that "The human being is the ultimate of ends, his free condition his highest condition, freedom of thought the most fundamental element in his freedom, and the library one of the first essentials in maintaining it." In matters of individual freedom, therefore, he sees the library as the principal institution standing between the individual and the coercive organizations of society, guarding individual freedom against intrusions of the state, religion, politics, morals, or other personal biases.

Broadfield's *Philosophy* certainly is, as Raymond Irwin (1950, p. 62) states so aptly, "a vigorous defence of the dignity and value of individual thought," and it is concerned only indirectly with practice, although he was a practicing librarian at the Leicester Public Library. The librarian's job, he says (p. 13), is to give the reader the resources that will give him the opportunity of making up his own mind freely, and without direction. But it is "not merely to satisfy the requirements of the thinker and the independent student of truth. He [the librarian] has the more fundamental task of helping to create such thinkers and students." Essentially, Broadfield believes (pp. 24–25) that if the librarian does his or her job properly, thinkers and students will be attracted to the library. Apparently a cynic in most instances, he may have been naïve in this one. Nevertheless, "The work of the librarian should be to assist a man to strengthen his conscience by liberal provision of all the necessary material of an intellectual or literary nature."

H. Curtis Wright (1928–)

H. Curtis Wright manifests considerable influence of Jesse Shera, depicting librarianship (1982, p. 8) as "a comprehensive synthesis of knowledge in which ideas about anything that is known can be located and correlated with ideas about everything that is known." But he finds instead (1979, p. 67) that "Virtually all of the user studies in both librarianship and information science study the ways in which people use *things* (like libraries, documents, or computers); they do not study the actual uses of information by human beings." Wright's library philosophy is expressed in a few writings that are brief, but terse and pregnant. He is opposed to what he sees as the aggressive scientism of the library profession, and urges (1982, p. 5) a rejection of "the physical concept of information-as-data, which reduces librarianship to notation science," and in its place a reassertion of "the metaphysical concept of information-as-ideas, which regards it as the cartography of knowledge." The only legitimate concern of the profession, he says (1982, p. 4), is "human subjectivity; and for that, the communication of information-as-ideas is absolutely indispensable."

Wright relates the ancient Greek philosophers' belief (1976, p. 297) that experience and intellection constitute the two worlds of human existence. "The disjunction of the senses and reason in man is the rock on which the Greeks built natural philosophy," he asserts, as a means of dealing with complicated human problems. The experiential world was called the physis, which included all realities existing in a physical way. However, in the view of the ancient Greeks, everything existing in a nonphysical way belongs to the metaphysis, which is a world "beyond physics" and discernible by reason, not by means of the senses. "Man is thus two men at once, an anthropopos somatikos whose body is linked with the sensed realities of the natural order, and an anthropos noetikos whose mind is tied to unsensed realities." Wright finds (1979, p. 71) that, over time, this ancient distinction has become "the most prominent feature of secular thought in the West. The sensed world is populated by physical existents, the objects of human experience." The metaphysical world includes the operations as well as the ideas of the mind, and therefore (1979, p. 72) "all of the meanings discovered, created, and utilized by human beings."

It is not surprising that H. Curtis Wright is very much at odds with the twentieth-century trend to infuse all aspects of librarianship with the appearance of rigid scientific theory and methodology, whether or not appropriate. By reducing ideas to data as a way of studying information and knowledge scientifically, he says (1982, p. 6), the effort illustrates "a classic instance of the hypostatic fallacy: we have transferred ideas, which belong to the noetic world of non-physical order/structure/form, to the world of physical realities by endowing them with a content and substance (*hypostasis*) they do not possess." H. Curtis Wright summarizes his philosophy of librarianship (1979, pp. 73–74) as follows:

> The librarian's object of study is human knowledge, or more precisely, metaphysical subsistents. The method of librarianship, which is determined by its formal objects of study, is metaphysical: it is rationalistic and recognitive by necessity, as in the humanities, because form must be present in the mind before its presence can be created or detected in the world. The librarian's goal, the reason for studying subsistents, is orientation to knowledge. It is the business of librarians to know their way around, and to help others find their way around, in the unsensed world of ideas created by the mind. The way to reach the goal, the librarian's means of orientation to thought, is the creation of formal knowledge (metaphysical concepts) about the physics of human expression and the effective utilization of communicative instruments.

H. Curtis Wright went very far toward establishing a philosophy of the concept of library, and surely he was on a track that would lead there. But there is little evidence that his ideas, as convincing as they are on their own, ever became as influential as this valuation suggests. Timing is usually crucial in these matters, and yet there also are other considerations that may have played a part in the profession's apparent quiet disregard of his ideas. Whatever else may have impeded his influence in professional thought, Wright did not place his philosophy in the kind of context that would help make it understandable and therefore acceptable either to the profession or to society.

John M. Budd (1953–)

John Budd has contributed a substantial number of works on various aspects of established philosophy that he considers applicable to library and information science, some of which are cited throughout this text. In *Knowledge and Knowing in Library and Information Science* (2001), Budd creates what he characterizes as a philosophical framework for the profession. The special importance of this book is twofold. First, it places the LIS profession in the context of intellectual history, primarily within formal philosophical systems and the development of science and social science theory, which is to say the development of knowledge. Second, this book is important because it very explicitly places the decisions and actions of librarianship and information science in a completely philosophic context. Budd critiques the philosophical debates that have been waged over the past four centuries and continue to be waged, and does so with the evident intention of enlightening theory behind the actions taken within the profession. He finds the most informative approach for this profession in hermeneutical phenomenology, the influence of interpretation on social phenomena. John Budd's book is a study in epistemological theory underlying the issues, decisions, and actions of library and information science. As such, the book highlights the distinction of *practice*, in its usual meaning in contemporary English usage, and *praxis*, in its Aristotelian sense. "We must continuously remind ourselves," writes Budd (p. 279), "that LIS has a social meaning as well as a technical application. We might even say that our praxis is a combination of all our practices *plus* the ethical basis of our being."

In a book titled *Self-Examination: The Present and Future of Librarianship*, Budd (2008) strongly encourages the profession to consider more closely its identity in terms of what it does and why. Fundamentally, he says (p. viii), "The phrase 'consciousness of purpose' is one that should be ever on our minds and should be the basis for our reflection." Ethos, politics, communication, and other social forces provide the context, he suggests, in which can be found opportunities for interactive reflection into unexplored possibilities.

Other Leaders

But there are many others, as well, who, through their published thought or their less visible activities, have advanced the consideration of library philosophy. Most noteworthy among them may be Antonio Panizzi (1797–1879), Edward Edwards (1812–1886), Herbert Putnam (1861–1955), José Ortega y Gasset (1883–1955), Lionel McColvin (1896–1976), Margaret E. Egan (1905–1959), Abraham Kaplan (1918–1993), Douglas J. Foskett (1918–2004), Joseph Z. Nitecki (1922–), Ajit Kumar Mukherjee (1908–), John E. Buschman (1960–), and Gary P. Radford (1961–). Their contributions are cited throughout this text, and it cannot be over-emphasized that this is but a small sampling.

Why the Need for a Philosophy Remains

Thus far in this book, reference has been made to barely a handful of library philosophers, although a substantial number of others' thoughts on the subject are cited throughout. With the need for a library philosophy having been expressed quite clearly and in various ways during the past three-quarters of a century and more, the next logical issue to address is the question of why an accepted set of ideas and principles in the form of a statement of philosophy to guide and explain the library has not been achieved. The reasons for this are varied, but run fairly deep in the motivations of the profession. The order of the following discussion of these motivations is both chronological and substantive, for they revolve around considerations that are never dropped, only reordered in degree of significance at any given time. In order of presentation they are: Simple neglect of and ambivalence toward a philosophy; the development of a belief system that rendered an agreed upon philosophy superfluous; the generally agreed near-fatal attraction of the practical side of the profession; the magnetic fascination, particularly in more recent decades, of information technologies per se; the invocation of the science model (scientism); and the influence of cognitive science.

Neglect & Ambivalence

Mentioned earlier is ambivalence of both the profession and society toward purpose of the library, the most consistent manifestations of which stem from the various possibilities for development of the collection.[4] Sponsorship of the library has changed hands frequently throughout history, moving from the nobility, the priesthood, private benefactors, voluntary associations , business and industrial enterprises, and a variety of governmental agencies represented in the public sector. Concurrently, however, the library increased dramatically in size, geographic ubiquity, and complexity; created for it was a body of rules and procedures as it evolved new patterns for its administrative control and constantly extended its clientele base. And through all that, as Jesse Shera points out (1973, p. 94), the library did not change its basic mission, "which is to maximize the social utility of graphic records," or "its special responsibility to operate in that complex association of record and human mind." Whether because of its history, or in spite of it, he writes (p. 94), "this relationship, which is at once intellectual, psychological, and physiological, is still only imperfectly understood." Elsewhere, Shera (1980, p. 314) expands on this conclusion, writing that "There are good historic reasons for the librarians' ambivalence, not to say indifference and neglect, concerning the philosophical raison d'être of the library as a social organism. Throughout the millennia libraries created, by their very existence, their own rationale, their own philosophical justification." With little or no guidance from the community it served, the library can flounder in the range of possibilities for the nature of the collection to be developed, any one of which could easily be construed to the benefit of society. "Public libraries have had the privilege and the satisfaction of determining their own objectives with considerable freedom," writes public librarian Clarence E. Sherman (1938, p. 45). "Few state laws, city ordinances or library charters define library aims and objects with more than rough approximations." A sense of privilege inferred from apparent autonomy, and organizational self satisfaction fueled by implications of that sense, may in time have led to disregard for purposes that could seem to extend beyond the daily operations of the library.[5]

More than seventy years ago, J. Periam Danton (1934, p. 545) characterized much of library activity as bewildered groping whose persistence is owed to the absence of a clear conception of purpose, and concluded with the truism that "we can scarcely expect society to think of the library in terms of its own constituent elements until we have made some progress in defining what the library's ends are or should be." These, he adds (p. 547), would be derived from the predominating ideals of that society. But ideals and special interests can be confounded, and if not given proper direction and interpretation can leave both the public and the profession in a state of ambiguity about library purpose. Shera (1966, p. 28) describes how, in the nineteenth century, a new credo of social progress on both sides of the Atlantic found universal education to be the solution to problems, so that there was great enthusiasm for bringing about "on behalf of the masses a fusion of popular culture and the traditional classical education of the upper classes. In the wave of enthusiasm for an expanded popular culture the librarians soon became immersed." Evidently these good intentions were not carried out well, because not only did the public become confused about the philosophy of the library, but so did the documentalists, writes Shera (pp. 21–53). For even as they had been making progress as a profession for several decades in the twentieth century, they determined that such confusion within the profession,[6] which was highlighted by an apparent thrust toward popular literature, was not in their best interests, so they separated themselves from librarianship.

Library historian James Thompson (1977, p. 12) suggests that the reason a philosophy has not developed is certainly not because libraries are new, but because the examination and interpretation of the history of libraries is. The pioneer here, he says, "as in so many other matters, acknowledged and unacknowledged, was Edward Edwards. His monumental two-volume *Memoirs of Libraries*—not published, after all, until 1859—was the first major attempt of this kind." More recently, library philosopher John Budd (2003) describes how librarians tend not to recognize or use the power they have placed at their command through library operations,[7] and therefore that it is not something on which they reflect.

Whatever may be the reasons for the profession's failure, as a profession, to come to grips with the formulation of a philosophy to support and guide their responsibilities, none alone is the likely consideration, which more likely is a complex of forces. The philosophy, objectives and role of the public library, as sociologist Bryan Luckham (1971, p. 1) states, for example "have sometimes been discernible only in retrospect by the historian, endowed with the objectivity given by distance."

In any case, it is not among the purposes of this essay to construct an apology for the LIS profession's lack of success in the search for a suitable philosophy, but only to provide some logic behind and understanding of the status of the issue. After all, the library has not persisted through time and turmoil as the result of decisions made and strategies designed by its curators or as the result of the efforts of a narrow special interest group, but in response to societal need, as strongly suggested by the fact that, libraries are not self sustaining. There has long been a lack of the kind of inquiry into the purpose of the library that would lead to something approaching agreement throughout the profession and, eventually, to an understanding within society. The idea of a philosophy is not an obvious part of the LIS discourse, even though it is a sporadically raised, apparently isolated topic. Other than through the initiatives and intellectual curiosity of a relatively minute number of the profession's membership, these questions tend not to be raised, let alone pursued. Lacking such sources of energy for sustained momentum, however, a form of belief system has managed to evolve.

A Belief System

In 1940, British librarian and theorist James Wellard (1940, p. 49) observed that "If one examines the professional literature, for instance, one reads numerous discussions of secondary problems, while the major functions and the main objectives of the service are inclined to be glossed over with an implied belief that the library exists by divine right and can do no wrong other than allow its circulation to drop." In 1955, library historian and Library Association leader W. A. Munford labeled this professional conviction or set of assumptions "the Public Library Idea," which is, according to library historian Paul Sykes (1979, p. 9), "a summation of thoughts and motives which originated with the pre-1850 pioneers [of the public library movement], whose basic philosophy was utilitarian and its application radical." Sykes adds that Munford's "succinct phrase connotes that abiding belief in a concept—almost an ideal—of a service of inestimable value which has been held by librarians (and a woefully small company of others) since the 1840s." In the United States, political scientist Oliver Garceau (1949, pp. 50–51) referred to this phenomenon in his report to the Public Library Inquiry of 1949 as "the library faith," which is "a fundamental belief, so generally accepted as to be often left unsaid, in the virtue of the printed word, the reading of which is good in itself, and upon the preservation of which many basic values in our civilization rest. When culture is in question, the knowledge of books, the amount of reading, and the possession of a library—all become measures of value, not only of the individual but also of the community." In the absence of demonstrable reason, a comforting faith fills the void.[8]

Perhaps for this very reason, analogies of the library and the church are not uncommon. Both are buildings; both are institutions; in differing ways both relate to mind and society; both are or can amount to something even greater than either of these. Again, library theorist James Wellard (1940, p. 87), for example, noted that "For the library, therefore, to concern itself only with the loaning of books to registered borrowers would be as inadequate as the church concerning itself only with the administration of grace to those who had already been saved" (1940, p. 87). More seriously, Pierce Butler (1933, p. xiii) had observed before Wellard that "the librarian has come to conceive his office as a secular priesthood, administering a sacrament of cultural communion to individual souls . . . At every suggestion that his activity be examined as an objective social phenomenon he draws back in terror because he fears that this can be done only by a sacrifice of all spirituality."

Without consensus about library philosophy, this belief system has at least fueled the continuation of efforts to support, perhaps even inspire, attention to the daily service demand, to the interests and liberties of the clientele, and to the library responsibility to posterity. The 'library faith', if that is what it is, has, de facto, kept the library on course. Library historian Wayne Wiegand (1988, p. 69) summarizes this value: "Throughout American history, librarians have tended to accept and perpetuate an 'ideology of reading' inherited from a European intellectual tradition and geared to the overall improvement of society. Through this unquestioning acceptance, the library profession has both limited and contributed to the development and preservation of democratic freedoms in America." But the faith alone has not been enough to help avoid a few misdirections.

Practicalities

Largely because of their limiting capacities for library administration the library faith and the grand tradition, as Lionel R. McColvin called it, according to library theorist K. H. Jones (1978, p. 123), energies that could otherwise have been directed to a guiding philosophy were turned instead to the many practicalities of providing a daily library service: the things one can do and see have been accomplished, and can even be quantified. Those who have expressed the strongest criticisms about the library profession's lack of a guiding philosophy have, almost without exception, complemented that observation with derision of the librarian's tenacious grip on routine and technicality. Noting that the profession had evolved highly efficient systems of practices while ignoring a system of theory, Pierce Butler (1933, pp. xi–xii) ridiculed the profession in a now classic denigration:

> Unlike his colleagues in other fields of social activity the librarian is strangely uninterested in the theoretical aspects of his profession. He seems to possess a unique immunity to that curiosity which elsewhere drives modern man to attempt, somehow, an orientation of his particular labors with the main stream of human life. The librarian apparently stands alone in the simplicity of his pragmatism: a rationalization of each immediate technical process by itself seems to satisfy his intellectual interest.

From his vantage point in England, James Wellard (1940, pp. 142–143) reached a similar, though less caustic, conclusion: "We can see now that both in England and the United States tradition and majority opinion in the profession emphasized the practical side of librarianship at the expense of the cultural aspects of the field... librarians had made an end of the means."[9]

Blame for this turn of events rests in no small part, according to some observers, on the American influence on librarianship. Library historian James Thompson (1974, p. 70), in urging the profession to establish a philosophy, argues that it must shed the all-pervading emphasis on technical matters, an emphasis he says has its origins in the United States. "From Dewey onwards we have had a succession of American experts on cataloguing, on library buildings, on storage methods, on circulation systems. We have been bowled over by American expertise and 'professionalism'." He agrees that this kind of professionalism has its place, but contends that it becomes "absurd when it is employed in a philosophical vacuum and when it distracts attention from considerations of what a library is, what roles it should play, and what a librarian should aim to be." Writing in similar vein, Raymond

Irwin (1949, p. 11) observed as pre-eminent among the differences between the professional literatures of Great Britain and the United States "a certain almost childlike faith in the value of statistical research as applied to librarianship." Chronologically preceding the terms librarianship and library science was that of library economy, which intends to raise the awareness of a need for efficiency in a profession that offers its host organizations no immediately recognizable recovery of the costs of its intangible services and products. In a paragraph that captures the spirit of his total library philosophy, A. Broadfield (1949, p. 56) cleverly ridiculed the pursuit of efficiency:

> At present the librarian is forced to be an efficient business man because of the niggardliness of society and its custom of placing a higher valuation on an external appearance of businesslike method than of free and active thought. One of society's duties to the librarian is to avoid presenting him with the dilemma of efficiency or poverty. Some argue for efficiency on the ground that it would be foolish to make things harder for ourselves by inefficiency. But it is only the single operation or isolated sequence of operations that is made easier for us by efficiency. On the whole, the result of the attitude of mind that is implied in devotion to efficiency is not that we are set free to do things that are supremely worth while, but that we are tied down to perform more of the operations in question. Our time and energy being limited, we are bound to deny to one kind of activity the time and energy that we expend on another. We ought therefore to retain and perfect the efficiency of the techniques which we use as means to our ends, but at the same time reduce greatly the quantity of time and attention which we allow them to claim from us.

To the extent that language can condition the way an organized activity perceives itself and chooses to project its image, it can be imagined that its usage not only excludes others, but also adds an element of mystery for the uninitiated. Looking at a broader scope of professional activities, philosopher of science Carl G. Hemple (1942, p. 47) observes that "In the contemporary methodological literature of psychology and the social sciences, the need for 'operational definitions' is often emphasized to the neglect of the requirement of systematic import, and occasionally the impression is given that the most promising way of furthering the growth of sociology as a scientific discipline is to create a large supply of 'operationally defined' terms of high determinacy and uniformity of usage, leaving it to subsequent research to discover whether these terms lend themselves to the formulation of fruitful theoretical principles." But the influence of pragmatic efforts to achieve the greatest intended results for the effort and financial resources expended was not limited to the kinds of practicalities addressed in the earlier part of this section, as will be seen in the next.

Technology as an End

The perceived propensity of the library profession toward detail, procedures, and routine—the readiness to discuss *how to* rather than *why*—is encountered as a major criticism of librarians in the literature contributed by both librarians and observers from other fields, and has been for many decades. The chief problem here is not the level of attention to the *how to* matters per se, but rather that those matters appear to be considered to the disregard of the *why* matters, again raising the issue of means becoming ends. The situation became even more prominent during the last quarter of the twentieth century, when information technologies emerged as the mainstay of library work in all areas. But it was not simply the all-pervasiveness of technology-driven operations throughout the library that brought about this situation. For the introduction of the computer made evident the ease of counting transactions and measuring operations that could not in practicality have been accomplished before; and it did so while adding an unprecedented level of acceptability to the *how to* matters. Technology lent an air of the scientific. It even smacked of an appealing glamour, perhaps longed-for and not owed entirely to the marvelously enhanced and innovative services it made possible. Library historian Wayne Wiegand (2003, p. vii) summarizes the influence of this phenomenon on research in the field:

> I argue that our current research preoccupation with information technologies, which facilitates the transfer of certain kinds of information that are heavily privileged mostly by powerful groups, has done a fundamental injustice to the democratic service goals of the profession, that it has exacerbated our tunnel vision and blind spots, that it tends to separate LIS researchers from library practitioners, and that it greatly limits what LIS research can contribute to future library planning.

Their services largely taken for granted, and cloaked in the security of the library faith and motto of the librarian as the guardian of the people's right to know, librarians for the most part continued their focus on technical and organizational matters to the near exclusion of matters of purpose, in spite of the occasional exhortations of observers of the changing professional scene. "The concept of the library as an institution designed to store information for particular groups has a rich heritage," writes Wayne Wiegand (1988, p. 70). "And because librarians want that institution to operate efficiently, managing the library has occupied much of their professional attention, especially during the last century." Librarians were not alone in their fascination with the innovative information technologies, but represented only a small and recent part of a much larger trend. Historian of science George Basalla (1988, p. 77) finds that "The fantasization of technology is so pervasive in our culture that it can be used to satirize the technological exuberance that brought it into being." Most of society has been amused by such cartoons, for example.

In view of this general social trend, in combination with the press of daily business and the unceasing pressure for efficiency, the lure of technology, which offered something quickly doable and infinitely measurable, proved to be intensely compelling to librarians individually and as a profession.

The Science Model

When the University of Chicago finalized planning for a Graduate Library School (GLS) in 1926, and followed it five years later with the inception of a new journal, *The Library Quarterly*, both of which were dedicated to advancing research, especially interdisciplinary research in a field called library *science*, a new era in librarianship very definitely was opened.[10] The emphasis would be on research, and the model would be science. Librarianship, whose term of designation was to have been replaced by library science, was not alone in adopting the science model at the time, for the social sciences in general already had taken the positivist direction. A strong start for the program was ensured by a grant from the Carnegie Corporate Foundation, with the intention (Richardson, 1982, p. xv) of supporting GLS influence on the library profession in the way it had supported the leadership of the Johns Hopkins University in medicine and that of Harvard University in law.

The growing pre-eminence of science, at least since the Renaissance and continuing to the present, is one of the great phenomena of social evolution, attracting much attention throughout society. Anyone reading this essay is quite familiar with the immense social influence wielded by science and the extent of admiration and respect that area of knowledge has been given. But how deep does this admiration and respect go? Almost a century ago, anthropologist and philosopher Lucien Lévy-Bruhl (1923, p. 35) posited an answer to this question:

> The uninterrupted feeling of intellectual security is so thoroughly established in our minds that we do not see how it can be disturbed, for even supposing we were suddenly brought face to face with an altogether mysterious phenomenon, the causes of which might entirely escape us at first, we should be convinced that our ignorance was merely temporary; we should know that such causes did exist, and that sooner or later they would declare themselves. Thus the world in which we live is, as it were, intellectualized beforehand. It, like the mind which devises and sets it in motion, is order and reason. Our daily activities, even in their minutest details, imply calm and complete confidence in the immutability of natural laws. The attitude of the primitive's mind is very different.

Contemporary society's admiration of and respect for science and things scientific has developed to a level of trust that largely is taken for granted and certainly unchallenged except in very specific instances. While it is true that the literature of investigation into the methods and motivations of science is voluminous and often questioning, there still remains an assumed order of things. The more immediate surroundings of the emergent library science, which are primarily the social sciences, lent a negative cast to this general sense, however, according to sociologist Roy Wood Sellars (1926, p. x), for "The prestige of the inorganic sciences made it difficult for the social sciences to have confidence in their own insights."

So it is quite logical that science would supply a model for the library that could give it acceptance socially, politically, and academically, and that did, in fact, present manageable means of operation and evaluation. The adoption of the science model was invasive throughout the social sciences for these reasons, all the more so because of the model's presumed objectivity and the facile manipulability of the numbers to which that objectivity could be reduced. "It is easy to assume that the ideas, concepts, or relationships or whatever phenomena we may wish to assign to those numbers, are being dealt with objectively," reasons Jesse Shera (1979, p. 315). Summarizing the long history of the influence of technology on society, which became a fertile part of the expansion of the social sciences, historian and philosopher John Herman Randall (1940, p. 623) concludes his monumental work with the thought that in view of the "appalling need to adjust their social structure to its technological basis, men have been driven to devote more and more of their intellectual energies to the problems of human and social relationships. Those who in another century would have taken their particular social order as a matter of course now bring all their problems to the focus of the maladjustments between group and group."

According to sociologists Peter L. Berger and Thomas Luckmann (1966, p. 16), it was in that context of high-profile technological advance and the rapid adoption of the science model in the academy and elsewhere, that "two of the most famous and most influential 'marching orders' for sociology" were established. They point out that Emile Durkheim (1950, p. 14), a founder of modern sociology and anthropology had claimed that "The first and most fundamental rule is: Consider social facts as things," while sociologist Max Weber (1947, p. 101) already had observed that "Both for sociology in the present sense, and for history, the object of cognition is the subjective meaning-complex of action." Librarianship also adopted the thrust toward the science model, as suggested by the movement to change the name of the practice librarianship to library science, doing so to the joy of some in the field and to the dismay of others. This immediately became a heated controversy[11] that rekindles on occasion.

And the controversy grew even more animated with the information science movement, which more readily accommodates the science model. Influenced, he says, by Sir Karl Popper, one of the pioneers in information science, Bertram C. Brookes (1980, p. 127), asserted that "What information science needs at its roots, it seems to me, is an *objective* rather than a *subjective* theory of knowledge. Any line of thought which claims to be scientific should be dealing with *objectivities* rather than *subjectivities*, though these are terms I need to clarify." At this point in the narrative, it is of some interest to note that three decades prior to Brookes' comment, forward-thinking mathematician and founder of cybernetics Norbert Wiener (1950, p. 125) had gauged that "The fate of information in the typically American world is to become something with a price which can be bought or sold." Although this notion takes some of the possibilities of the application of scientific methods to librarianship to an extreme, and certainly represents a perversion of the intention of the concept of library, Wiener was indeed prescient, for society has become, in the twenty-first century, well acquainted with the concept of information as commodity.

Economist and philosopher Kenneth E. Boulding (1978, p. 126) identifies the underlying cause of the problem to be encountered when mixing the rigid criteria of science with the necessarily more malleable criteria demanded by the social dimension of humanity: "In the absence of any clear measure of complexity, it is hard to say whether social processes are more complex than biological ones, but they are different. The differences arise primarily because social processes are the result of the intervention of an extraordinary organ, the human brain, and its associated nervous system into its environment." While it may be true that the brain and nervous system consist of no more than a combination of physics, biology, and chemistry, as the biologistand philosopher Edward O. Wilson reasons (1998, esp. pp. 266–298), at present there evidently is no way yet to understand in depth and with certitude just how these capacities work together in interaction with their complex environment; at least not sufficient understanding to support that trustworthy criterion of science called prediction. Thus, writes library administrator and educator Lewis F. Stieg (1978, p. 354), it remains that "many phenomena in librarianship are not amenable to scientific observation, classification and measurement." Some aspects of science, such as rationality, the gathering of facts and perspectives, and the highly conscious effort to be objective while recognizing that absolute objectivity is not only unachievable but sometimes even undesirable, should be applicable to the library, but not all.

The Cognition Model

"Man's toughest problem is himself," writes educator Lyman Bryson (1947, p. 180), as the final statement of his book on science and freedom. Similarly, neurologist Antonio R. Damasio (1999, p. 82) writes that consciousness in general "is an entirely personal and private affair and that it is not amenable to the third-person observations that are commonplace in physics and in other branches of the life sciences," which, he says, is a challenge that "applies to all other cognitive phenomena." Thus the single most daunting challenge in librarianship is that of achieving an understanding of the cognitive aspects of motivation relative to information and knowledge; understanding the meaning and the values of the various transactions that take place in a library or other setting of similar purpose. So the library and information science field is, of course, not alone in its struggle with these considerations for, as cognitive psychologist Howard Gardner (1985, p. 295) also concludes, "the history of philosophy and psychology testifies to the difficulty of finding acceptable accounts of how ordinary percepts come about." In the least complex of terms, this is the difference between the social and natural sciences, and it is a difference that falls squarely on the cultural function of the library.

Cognitive science emerged in the early 1970s and developed rapidly. Gardner (1985, p. 6) defines cognitive science as "a contemporary, empirically based effort to answer long-standing epistemological questions—particularly those concerned with the nature of knowledge, its components, its sources, its development, and its deployment" Gardner says he is "interested in whether questions that intrigued our philosophical ancestors can be decisively answered, instructively reformulated, or permanently scuttled. Today cognitive science holds the key to whether they can be." Of the many areas of interest that such a broad field has to offer to the library, some of those summarized by Gardner are directly on target. He writes (p. 5) that cognitive scientists "reflect on language, noting the power and traps entailed in the use of words and their possible predominant influence over thoughts and beliefs. And they speculate at length on the nature of the very activity of knowing: why do we want to know, what are the constraints on knowing, and what are the limits of scientific knowledge about human knowing?" This is the subject matter of the library.

In that connection, the problems that plague library use and user studies, which tend to result in far more questions than answers, constitute a microcosm of the problems confronting theory generally in librarianship. Pierce Butler (1933, p. 106) summarized this situation in the library context three-quarters of a century ago: "For all this there must be a sympathetic understanding of that individual's [the library client's] motive and mental ability. Effective librarianship is largely a matter of accurate psychological diagnosis." The most critical questions can be reduced to these few: what motivates individuals to seek one of the varied experiences the library has to offer (which will be discussed more fully in Chapter 6); how do they determine the approach that should be taken; how does the individual, and eventually society, benefit from the experience? Answers to these questions are to be found in a much better understanding of the mind as both an individual and a social phenomenon than is readily accessible to the profession at this time.

Thus, more directly tailored to the library, Jesse Shera (1972, p. 500) describes the environment in which the librarian operates, the aspect of the library that is timeless and unique, noting that "The librarian operates in an environment of ideas, ideas expressed in bibliographic form." The library is about people and ideas; it is not about books and computers. Meaning, about which the natural sciences need have no concern, but because of which the library environment flourishes, is described by communications scholar Wilbur Schramm (1971, p. 30) as "a cognitive and emotional thing; it exists within the participants."

Douglas J. Foskett (1984, p. 38) has managed to construct a very insightful scenario of how these complexities play out in library transactions. He sets the stage by repeating what most librarians seem to know from experience with various categories of clientele, observing that they are "notoriously vague in their statements of need," even when the need is of an evidently trivial character. Foskett continues (p. 93) his perceptive narrative:

> He [the client] first of all puts into words what he conceives to be the subject of which he requires information. This is a considerable mental discipline, and it is well known to librarians that users rarely succeed in stating their requirements with any precision... This is a phenomenon that we might expect. When a user has been stimulated to make a reference it means that he has become aware of a gap in his knowledge. He wants new information, or maybe information that he once knew but has forgotten—it has lapsed from his own memory and he needs recourse to a record. He finds that he has only an anomalous state of information, that the sum of what he knows of a particular subject does not make a complete or coherent picture; something is lacking. The word or words that he chooses to state his need are more likely to describe the part of the subject that he does know, because he is probably unsure about the missing pieces. It is hard for him to do otherwise, since a considerable mental effort is required to visualize and describe clearly the nature of what one does not know. The fact that something is lacking impresses itself clearly and urgently enough, but the shape and size of the gap are vague and often simply cannot be known at all.

The cognitive challenges of the client are at least doubled for the librarian who wishes to assist, for intellectualizing someone else's cognitive processes must be considerably more difficult than understanding one's own.

It is easy, then, to see why the adoption of the science model might be more attractive to the library world than the adoption of a more cognitive approach to an understanding of the library in society. But physiologist and Nobel laureate Sir Peter B. Medawar (1969) suggests that a closer examination of the workings of science does not completely support the notion of a transparent clarity that society so often seems ready to accept. He notes that few scientists have attempted to analyze their own thought processes, which normally proceed without deep consideration of their mental pathways. Those who do analyze the scientist's method of thinking tend to be philosophers, not scientists. And when scientists do attempt to account for these cognitive processes, their account tends to be untrustworthy. Medawar (p. 10) quotes Einstein: "'If you want to find out anything from the theoretical physicists about the methods they use,' said Albert Einstein, 'I advise you to stick closely to one principle: don't listen to their words, fix your attention on their deeds'." With less detail than Foskett used above in his description of the typical library client's intellectual system, Medawar (p. 46) proposes a narrative of that of the scientist, calling scientific reasoning an exploratory dialogue in two alternating and interacting episodes. "In the imaginative episode we form an opinion, take a view, make an informed guess, which might explain the phenomena under investigation. The generative act is the formation of a hypothesis . . . The process by which we come to formulate a hypothesis is not illogical but non-logical, i.e. outside logic." The method of the scientist is likely more ordered by reason and purpose than that of the typical library client, but still is complex and more than a bit murky.

For the librarian, the issues raised many decades ago by library educators Douglas Waples, Bernard Berelson, and Franklyn R. Bradshaw (1940) remain central to the purpose of the library and the responsibility of the librarian: they pose questions of what reading does to people. And we have understood the centrality of that invisible activity for much longer,[12] of course, but continue to find the answer so far beyond our grasp that we do precious little even to contemplate it, even in a philosophical mode. As the writer C. S. Lewis reportedly said, according to library administrator and educator A. W. McClellan (1973, p. 133), "We must never assume that we know exactly what is happening when anyone else reads a book." Reading is, of course, at the core of the principal concerns of librarianship, for there is considerable transfer from the cognitive processes of reading to the concepts of use and user and their derivatives. But these phenomena surely are worthy of further consideration and research.[13]

Communication, as has been demonstrated for a long time throughout the library literature, is the most basic function of the library. And, like the experiences of both library and reading, human conversation is so common as to be taken for granted. Yet actually, according to Kenneth Boulding (1985, p. 134), "it is a process of almost literally inconceivable complexity in terms of communication and change of structures. In physical systems themselves perhaps the closest parallel to communication is in the phenomenon of catalysis." Jesse Shera (1970, p. 34) spent a substantial part of his career describing librarianship as communication in a special sense, "which is implicit in the transfer of knowledge from a printed page, or a picture, or some other form of graphic record to an individual and the impact of that message upon his conduct." One of the complicating factors in this transfer is that it is not a simple and one-time transaction that can be observed, but rather the accumulation of experiences and lessons that forms the mind. Cultural historian

Raymond Williams (1983, p. 313) ultimately states that "The minds of men are shaped by their whole experience and the most skilful transmission of material which this experience does not confirm will fail to communicate. Communication is not only transmission; it is also reception and response." These are conditions over which the librarian can have no control and into which the librarian can gain precious little insight.[14] More than any others, these also are the conditions that would be made more manageable in the library setting with the guidance of a philosophy.

Summary

Chapter 1 has reviewed the principal reasons for the need of a library philosophy that have been expressed principally throughout the twentieth century by library practitioners and theorists, founded on the practices and thoughts of the earliest influential librarians. It also has summarized the major steps made toward meeting that need, although presenting only enough to make clear that excellent thinking and some debate about purpose and philosophy have been taking place. While these and other scholars and theorists have, indeed, contemplated a library philosophy, or criteria for a philosophy, few have done so in a comprehensive manner, and none has consolidated pertinent thought in a single, integral, work in broad context. So the need continues unmet for many reasons, among which are ambivalence and an attendant neglect, a strong belief system held in the profession and in much of society, the non-threatening comfort of attention to the most pragmatic of matters, the fascination with information technologies, the brilliantly successful, and therefore influential, model of science, and finally the challenges of recognizing that cognition, the function so elusively interwoven in the mind, resides at the center of the library experience in any type of library. This is a daunting list of impediments to the design of a credible philosophy for the total function of library. In her discussion of theory, however, biologist and neurophilosopher Patricia Smith Churchland (2002, p. 133) finds a general lesson: "*theories* about certain things and *definitions* as to *what in the world count* as those things evolve together, hand in hand. Firm explicit definitions become available only fairly late in the game, as the science that embeds them firms up and matures." We may have achieved that level of understanding in the LIS professions.

At bottom, however, these library problems may be subsumed under one concern relevant to this investigation; that concern is that what is seen most clearly, and therefore is studied most readily and understood most easily, often is the *practice* of library and information science, not the *function* of the library. The list of impediments in the way of identifying the philosophy amounts only to a list of parts or aspects of the library function in society. A leading sociologist who specializes in the professions, Andrew Abbott (1998, p. 431) observes that "The sociology of professions has yet to catch up with the wildly dynamic world of contemporary librarianship." His conclusion, however, captures in a few words the formal problem of focusing only on what librarians appear to be doing at any given moment, without regard for the consequences of what is being done, or the ultimate function. Thus (p. 441), like engineering, which in Abbott's terms is a federated profession, librarianship "has always consisted of a loose aggregation of groups doing relatively different kinds of work but sharing a common orientation."

Archeologist Stephen Shennan (2002, p. 43) observes that because of the passing down function of cultural evolution, traditions persist in the face of changing environmental conditions, his point being that "cultural patterns cannot be explained simply in terms of present-day adaptation but also need to be understood in terms of their past history." Adaptation is a stage in a much longer continuum. To the extent that one cannot realistically discuss the social function of library without allusion to librarianship, it is the "common orientation of the profession" that appears as the de facto locus of library philosophy. In her survey of the recent historiography of libraries in Mexico, Rosa María Fernandez de Zamora (1997, p. 241) concludes that "Librarianship, like any other profession, needs to know its origins, to understand why and how libraries of the past were organized; the role they played within their communities; their contribution to the cultural growth of the societies they served; and how they informed the identity of modern Mexican libraries." The desired philosophy must be drawn from the identity of the library, not from the entities and activities with which the practice is identified. This obstacle to the design of an acceptable philosophy is analyzed further in Chapter 2, for it constitutes the single greatest obstacle.

Attempts to perceive the significance of aspects of the cognition model, which would move the proposed philosophy closer to the epistemological function theorists now seem to agree is of greatest significance, and therefore closer to a focus on people and ideas, tends to lack, above all, a penetrating integration into the forces of culture. They lack the dimension of history and continuity so central to a full understanding of the place of library function in society. The science model and the cognition model at least suggested philosophical perspectives for consideration, but they were not appropriate to the library profession in all respects. The problem is that these models consisted in attempts simply to add a veneer that had proved successful in other venues; they seem not to have been models to be molded and fitted as systems in a special environment. Still more recent efforts to arrive at a library philosophy by setting it in the context of philosophical development, while in fact historical, seem to be circumscribed by formality and an attendant rigidity. But the library continues to exist precisely because it is a flexible phenomenon. For a while, perhaps even for a long while, the profession seemed passively satisfied with the study of *libraries*, rather than of the *library*, which is a conclusion summarized thirty years ago by library administrator and educator Lewis F. Stieg (1978, p. 358):

> The unique characteristics of the institutional setting as well as the inadequacy of data prevent generalization on any broad scale. There are, however, similarities in purpose, materials and methods, and administrative structure. Investigations in these areas can provide the data for identification of general principles. The unifying theme may well be the socioeconomic implications of those principles. Although it may be self-defeating to search for theory in the strict interpretation of that term, those general principles can . . . be of help in understanding and explaining particulars.

More than seven decades ago, however, public librarian Clarence E. Sherman (1938, p. 46) suggested that the accumulation of opinions and trends in the thinking of community representatives and librarians could lead to appropriate objectives, "And from these objectives there possibly may be developed, as a by-product, that long awaited and essential intangible—the philosophy of the American public library." In the present book the library and its community are surveyed through the reasoned analyses of many observers, and examined under the organizing lens of cultural evolution. My conclusion is that what has been overlooked in all the efforts to identify an appropriate model for library philosophy is quite simply that the library is its own model. Perhaps that is the message to be taken from the long resounding echoes of philosophy.

CHAPTER 2

Strategic Considerations

> There is, upon the whole, nothing more important in life than to find out the right point of view from which things should be looked at and judged of, and then to keep to that point.
>
> —Karl von Clausewitz, 1932

Introduction

The library is not an assemblage of books and other information formats that contain information. Indeed, the library is that, but it is also much more. It is made up of all the acts and transactions that are initiated on a daily basis in the name of library service: selection, preservation, organization, assistance, assurance of freedoms, and the myriad processes of communication that accompany these functions, which have been conceived as means to bring recorded knowledge and experience to the support of society and individual. In the course of these transactions between library clientele and their respective libraries, library function adjusts technique incrementally to remain an intellectual reflection of society; and in their accumulation through centuries and millennia, society and library increasingly have become interlocked. Library function consists of these acts and transactions as they have accumulated over time—vast expanses of time—to interact with humanity in a way that facilitates and expedites human adaptation to both the challenges and the opportunities posed by environmental conditions as they change. All these overt activities are representative of library function in society, which carries a much more profound significance than the sum of all these many parts.

Among the purposes of the present study is to demonstrate that the library is not only a physical entity held together by a set of policies, procedures, and transactions, but also a conceptual entity of much greater function because of the manner of its integration into the condition of being human. As such, library as concept is presented as an extension of human nature. This is the principle that underlies the present examination to identify an explanatory and guiding library philosophy.

Human beings differ significantly from other natural beings in a number of ways. Foremost among the differences that set human beings apart is their interaction with an extraordinarily strong culture that has evolved to alter their condition from that of the cave dweller to that of the outer-space dweller, and that continues to evolve; it is a culture that humans create, and which then further recasts humanity in its individual and societal manifestations. Essential to the present exploration for library philosophy is an understanding of the library's place in the evolution of culture. Although the evolution of culture is imperceptible at any given point in time, over long stretches of time it is, to the contrary, highly perceptible, because it is marked by the accumulation of continuous changes great and small. And because humans interact with their culture every day, it is above all in the combination of daily and millennial perspectives that the library function in cultural evolution can be seen most clearly and completely as one symbiotic function.

The search for library philosophy logically begins with the location of the most promising site in which to find the appropriate kind of philosophy, which I believe is its purpose in culture, rendered most visible in cultural evolution. Many excellent minds throughout the ages, both within and outside library and information science, have been applied to the challenge of elucidating the purpose of the library, because an understanding of its purpose, of its ultimate function in society, constitutes the framework of a library philosophy. But only a very small part of this scholarship has focused explicitly on the library's development within its larger context, while, taking the other extreme, much more work extending well beyond the scope of library and information science, has concentrated on the cultural context, although with reference to the library only by implication. The present study distills from the most cogent of the latter analyses, interpretations, and theories about culture, society, and the individual the essence of library purpose and thus its philosophy. It is within the motivations of humanity, which is to say the thought processes identified as belonging uniquely to humans, that resides the most fundamental purpose of the library. The library is woven tightly into the fabric of cultural evolution, along with all its principal elements of language, literacy, communication, cooperation, experience, knowledge, values, memory, reasoning, decision-making, beliefs, orientation to the future, imagination and creativity, entertainment, understanding, concepts and percepts, progress, and democratic ideals, all of which support the definitions of self-identity and world view.

Scholars who theorize about cultural evolution do so from the special perspective of their primary discipline, yet within even that relatively narrow range of possibilities there are conflicting schools of thought. Consequently, academic debates about cultural evolution do abound, as well they should, since through that process glimpses into understanding can be refined, perhaps even achieved at a much higher level. The present synthesis addresses only a few of these conflicts or exceptions directly with explanation, and are chosen for that abbreviated treatment only when judged of special significance to an understanding of the place of the library in cultural evolution. And it is very definitely from the library perspective that this essay examines relevant scholarship.

Certain concepts need to be addressed at the beginning of this exploration in the search for library philosophy to ensure that it stays on course. They are fundamental, yet can cause some confusion if not considered with the explicit intention of precluding or minimizing confusion. In order of discussion, these concepts are: philosophy, social sciences, evolution in contrast with history, the relations of history and philosophy, the word "library," the place of the practice of librarianship, and the concept of function as it relates to library. They are concepts that will re-appear frequently in ever-narrower contexts as the present study progresses. In view of the need to address these concepts in just the right way to perceive the function in which philosophy resides, they are very strategic considerations.

Philosophy

The development of philosophy, science, and scholarship are closely intertwined. As reflected in the contemporary French and German languages, for example, science and Wissenschaft respectively continue generally to mean knowledge well founded on critical thinking, while in English the word science usually signifies knowledge only of the natural world, narrowly defined. Moreover, the word science, as science historian Rachel Laudan (2003, p. 632) calls to memory, "comes from the Latin *scientia* (itself a translation of the Greek *episteme*), meaning certain knowledge as opposed to mere opinion or *doxa*." But philosophy is knowledge of a less certain type, a quest for comprehension solely by way of reason, that state we refer to as understanding, more about which will be said in Chapter 7. Philosophy is also a love of knowledge, a love of learning. Philosophy does not address questions of *what* or *how* nearly so much as it addresses questions of *why*. It provides the subconscious context in which we engage thought processes that lead to actions. As this text continues it will become evident that what constitutes science is not just investigation and consideration undertaken in select disciplines, but is a rational process engaged in, more or less self-consciously, by all humans relative to concerns even of the most mundane kind.

Given this context, throughout the present essay philosophy is treated as a concentration on not just the surface appearance and surface significance of those actions, but on the significance that lies beneath, the elements that constitute reasons for the surface activity. Philosophy is a search for understanding through questioning, relating, and integrating, and attends to the implications of the actions and the considerations that give rise to the actions. In the process of asking why, philosophy concerns itself with all that is or might be embraced by a particular concept at issue. For present considerations in introducing the subject of this book, library philosophy is an attitude about how we perceive the underlying purpose of and principles behind what we do. By way of illustration through comparison, the philosophy guiding the medical profession would inform the principles behind the actions that are in most evidence, such as listening to the heart, looking into the throat or at an X-ray, and other visible or otherwise apparent activities. Then there are clearly medical actions taken, such as surgery, setting a broken bone, prescription of medication, or other therapy. Such actions are categorized into basic parts, such that evaluation leads to diagnosis and diagnosis leads to treatment. The philosophy is the part that incorporates these meta actions into the even broader scope of health care, explaining by statement of professional mission or philosophy why the health care provider follows certain principles and initiates certain procedures. The philosophy is to ease suffering and prolong life, and to do so without causing harm. In this way the forest issues are distinguished from the trees issues. What transpires is clear to the practitioner and as understandable as reasonably possible to the outsider.

In the case of any professional practice, a philosophy serves several purposes: to *provide a readily understandable context* for communicating to others intelligently and as fully as reasonably possible what is done and how it is done; to *explain* why it is done; to *evaluate* what is done and the manner in which it is done; and, above all, to *guide* the what and the how of the activity. Answering the question *why?* is fundamental to doing the right things the right way. The library profession categorizes its activities into basic operations called selection, organization, guidance in information seeking and interpretation, and preservation, among others, each of which is accompanied by many principles and procedures. They are separate but mutually dependent manifestations of function and modes of expressing in action the philosophy that underpins the principles developed for each. It is quite orderly. There is no mystery to any of it.

Social Sciences

Library science and information science generally are considered social sciences among the various disciplinary clusters, even though that designation is found by many to be unsatisfactory. Anthropologist John Tooby and psychologist Leda Cosmides (1992, p. 23) observe that the social sciences, even after more than a century of their existence as an accepted scientific cluster, generally are still adrift, "with an enormous mass of half-digested observations, a not inconsiderable body of empirical generalizations, and a contradictory stew of ungrounded, middle-level theories expressed in a Babel of incommensurate technical lexicons." They note, however, that by the late twentieth century this impression was accompanied by a growing malaise, so that the single major trend came to be one characterized by rejection of the scientific enterprise as it applies to humans. The research team further suggests (p. 23) that this lack of progress, this "failure to thrive," has been caused by the failure of the social sciences to explore or accept their logical connections to the rest of the body of science—that is, to causally locate their objects of study inside the larger network of scientific knowledge. "In place of the Standard Social Science Model, there is emerging a new framework that we will call the Integrated Causal Model. This alternative framework makes progress possible by accepting and exploiting the natural connections that exist among all the branches of science, using them to construct careful analyses of the causal interplay among all the factors that bear on a phenomenon." Based on their general outline of this approach to research and theory, it seems to fit most closely the approach adopted in the present study, where there will be frequent reference to the appropriate situation of LIS theory among all the sciences.

Evolution & History

A word about the professional disciplines of cultural evolution and history may be in order here. These two areas of study bear similar features, both sharing an interest in the past and offering a dubious predictive capacity, and they both, of course, strive to achieve a fuller understanding of the human world. Yet the study of history and of cultural evolution are not the same.

Concluding his landmark study of societal evolution well over a century ago, anthropologist Edward Burnett Tylor (1871, vol. 2, p. 402) observed "It has to be maintained that the early history of man has its bearing, almost ignored as that bearing has been by those whom it ought most stringently to affect, on some of the deepest and most vital points of our intellectual, industrial, and social state." Perhaps the influence of humanity's early state largely had been ignored prior to Tylor because it had not been perceived a relevant part of the present, but instead as something completely unattached to it, different and not at all related. Charles Darwin's (1859) study of biological evolution, however, triggered a flurry of systematic inquiry into the story of humankind through a new but analogous perspective that soon came to be understood as cultural evolution. This is a science that looks at humanity as the product of a continuous process rather than a series of events. The human past is viewed as very much a part of the present, having gone through a staged and gradual process of change, not necessarily with a beginning or an end.

Philosopher Maurice Halbwachs (1980, pp. 80–87) offers insight into the subtle distinction of history and evolution by separating history and collective memory, without which there would be no cultural evolution. "Collective memory differs from history in at least two respects. It is a current of continuous thought whose continuity is not at all artificial, for it retains from the past only what still lives or is capable of living in the consciousness of the groups keeping the memory alive. By definition it does not exceed the boundaries of this group." Halbwachs finds another distinction, which is that "In effect, there are several collective memories. This is the second characteristic distinguishing the collective memory from history. History is unitary, and it can be said that there is only one history." He subsequently explains the latter distinction at length.

Whereas history is indeed about the past, cultural evolution is about the past, present, and future. This difference derives largely from the fact that history is about a situation within human life, while culture is about a condition of human life. For example, in his study of technology, historian George Basalla (1988, p. 209) finds that "History and the social or psychological sciences provide inadequate explanations for the appearance of novel artifacts within the made world . . . The importance of play and fantasy in the creation of technological innovation has been stressed here because their significance has been overlooked by scholars who believe necessity is the sole spur to invention."

The examination of history is about an event or series of events having already occurred; thus, says historian Penelope Corfield (2007, p. 246), it is always a work in progress. This is because "all our evidence and experience are situated within an asymmetrical time and are therefore always expanding and changing the perspectives. Yet this developmental component is an essential part of the subject's strength. If human understandings of history become ossified, then the result is like a "stuck" collective memory, which is ultimately as damaging to a community as it is for individuals who cannot adjust to changing times." The history of an event or time or place or person commences and concludes at finite points in time except as it is re-interpreted or as new information is added. By contrast, evolution addresses a never-ending process in motion, only achieving stages as designated by scholars. History is about specific individuals and societies; cultural evolution is about humanity. As history may be about societies, cultural evolution is about society; and whereas history studies the economic and political order of society, evolution studies the symbolic order of society.

As a consequence of these specific differences, history relies on evidence, preferably objective proof, of an accomplished event, whereas cultural evolution relies on reasoned understanding of cognition linked to human motivations. Anthropologist Robert Boyd and environmental scientist Peter

J. Richerson (2005, p. 288) offer insight into distinctions between the methodologies:

> There is (or ought to be) an intimate interplay between the study of the unique events of given historical sequences and the generalizations about process constructed by studying many cases in a comparative and synthetic framework. The study of unique cases furnishes the data from which generalizations are derived, while the generalizations allow us to understand better the processes that operated on particular historical trajectories. We cannot neglect the close, critical study of particular cases without putting the database for generalization in jeopardy... On the other hand, it is from the study of many cases that we form a body of theory about evolutionary processes. No one historical trajectory contains enough information to obtain a very good grasp of the processes that affected its own evolution.

To avoid being judged too harshly for splitting hairs, it should be noted that not all who study history or cultural evolution see them as mutually exclusive sciences. Social anthropologist Tim Ingold (2002, p. 63), for example, reasons that they are clearly related in the most fundamental ways:

> For while we may grow out of certain ways of doing things, and grow into others, no-one has ever grown out of biology, or grown into culture! Now if evolution is about the changing forms and capacities of organisms, then we must conclude that whatever capacities have emerged in history, and which may be taken to distinguish humans of one tradition from those of another, have themselves evolved. History, it appears, is no more than a continuation, into the field of human relations, of a process that is going on throughout the organic world. The distinction between history and evolution is thus dissolved. Indeed evolution is proceeding around us all the time, in the very historical unfolding of our lives.

In many respects, the situation Ingold describes is much the reverse of that created in the LIS field by its failure to distinguish between library the concept and librarianship the practice, which is addressed further in this chapter and treated in Chapter 5 as the single most significant impediment to a determination of library philosophy. Somewhat akin to Ingold's description of historical scholarship is intellectual historian Charles Van Doren's (1967, p. 199) account of the conclusion reached by nineteenth-century Renaissance scholar Jacob Burckhardt, who denied any single, overall pattern of history. Burckhardt, he says, found that in every developed civilization, various aspects of culture continually affect and modify one another so that all that one can see at any given moment is the temporarily dominant factor. In this view, "History presents a constant shifting of values; progress in one respect is made at the expense of regress in another, with the result that both progress and regress are merely apparent. In short, gains are canceled by losses, and the sum remains zero." Related to this understanding, according to Van Doren, is Burckhardt's notion that "human nature remains essentially the same at all times." This could be interpreted as a partial reconciliation of history and cultural evolution.

But another, very basic difference traditionally has separated research in history and research in cultural evolution. Published in its first version in 1942, science philosopher Carl G. Hempel's landmark essay (1965) on the application of general laws to the study of history makes it clear that, at least in Hempel's estimation, historians in mid-twentieth century tended not to accept the application of general laws to their field in the manner of scholars in the natural sciences and of some in the social sciences, and certainly in cultural evolutionary studies. But, to the contrary of that tradition, Hempel sets about to show (p. 231) that "general laws have quite analogous functions in history and in the natural sciences, that they form an indispensable instrument of historical research, and that they even constitute the common basis of various procedures which are often considered as characteristic of the social in contradistinction to the natural sciences." By general laws, Hempel means (p. 231) "a statement of universal conditional form which is capable of being confirmed or disconfirmed by suitable empirical findings. The term law suggests the idea that the statement in question is actually well confirmed by the relevant evidence available." Cultural evolution, on the other hand, is based very squarely on general laws, as will be seen in Chapter 3.

Six decades following Hempel's remarks, the discipline of history is advised also by one of its leading theorists, Reinhart Koselleck (2002, p. 9) to work with "hypotheses that introduce constant factors, against which variables can be measured." Historical research has become isolated, he says, and therefore is of less value, because "Ever since the era of new-Kantianism, our academic field has been caught in a self-definition: History has to do with what is individual and specific, whereas the natural sciences concern themselves with what is general" (p. 1). So, perhaps the discipline is beginning to move along a gradation toward the general application of scientific laws. But as far as history's adoption of the expansive characteristics of cultural evolution, there is still a fuller range of differences that distinguish research in history and research in cultural evolution.

The present study is in no way a study in history. It is intended to be a synthesis of scholarship in the broad field of cultural evolution, using as its focus the role of the social institution called library. That said, it is no surprise that in the course of entering into research and theory produced in the many diverse fields that are essential to it, I have assumed the very risks outlined by historian Arthur O. Lovejoy (1936, p. 21), who alerts his readers, as I do through his words, that "Because the historian of an idea is compelled by the nature of his enterprise to gather material from several fields of knowledge, he is inevitably, in at least some parts of his synthesis, liable to the errors which lie in wait for the non-specialist."

History & Philosophy

The relation of philosophy to historical scholarship also has bearing on this book. Any standard desk dictionary would likely define the word philosophy as the pursuit of wisdom; a search for a general understanding of values and reality chiefly by speculative rather than observational means; an analysis of grounds and concepts expressing fundamental beliefs; a theory underlying or regarding a sphere of activity or thought. In that context, the concept of understanding is critical to the present study and will be examined more closely in Chapter 7. Further defining what is meant by philosophy, philosopher of history R. G. Collingwood (1999, p. 114) cites the distinctions traditionally drawn between philosophy and history on the bases of their method and the objects of their study:

> With regard to their methods, philosophy has been conceived as working by means of demonstration, staking its very life on its ability to prove with conclusive force the doctrines it asserts, and accomplishing nothing unless that is accomplished: history as working by the acceptance of what authorities have to say, or alternatively (since the notion of an authority has long been obsolete among working historians) as unable to reach demonstrative certainty from interpretation of its evidence . . . With regard to their objects, philosophy has been conceived as thought about the universal, the timeless, the eternal: history as thought about the individual, the temporal, the transient.

Establishing a philosophy means inferring it from the general, because it is the essence of any object of study that provides the frame for perceiving its particulars and for identifying the relations and connections of the particulars. A philosophy therefore is not for today, yesterday, or tomorrow, but for all time.

For immediate purposes, philosophy is an approach or attitude that encompasses all types of libraries and all operations within them for all time,[1] taken in the aggregate. But the various types of libraries and the multitudinous procedures and transactions carried out within them as means of library service appear to be determined in the absence of an underlying philosophy. Surely that is not a valid perception, for those transactions respond to the surrounding society. Not in detail, but in gross outline, their purpose is determined by the library's cultural function in society. Library philosophy is only tangentially about a physical structure or a geographic setting, for it relates directly to a cultural function in society from which the library's structure, mission, goals, objectives, strategies, and operations are derived. Library philosophy thus will be seen as the context that gives definition to the relevance of the concepts and theories employed to inform programs of professional preparation, practice, and research.

Not long ago, sociologist Régis Debray (2000, p. 60) pointed out that, contrary to all the earlier predictions about the rapid expansion of dependence on the automobile leading to an atrophy of the human leg, it turned out to lead in quite the opposite direction: to jogging. Calling this the jogging effect, he related it to the ironic influence of the rising digital society on the concurrent wave of monumental library construction: "These technologically superfluous extravagances are yet deemed necessary *ethnically* [culturally]. Rather than erasing sites of memory and commemoration, digital delocalization and audiovisual amnesia generate them in profusion. The spirits of marble are revived by the flux around them." The technologies that help advance society do change with relative swiftness and apparent ease, while the way we think and feel about the essentials of life prove to be far more stable. Similarly, writing about the millennia of library development, library philosopher and historian Jesse Shera (1973, p. 94) wisely advised that the library "has not changed its basic mission, which is to maximize the social utility of graphic records, and it is its special responsibility to operate in that complex association of record and human mind. Yet this relationship, which is at once intellectual, psychological, and physiological, is still only imperfectly understood." That complex relationship is the subject matter of this study, for it contains the library philosophy.

Librarianship the Wrong Focus

A problem encountered by anyone contemplating library philosophy is posed immediately and simply by the word library, for its linguistic and conceptual derivatives tend at times to be used indiscriminately. Too frequently it is easy to confuse the root word with concepts represented by other manifestations in the words *librarian*, *librarianship*, *library science*, and even *information science*; derivatives of the concept in question do not, in fact, constitute the concept itself. To further complicate matters, the purposes of differing types of libraries, each fulfilling differing missions, figure into this mix of problems in communication and understanding. Such differences in management and operation, about which many books and articles are written, do not constitute the library function; they are not about *why* the specific operations are performed. Such scholarly and professional contributions are instead about *how* the operations, which stem from function, can best be performed.

Being a term of recent vintage within library history, information science is in the midst of a struggle for own identification, not to mention a search for guiding philosophy, which seems hardly to have been undertaken. Pioneering information scientist Harold Borko's (1968, p. 5) classically clear statement of definition of information science has been influential for the past four decades. For him, information science "is an interdisciplinary science that investigates the properties and behavior of information, the forces that govern the flow and use of information, and the techniques, both manual and mechanical, of processing information for optimal storage, retrieval, and dissemination."

In a more recent paper advocating and justifying a name change from information science to knowledge science, and in which the author also considers message science and content science as logical possibilities, the reader is advised by Chaim Zins (2006, p. 448) to "Note that 'knowledge science' can explore knowledge and its building blocks, information and data, but 'information science' cannot explore knowledge, since the latter is of a higher order." And as will be seen in Chapter 4, knowledge is of the highest order in cultural evolution. Zins observes further (p. 459) that "As the field of information science has reached maturity, it enters into an age of reorganization" (p. 459).

But the formal signs of maturity, which at least should have to include agreement on the substance of the profession, seem not to have been attained yet in information science. For the time being, it seems to occupy responsibilities that fall primarily among those daily procedures and transactions that culminate in the library and information service to society. Prior to Zins's assessment, library historian Margaret F. Stieg (1992, p. 13) had summarized the situation of the varied approaches to services connecting society to information, with her conclusion that ultimately the relation of librarianship and information science depends on the individual's perception of each. "One can regard the two as identical; information science is simply librarianship under another name. Then there is information science as a branch of librarianship, junior partner in an ancient enterprise. Others consider information science the theoretical foundation of all the information professions and librarianship one of its applications. And finally, there is library-and-information-science, the new federated discipline." The contention of the present essay is that this situation remains highly amenable to confusion primarily because the ultimate purpose of the specific activities entailed in the object of study are not being considered in the context of an encompassing greater purpose that reaches beyond those activities per se.

For reasons similar to those cited above, one also encounters confusion among several related concepts that raise the question of whether library is a function, a concrete structure, or a discipline-dependent branch. And then there are the questions about whether it is an art, a craft, a science, a social science, a corrupt branch of the humanities, a part of something else, or something of its own, and whether it is a thing or a process. One could easily conclude, solely on the basis of this variety of possibilities, that such ambiguity has hindered, perhaps in seemingly minor yet tenaciously frequent and consistent ways, the establishment of a library philosophy. To repeat: in the present study, the practices of librarianship, library science, and information science are understood to be focused on the ways and means by which the mission of library as a cultural concept is fulfilled. These matters, as important as they are, do not constitute the library in the present study, nor do all of them taken together amount to the library concept. The library concept is greater than the sum of all its parts, for it is intensely and significantly integrated into cultural evolution. It is the basis from which this essay proceeds.

While the concept of library is of greater magnitude than the sum of all its many parts, the two components most often are mistaken to be one and the same, calling to mind philosopher Gilbert Ryle's (1949) category-mistake. His idea addresses the situation whereby the parts and actions of an entity can be confused with the category of which they are constituent, taking the part or parts to be the category, and thereby missing the true significance of the greater, inclusive category. The subject of the present essay is library as a concept of considerable significance in cultural process. It is not about *how* the library functions, how it *should* function, or about how information behaves; it is about *why* the library functions in the first place.

Within the library profession libraries are classified foremost according to the line of their administrative accountability, which indicates their particularized mission. While this classification is useful for practical purposes engaged in by those in the profession, such as grouping by library type and size as a means to understand common situations and conditions and to establish benchmarking performance practices, it can be misleading for other purposes. Moreover, the very existence of all these types and sizes of libraries, each with differing missions and emphases in the service of differing clientele, contributes to the perception of multiple, perhaps even conflicting, purposes of the library in society. Library administrator and educator Lewis F. Stieg (1978, p. 354) reasons that "If libarianship's scientific manifestation is legitimately classified as a social science, it seems axiomatic that any search for the kind of theory that it may be able to achieve must at some point include analysis of its relationship to the social forces that brought it into being and continue to chart its course." His discussion revolves specifically around the emergence of the academic library within the academy, but the essential idea applies to the library generally in its evolution within culture, understood in the broadest sense. The contention of the present study is that there has been and continues to be a library philosophy at work, quietly and all but imperceptibly, for a very long time and that it provides a basis of understanding, explanation, and guidance to all libraries and all of their operations.

Library the Focus

The library has been defined in many ways for at least many centuries. Socrates saw it as the delivery room for the birth of ideas (Braverman, 2000, p. 100); for Horace Mann the library was the crowning glory of our public schools (Shera, 1973, p. 93); Oliver Wendell Holmes imagined it as a nest to hatch scholars (Shera, 1972, p. 140); William S. Learned described it as "the community's intelligence service" (Learned, 1924, p. 26); S. R. Ranganathan concluded that the library is an externalized memory (Foskett, 1984, pp. 43, 89); social economist Alvin Johnson judged the library to be the peoples' university (Johnson, 1938); and Jesse Shera himself saw it as an agency of communication (1970, p. 67). Above its portal in ancient Thebes the library is labeled The Medicine Chest of the Soul (Braverman, 2000, p. 100); and also in ancient Egypt, the library of King Osymandyas was The Soul's Dispensary (Edwards, 1865, p. 4). This is but a small sampling of the epithets assigned throughout at least the past two thousand years to the library in efforts to crystallize its positive social significance.[2]

Emphasis in the present synthesis is on library as a cultural concept. "Whatever its external form may be," writes information scientist Kevin McGarry (1993, p. 106), "the essence of a library is a *collection of materials organized for use*. The outer forms of these materials have changed with each innovation in communications technology from clay tablets to the computer." And that simple fact carries with it the potential for misunderstanding about libraries being, in the most specific sense, a location where books are stored. There are etymological reasons for this, but the resulting images of both book and library grow less valid each day. Like McGarry, but four decades earlier, library philosopher and historian Pierce Butler (1952, p. 90) referred to all the things gathered and made accessible by the library as "books, the actual packages of ideas the library must use," and in the present study all those formats of recorded knowledge and experience are understood as the "generic book," that is, whatever may constitute the graphic record conveyed through the social transcript. This also is the sense in which information scientist Bertram C. Brookes (1980, p. 132) explains that "A book is both a physical thing and a potential source of knowledge. So in using the term book we have to make our reference clear in this context: are we referring to the physical or the mental aspect of the book? . . . To analyse information and knowledge we have to operate on purely mental entities." To be sure, it is the cognitive aspect that is the focus of the present study, while also recognizing a significant symbolic value of the physical book in culture.

Raised earlier in this chapter is the matter of misunderstanding that can be incurred through confusion of the terms *library* and *librarianship*. Attention is now turned momentarily to the practice of librarianship, which bears the responsibility for whatever actions are taken in fulfilling the concept of library.

And because the concept of library has very broad connotations, as will be demonstrated in the course of this essay, the practice called librarianship embraces activities that appear in the ongoing press of business to be quite remote from the concept[3] of which they are a part. But those activities do relate to the concept when they are considered in their incremental dimension and over a great expanse of time, just as culture itself evolves. Sometimes society even seems to be no more aware of an evolutionary function of the library than it is conscious of the many other evolutionary forces at work in its surroundings every day. In other words, the grand evolution of culture may proceed along lines that are relatively logical, albeit unpredictable, as does the library; but within the moment, the degree of awareness of that process varies among individuals from not-in-the-least to a fairly sound understanding of its place.

Clearly, the *definition* of library is a much less complex notion than the *concept* of library. Thus, definition and concept are distinguished by information scientist Nicholas Belkin (1978, p. 58) in his analysis of information: "The distinction is that a definition presumably says what the phenomenon defined *is,* whereas a concept is a way of looking at, or interpreting, the phenomenon. Although there have been various reasons proposed for the significance of this distinction, the crucial one for this argument is that by accepting the idea of a concept one becomes free to look for a *useful* concept, rather than a universally *true* definition, of information." The *concept* of library definitely is of greater value to a discussion of its function than is a *definition* of library. As philosopher and cognitive scientist Paul Thagard (1992, p. 25) emphasizes, "explanation is one of the roles that concepts must serve," and an explanation of the library's function is exactly what is sought here.

The definition of *librarianship*, on the other hand, is of value in this discussion to the extent that it addresses the more visible, the practical or daily, contribution to the library's function in cultural evolution. According to library theorist Ronald C. Benge (1970, p. 222), all the available definitions of librarianship include four main areas of activity: The collection of material appropriate for libraries; the preservation of the material; the organization of the collections; the dissemination of the material or the information which it contains. He adds that "This may include interpretation." Practice in each of these areas of librarianship, which is to say routine daily activities, entails many kinds of operations, skills, and knowledge in a complex of processes. "Librarianship is a process," says library educator and theorist Douglas J. Foskett, (1962, p. 8) "and like all processes is a dynamic continuum." Library and information science constitute culture and social transcript in the making at the point of change. They are scientific in daily service and humanistic in the long-term function of ensuring communication between the past and the future, which is the transmission of culture. Foskett (p. 6) encapsulates the latter notion: "As librarians, we are the guardians—not the owners, but the guardians—of knowledge." But it is to both the long- and short-term considerations of librarianship that library philosopher Jesse Shera (1966, p. 70) refers in a paper he gave in 1962 in his concise but pregnant definition of librarianship as "the management of human knowledge." And he refers specifically (p. 71) to the humanistic traditions and scientific predispositions of librarianship in carrying out the library role in the synthesis of the total human experience. It seems that in the practice of librarianship, much like that of the field of anthropology, as anthropologist Robert Redfield (1962, p. 123) describes it "the science is sought while the human reality is never forgotten." Such a notion hints at a duality in the purpose of the library. From his perspective as a cultural historian, Raymond Irwin (1949, p. 62) defines librarianship as "that branch of learning which has to do with the recognition, collection, organization, preservation and utilization of graphic and printed records."

A very succinct, yet broadly inclusive, definition of librarianship is the statement that is crafted by information scientist J. G. Meijer (1982, p. 26) to be scientifically tenable:

> Librarianship is a form of cultural enterprise whose main characteristic is the stimulation of the optimum use of mankind's cultural heritage insofar as it consists of coded thoughts recorded in documents that are and must be held in readiness for use with the ultimate objective of making possible cultural progress (also in the fields of religion and science) in its particular sphere.

There are those who predict that the operations and services of librarianship, library science, and information science will one day be performed by organizations not called libraries, that relevant services will no longer be managed by people identified by designations that recall those supplanted activities, and consequently that the library will no longer exist. It is not at all difficult to point to budding stimuli for this shifting image. Such predictions, however, are neither challenged nor supported in this essay, for they are irrelevant to the essay's purpose in describing function. That function is part of culture no matter how, where, or by whom it is effected.

This essay contends that there is a fundamental cultural need for the function of which humanity has availed itself for many generations because it was invented and has been sustained to accommodate human need. It is a cultural function that pertains to stewardship of the recorded social transcript and, therefore, is a cultural technology that transcends location and method. Communication technologies that have been developed primarily during the past forty years, along with the services they make possible, are being applied and will continue to be applied to the management of library function, just as new strategies always have been; some of these services may even be developed into as yet unknown dimensions of the library function. But, regardless of the term or terms employed to identify what is called in these pages the library function, regardless of the management strategies followed to fulfill the social requirements of the function, and regardless of new dimensions that may be added to it, that function remains because the library function is natural to cultural evolution. This is the foundation of its guiding and explanatory philosophy.

Function of the Library

To understand the library as a concept is to know that its function is highly social, perhaps more profoundly social than that of any other institution, as will become evident in the following chapters that address fundamental motivations of both the individual and society. Proceeding from the premise of the library's social nature, it may be useful to consider that developmental psychologist David F. Bjorklund and educational psychologist Anthony D. Pellegrini (2002, p. 203) conclude from their work that "Perhaps the single most basic ability underlying human social interaction is the understanding that other people have knowledge and desires that may be different from one's own." They elaborate that "We understand that our own behavior is based on what we believe (know, expect) and what we desire (want, wish)—and we assume that others' behavior is based on their beliefs and desires—and that our beliefs and desires can be different from those of others" (p. 204). This apparently simple human ability will be seen to manifest many cultural implications that have drawn upon the library and have sustained it for many generations.

One can readily understand that the function of the library is permeated with various purposes that are guided by as many possibilities as there are ideas. Ideas are valued highly by culture, but they are temporal, being assigned a relative value. Thus the library purpose is layered by values that change as the human environment changes and as the culture evolves. But ideas always are valued. Some of these ideas address the needs of the moment, while others quite consciously address the likely needs of future generations. And some of the needs are those experienced by individuals, while others are experienced by society.[4] But in any case the library exists to meet the need and to stimulate new ideas because it maintains the store of ideas for use, re-use, and modification. The essential force in the library's development is the degree of consciousness of purpose held for it within the profession and by the greater society. And that degree of consciousness varies with the nature of challenges confronting society at any given time, along with the responsibilities assigned it by society and assumed by the profession on a sliding scale that registers on calibrations extending from the library as a topographical point in the confines of the community to the library as a concept in cultural evolution. The library as a topographical point in the community dominates the literature of library and information science, but the remainder of this essay will address, with sporadic exceptions as necessary for clarification, the library as a concept in cultural evolution.

In his study of the current British public library, historian Peter Brophy (2001) reminds us that the original and consistent purpose of the library generally has been viewed to be its social function in terms of preservation and organization of materials for use. He demonstrates that until the nineteenth century the emphasis of librarianship was on the collection, rather than on the community, and that innovations such as the institution of legal deposit and systematization of knowledge organization schemes led to a refocused emphasis on the community. With the development of these concepts, the public library pioneers became conscious of the major role that is played by the library, that it is a social institution with an ongoing function in the organization of society. "While some saw this as social control," Brophy explains (p. 49), "others took a more liberal and progressive view, seeing in the public library a means to spread literacy and a love of learning." He finds emerging in the second half of the twentieth century a clear focus within the LIS professions on the needs of *individuals* related to information, knowledge, understanding, and learning. Expressed in the so-called grand tradition of the public library, for example, the function is liberal, humane, and rational.[5] This tradition, characterized by library theorist K. H. Jones (1978, p. 123), considers the public library as

> an institution helping to sustain an "open society," an institution which will serve to open the mind of the rational, truth-seeking citizen to a whole range of opinion, giving him both sound judgement and tolerance. It will supply literature and information to sustain technical innovation and progress in the national and individual interest. It will provide the means for ordinary people to broaden their cultural vision and understanding and thus enrich society as a whole.

Specifically relevant to library purpose, the assertion of library historian James Thompson (1974, p. 42) is that "The principle J. H. Shera invoked is the most significant in librarianship to-day," because, while Shera sees the library primarily as an agency of communication, he does so in a very special way that depends on the librarian's intention. Thompson's interpretation of Shera's understanding of the library's social role in communication is that in a time of increasing specialization and social fragmentation the library can become a great force for cohesion. However, Thompson (p. 42) says, by 'cohesion' Shera does not mean the achievement of conformity, but that "whereas the mass media such as newspapers and television are declaratory, 'the library is interrogative'... Shera stresses that a library is a unifying, not a homogenizing force."

Again, however, two dimensions of communication are at issue in the determination of the library function, and the two are mutually dependent. One dimension relates to current service and has primarily to do with relevance and flexibility. And so it is the library's function, Douglas J. Foskett (1962, p. 10) emphasizes, "to serve as a store of information from which each reader can draw as he requires. It is an automatic memory, relieves the reader of the necessity of remembering everything he has ever learnt. A store needs a key; the librarian and his professional techniques provide it." Ultimately, Shera (1970, p. 77) writes, it is the librarian's responsibility to "Make the communication process as useful as possible and employ all techniques that seem to have any promise at all to the achievement of that end."

But the other function is manifested within the quotidian activity of the Library, and is an even larger and ever growing dimension of communication that is determined by the library in its selection, organization, and interpretative and preservation services, and that connects the two apparent dimensions of library function. At the point of this connection, however a compromise has to be struck between universality and selectivity. "This compromise," writes sociologist Bartholomeus Landheer (1973, p. 76), "seems to lie in the realization that the library has the function of long-term preservation of those materials which have long-term significance, whether this be interpreted in terms of time, space or social distance." What he characterizes as compromise in the library function is treated in the present essay as the library's primary function in cultural evolution. The librarian, Jesse Shera (1970, p. 84) summarizes, "must in effect carry on a kind of schizophrenic existence, keeping his eyes constantly on the informational, and intellectual and knowledge-needs of the individual, while at the same time, not forgetting the knowledge-needs of society. It is, then, in this complex individual-social relationship that the librarian must operate." In a sense, the compromise comes down to a statement that distinguishes content and container. This essay is foremost about content.

A long-time leader in the changing library scene during the middle and second half of the twentieth century, Maurice B. Line (1965, p. 270) has observed provocatively that "The library is a social weapon of some power, and we should be careful how we wield it." His admonition would first require knowing what it is that we are wielding and understanding the context for serious consequences. In Chapter 1 of this book, philosophies, mostly partial philosophies that have come forward, were examined. It is useful to summarize at this point, however, that the few systematic reviews of this activity that have been published to date (Benge, 1970; McCrimmon, 1975, 1994; and Rogers, 1984), can provide only a patchwork picture of the status of this aspect of the library and information profession. The reader comes away from these reviews with little sense of or insight into the philosophy behind what goes on in the library, no fault of the reviewers. For example, the concluding comment of Ronald C. Benge (1970, p. 254) is that "One is obliged to conclude that the theoretical foundations of librarianship are weak, not because of the limitations of library education or because of the Anglo/American anti-metaphysical tradition, but because there are certain unresolved and possibly inherent contradictions." Likewise, the summary statement of A. Robert Rogers (1984, p. 29) in his review of writings on pertinent philosophy is an attempt to be positive on the basis of little substance, suggesting that "The quest for a philosophy of librarianship has sometimes seemed remote from the day-by-day work of librarians. This perceived remoteness, however, is more apparent than real. How we think about librarianship has practical consequences in the ways we act." The consequences of the librarians' actions may be quite subtle, but they may also have the effect of very slight, countless, nudges on the rudder of a large ocean-going vessel.

Much of the problem of establishing a philosophy, I believe, lies in failure to achieve proper focus: the attempts are premised on, and therefore pursued in, misleading directions. The usual premises range from a set of beliefs and general faith, to weaknesses in library education, to the personal appreciation of reading rather than of people and ideas, to the desired professional and personal characteristics of the librarian, to the very nature of information and knowledge, and to the elusive discovery of an appropriate combination of existing philosophic systems.

Most of the published philosophy related to the library confuses *why* something is done with *how* it is done. It attempts a philosophy for aspects of librarianship rather than a philosophy of library as a conceptual construct in culture. Confusion of objectives for the establishment of a philosophy explains the apparent complexity and general difficulty experienced in the profession's efforts to achieve a satisfactory statement. The answer to the question of *why* the procedures and transactions of librarianship are performed cannot be found solely within the fact that they *are* performed. The answer to why librarianship exists is found somewhere outside its own activities; it is found in a philosophy that transcends the doing. It is in the ultimate result of the doing, that which is expected beyond the activities. These library things are done for a purpose beyond the doing itself, and it is within that purpose that library philosophy must be embedded. Library philosophy is to be found within library function.

Summary & Prospectus

Chapters of this book are organized to lead from the general to the specific, thus recasting some concepts as they assume more particular meaning in a narrowing context, and the study proceeds in the knowledge that theory, like the research that both advances from it and yields it, is never finished.

Social forces behind theory and research lead to the continuous forming and re-forming of understanding, and it is by this manner that library philosophy can most likely become discernible, embedded deep within cultural evolution.

Part One of this study, incorporating its first two chapters, addressed problems encountered in defining a library philosophy, problems that will reappear throughout the text. Its purpose is to locate the perspective most likely to yield the conditions appropriate to uncovering library philosophy. More than six decades ago, Pierce Butler (1942, p. 3) warned that "Until librarianship develops an adequate theory, its members must continue to be inarticulate no matter how vociferous they may become." While Chapter 1 demonstrated that many elements suitable for a philosophy do exist, it also concluded that no single statement has proved adequate in focus, breadth and depth to achieve wide acceptance. Most significant among these, proper focus for a philosophy has proved especially elusive. Vannevar Bush (1950, p. 87), then President of MIT and the eminently successful Director of the U. S. Office of Scientific Research and Development during World War II, tells an amusing but instructive story that fits this discussion of focus: On learning from her professor's clarification that the earth was coming to a cold end in two billion years, rather than the two million she mistakenly had thought he said, the student replied: "Oh, I feel very much relieved." Bush explains the moral of the story, saying "To my mind, there is a hazard in the general topic with which we are concerned [the social implications of scientific progress]. The pragmatic details of methods to meet immediate needs may by their very fascination become the focus. They may thus divert attention from the broad philosophical implications of the subject."

Similarly, A. Broadfield (1949, p. 6) seemed to point in an advantageous direction, contending that any "Philosophy of librarianship should be concerned only indirectly with library practice, otherwise it would merely augment the literature of the techniques." Continuing this thought, he also wrote (p. 7) that "The philosophical ideal is to interpret the whole of the subject matter in the light of a single principle: if this principle is sound it will give the character of necessity to everything else." His principle of choice was intellectual freedom, which certainly is essential, but he relates it more to a principle of management than to an explanation of library function. Broadfield was discussing the practice of librarianship, not the library as cultural phenomenon, yet it is a principle so essential to the library environment that it will be examined further in Chapter 6. Numerous other attempts to establish a guiding philosophy have displayed impressive insight into and understanding of the library function. Nonetheless they have not yet resulted in a philosophy that could reconcile two differing images of the library, images held in mind by both the profession and the society it serves. That said, it must be acknowledged that the library has continued its service in the absence of an explanatory and guiding philosophy, most evidently because something has been present to sustain the institution even in the absence of such potential influence.

Chapter 2 turned attention to a selection of terms and concepts, referred to as strategic considerations, that inadvertently have come together in forming obstacles to the development of a philosophy. Some of these obstacles have resulted very definitely from terminology that has clouded meanings by dint of imprecision in scope; concepts both within the LIS field and outside it often are employed carelessly and have been misleading. The purpose of library as a concept in cultural evolution, which is viewed in the present book as the basis of library philosophy, is different from, yet closely related to, the purpose of LIS work, which attends to how the library purpose is best achieved. The term theory relates more to LIS services and operations than to the concept of library, where the term philosophy is more fitting. There are many theories at work in LIS; but there is only one philosophy that underpins the concept of library and therefore also LIS. Library administrator and theorist John E. Buschman (2006, pp. 295–296) concludes his assessment of Jürgen Habermas's philosophy in the context of a survey of LIS theory with the thought that "Perhaps our task should be framed more modestly: the goal of LIS theory—and the librarianship it would shape—must point us toward a society such as he [Habermas] describes, grounded in a hopeful, humane, cosmopolitan, and suspicious disposition, which is respectful of the obstinacy of human intellectual creation." These ideal social characteristics are in fact identified very closely with library function as it will be described in the following chapters.

Part Two will address cultural evolution, with an emphasis on the interactions of mind, society, and communication. Language is accorded prime significance in its various forms for both culture and the library function, whose responsibility is the maintenance of the recorded social transcript. Part Three begins with an assessment of the areas that seem to be most amenable to a library philosophy; that is, those areas that create the immediate context for an appropriate philosophy. Consequently, it focuses on the intersection of processes of mind and concept of library, emphasizing the distinctively human elements of both. These three chapters are intended in part as a reminder that the library has survived through so much for so long simply because it is needed by humanity for reasons that are not so simple, and certainly not self evident. Proof that it is needed by humanity in the most profound ways is found in an understanding that the library is at once a concept and a function created and maintained by humanity's culture, which is the replenishing source of library philosophy.

PART II

A Creation of Culture for Mind

CHAPTER 3

Cultural Evolution

The story goes round among biologists everywhere that teleology is a woman of easy virtue whom the biologist disowns in public, but lives with in private.
—Michael Polanyi, 1964

Introduction

The terms culture and society and their derivatives are not subject to neat definitions, so this essay describes these two concepts primarily in their situation as the providers of context for the library function. There are other aspects of culture that affect society quite markedly, among them family and law, for example, that do not relate immediately to the library except as part of the general dimension of culture. In later sections of this chapter the significance of culture will be examined more closely, but for the time being it may suffice to observe that culture is a human force within society, a force that exerts considerable influence on all dimensions of society over a long duration. Consequently, Chapter 3 begins with a brief review of the concept of 'society' as the stage upon which culture plays out, then proceeds to an examination of the latter concept as employed in the formal study of culture and cultural evolution. It then examines the function of culture in society and culture's place in determining the definition of humanity. The notion of cultural progress, whose validity is justly contested from time to time, is explored with a focus on the causes of progress and the ways by which progress usually is identified. Underlying all of culture is the individual phenomenon of reasoning in depth which, according to most scholars, is exclusively a human phenomenon, and which in turn is greatly influenced by culture.

Society

Although cultural historian Robert Redfield (1962, p. 125) characterizes society rather simply as a group personality, use of that concept in conjunction with culture begs further explanation and distinction, which will follow in the next few pages. Meanwhile, Redfield further observes about society that it is comprised of people with common ends, engaged in work and getting along together while sharing common convictions about what the good life means. More than a system of production and services (p. 418), society is a shared view of what constitutes good and bad conduct and bears a sentiment of belonging together, of solidarity against those who are not a part of that society. Stated another way, a society is a collective based on ideas, says sociologist Célestin Bouglé (1926, p. 187), "When it has been demonstrated that an idea has a collective form, it has not yet been demonstrated that it possesses universal value. The collective is an intermediary between the individual and the universal." Common to humans and other social animals, according to philosopher John Searle (2007, p. 7), "is what I call 'collective intentionality' cases where humans and other animals are capable of cooperating and thus sharing common forms of intentionality" for the group.

Addressing many of the key issues incorporated in the concept of society, sociologist Leon H. Mayhew (1968, p. 585) offers explanations pertinent to the purpose of the present synthesis: "To start with the concept of a population is not to define a society as consisting in its population. The society is not the population but the complex systems of action in which the units of the population participate." And, Mayhew adds, "'Society' often is used as a general term supplying context to the examination of a particular aspect of social being, an encompassing network of social relationships that enclose some more specific phenomenon which is the primary object of analysis" (p. 577). The so-called self-sufficient society is a constant theme in most concepts of society, writes Mayhew (p. 584), meaning that "the system contains within itself cultural materials and role opportunities sufficient for carrying on controlled relations with an environment." He clarifies this statement, adding that "To call a society self-sufficient implies not that it is isolated but that its social system contains within itself cultural materials and role opportunities sufficient for carrying on controlled relations with an environment." Society collectively is greater than the sum of its individual parts, and thus is amenable to study as a system, says Mayhew (p. 578). Societies are population units that convey culture.

Cultural historian Robert Nisbet (1969) stresses the point that the notion of evolution in society had taken hold in the eighteenth century, when it was linked to that of social progress. He writes (p. 161) that "it is one of the more curious misconceptions of much modern writing in the history of social thought that nineteenth-century social evolutionism was simply an adaptation of the ideas of geological evolutionism . . . In the first place, all of the principal works in the formation of the theory of social evolution had made their appearance before publication of Darwin's book." In fact, he points out (p. 160) that "the assumptions concerning the nature of change in time which underlay the theory of natural history passed directly into the nineteenth-century theory of social evolution," although naturalist Charles Darwin's *Origin of the Species*

(1859) did stir a level of self-consciousness about the connection that resulted in an unmistakable upswing in scholarship dedicated to cultural evolution, as will be seen in subsequent sections of this chapter.

From another perspective, Leon Mayhew argues (p. 578) that the notion of society "as something clearly prior to and outside of the state" emerged when philosophers began to search for secular foundations for critical analysis of existing political institutions. Society is not a population. It is a combination of complex systems of actions in which a population participates; it is an encompassing cultural network of social relationships.[1] Noted anthropologist Margaret Mead (1949, p. 30) concludes that "Human beings are perceived within a set of categories which permit ready interchangeability," and therefore that there is no international policy or coordinated domestic policy to guide these phenomena. There are instead "many distinct programmes advocated by groups or parties who show very little recognition of the inconsistencies among and within the programmes they advocate."

The spirit of the society is supplied by its culture, which is embodied in traditions and institutions, and it evolves over time, says Mayhew (1968, p. 580), "according to whether the changes are consonant with the cultural distinctiveness of the larger society." A social system, he declares, is an organized set of interdependent social persons, activities, or forces. "It is called a system because its organization includes mechanisms for maintaining an equilibrium or some other constancy in the relations between the units" (p. 583). Social anthropologist A. R. Radcliffe-Brown (1948, p. 90) employs the medical term coaptation to explain this set of phenomena: "*Coaptation* means 'fitting together.' The most characteristic thing about any society, human or animal, is that the individual members of the society have their behavior fitted together in some way so as to maintain a social life as a result of that fitting together . . . Social coaptation in this sense is the fundamental characteristic of all societies." Sociologist Shmuel N. Eisenstadt (1968, p. 233) adds that "An evolutionary perspective, from the point of view of human societies, makes sense only so far as at least some of the processes of change that are inherent in any social system create the potentialities for the institutionalization of more differentiated social and symbolic systems." Chapter 5 will demonstrate that the library is a cultural invention, a technology intended by societies within their broader culture both to maintain the equilibrium of the respective society and to facilitate its processes of change through cultural evolution.

Culture

It is largely as a result of progress in the understanding of evolutionary processes, according to neurologist Sir W. Russell Brain (1961, p. 61), that there is a comprehensive view of the mind, because the mind inheres "in the evolutionary process, growing from elementary beginnings into a subordinate, and finally the dominant factor in evolutionary advance. We see the great transition from individual to psychosocial evolution [a term also used by Huxley, 1958, p. 442], the latter the matrix for the development not only of conceptual thought and the techniques that it has produced, but also of 'spiritual' values, ethics, and artistic creativeness." The interaction of mind and culture suggests the importance not only of the one or other force, but of both conjoined, which is essential to the discussion of knowledge in Chapter 4. Moreover, related is the fundamental theory expressed in simplest terms by anthropologist Robert Boyd and environmental scientist Peter J. Richerson (1985, p. 33) that "Culture is information capable of affecting individuals' phenotypes which they acquire from other conspecifics by teaching or imitation." This theory is essential to explanation of the social transcript in Chapter 5, where it will be examined more fully.

Perhaps the single most important fact of cultural evolution, however, is also the simplest and yet most frequently taken for granted, but cultural anthropologist Jérôme Rousseau (2006, p. 238) presents this important fact in one cogent sentence: "People accept as *the* reality the social environments in which they are brought up." This is the first and perhaps most evident power of culture. Anthropologist and philosopher Milton Singer (1968, p. 527) traces the development of the concept of culture in the science of anthropology, beginning with pioneer anthropologist Edward B. Tylor's (1871) borrowing of the term from German historians and his definition of the concept as that which, "'taken in its wide ethnographic sense is that complex whole which includes knowledge, belief, art, morals, law, custom, and any other capabilities and habits acquired by man as a member of society" (Tylor, 1871, vol. 1, p. 1; cited by Singer, 1968, p. 527). Singer finds that many others have been reasonably satisfied with Tylor's explanation,[2] and concludes with the thought (p. 539) that "Tylor's omnibus conception of culture is still the basis of most modern anthropological theories of culture, although the conception has been refined and developed in several different directions." Kenneth Boulding (1964, p. 57) points out that in the wake of the influence of Darwin in the mid-nineteenth century "the evolutionary view of the history of life and of the universe led to an enormous expansion of man's image of the time scale, by contrast with the folk image of special creation and a history of only six thousand years." Related to that heightened sense of time, and perhaps of even greater significance, Boulding also observes (p. 63) that the accompanying shift "from the folk image of man and society to a scientific image involves man in at least two large, irreversible, and related changes. The first of these is the increase in self-consciousness, not only of the individual himself but also of the society in which he has been placed," and that "With the development of social self-consciousness, man, as it were, steps outside his own social skin and looks at himself and at his own society from the outside" (p. 64). The importance of these shifts in self and world view is great, holding considerable potential for the evolution of culture, while the strengthening of social self-consciousness is essential to the sustaining of the mechanisms developed to preserve the culture, adjust it gradually to changing needs, and pass it all along.

Anthropologist Elman Service (1968, p. 222) observes about culture that "The sum total of the social and political rules, technological inventions and economic institutions, the arts, shared beliefs and practices—that is, the culture—tends to persist through time because any particular society maintains these parts integrated with each other and with its environment."[3] But anthropologist Theodosius Dobzhansky (1983, p. 64) abbreviates this definition to "Culture is the totality of information and of behavioral patterns that are transmitted from individual to individual, and from generation to generation, by instruction and learning, and by example and imitation." An extraordinarily concise and pithy definition of culture is designed by evolutionary psychologists Louise Barrett, Robin Dunbar, and John Lycett (2002, p. 352), who state "We define culture as beliefs or rules of behaviour (or perhaps more generally as knowledge about the world) that are passed on from one individual to another by some form of social learning (including teaching)." This definition encompasses a vast part of the human condition. And it is in the context of culture that developmental psychologists David F. Bjorklund and Anthony D. Pellegrini (2002, p. 335) find the basis of what is called human nature, writing "Moreover, from our perspective, "human nature is not simply something one is born with. Rather, human nature develops, being expressed as evolved dispositions that interact with a species-typical environment over the course of ontogeny." Thus, in any setting, says Dobzhansky (1968, p. 236), "Of the many existing forms of human culture, the particular one an individual acquires is determined by the society in which this individual is brought up rather than by his genes." Because culture is so ubiquitous and powerful a force, the research of anthropologists Clyde Kluckhohn and William H. Kelly (1945, p. 104) leads them to add to the definition of culture the important idea that "Every culture is also a structure of expectancies." An understanding by both individual and society that knowledge and beliefs have been handed down from the past makes possible and stimulates thoughts about the future.

Cultural historian Raymond Williams (1983, xviii) contends that the concept of culture[4] emerged in the West during the late eighteenth and first half of the nineteenth centuries. Its emergence consolidated two more general trends: that of "the intellectual activities for the driven impetus of a new kind of society;" and "the emphasis of these activities as a court of human appeal, to be set over the processes of practical social judgment and yet to offer itself as a mitigating and rallying alternative. Where *culture* meant a state or habit of the mind, or the body of intellectual and moral activities, it means now [by the mid nineteenth century], also, a whole way of life." Williams concludes that the development of the idea of culture throughout the period under his investigation was a criticism of what is sometimes called the "bourgeois idea of society." The contributors to its meaning, according to Williams (p. 328), started from widely divergent positions and eventually reached equally divergent attachments and loyalties. But they were alike in one major regard, he says. They were "unable to think of society as a merely neutral area, or as an abstract regulating mechanism. The stress has fallen on the positive function of society, on the fact that the values of individual men are rooted in society, and on the need to think and feel in these common terms. This was, indeed, a profound and necessary response to the disintegrating pressures which were faced."

Values may be considered the central and deepest motivation in creating and molding a culture. Economic philosopher Kenneth Boulding (1964, p. 45) observes, for example, that "a considerable part of the success of the scientific community in advancing knowledge must be attributed to its value system in which an impersonal devotion to truth is regarded as the highest value to which both personal and national pride must be subordinated." And sociologist Roy Wood Sellars (1926, p. xxxv) argues in his Introduction to the work of Célestin Bouglé that "The basic principle is that values are objective because imperative and imperative because collective. It is society that creates values. They express social aspirations or ideals. Society is not alone an exchange of services or a collaboration of forces; it is, above all, a communion of feelings. And it is especially by the transmission of values that societies perpetuate themselves." The level of social awareness held by the individual is of course essential to this function of cultural evolution, which demands not only the passing along of cultural identities but also the individual willingness to fit in the group. And humans seem well suited to this function, according to social psychologist William R. Thompson (1958, p. 295), who cites research that refers to the collective roles taken on by an individual as the generalized other. "This ability to be someone else, to take on the characteristic of 'the other' is regarded as the very core of social behavior and as being uniquely developed in man." It is an essential capacity that will be examined as theory of mind later in this chapter.

Anthropologist Leslie A. White, who figures among the most prolific and influential authorities on cultural evolution in the second half of the twentieth century, has elaborated on the Tylor definition in a number of works. Repeating (1973, p. 31) that culture generally "consists of ideas, attitudes, acts, and objects," he (p. 29) also places a more explicit emphasis on the concept of culture "as that class of things and events dependent upon symboling, products of symboling, considered in an extrasomatic context," the idea referring specifically to the use of language in intellectual activity. Elsewhere, White

(1949, pp. 363–364) states that "Culture is, so to speak, a form of social heredity. We thus view culture as a continuum, a supra-biological, extra-somatic order of things and events, that flows down through time from one age to the next," and (1975, p. 7) more simply that "It is man who has made the existence of culture possible. Culture, in general, is what it is because man is the kind of animal that he is; had he been different, culture would have been correspondingly different." The diversity of concepts incorporated in culture and the stability that can be maintained throughout their large-scale evolution combine in a uniquely human phenomenon. Particularly human in this phenomenon is not just the recognition of the role of culture, but also the ability to design mechanisms that meet the need.

A sociologist specializing in the social institution, Joyce O. Hertzler (1946, p. 26) proffers a useful summary definition of the concept of culture:

> The most inclusive overview of social phenomena by the sociologists and anthropologists is that which conceives of *all* that man has wrought as culture or the social heritage... Culture, thus interpreted, is wholly man-made; it is the total product of man's trial and error, his accidents, his observations, his discoveries, his inventions in dealing with nature and his fellow men; some of it is a matter of deliberate planning and invention; most of it is a matter of hit-and-miss, automatic formation.... Almost all of the essential elements of this experience summarized as culture are looked upon as precious, since they are techniques of adjustment to the physical and social universe, and are reputed to have survival value.

Created by humans for humans, the kind of culture under discussion here functions to make life secure, continuous, and enduring by exploiting all the resources available to meet the needs of humanity. Leslie A. White (1959, p. 9) considers needs to fall in two fundamental categories: those that can be served only by exploiting the resources of the external world, which is to say outside the self; and those that can be served only by drawing deeply on the inner self. The former category consists of clothing, utensils, and other material entities; the latter refers to psychic, social, and similar spiritual resources, such as "courage, comfort, consolation, confidence, companionship, a feeling of consequence in the scheme of things that life is worthwhile, and some assurance of success," a conclusion White subsequently reaffirms.[5] Similarly, in writing of the significance of the concept of culture, sociologist and anthropologist Clyde Kluckhohn (1945, p. 103) declares that "First and foremost I would insist that its use lies in the aid the concept gives to man's endless quest to understand himself and his own behavior." It is in that spirit that psychobiologist Henry Plotkin (1998) entitles the sixth chapter of his book on the evolution of the mind: Culture: One of the Last Great Frontiers of Science.

Functions

"The most significant product, and the paramount determining factor, of human evolution is culture," writes geneticist and anthropologist Theodosius Dobzhansky (1968, p. 236). But the force of culture got a late start in its function in the development of humans, adds anthropologist Adam Kuper (1994, pp. 90-91). "If by culture we mean learned, adaptable symbolic behavior, based on a full-fledged language, associated with technical inventiveness, a complex of skills that in turn depends on a capacity to organize exchange relationships between communities... But once cultural development got into its stride, it operated at a rate quite foreign to the slow, blind mutations of biological evolution. The outstanding characteristic of cultural history is its accelerating pace of change." Anthropologist V. Gordon Childe (1951, p. 176) points out that the process can be much faster in human than in natural history, owing to the different methods of transmission. He explains that "An acquired adaptation—say the musculature of an acrobat—cannot be transmitted to the offspring by biological heredity. But the acrobat may teach his children-and people quite unrelated to him genealogically—the movements and exercises that developed his muscles." Psychobiologist Henry Plotkin (2002, p. 106) sees the fact of the gradual and orderly process of biological evolution as different from that of cultural evolution because "Enculturation is not a discrete event in the way that gene transmission is a discrete event. It is a gradual, 'smeared -out' process covering a period of years and intimately bound in to social interactions." The process is so gradual and 'smeared out' as to be imperceptible to contemporaries. Cultural anthropologist Jérôme Rousseau (2006, p. 224) points out that in any given society "Social change can be continuous or discontinuous; most major changes involve significant discontinuities because human life is organized and controlled in order to establish a status quo. As pressure for change increases, a new status quo is established." Or, as sociologist Joyce O. Hertzler (1946, p. 237) would have it, "One generation's commonplaces are another generation's antiquities." And this comparative speed of cultural evolution can be a source of stress.

The individual thus inhabits a world of pressures established by the culture. Social philosopher John R. Searle (1995, p. 145) refers to the force of culture on the individual as the rule structure, to which we evolve a set of sensitive dispositions. He says (p. 147) "The point is that we should not say that the man who is at home in his society... is at home because he has mastered the rules of the society, but rather that the man has developed a set of capacities and abilities that render him at home in the society; and he has developed those abilities because those are the rules of his society." Sociologist Roy Wood Sellars (1926, p. xxxii) acknowledges the influence of Emile Durkheim in describing how, at certain intense moments, society creates ideals that influence and control the lives of individuals. "The individual feels himself to be in a social medium which constrains him. These ideals are not abstract, cold, intellectual representations, robbed of all efficacy. They are essentially motor; for behind them there are real and active forces. These are collective forces, which are consequently natural forces, although moral; and they are comparable to those which play their part in the rest of the universe."

Looking beyond the individual, sociologist Joyce O. Hertzler (1946, p. 27) finds that "Culture gives continuity to human experience. Culture in general accounts for most of the organized behavior of man; it is a large-scale molding-matrix, the patterning of the behavior of men interacting in groups." One of the most influential anthropological studies, Margaret Mead's *Coming of Age in Samoa* (1928), was an attempt to investigate the way in which individual personality reacts to culture. Bronislaw Malinowski (1930), among the foremost exponents of anthropological functionalism in the twentieth century, which is an approach that describes culture as an organic whole rather than as a series of discrete characteristics. He presents (p. 645) a different kind of analogy by which to consider the value and function of culture in this classic statement:

> Culture endows man with an additional extension of his anatomical apparatus, with a protective armor of defenses and safeguards, with mobility and speed through media where his direct bodily equipment would have entirely failed him. Culture, the cumulative creation of man, extends the range of individual efficiency and of power of action; and it gives a depth of thought and breadth of vision undreamed of in any animal species. The source of all this consists in the cumulative character of individual achievements and in the power to share in common work. Culture thus transforms individuals into organized groups and gives these an almost indefinite continuity.

Human actions stem from ideas, which are not always positive, however. Most scholars in the fields of neurology, psychology, and culture are quick to acknowledge this fact, and library educator Pierce Butler (1952, p. 82) calls to mind that fact when he notes in staccato tempo that "Ideas mishandled may be lethal. The Devil can quote Scripture to his purpose. No lie is so false as a tissue of carefully selected truths." So it is useful to bear in mind that the root proposition of the sociology of knowledge which, according to sociologists Peter L. Berger and Thomas Luckmann (1966, p. 5), is that "man's consciousness is determined by his social being," and Leslie A. White's (1968, p. 548) conclusion that "the behavior of a people is a function of its culture." In order to understand the mind, it is essential to have an appreciation of surrounding cultural factors as determinants of thinking, feeling, and acting. "But if your interest is in action rather than thought," writes Clyde Kluckhohn, "the principal claim which can be made for culture is that it helps us enormously toward predicting human behavior" (Kluckhohn & Kelly, 1945, p. 103).

In the same spirit, neuropsychologist Merlin Donald (1991, p. 14) takes these ideas a step further: "Cultures restructure the mind, not only in terms of its specific contents, which are obviously culture-bound, but also in terms of its fundamental neurological organization." Memory is a central capacity of the mind, as will be discussed throughout this book, especially in Chapter 4, and is of special significance to library function, as discussed especially in Chapter 6. Donald (2001, p. 164) shows that culture is a guide in encoding memories and more even than that, that it provides the system used to recall them at will. In turn, he says, "Access to memory is the key to our symbolic cultural system. It is the foundation, as well as the product, of that system . . . Culture provides more than mere programming for explicit recall. In its deeper aspects, it provides something that is perhaps more akin to an operating system. It gives us a shared structural framework for public, conventional systems of thought."

As a systemic process, culture receives its energy from within its subsystems and operates in its own interest, which is the interest primarily of groups, but also of individuals. It is highly susceptible to change brought about by new additions, distortions, elaborations, variations, syntheses combinations, and inventions, which are continually emerging. "One trait, or combination of traits, is the result of antecedent and concomitant traits and the cause of subsequent traits and trait combinations," writes Leslie A. White (1968, p. 548). "One form of language, writing, social organization, technology, or of culture as a whole, grows out of a previous stage or emerges from an anterior condition." The strength of cultural evolution is that it is in fact an evolution, not a series of revolutions, not a series of concatenated events, but a continuation of one moving phenomenon more like a wave in the ocean; if what went before the wave and what follows it is not there, the wave is not there. In cultural evolution nothing is lost, even if it is not immediately visible, because the past, the present and the future are composed of redundancies. Though subject to much continuous change, culture nonetheless "is highly durable, even perpetual," says Joyce O. Hertzler (1946, p. 27). "While peoples and civilizations rise and fall, much, perhaps most, of their culture goes on–somewhere." The process incorporates culture traits that combine and permute, and act and react among themselves in accordance with the principle of cause and effect.[6] In summary, White (1975, p. 6) makes it clear that "culture determines and causes culture; culture is to be explained in terms of culture."

Processes

Above all else, culture is a human phenomenon. "Man becomes human only as he departs from nature," writes Pierce Butler (1952, p. 80). "In culture man moves through realms of experience that no animal can enter–rational consciousness of himself, of nature, and of values. Thus he ceases to be merely a denizen of the world and becomes an agent in it." While the existent culture is comprised of individuals, it is essential to an understanding of cultural evolution to recognize that the individual is formed in what have been identified as cultural matters largely by the surrounding society. Psychobiologist Henry Plotkin (2002, p. 106) reminds the reader that "Much of what humans communicate to one another in the course of everyday life is based upon an enormous reservoir of knowledge," which is held in memory, and that "Knowledge structures are built cumulatively." He refers elsewhere (1998, p. 159) to a developing body of theory on social or cultural change, among the components of which is that "what is transmitted between individuals in a social group is equivalent to genetic transmission in biological evolution. These memes, as opposed to genes, are essential units of the social group's common cultural currency." The significance of this concept will be examined further in Chapter 4.

Sociologist Charles Horton Cooley (1920, p. 21) concludes from his study of cultural processes that "Generally speaking, social organisms feel their way without explicit consciousness of where they want to go or how they are to get there, even though to the eye of an observer after the fact their proceedings may have an appearance of rational prevision." Anthropologist Robert Boyd and environmental scientist Peter J. Richerson and anthropologist Robert Boyd (2005, pp. 270–271) find it plausible that processes of cultural evolution led to group selection being a more powerful force on cultural, rather than genetic, variation. In their view, the cultural systems of inheritance probably arose in the human lineage as an adaptation to the increasingly variable environments of the recent past, and, "Over a long period of coevolution, cultural pressures reshaped 'human nature', giving rise to innate adaptations to living in tribal-scale social systems . . . culture is, prima facie, a plausible key element in the evolution of human cooperation." The reverse conclusion may be of equal validity.

Charles Darwin (1859) long ago succinctly stated his assessment of the significance of culture in the evolution of humanity,[7] observing that of higher human value than survival are the moral qualities developed through social influences. And since then there is a large and growing body of theory and research showing, as ethologist and evolutionary biologist Richard Dawkins (2006, p. 189) expresses it, that "Cultural transmission is analogous to genetic transmission in that, although basically conservative, it can give rise to a form of evolution." This idea will be examined more extensively as it applies to cultural technology in Chapter 5.

Individuals and groups generate culture while, in turn, culture forms the individuals and groups, but this is anything but automatic. For the key point is that "One must have thought and doubted before the view of another can be accepted with spiritual profit," surmises sociologist Robert MacDougall (1912, p. 7). And, furthermore, "One must have struggled for power, directly and blindly, before the beauty of obedience to a common law can be apprehended." Moreover, in examining some of the most fundamental and common place operations of thinking, social psychologist Sir Frederic C. Bartlett (1958, pp. 182–183) concludes that

> . . . the number and sweep of the generalizations used in everyday thinking are such that no ordinary person could possibly arrive at them by a gradual process of abstracting common features from a lot of different settings. The great majority of these generalizations are, in fact, taken over ready made, by the thinker, from the society into which he is born . . . One thing that is very common is formula making by model. When a lot of social conventions are established and available, all of which when they are formulated have that sort of sweeping range which can cover all manner of particular occasions, it becomes easy for anybody to treat them as models, and so to cast the apparent results of his own single and limited experiences into the same sweeping form.

Sociologist Charles Horton Cooley (1920, p. 379) places this process in perspective, writing that "it is only as agreement that opinion can function," and further (p. 381) that "There is nothing more democratic than intelligent and devoted non-conformity, because it means that the individual is giving his freedom and courage to the service of the whole. Subservience, to majorities, as to any other authority, tends to make vigorous democracy impossible."

Thus, the human being is something other than a domesticated animal, for such domestication began with the origin of culture in the form of rules of conduct for individuals and the "subordination of individual right to general welfare, the origin of ethics," writes anthropologist Leslie A. White (1959, p. 367). "It is true that man subsisted upon wild foods as did other animals, but even here the art of cooking elevated him above the beast." White's analysis of the cultural system gives considerable insight into its workings. He sees the system as comprised of three major parts: technological, sociological, and ideological or philosophical. The technology subsystem, which he sees as the foundation of culture, consists of tools and weapons and techniques of using them; the sociology subsystem includes customs, institutions, codes, and understood rules and regulations. The ideology or philosophic subsystem is the final product, consisting of ideas, concepts, and beliefs. White's research leads him to the conclusion that all cultural systems are composed of these three classes of elements. But he points out that this is not a simple matter, because the subsystems are inter-related, each bearing meaning only in terms of its relationship to the other two, and to the system as a whole.

Even more significantly, White emphasizes (1949, pp. 390–393; and 1975, pp. 17–18) the lead taken by technology,[8] upon which the other two elements and the cultural system as a whole depend. Technology, incorporating its development, its enabling and facilitating capacities, and its suggestion of further possibilities, clearly is a key factor in the evolution of humanity in all its features that separate it from the rest of nature. Of particular interest to the present synthesis, White (1959, p. 7) describes the most significant and profound difference between the way humans and animals employ tools, writing "The use of tools in the human species is, on the whole, a cumulative and progressive process; it is this that distinguishes Neolithic from paleolithic cultures, and the Age of Coal and Steel from the Middle Ages. In the human tool process, one generation may begin where the preceding generation left off." The library as a cultural technology is examined in Chapter 5.

Throughout his monumental study of cultural change, sociologist F. Stuart Chapin (1928) finds the fundamental processes at work in culture to be invention, accumulation, selection, and diffusion, more about which is considered throughout the remainder of this text. "The behavior of societies is explained in terms of their cultures," says White (1968, p. 548), "each is a function of the culture," but the reverse does not hold. "We do not and cannot explain their cultures in terms of the respective 'psychologies' of the peoples." Elsewhere (1949, p. 125), he writes "The specific 'psychologies' are psychosomatic expressions of the cultures, not their causes. The cultures must be explained in terms of culture; culturologically rather than psychologically." Zoologists Peter and Jean Medawar (1977, p. 55) write that "Exosomatic [extra-somatic, in Leslie White's lexicon] evolution is the great evolutionary innovation of mankind—the process to which we owe our present biological supremacy and our hope of future progress." Thus, reasons sociologist Régis Debray (2000, p. 50), for example, the rejection or the acceptance and uses of a new technology is determined by the culture, its readiness being the pivotal factor. "Invention proposes; community disposes. Each of the two agencies holds half the program." Timing is everything.[9] For it is neither by chance nor by simple coercion that changes are adopted by a society, whether they are technological or philosophical. "Imitation, in other words," concludes sociologist Robert MacDougall (1912, p. 13), "is never a passive receptivity but an aggressive assumption of the function imitated, involving anew the establishment of a circle of human wills through which it is mediated." We will examine in Chapter 4 the facilitating function the library extends to imitation through memetics.

Selection & Adaptation

Geneticist C. H. Waddington (1961, p. 71) is emphatic that "The overwhelmingly general view of biology, indeed, is that there not only is a natural order but that this is an evolutionary order, the higher stages having appeared on the earth's surface later than, and by derivation from, the earlier." It is easily arguable that the same is true for human culture, notwithstanding differing definitions of progress, so that cultural humanity is always in a state of becoming, as is biological humanity. This is made clear in another statement of geneticist Waddington (p. 69), who writes, "all biological organization, whether of cells, individual organisms or populations, is involved in temporal change. Any mode of thought which attempts to attribute to man or any other organism any form of unchanging essence, or any character that is conceived as *being* rather than *becoming*, flies in the face of our whole understanding of biology." This process of ever-becoming is motivated by selection for the purpose of adaptation in evolution, both biological and cultural.

Diversity, selection, and adaptation are key concepts in biological evolution, and have been since Charles Darwin (1859) advanced his theories a century and a half ago. "The one area of modern evolutionary biology that is unambiguously adaptationist," says philosopher of science Michael Ruse (2005, p. 194), "is the study of animal social behavior, a topic to which Darwin himself gave considerable attention in the *Origin*." The effective action of evolution is natural selection, as it is described by anthropologist Bernard G. Campbell (1974, p. 27), who asserts that "*Evolution* is an adjustment in the mean characters of a population as a result of natural selection which results in an increased likelihood of its survival in its particular environment. There is no force operating within individuals that causes evolution, nor are systematic changes in the genetic structure of a population necessarily 'advances' on the *status quo*; they are changes which maintain that status."

In this regard, selection in cultural evolution occurs as a result of interactions between the individual, or society, and the environment, much as geneticist Theodosius Dobzhansky (1977, p. 97) describes selection in the biological sphere: "Natural selection has no selector, it is a self-generated outcome of interactions between organisms and their environments." But the notion of selection does presuppose an identified array of possibilities, or a diversity of options, and selection for the purpose of adaptation to environmental conditions is of equal significance in cultural evolution. Biologist and Nobel laureate in physiology and medicine François Jacob (1982, p. 66) sees in diversity "a way of coping with the possible. It acts as a kind of insurance for the future. And one of the deepest, one of the most general functions of living organisms is to look ahead, to produce future as Paul Valéry put it. There is not a single movement, a single posture that does not imply a later on, a passage to the next moment." Providing guidance to non-biological selection is the powerful fact that "A culture is an organic whole, not a mechanical aggregate of traits," writes V. Gordon Childe (1951, p. 14).

Criteria for selection appear in the form of norms accumulated over generations and millennia that make the timing of an innovation fortunate or not, and that either earn the support of the society in that time and place or do not. Psychologist and anthropologist Donald T. Campbell (1974, pp. 450–451) proposes that the process of successful selection leading to adaptation applies to most, if not all, mental faculties, and more specifically that "The variation and selective retention process of evolutionary adaptation is generalized to cover a nested hierarchy of vicarious knowledge processes, including vision, thought, imitation, linguistic instruction, and science." Social theorist Stephen K. Sanderson (2001, p. 130) concludes that "since the social changes over the past 10,000 years have been the result of human action, it is reasonable to assume that these changes have reflected human limitations and predilections and thus have been adaptive products." The most fundamental conclusion about the connection between biological and cultural evolution is stated by clinical psychologists Freedman and Roe (1958, p. 456), who write that "Adaptation and survival are the themes which relate man's psychology and his evolution," because humanity's "greatest promise and most fearful potentialities spring from the nature of these human dependencies." As described by biologist Colin S. Pittendrigh (1958, p. 399), adaptation in biological and cultural terms are highly analogous:

> Adaptation is thus relative to past genetic alternatives realized by the population, as well as to the particular environment the population inhabits. And since the environment is itself continually evolving we are surely confronted in many contemporary forms with organization that is, as it were, an adaptive anachronism; much of the organism must have evolved as adaptation to conditions—and in terms of genetic potentialities—long since past.

Of special interest to the present study of the function of library in culture is the work of biological anthropologist Donna Hart and anthropologist Robert W. Sussman (2005, esp. pp. 245–250). Drawing on recent anthropological findings in their quasi fictional-anthropological account of early humanity, they reassess earlier ideas about man as the hunter, which were founded on the innovative use of weapons to defeat larger and more fierce animals. Their interpretation of the facts, including especially the relatively small size of human anatomy and other anatomical evidence, along with the large tooth marks found frequently in human skulls, is that the human was in fact the hunted among the animals of the time, rather than the hunter. Throughout their study, Hart and Sussman demonstrate consistently that humans devised ways of coping with this desperate condition by collecting their forces in fairly large groups for protection, which meant honing their social skills, and exercising their collective brain power to devise strategies for survival. This is an excellent early example of cooperation for the purpose of adapting to environmental conditions.

Social institutions are the formalized embodiment of successful innovations that have been nurtured and protected by society because they offer considerable assistance in relating the diversity of options to established, though ever-evolving, criteria. As do all social institutions, the library exists as a selection from among many other technologies, physical and intellectual, at the disposal of the culture: the brain, the memory, speech, writing, and literacy. All preceded and suggested the library concept, not simply as a means of adaptation to environmental conditions but also as a means of extension of those capabilities that are uniquely human.

The present synthesis has made frequent allusion to analogies between biology and culture in human evolution, as have most other analyses of cultural evolution. Statements by leading scientists since Darwin, such as that offered by Theodosius Dobzhansky in the title of his paper, "Nothing in Biology Makes Sense Except in the Light of Evolution" (1973, p. 125), do stimulate these considerations. And as frequently as scholars make such analogies, rarely if ever do they claim that the two evolutionary tracks are identical, or even that culture operates at the level of exactitude often expected in the biological sciences. But surely there is more than a coincidence of connections between them if the intellect is related to genetic and other biological features, and if individual behavior is related to group behavior. While psychobiologist Henry Plotkin (2002, p. 114) pragmatically observes that "There are . . . difficulties for anyone trying to adopt an adaptationist perspective on culture," there is no denying that culture has evolved, that it has evolved as the result of choices in the context of diverse options, that an organ—the human brain—ultimately makes decisions leading to actions that affect other, perhaps millions, of humans.[10]

Plotkin's (p. 115) assessment of the appropriateness of these analogies of cultural and biological evolution is that "culture is a special manifestation of human intelligence and hence difficult to place within the normal conceptual landscape of biology," and more aptly (1998, p. 232) that "Our biology can influence our culture, and our culture can influence our biology. This two-way interaction involving both upward and downward causation, to use 'hierarchy speak', means that reductionist explanations of culture are ruled out, but neither can culture be seen as isolated from our biology." At very least, the analogy of biological and cultural evolution opens a path toward useful perspective and fuller understanding, and specifically toward ever greater knowledge of the relationship that may be possible between biological and cultural evolution.

Selection does not necessarily entail the sacrifice of self for society, in an altruistic sense. Most often it surely is a decision, but a very conscious decision based on reason and fashioned through trial and error with the intention to adopt the most likely successful adaptation for the society from among the many available at the time. "Many, probably most, of the features of human social life are the adaptive consequences of people struggling to satisfy their interests," writes social theorist Stephen K. Sanderson (2001, p. 148). "Adaptation is the process whereby individuals originate (or inherit or borrow) social forms that are devoted to serving their interests and fulfilling their needs and wants." Jérôme Rousseau (2006, p. 244) reasons that "Societal choices are limited by circumstances. The prevailing conditions of existence are the backdrop for any change; this is why it is unsatisfactory to explain social change as an adaptation to ecological or social constraints. A focus on individual interests must acknowledge the predominance of some people's interests at the expense of others, and this differentiation begins within the domestic unit." Whereas biological and cultural evolution both go through the processes of selection and adaptation, the former requires a far greater expanse of time because, as noted earlier and as sociologist W. G. Runciman (2002, p. 10) observes from a different perspective: "In cultural selection, the bundles of instructions can jump across lineages in a way that they cannot in natural selection; their mutations arise less from random copying error than from active reinterpretation by the receiving mind; and they can be accepted, rejected, and reaccepted over the course of the lives of the organisms whose minds are their carriers." This idea relates to the notion of redundancy mentioned earlier in connection with culture traits.

Selection for the purpose of adapting to the environment, not just for reasons of survival but increasingly for reasons of all those other human wants and needs, is what motivates cultural evolution. Selection is guided by purpose. This may not be probative, but as social philosopher Talcott Parsons (1978, p. 364) suggests,

> only man among known living systems has telic problems in the sense in which we have defined that concept. This we think is because they are problems of an order that do not arise unless the capacity to learn and use symbols and their meanings already exists... It is in this sense that we consider telic problems, and hence the telic system, to be internal to the human condition... It seems to follow that if human action is subject to the rational form of cognitive understanding, then there can be no cogent reason why the telic area should be excluded from this possibility of rationally apprehending. On the contrary, it is our view that *all* of the essential modes of human action orientation are relevant to man as actor's orientation to all of the environments to which, in the human condition, he is exposed.

It is in the context of culture that purpose comes forth to help organize the thought processes leading to the selection of an action or a useful idea. All aspects of human social life participate in this pattern of decision making. Physicist John Ziman (2002, p. 5) points out that "material artifacts are the most tangible, and scientific theories the most intangible, of the many types of cultural entity to which evolutionary reasoning is applicable," citing as specific examples the role of selection in the evolution of natural languages, systems of common law, economics, and general social behavior. And he makes the role of selection quite clear (p. 4): Technological sciences, he emphasizes, "produce material artifacts, which are caught up in evolutionary cycles through market selection." It is not too remote from the realm of possibility to draw an analogy between this kind of cultural trait and a biological trait that facilitates adaptation in the manner described by evolutionary psychologist David J. Buller (2005, p. 35):

> A trait that is present in a current population because it performed a function (solved an adaptive problem) that enhanced fitness in an ancestral population, and was thus preserved or proliferated under selection for it, is called an *adaptation*. In other words, an adaptation is a trait that has a history of having been preserved, and possibly modified, by selection for the beneficial role it plays in an organism. Thus, an adaptation is a trait that contributed to its own persistence or proliferation; for, by enhancing the fitness of its bearers, an adaptation contributed to the reproductive success of it bearers, which contributed to the transmission of the genes for that adaptation, which in turn contributed to the development of that trait in other organisms. Adaptations, in short, are self-perpetuating design features of organisms. Organisms have those traits *because* they were beneficial to their ancestors.

V. Gordon Childe (1956, p. 63) underlines the significant idea that the raw data for knowledge are not poured indiscriminately into a "communal reservoir, but are co-operatively shaped, fitted together and built up into a structured edifice. The component experiences no more automatically come together to form a pattern than do the scraps of painted plaster that have fallen from the collapsed walls of a ruined building." For his part, F. Stuart Chapin (1928, p. 417) focuses on the function of selection in cultural accumulation, showing how the advent of language, especially written language, led to the emergence of scientific method, or clarified reasoning, upon which selection is based. "As an auxiliary to the logic of scientific method," he writes, "certain important abbreviating devices have been invented, and these serve as selective criteria over the increasing elaboration of language symbolisms and the growing volume of printed matter," and his primary example of the preliminary sort through all available printed sources reveals the major abstracting services and no mention of the library. In the scheme of the present book, however, this is precisely where the library function fits within cultural evolution. It has to do with an abbreviating device that serves also as the social memory; it is the social transcript, which is described in Chapter 5.

Progress

Discussion of adaptation and selection seems inseparable from contemplation of concepts of progress and purpose, as is reflected in the literature of cultural evolution. Moreover, historian Charles A. Beard (1932, p. xl) concludes from his study of the matter that, "it is evident that the idea of progress is both an interpretation of history and a philosophy of action." In fact, Beard (p. xi) writes, "among the ideas which have held sway in public and private affairs for the last two hundred years, none is more significant or likely to exert more influence in the future than the concept of progress."

The publication of Charles Darwin's general theory of evolution in 1859, was followed immediately by a burgeoning of scholarly and scientific interest in the progress believed to be depicted by theories of human evolution. The idea made clear by anthropologist Bernard G. Campbell (1974, p. 36) that "Progress in human evolution is seen as the appearance of new homeostatic mechanisms that make possible survival in the face of ever greater environmental variation" quite likely was found appealing by natural scientists. And of equal likelihood, anyone who might have taken the time to consider present culture in relation to the past would have been pleased to find a scientific basis for the notion that current culture was the goal of many preceding generations of purposeful effort. Historians are among those who do take the time to examine the past in relation to the present. Cultural historian Robert Nisbet (1980, p. 176) finds that "In historiography the idea of progress became with rarest exceptions the very foundation of the field. On both sides of the Atlantic there were literally hundreds of historians to echo in one way or other the faith in progress." And in a more qualitative sense, he asserts (p. 8) that "The history of all that is greatest in the West—religion, science, reason, freedom, equality, justice, philosophy, the arts, and so on—is grounded deeply in the belief that what one does in one's own time is at once tribute to the greatness and indispensability of the past, and confidence in an ever more golden future. But, as I say, the record is not always a clean one for the consequences of belief in progress." More positively, Nisbet (1969, p. 171) argues elsewhere that "what had made indefinite human progress certain to philosophers of the eighteenth century was the fact that it came from forces internal to mankind, not from willful or adventitious elements external to mankind. The same assumption of immanence is present in the nineteenth-century theory of development."

As in historical study, the concept of cultural evolution also is accompanied typically by a notion of progress. "Progress is development or evolution in a direction which satisfies rational criteria of value," writes sociologist Morris Ginsberg (1972, p. 42). He finds (pp. 2–3) three stages through which the idea of progress has passed: First it was "an ethical ideal towards which humanity was considered to be moving;" then attempts were made "to define the notion of progress more clearly and to formulate and establish general laws of progress;" finally it was realized that if progress has occurred, "it is neither simple nor continuous, that advance in one direction is frequently accompanied by retrogression in another." Historian of ideas Peter J. Bowler

(1989, p. 3) describes the Victorians' fascination with the past as the product of an age obsessed with change and desperately hoping that history itself might supply the reassurance that could no longer be derived from ancient beliefs. "The Victorians sought reassurance through the belief that social evolution was moving in a purposeful direction. The idea of progress became central to their thinking precisely because it offered the hope that current changes might be part of a meaningful historical pattern." And he finds further (p. 5) that "Evolution became a central theme of late-nineteenth-century thought because it brought together parallel changes in attitudes towards human history, human origins and the development of life on earth."

One could easily reach the conclusion that there is progress of various kinds in cultural evolution, emerging through a positive cause and effect sequence, simply by comparing conditions of life that are possible in the twenty-first century A.D. to those of the twenty-first century B.C. Except perhaps when the potential of the atom bomb and emerging environmental conditions are taken into account. And shortly following World War II, this issue had become unavoidable in a gathering of leaders in science and government on the topic of the social implications of scientific progress, where it was addressed directly by science leader Vannevar Bush (1950, p. 87):

> What does it mean, to say that we recognize that knowing is hazardous, but to declare it well worth the risk? That statement means that we recognize that the consequences of an advance in knowledge cannot be fully predicted, that some of them may bring difficulties and abuses, that they may also bring material and other benefits as well, but that apart from these the search for knowledge has its absolute justification in the fact that it expresses the fundamental urge of the human spirit to go forward in the long quest for truth.

This response goes directly to the heart of the ideal of intellectual freedom, which is discussed in Chapter 6.

The common understanding seems to be that cultural evolution and progress are pretty much synonymous. But historian John B. Bury (1932, p. 335), whose name is practically synonymous with the study of the idea of human progress, points out that "Evolution itself, it must be remembered, does not necessarily mean, applied to society, the movement of man to a desirable goal." And in his analysis of cultural evolution, philosopher David Kaplan (1970, p. 74) concludes that culture has evolved in two fundamental directions: toward an increasing heterogeneity of the higher cultural type; and toward an increasing homogeneity as the diversity of culture types is reduced. And he sees this divergence continuing at an ever-accelerating rate in the future.

Cultural evolution is defined by Leslie A. White (1959, p. 30) as "a temporal sequence of forms: one form grows out of another; culture advances from one stage to another. In this process time is as integral a factor as change of form." And to his definition he adds the significant consideration that "Only systems can evolve; a mere aggregation of things without organic unity cannot undergo evolution." Literary scholar and philosopher Raymond Williams (1983, p. 338) brings the definition closer to everyday life by explaining that "To take a meaning from experience, and to try to make it active, is in fact our process of growth. Some of these meanings we receive and re-create. Others we must make for ourselves, and try to communicate. The human crisis is always a crisis of understanding: what we genuinely understand we can do." From that perspective, anthropologist Bronislaw Malinowski (1930, p. 645) synthesizes accordingly, "Culture is then essentially an instrumental reality which has come into existence to satisfy the needs of man in a manner far surpassing any direct adaptation to the environment." Bury (1932, p. 338) simplifies some fundament definitions relevant to this discussion, saying "Civilisation represents the adaptations which have already been accomplished. Progress means the successive steps of the process."

How the idea of progress in civilization developed as a part of general understanding is the subject of John B. Bury's major examination of that aspect of the history of ideas. In his introduction to the American edition of Bury's work, historian Charles A. Beard (1932, p. xv) recounts two significant discoveries critical in the development of Bury's thinking: one was that in the fifth century B.C. "man had become conscious of himself as a wonder-working force in the world—a conqueror of the beasts of the field, the fowl of the air, the wind of the sea, and the patient earth." The other discovery Beard (p. xvi) says Bury made was that a point was reached in human evolution when "mankind became conscious of what could yet be done, when the idea of progress broke in upon the belief in the vicious circle or contentment with status."

And, more generally, historian and philosopher John Herman Randall (1940, p. 462) summarizes the considerations that fueled the spread of the idea that progress throughout society is linked to cultural evolution.

> The very changes which in the Revolutionary period succeeded one another so rapidly gave to most men a new sense of the mutability of human affairs, and shook them from their belief that society was a mechanical and timeless kind of thing like the state of the solar system. Moreover, men of all faiths were led to appeal to the past in justification of their present policies: all the new social philosophers, from the traditionalist de Maistre to the radicals Comte and Fourier, felt it necessary to preface their own criticisms of the existing order and their recommendations of change with a philosophy of history explaining how they stood in the direct line of social advance.

The later development of ideas about progress is summarized by concept historian Reinhart Koselleck (2002, p. 225), as follows:

> Although the Renaissance did evoke the consciousness of a new time, this consciousness was not yet that of the progression to a better future as long as the Middle Ages appeared as a dark interim period beyond which antiquity was considered the model. Only the growth of knowledge about nature, by way of which the authority of antiquity was displaced through the autonomous use of reason, opened up—at first only partially—a progressive interpretation of the future. Nature itself would remain the same, but the discovery of it would be methodically driven forward, and thus, so would its increasing domination. Farther-reaching inner-worldly goals, such as a general improvement of life, followed from it, allowing the doctrine of Last Things to be displaced by the gamble of an open future. Since then, past and future differentiate themselves qualitatively from one another and, to this extent, a genuinely historical time is discovered that is finally encapsulated in the term 'progress'.

As noted earlier, an understanding of the concept of culture enhanced the capability to contemplate the future, even before that of evolution entered the scene. As will be demonstrated in Chapter 7, the importance of the idea of progress to this text is that humanity possesses a sense of the significance of what it does, a sense that its decisions and actions overall lead somewhere and that the results usually are and should be positive.

We have examined briefly some definitions of the concept called culture, and have outlined its major functions in society, as well as its significance to humanity. As a cultural force that functions as a system, writes anthropologist Leslie A. White (1975, p. 19), "it must obtain energy in increasing quantities from the external world." Thus, among competing cultural systems, according to philosopher David Kaplan (1970, p. 75) in his paper describing what he calls the law of cultural dominance,[11] the system that "more effectively exploits the energy resources of a given environment will tend to spread in that environment at the expense of less effective systems." From this perspective, the notion of progress is related directly to the energy it requires, in a cause and effect relation, and thereby determines the extent to which one can ascribe the notion of progress.[12]

Anthropologist Wilson D. Wallis (1930, p. 203) discusses this phenomenon as well, but by taking a mirror reflection of the energy consumed and converting it to the human power developed. "Civilized man possesses power undreamed of by the savage. Life is power, civilization is socialized power, and the absence of power is death and decay. Progress, therefore, implies increase in power." So evident is this relation that sociologist F. Stuart Chapin (1928, p. 203) claims the theme of his book on cultural change to be that it is selectively accumulative, citing more than a half dozen earlier scholars who had reached the same conclusion. He asserts that culture proceeds by discontinuing some elements while adding new ones through invention and borrowing. "There is a dropping out of elements, but there is also the adding of new elements by invention and borrowing." He also advises (p. 206) that "Selective culture accumulation is a description of the upward rise of the culture cycle." The energy required by cultural evolution is contained in ideas. "In a very real sense the progress of the scientific activity of men in culture," writes educator Lyman Bryson (1947, p. 167) in speaking of all scholarship and reasoned thought, "the growth of those institutions that are based on an attempt to describe events without adjectives of value, has been achieved by the gradual extrication of man himself from the event he is trying to control. The 'objective' judgment is a deep and severe reversal of the naïve impulse to master brute fact."

But simply the introduction of new ideas is not sufficient to influence culture, much less energize it in a progressive sense. Again, the sequencing of events, timing, plays a significant role; culture must be ready to receive new ideas, because it is a system. For example, "Without the quasi-chromosomal conjunction of cultural breeding ground with new technology," writes Régis Debray (2000, p. 51), "an innovation will not come forward and take over." Philosopher Andrew Edgar (2006, pp. 137–138) elaborates on this description in his interpretation of the relevant views of sociologist and philosopher Jürgen Habermas. Thus, social evolution is

> the process by which societies change and grow in complexity... If a theory of social evolution is to be an account of social change that has general applicability, then for Habermas it must deal with the development of basic human capacities. This is to say that human history, taken as a whole... is understood in terms of the growing intellectual, technical and social sophistication of humanity. Homo sapiens does not come on to the evolutionary scene fully developed. While the species may be full of potential, that potential is only going to be realized by living in, and indeed responding to the challenges of, historically changing societies. The sophistication of a society is thus, in large measure, a result of the sophistication of the people within it... It is the fundamental character of the relevant human capacities here that is all important.

This is not as simple as discovering a new idea; nor is it a coincidence that most people in an industrial setting consider life to be growing ever more complex.

Purpose

A more meaningful perspective may be offered by psychologist Leda Cosmides and anthropologist John Tooby (2002, p. 149), who observe that over the years the technological metaphor used to describe the structure of the human mind has been consistently updated, from blank slate to switchboard to general-purpose computer, and that evolutionary psychology represents an alternative proposal about how to organize our understanding of the human mind and the nature of human intelligence. In this view, they find (p. 150), "all normal human minds reliably develop a standard collection of reasoning, emotional, and motivational circuits or programs. These programs were functionally designed over evolutionary time by natural selection acting on our hunter-gatherer (and more distant) ancestors. They are individually tailored to the demands of particular evolutionary functions and often come equipped with what philosophers would once have called 'innate ideas'."

Beyond the set of human needs that evolve the culture, as discussed earlier, there are even more sweeping purposes motivating evolution. "I have said that for me the central problem of evolution lies in the rise of higher beings from lower ones and, above all, in the rise of man," states Michael Polanyi (1964, p. 72). "A theory which recognizes only evolutionary changes due to the selective advantage of random mutations cannot acknowledge this problem. For the capacity to survive is no criterion of evolutionary achievement in my sense" (pp. 72–73). And, also as mentioned earlier, human needs include the control of nature and an infinite array of psychic needs. Accordingly, bio-chemist Lawrence J. Henderson (1924) examines life and the universe in terms of a system with purpose.[13] He observes how the mechanistic aspects of building a house can be described in total and logical detail without mention of the thought involved in the architect's plan. Yet, he says, the purpose is no less an integral part of the finished product as the mechanistic aspects. Therefore, he concludes, an analogous tendency is at work through the evolutionary process. "In short," writes Henderson (p. 308), "our new teleology cannot have originated in or through mechanism, but it is a necessary and pre-established associate of mechanism. Matter and energy have an original property, assuredly not by chance, which organizes the universe in space and time." It is not essential to the concern of the present synthesis that there is or is not purpose to the continuity of cultural evolution, although the notion of continuity is rather important. In that regard cultural historian Robert Nisbet (1969, p. 174) concludes that "The importance of the concept of continuity in the theory of [societal] development is obvious. How else can change be declared directional, predictable, save on the grounds of its continuity."[14] And geneticist and science philosopher Theodosius Dobzhansky (1977, p. 95) makes his position quite clear: "Purposefulness, or teleology, does not exist in nonliving nature. It is universal in the living world."

Complexity

Continuity, but with increasing complexity. The most general guideline to be followed in distinguishing cultural traits that have evolved from traits that are there for other reasons, according to psychobiologist Henry Plotkin (1998, p. 224), is that "the more complex a characteristic, the more likely it is that it has been selected and shaped by evolutionary forces." Assessing the affect of cultural development in increasing life's complexity, anthropologist Wilson D. Wallis (1930, p. 201) suggests that "If complexity has value it is because it simplifies the goals or the methods of reaching them, and facilitates the accomplishment of a purpose, or stimulates new purposes which afford more or deeper satisfactions," and he concludes (p. 202) that "Civilization is not superior to primitive culture because it is more complex; its complexity is an attribute, not the essence of its superiority; it is superior in spite of its complexity."

Of course, there is no single culture, although cultural anthropologist Jérôme Rousseau (2006, p. 245) theorizes the fundamental point that "Without being teleological, we can see a tendency towards complexification; this is because more complex systems have the means, materially and ideologically, to absorb simpler systems. The possibility of complexification will realize itself in some cases and it may even have a global impact." Humanity is organized in many societies characterized by differing cultures that evolve at differing rates for differing reasons,[15] as summarized earlier. And as Régis Debray (2000, p. 55) finds, "All cultures are hybridizable, their traits exportable and their peoples mixable" in a fashion such that "cultural diversification has been the principal regulator of evolution at the level of Homo sapiens." There is no culture without individuals, and the nurturing of both the culture and the individual is a complexity of sorts. Robert MacDougall's study (1912, p. 14) of the relation of social evolution and the evolution of the individual suggests this special complexity.

> The individual as well as society has been brought into existence through the development of human civilization. The results of that process are at once socialization and individualization. On the one hand appear progressive differentiation of function, complication of relations and integration in a system of continuously increasing mutual dependence. On the other hand appears an individual life which grows endlessly more manifold and significant through the progressive enrichment of its own inner content.

The development of technologies has the effect of accelerating cultural evolution and making it more complex. Science historian George Basalla (1988, p. 208) provides insight into this phenomenon, writing that "The history of technology is not a record of the artifacts fashioned in order to ensure our survival. Instead, it is a testimony to the fertility of the contriving mind and to the multitudinous ways the peoples of the earth have chosen to live. Seen in this light, artifactual diversity is one of the highest expressions of human existence." Flexibility and capacity, leading to diversity, are the enabling features of the mind. In the course of a brief discussion of one economic aspect of culture, psychobiologist Henry Plotkin (1998, p. 223) notes that the problem is reminiscent of the noted social scientist Herbert Simon's comment about how complexity can turn an in-principle reductionist into a pragmatic holist. He concludes that it is not just complexity that distinguishes culture from all other issues in the biological and social sciences: "Culture seems to involve the creation of something whole, something cohesive, and possibly something which seems to be greater than its constituent parts, all of which are properties that are hard to conceptualize within the usual framework of thought characteristic of the biological sciences... Culture really is big science."

Mind

Neuroscientist Jean-Pierre Changeux (1986, p. 272) reasons that "One of the advantages of the evolutionary divergence that led to *Homo sapiens* is, of course, the increased capacity of the brain to adapt to its environment, with an accompanying increase in the ability to form and combine mental objects. Thought develops and communication between individuals becomes richer." Among the remarkable features of the human brain commented on by Changeux (p. 242) is that its development continues long after birth, extending to adulthood. And consciousness, writes social philosopher John Searle (2007, p. 49), "is a feature of the brain in a way that solidity is a feature of the wheel." His statement is intended as an illustration that consciousness is a physical condition of the mind, no more than or less than the roundness and hardness of the wheel. But Jesse Shera (1975, p. 166) cites research supporting his own belief that "The human mind can no more tolerate a vacuum than can nature, for the brain must constantly receive a flow of information upon which it can operate," information being the raw material of knowledge.

Philosopher Henri Bergson (1944, p. 182) even suggests that "The intellect is characterized by a natural inability to comprehend life," and that is why it continues groping. In that regard, consciousness of the brain may be somewhat different from, or at very least far more complicated than, other organs of the body. The human being cannot discontinue thinking without effectively discontinuing life and, as Pierce Butler (1952, p. 83) categorically states, "Man cannot think without thinking of something and to some purpose." The phenomenon of thinking is defined briefly by social psychologist Sir Frederic C. Bartlett (1958, p. 75) as "The extension of evidence in accord with that evidence so as to fill up gaps in the evidence: and this is done by moving through a succession of interconnected steps which may be stated at the time, or left till later to be stated." And sociologist Robert MacDougall (1912, p. 18) more closely links the individual and society:

> The system of objects with which anyone concerns himself is not created by him; it is a social product which is enriched generation by generation and constitutes the spiritual inheritance of each individual born to the culture in question. To each such individual it affords a system of specific stimulations, which both provokes and directs his psychical activity at every moment. The richness or inner complexity of individual experience can thus never be logically separated from the objective form of human society in which the life is cast.

This is what is meant by chemist and social philosopher Michael Polanyi (1964, p. 62), who observes independently of MacDougall that "by saying that we live in our body by using it as an instrument for knowing things outside, our confidence in our knowledge of such things expresses our commitment to life in our body."

And the mind is an instrument for knowing or learning how to modify things outside our body, as anthropologist Theodosius Dobzhansky (1968, p. 236) writes: "Human acquired, extrabiological culture is man's most potent adaptive instrument; it is chiefly by brain, not by brawn, that man controls his environments." Linguist James Paul Gee (1992, p. xix) would confirm this perspective in linking language, mind, and society in a work whose goal "is to persuade the reader that the study of the mind is a study of social practices, which are inherently ideological and political." He elaborates by contending that to study "writing, speaking, believing, valuing, memories, or meaning is not primarily to study what is going on" inside one's head. "It is to study what is going on in the material and social world." The mind, he concludes (p. 151) "lies about out in the material, political, and social world. To retreat from this world is to retreat both from any viable linguistics or psychology, and from any hope of changing the world we live in."

Of course, other persons inhabit that world, and by force of the culture they cause to pervade each society at any given point the individual is constantly subject to the influence of those others. And this can be in the most subtle ways. Philosopher Maurice Halbwachs (1980, p. 34) explains how even when one is alone for a period in a physical sense, that is only an appearance because one's "thoughts and actions during even this period are explained by his nature as a social being and his not having ceased for one instant to be enclosed within some group." Writing particularly about the role of individual and collective memory in thought processes, Halbwachs (p. 49) goes on to say, "The succession of our remembrances, of even our most personal ones, is always explained by changes occurring in our relationships to various collective milieus—in short, by the transformations these milieus undergo separately and as a whole."

Mind and body are not separate, and we should not be constrained by such thinking, advises philosopher Gilbert Ryle (1949, pp. 15–16), who refers to this understanding as the faulty "dogma of the ghost in the machine, " in ridicule of the traditional mentalistic theory that would divide mind and body. Linguist Leonard Bloomfield (1933, p. 32) describes it well, writing that "The *mentalistic* [as opposed to the materialistic or mechanistic] theory . . . supposes that the variability of human conduct is due to the interference of some non-physical factor, a *spirit* or *will* or *mind* (Greek *psyche*, hence the term *psychology*) that is present in every human being. This spirit [prefiguring Ryle's ghost], according to the mentalistic view, is entirely different from material things and accordingly follows some other kind of causation or perhaps none at all." Like Ryle, philosopher Mark Johnson (2007, p. 15) emphasizes the place of external considerations in determining meaning: "I try to show why disembodiment is *not* purity of thought but would, in fact, amount to the loss of all the means we possess for making sense of things." Such profound and complex considerations of the mind lead biologist and philosopher Edward O. Wilson (1978, p. 77) to the inescapable conclusion that "The mind is too complicated a structure, and human social relations affect its decisions in too intricate and variable a manner, for the detailed histories of individual human beings to be predicted in advance by the individuals affected or by other human beings." But progress is being made, and neurologist Antonio R. Damasio (2002, p. 6), who specializes in the phenomenon of consciousness, is confident that "by 2050 sufficient knowledge of biological phenomena will have wiped out the traditional dualistic separations of body/brain, body/mind and brain/mind."

Cognitive psychologist Michael Tomasello (1999, p. 215) connects the mind very significantly to culture, currently and in its evolutionary function, in his statement that, "like evolution and history, ontogeny really matters. Human beings have evolved in such a way that their normal cognitive ontogeny depends on a certain kind of cultural environment for its realization." And he elaborates (p. 216) in his specific integration of the genetic and the cultural, writing that "Modern adult cognition of the human kind is the product not only of genetic events taking place over many millions of years in evolutionary time but also of cultural events taking place over many tens of thousands of years in historical time and personal events taking place over many tens of thousands of hours in ontogenetic time." In consideration of the many complexities encountered through cultural evolution neuroscientist Jean-Pierre Changeux (1986, p. 272) even sees as a paradox the "increase in cerebral complexity with a constant set of genes." Chapter 5 will address at least a part of this paradox.

Psychologist and neuroscientist Merlin Donald (2001, p. 202) finds in a radically improved conscious capacity the essence of human uniqueness. He concludes that humans are specialized in making action decisions, which is a function that places very large demands on the mind's capacities. This executive functioning, as he calls it, "requires a larger perspective on time and space and a more flexible mentality. We are specialists, like all other mammals, but our particular specialization is for high-level executive control." Donald

(p. 322) points to evolution as the force behind the emergence of this capacity, which is characterized by an interlocking of "brain and culture, toward the absorption of individuals by communities of mind. The human conscious process is a specialized adaptation for navigating the turbulent waters of culture as well as the primary channel through which cultural influence can be transmitted back to us." These ideas will be given further attention in Chapter 5 on cultural technology.

As the knowledge held by one individual is the source of that individual's behavior, so is it multiplied billions of times over when considering the earth's population. That global knowledge structure, which is to say the diverse images held in the minds of all human beings, is referred to as the noosphere, the coining of which term Kenneth Boulding (1983, p. 1) attributes to the Jesuit philosopher Pierre Teilhard de Chardin. It reflects and affects the culture as it evolves. For knowledge is considerably more than an isolated condition of mind, whose function will be explored below. Meanwhile, "The behavior of each human being," Jesse Shera (1975, p. 167) stresses, "depends upon his knowledge of the world, and with that knowledge, be it personally experienced or vicariously derived, rational or irrational, he weaves a pattern of conduct that is his individual and social life." Biologist and neurophilosopher Patricia Smith Churchland (2002, p. 31) observes that the primary function of the brain is to guide adaptation to changing circumstances, and adds that "The human brain, as a rather fancy defense against variability and disaster, also generates stories—call them *theories*—to explain *why* things happen and thus help predict what *will* happen." In conjunction with the brain, she continues (p. 40), if the primary function of the nervous system is to allow the organism to take action "then an important job of cognition is to make *predictions* that guide decisions."

It is clear that science has been widely recognized as a marvel of humanity for at least the past five hundred years, and it constitutes an area of scholarship that most would agree is to be credited in large part for whatever progress civilization may have achieved. But physicist John Ziman (1978, p. 150) puts that idea into perspective when he writes that "The key factor in the evolution of science remains, nevertheless, the power of the human mind to recognize a comprehensible pattern in a mass of detail." Following are the principal functions of mind that pertain to the central theme of this book.

Truth

What motivates this strong inclination to think? Michael Polanyi (1964, p. 54) says he founds his theory of knowledge on the notion "that we can know more than we can tell," which is an inference he draws from psychological research. Science has long been held as a model for understanding how an idea becomes knowledge; with some stretching here and there that model can be made to fit society in general, well enough at least to provide broad insights into the dynamics of knowledge. Polanyi (1966, pp. 82–83) also argues that scientific tradition derives its capacity for self-renewal from its belief in the presence of a hidden reality, and he reasons that any tradition that fosters the progress of thought must share the intention of teaching its current ideas as stages leading on to unknown truths that may even prove eventually to disagree with the teachings that had led to that point. Such tradition assures the independence of its followers by transmitting the conviction that "thought has intrinsic powers, to be evoked in men's minds by intimations of hidden truths... Such are the metaphysical grounds of intellectual life in a free, dynamic society: the principles which safeguard intellectual life in such a society: I call this a society of explorers. In a society of explorers man is *in thought.*" The highly influential work of Jürgen Habermas on social evolution is not concerned with particular human achievements, says Andrew Edgar (2006, p. 138), however widespread their influence might be. Instead, he says, Habermas concerns himself with the human capacity for rational thought and inquiry, with the interactive and communicative competences that make them possible.

With the apparently simple statement that "From individual experiences we try to establish universal truths," D. J. Foskett (1962, p, 4) suggests a vast area of motivation behind cultural evolution. It is the seemingly innate propensity of the human to seek something identified as truth, an idea or fact or interpretation that is sufficiently valid for individual and society to survive in relative safety and comfort, both physically and psychologically. Philosopher Karl Popper (1994) sees dialectic as the fundamental social tool that has guided this search, just as it most evidently has become the cornerstone of any scientific inquiry.[16] "I believe that this respect for truth," he writes (p. 203), "is indeed one of the most important and most precious traits of European civilization, and that it is rooted nowhere more firmly and deeply than in science. It is a priceless treasure we find in the treasure-house of science, a treasure which, I believe, far surpasses her technological utility." Michael Polanyi (1959, p. 27) would probably concur, for he states that the capacity of our minds to make contact with reality and the intellectual passion which impels us towards this contact "will always suffice so to guide our personal judgment that it will achieve the full measure of truth that lies within the scope of our particular calling." He strongly affirms this notion by making it the subject of *Personal Knowledge,* which is one of his most comprehensive statements.

The effort of humanity to distance itself from nature has been mentioned in this text as one of the key features to distinguish humanity from other species, and is a concept very much analogous to cultural evolution, itself. But it is not just the distancing of humanity from the rest of nature that is a characteristic result of cultural evolution. Taking that notion a step further, there seems to be an inborn human drive to control, if not conquer, nature. Sir Karl Popper (1994, pp. 193–194) describes in a few short paragraphs the development of the place of knowledge in society. He says that as technologies and science began to develop to the point of receiving wider public recognition, a variant on the Platonic idea that the philosophers, who were the learned of Plato's time, should be the leaders of the society, that they should wield the power. Knowledge was seen as power. It is Popper's thesis that "both the industrial and the scientific development which took place since the Renaissance are realizations of this philosophical idea—*the idea of the mastery of man over nature.*"

In writing of the tacit mental powers (the kind of knowledge we may not even be aware we ever acquired) of an adult human, Michael Polanyi finds that at their highest level they may not exceed and perhaps may fall short of those of an animal or an infant. Nonetheless, "the adult's incomparably greater performances are to be ascribed predominantly to his superior cultural equipment." (1959, p. 19)[17] Truth is a human concept. If there is an innate drive to find truth, even though it cannot be proved that whatever may be in question, has general validity, then the idea must have directly to do with survival; at least survival of the human species in its most characteristic considerations. It is the search for truth that invokes the need for knowledge about the physical world, the social world, and about the exercise of political power, which ultimately results in its creation and any action that might flow from it.[18]

Mathematician, historian, and philosopher Jacob Bronowski and historian Bruce Mazlish (1960, p. xii) introduce their study of Western intellectual tradition with the summary that "Ideas are not dead thoughts, even when they are no longer contemporary; for they remain steps in the evolution of contemporary ideas." This brief declaration embraces the structure of library function and, therefore, describes the foundation for library philosophy.

Dialectic & Decision Making

Philosopher Karl Popper (1994, p. xii) summarizes his own conscious motivation in thinking and even, he says, his way of living, with a method he formulated around 1932 to ferret out the truth. He proceeds in a straightforward manner that "I may be wrong and you may be right, and by an effort, we may get nearer to the truth." What he is emphasizing here is communication, an exchange of ideas between individuals and groups that can develop into a common understanding and perhaps a dialectic from which a new thought or perspective can emerge. This is a key mechanism in the evolution of culture. Peter L. Berger and Thomas Luckmann (1966, p. 165) also argue that dialectic is an ongoing function in the human condition, and that in the individual it comes into play in an already structured socio-historical situation. They conclude that, externally, the dialectic takes place between the individual and the surrounding social world while, internally, it works between the individual's biological substratum and his socially produced identity. Thus, "It is possible to speak of a dialectic between nature and society."

Dialectic and decision making are complex matters that give direction to thought and eventually to action. Most often, humans, and other animals, as well, face the challenge of, or the opportunity presented by, a choice of actions to take. In this process, the determining factor hinges on the individual's view to the future, for it is a capacity that involves thinking about the likely consequences of the action. Kenneth Boulding (1978, p. 132) explains that something even as fundamental as making the first tool had to have required an image of the future, that is to say an understanding of the utility of the tool, rather than some other kind of stimulus. Purpose had to be the motivation behind the crafting of the tool. This capacity of the mind to form complex images of the future, as well as of space and time, became "an increasingly important element in the dynamics of the individual human being and his society... The human race is not merely pushed by past events or present circumstances, but it is also pulled by its own images of the future," and values play a very important part in that process. Boulding (1985, p. 89) also reminds us of this consideration, in asserting that "Decisions, it can hardly be stated too often, depend not only on images of the future but also on the valuations that we apply to these."

Social anthropologist Jack Goody and literary critic and historian Ian Watt (1988, p. 20) recount a story about Thomas Jefferson who once complained that "'The printers can never leave us in a state of perfect rest and union of opinion'." Jefferson's reference was to the criticism of ideas that is both invited by and made convenient by the printed text, for reading and writing. And because of the printed text, which, owing to its physical attributes, is a nearly permanent record, literate societies cannot dispose of ideas, beliefs, and accepted knowledge, one way or another, as easily or carelessly as oral societies can. With the capability to contemplate the past quite separately from the present, historical enquiry is made possible. "This in turn encourages skepticism," write Goody and Watt (p. 26), "and skepticism, not only about the legendary past, but about received ideas about the universe as a whole. From here the next step is to see how to build up and to test alternative explanations; and out of this there arose the kind of logical, specialized, and cumulative intellectual tradition of sixth-century Ionia."

Here we need to consider, again, the importance of dialectic, of which a significant implication is criticism. It is by means of dialectic that science develops in its most formal mode through peer review. Just as it is the role of science to make the universe around us understandable and, therefore, useable, so criticism carves the path toward truth in all spheres. Analogous to the dialectic of science, criticism is a method of reason, while reason is sharpened through criticism. Sir Karl Popper (1977, p. 451) argues that the emergence of criticism had to be preceded by that of language. "Real criticism—the criticism of ideas, of theories—arises, I think only with language, and it seems to me that this is really one of the most important aspects of language." He finds it (1994, pp. 40–41) highly improbable, for example, that prior to the development of language tools would be subject to criticism except in the most rudimentary way, such as by the discard of an implement found to be of little value. One of the components of reason is what he calls poetic inventiveness, which is the explanation of the surrounding universe through story-telling or myth-making. The other component of reason is the critical discussion of the explanatory myths with the aim of consciously improving upon them, which was not in place until the establishment of writing in ancient Greece. Whether about science or mythology, these are theories to be tested and discussed with the purpose of achieving clearer and deeper understanding.

Imagination & Creativity

The brain is an organ of the body that is stimulated by the rest of the body surrounding it and by the external influences of all kinds that affect body and brain. The composite function is the mind. The mind is conceived of as a much broader entity than awareness, consciousness, or even introspection. An understanding of the mind in the sense of explaining it has not moved much beyond the establishment of theories which seem yet to be distant from proof, although philosopher David Malet Armstrong (2004b, p. 605) finds that current work "identifies mental processes with purely physical processes in the central nervous system." In that context, an especially important feature of the human brain, one that distinguishes it from other natural beings, is its extraordinary capacity to create, and it is a feature that operates through the mind. Eighteenth-century Scottish philosopher and historian David Hume (2007, p. 13) described the elusive qualities of this important human capacity:

> What never was seen, or heard of, may yet be conceived; nor is any thing beyond the power of thought... but though our thought seems to possess this unbounded liberty, we shall find, upon a nearer examination, that it is really confined within very narrow limits, and that all this creative power of the mind amounts to no more than the faculty of compounding, transposing, augmenting, or diminishing the materials afforded us by the senses and experience.

Creativity generally is considered the act of introducing something that is accepted as new, whether through manufacture or visualization. In either case it is generated by the imagination. Cognitive psychologist Robert W. Weisberg

(1993, p. 241) finds two essential ways of viewing creativity: "the 'genius' view, which conceives of creativity as the result of extraordinary thought processes; and the 'ordinary' view, in which creativity is seen as resulting from thought processes possessed by all of us, seen most clearly when we solve problems." Creativity can be based on the so-called real world, which is outside and around us, or it can be fantasy. Kenneth Boulding (1978, p. 127), for example, believes that because of its extraordinary capacity for complex images, "the human brain exercises its genetic function in the form of human artifacts." And it is through the magic of human language and other forms of human communication, says Boulding (p. 128), that "The human mind can form images of large, complex, and integrated systems of which it has no personal experience." In any case, imagination seems to be the vehicle for creativity, for it is a mental stimulant. One of the characteristically human powers, writes anthropologist Tim Ingold (1993a, p. 431), is "the capacity to turn attention inwards towards the self rather than outwards towards the world–to explore, that is, our own past experience and to construe future possibilities of being. That is the power of imagination." Somewhat similarly, archeologist Iain Davidson and psychologist William Noble (1993, p. 382) conclude that effects of primitive humans they have studied "exhibit the marks of planning that seem to entail a capacity for consciousness of what is being done, not just responsiveness to the unfolding contingencies of the here-and-now environment. It is language that makes possible this 'reflective turn', the capacity to express . . . 'second-order intentionality' (having 'beliefs and desires' about one's 'beliefs and desires')." Cell geneticist François Jacob (1982, p. 10) reasons that it is probably a need of the human brain to have a representation of the world that is unified and coherent. "A lack of unity and coherence frequently results in anxiety and schizophrenia. It seems only fair to say that, as far as coherence and unity are concerned, mythical explanation often does better than scientific explanation." And he adds (p. 11) that "Whether mythic or scientific, the view of the world that man builds is always largely a product of his imagination."

Psychologist Ilona Roth (2004, p. 444) summarizes the essential role of imagination in evolution: "A hominid capable of imagining the possible outcomes of different actions, or the possible responses of its peers, would have the selective advantage of control over its physical and social environment, uncompromised by expenditure of energy in physically enacting and evaluating alternative outcomes." It is to the imagination that is owed the development of technologies, as will be discussed below, and to modes of socialization. Research in the fields of cognitive archaeology and evolutionary psychology suggest that the imagination likely emerged only in the last hundred thousand years. But its capacity began to resemble the modern imagination, which is characterized by the use of imagery, symbolism, counterfactual thinking, novelty and creative output, only about fifty thousand years ago, when other evolutionary features, especially linguistic symbolism, gained strength. Biologist Sir Julian S. Huxley (1958, p. 453) also gives great credit to human imagination as a force in cultural evolution arguing that "in all man's creative activities, including the construction of 'visions of destiny', imagination and intuition are as essential as logic and reason. And there is the further fact that if knowledge is lacking on which to build a coherent and satisfying vision, imagination will almost universally be called on to provide mythical explanations and interpretative extrapolations of actuality; and that these imaginative formulations may then canalize and condition the whole culture."

Similarly, how the human brain evolved to cope with complex intellectual considerations—to be able to work through issues and make complex decisions, to ponder the future, to create concepts or, in a word, to be able to reason, is not known precisely, but there is no shortage of relevant theory and research. Much of it, however, relates to the development of a high level of language and will be explored in Chapter 4. Archeologist V. Gordon Childe (1956, p. 12) describes the capacity at issue: "Finally, our unique evolutionary success is due not only to our ability to communicate knowledge, but equally to our capacity to use the symbols with which we communicate also for 'reasoning'. For reasoning has been defined as 'operating with symbols in the head instead of going through a physical process of trial and error'." In describing the element of cognitive modeling, neuropsychologist Merlin Donald (1991, p. 10) concludes that all animals do not have the same cognitive capacity and that "In fact the uniqueness of humanity could be said to rest not so much in language as in our capacity for rapid cultural change," which raises the issues of mind and body, mind and brain as they relate to culture. None the less, social psychologist David Loye (1998, p. 175) observes that "Though the force of creativity as the basic driver for cultural evolution has been shown in hundreds of ways in primarily psychological studies . . . the battle to inject this perspective into evolutionary theory has been uphill all the way." Chapters 5, 6, and 7 will demonstrate that the library was created as a cultural technology to extend the mind, with the purpose of greatly accelerating cultural evolution, for, as neuropsychologist Merlin Donald (2001, p. 324) concludes, "The human brain is the only brain in the biosphere whose potential cannot be realized on its own."

If ideas constitute the substance of the energy needed to generate and evolve culture, then thinking—human thought—is the engine for those ideas. What is thinking? Plato defined it as a dialogue in the soul, and his view on this is echoed two millennia later by philosopher Gilbert Ryle (1949). Ryle (p. 309) finds that "Didactic discourse is the vehicle for the transmission of knowledge," and (p. 311) that "All talk is meant to exert some specific influence," just as (p. 312) "Didactic talk is meant to instruct." These thoughts merge (p. 312) in his conclusion that "Didactic influence can be exerted not only by one person upon another but also by one person upon himself." Such is Ryle's explanation of thought. Another commentator, A. Broadfield (1949, p. 12), observes that this dialogue is so much a part of human existence that it is tenaciously unstoppable, that man "can be prevented from eating, sleeping, meeting or voting, but not from thinking" and, as if to make the point extra clear in its simplicity, Peter L. Berger and Thomas Luckmann (1966, p. 165) remind us that "Man is even capable of eating and theorizing at the same time."

Yet the phenomenon of thinking seems to be even deeper and more complex than such ideas suggest. Conceptualization, which is a particularly powerful tool for thinking, is an abstraction of ideas that can lead toward understanding (which is discussed further in Chapter 7), and can become part of a theory or be explained by theory. Philosopher Abraham Kaplan (1964, p. 46) observes that "Since Kant, we have come to recognize every concept as a rule of judging or acting, a prescription for organizing the materials of experience so as to be able to go on about our business." Conceptualization is essential to thinking, and as anthropologist Bernard G. Campbell (1974, p. 334) says, "as generally defined, is an abstraction from the particular to the class." Cognitive psychologist Ziva Kunda (1999, p. 16) describes conceptualization as an act of relation and integration, writing that "Concepts are the building blocks of cognition. A concept is a mental representation of a category, that is, a class of objects that we believe belong together... It embodies our knowledge about the category and its members." And psychologist Paul Thagard (1992, p. 25) suggests how this action comes about even in the absence of any intention to call upon its capacity, concluding that "A concept is not a structure stored in the brain the way a data structure is stored in a digital computer. Rather, it emerges when needed from the interaction of large numbers of connected nodes." Thinking with concepts is not a straight-forward activity, as John Wilson (1971, pp. 14–16) writes in his book on the subject. He observes that when considering the meaning of a concept it is as though we are asked to become

> selfconscious about words which hitherto we had used without thinking—not necessarily used wrongly, but used unselfconsciously. This is rather like the process of psychoanalysis, or the self-examinations and confessions practised in religion. In these we are asked to become more conscious of our actions, to look at them objectively and think about them: hitherto we had been content to act, but now we have to become aware of the significance of our actions. In the same way, when we deal with questions of concept, we are asked to become aware of the significance of our words... the process of becoming conscious is not a simple one: not so simple, for instance, as learning a factual subject like physics, or a subject governed by strict rules like mathematics.

Paul Thagard also provides a useful list (p. 22) of "various roles that concepts have been deemed to play."

At some point in cultural evolution, the emergence of a new power to contemplate the future is evidenced, as discussed earlier in this chapter, by the production of tools in advance of their use, and the construction of dwelling sites with an evident protracted period of occupation in mind. But other changes also emerged, although not so easily related to basic survival, such as cave painting, the diversification and stylization of tools, the manufacture of body ornaments and innovation in burial practices. Archeologist Steven J. Mithen (1996, p. 195) refers to this critical capacity in the evolution of the brain as 'cognitive fluidity. "The critical step in the evolution of the modern mind was the switch from a mind designed like a Swiss army knife to one with cognitive fluidity, from a specialized to a generalized type of mentality." This enabled humans to design complex tools, to create art and believe in religious ideologies, and Mithen adds that "the potential for other types of thought which are critical to the modern world can be laid at the door of cognitive fluidity." This strictly human feature of the brain (or mind) is what made possible the development of a relatively powerful and flexible tool in cultural evolution, which is manifested in the various forms of language usage,[19] which is examined more closely in Chapter 4.

The field of evolutionary psychology is of special interest to understanding library function in cultural evolution, as can be judged from the rationale behind research in that field, described by psychologist Leda Cosmides and anthropologist John Tooby (2002, p. 145): "Evolution brought brains and minds into a world initially devoid of intelligent life. The evolutionary process designed the neural machinery that generates intelligent behavior, and important insights into how this machinery works can be gained by understanding how evolution constructs organisms."

Summary

While the individual's mind works with that of others to create the culture, the culture in turn plays a very substantial role in forming the most significant social aspects of the mind. "An understanding of the human mind, therefore," advises anthropologist Leslie A. White (1949, p. 188), "calls for an appreciation of the role of cultural factors as determinants of thinking, feeling and acting." And the mind's influence can be unconsciously directed to the most essential considerations, for as neurologist Antonio R. Damasio (1999, p. 139) advises, "Brains permit the life urge to be regulated ever so effectively and, at some point in evolution, knowingly."

That such power of culture is well recognized by societies is evident in the effort seen almost everyday to create a cultural dependency on and acceptance of an innovation by introducing something as a long-valued expression of the society. Historian Eric Hobsbawm (1983, p. 1) explains this kind of social engineering drawn from the recognition of power inherent in tradition. "'Invented tradition' is taken to mean a set of practices, normally governed by overtly or tacitly accepted rules and of a ritual or symbolic nature, which seek to inculcate certain values and norms of behaviour by repetition, which automatically implies continuity with the past. In fact, where possible, they normally attempt to establish continuity with a suitable historic past."

Among the more important aspects of cultural evolution is the fact that, while selection supports the individual in his or her individuality, it will ultimately be society that determines most of the selections made by the individual. Psychobiologist Henry Plotkin (1998, p. 230) formulates the idea this way: "Human evolution, therefore, will have favoured behavioural traits that enhance the fitness of individuals, but some of these will do so because they operate at the group level." Attempting to avoid the complex knot of ambiguities and unknowns of cultural evolution, yet account for them in a meaningful way, social anthropologist Adam Kuper (1994, p. 101) concludes that "There is no obvious point of origin that fixed what human beings were to be. In very many ways, we are not what we were. As we become more like each other, we become more different from all the people who have lived before. We may now be converging with each other, but in the process we are distancing ourselves with unprecedented rapidity from even our recent ancestors." If ultimate origins are supposed to explain the essence of what we are, he says, "we might just as well go back to the first insects that spread over the world, or forward to the origins of capitalism." The attraction to fit the culture is so fundamental and strong that even in recounting personal experience, writes sociologist John Shotter (1990, pp. 122–123), that "our ways of talking about our experiences work not primarily to represent the nature of those experiences in themselves, but to represent them in such a way as to constitute and sustain one or another kind of social order."

By way of perceptions and the meanings assigned to them, all our surroundings have been incorporated into our world view and our place in the world, including the smallest living entity, by way of perceptions and the meanings assigned to them. Geneticist and science philosopher Bentley Glass (1985, p. xiv) theorizes that "Human thought has been formed through centuries of man's consciousness, by perceptions and meanings that relate us to nature. The smallest living entity, be it a molecule or a particle, is at the same time presenting the structure of the Earth and all its inhabitants, whether human or manifesting themselves in the multiplicity of other forms of life." Part of the complexity toward which cultural evolution seems to lead is the concomitant, perhaps resulting, sense within humanity of the increasing velocity at which time passes. As Nobel laureate physicist Ilya Prigogine and co-author Isabelle Stengers (1984, p. 301) observe, "It is interesting that with an increase of complexity, going from the stone to human societies, the role of the arrow of time, of evolutionary rhythms, increases." Historian Penelope

Corfield (2007, p. 74) concludes, as do most others, that particularly since the eighteenth century, a significant cultural strand of confidence in long-term processes has developed. This attitude, she writes, "while emphatically not shared by all, was based upon admiration for the consolidation and continual updating of the human stock of knowledge in accessible forms. Theory and practice would alike benefit, gaining from the accumulated wisdom of time. So things would 'progress'.... Later generations had the advantage of a much larger stock of knowledge, observations and experimentation. The achievements of one age would assist the next." Library function occupies a key place in this evolutionary phenomenon, for, without detailed knowledge of past thinking and experience, how could one imagine the possibility of progress and, indeed, how could society advance without that knowledge?

What of the role of intelligence in cultural evolution? Sociologist Morris Ginsberg (1961, p. 113) answers, "There is no evidence of any general change in inborn faculty. What has grown is the body of knowledge and its better organization. This is a social product, the result of co-operative effort, mutual stimulus and cumulative experience. Furthermore, there is not only development but progress." But this is where the function of diversification becomes critical, for it is an area where biological and cultural evolution merge. Bentley Glass (1985, p. 160) underlines the significance of biological diversification in the adaptation of humans to their environment:

> The intelligence of man is an evolutionary product of natural selection for adaptability to great variation of surroundings to tremendous vicissitudes of experience, as Henri Bergson concluded seventy years ago. Such evolved intelligence depends upon a genetic pool in human populations to which many genes contribute, in ever-shifting combinations produced by the patterns of heredity and reproduction. A pure line, no matter how perfectly selected for special excellence under given conditions, could be well adapted only to particular conditions. Unless man's power produced a world not only stable but unvarying and unvaried, the maintenance of human diversity should remain a paramount aim. As long as our brave new world presents an abundance of choices and as long as we have freedom to choose, just so long will human intelligence based upon genetic diversity continue to be a primary requirement.

A questioning, reasoning mind that is more than a brain has evolved and continues to evolve aided by the technologies needed to extend the encased power and more fully realize the being's most human qualities.

In considering the conceptual stages of evolutionary development that can be applied to the human situation, geneticist Conrad Hal Waddington (1961, pp. 71–72) eliminates stasigensis as an appropriate concept on the basis of the radical change the species has experienced in evolving from non-human ancestry; and he rules out cladogenesis because mankind's "mastery of conceptual thought and social communication mark off his biological organization as something radically different from that of his nearest biological relatives, the apes." Waddington concludes that the human being "must be considered to have resulted from anagenesis, a real progressive change and not a mere modification in detail." It is not the intention of this book to cast the library as that real progressive change, but rather to argue that the library is the clearest, most powerful technological advance in cultural evolution to reflect such change.

Of the many motivations that find influence in cultural evolution, however, the most consistent and perhaps the strongest is that of values shared among individuals and groups. The highest levels of culture are those that relate directly to values. Writes sociologist Roy Wood Sellars (1926, p. xxviii): "Clearly values are intrinsic to reality at this high level. In values we are *in* culture, *in* civilization, *in* the very pulse of selective and creative human life." Values exert a strong yet usually unobtrusive form of influence, but as subtle as they may be in and of themselves, they can be shared easily through the medium of language. The development of language, with its penchant toward refinement and nuanced shades of meaning, in combination with its capacity for clarity and ease of communication, has proved to work in natural symbiosis with the mind. The joining of that set of exclusively human powers to the library function is the recurrent theme of the following chapters.

CHAPTER 4

Communication

The seeming novelty of many a system is due solely to the novelty of the application or arrangement of the old elements which enter into it.

—Arthur O. Lovejoy, 1936

Introduction

Language has played the central facilitating role in cultural evolution, and by most accounts also is in large part a product of evolutionary forces.[1] It has enabled humans to think at relatively high levels in the creation and understanding of concepts and in reasoning, and ultimately in generating and communicating ideas. Language arises from the articulation of thought, for as psychologist Lev S. Vigotsky (1962, p. 150) reasons, "Direct communication between minds is impossible, not only physically but psychologically. Communication can be achieved only in a roundabout way. Thought must pass first through meanings and then through words." This fact, along with its corollary that language stretches the potential of the brain, is the basis for the present chapter.

"Man gets his ideas from two sources," comments Pierce Butler (1952, p. 82), "his own experience and the experience of others . . . Without communicated experience man can hardly become rational." Communication, in the words of communication theorist Wilbur Schramm (1971, p. 5), is "the fundamental social process," for, according to linguist Edward Sapir (1931, p. 78), "every cultural pattern and every single act of social behavior involve communication in either an explicit or implicit sense." The modes of human communication, with its range and potential for both relative specificity and depth in human communication, are unique among primates. The potential of human communication and the ways in which that potential are realized constitute the essence of process in cultural evolution.

The value of human communication to culture and its evolution is to be found in the sharing of information, ideas, experience, concepts, and images so that they may be useful to the security and success of the surrounding society, as well as to the individuals it incorporates. "The organization of common experience constitutes society," explains D. J. Foskett (1984, p. 6), and it is from this source that information derives its value. It is also through our experience that we associate concepts and ideas of the world around us, and we are often impelled to pass them on. Foskett continues that "A structure of society develops out of the ever-increasing stock of socially available concepts which have common acceptance." And communication theorist Frank E. X. Dance (1985, p. 72) holds that language facilitates a blending of subjectivity and objectivity early in a child's development, leading to a sense of contrast that is fundamental to the fine tuning of ideas. But the relative quality of the information that is communicated has some bearing on this. Library theorist Margaret Egan (1951, p. 254) contends that "no communication has any social value unless it stimulates or modifies behavior which has some impact upon the community. The greater the impact, the greater the importance to society. Such behavior may be individual or it may be corporate . . . the impact may be immediate, long-delayed, or gradual." As will be shown in Chapter 6 on library function, the power of language is not only instrumental, but even more profound than that. For example, linguist Benjamin Lee Whorf (1956, p. 263) synthesizes this potential in his assertion that "A change in language can transform our appreciation of the Cosmos," and further (p. 267) that "What is significant for our thesis is that language, through lexation, has made the speaker more acutely conscious of certain dim psychic sensations; it has actually produced awareness on lower planes than its own: a power of the nature of magic." Language will be a recurring theme throughout the following chapters because of the unique powers it affords humanity.

Memory

Memory plays a key role in providing the substance of thought and also, therefore, of communication, whether over a short or long duration, for it holds in readiness the store of knowledge that has been accumulated through the culture. But there is a reciprocal process of memory and social context, as sociologist John Shotter (1990, p. 132) emphasizes. Without being situated within an organized setting, "our behaviour would become pathological: we would be unable to formulate goals, to act from the past towards the future; to remember who we were or what we were about. In short, we would be unable to act as self-determining agents. Disorganized memories, irrelevant to our lives, would come and go wholly undirected by 'us'—our actions would bear no relation to our social identities."

A memory, something remembered, writes philosopher Maurice Halbwachs (1980, p. 69), "is in very large measure a reconstruction of the past achieved with data borrowed from the present, a reconstruction prepared, furthermore, by reconstructions of earlier periods wherein past images had already been altered." The phenomenon of memory (p. 51) "is not completely sealed off and isolated. A man must often appeal to others' remembrances to evoke his own past. He goes back to reference points determined by society, hence outside himself. Moreover, the individual memory could not function without words and ideas, instruments the individual has not himself invented but appropriated from his milieu." Halbwachs adds that, what becomes fixed in memory "are not just facts, but attitudes and ways of thinking from the past" (p. 64). Social psychologist Sir Frederick C. Bartlett (1932) used the concept of the schema, an organizational frame that influences the character and content of an individual's memory, while concurrently and for similar purposes behavioral psychologist Edward C. Tolman (1932) used the term cognitive map, meaning more specifically internal representations that allow animals and humans to amend performances in accord with new contexts. Both concepts relate memory to cognition and action. But Halbwachs (p. 23) stresses the importance of the social derivation of memory, writing that "Our memories remain collective, however, and are recalled to us through others even though only we were participants in the events or saw the things concerned." And he adds another dimension to this idea by saying, "In reality, we are never alone. Other men need not be physically present, since we always carry with us and in us a number of distinct persons." Halbwachs' depiction of memory suggests an unusually vast and fertile field for the intellectual seeds that can be sown by the convergence of humanity and library.

Psychobiologist Henry Plotkin (2002, p. 107), whose reference in Chapter 3 to emerging theory on memory that accounts for the accumulation of memes in the function for memory that parallels the function of genes in genetics, describes the functioning of these higher-order-knowledge structures involved in memory as a process of creative reconstruction. The idea was not his, and in fact is traced far back in philosophy, for it is the substance of culture. The term memes in reference to this concept was coined by ethologist and evolutionary biologist Richard Dawkins (1976), a term he also popularized in an analogy of memes and genes. He writes (p. 215) that "We are built as gene machines and cultured as meme machines." Much like genes, theorizes Dawkins (p. 208), memes are replicators, whose function depends upon three qualities: longevity, fecundity, and copying fidelity. He calls these the "units of variation" in evolving cultures. Elsewhere Dawkins (1999, p. 297) defines meme as "A unit of cultural inheritance, hypothesized as analogous to the particulate gene, and as naturally selected by virtue of its phenotypic consequences on its own survival and replication in the cultural environment," and states further (1999, p. 109) that "A meme should be regarded as a unit of information residing in a brain. It has a definite structure, realized in whatever physical medium the brain uses for storing information." Mind and culture are designed by memetic selection, just as organisms are designed by natural selection acting on genes.

Dawkins' ideas in this matter have become influential but are not accepted in their entirety by the scientific community, as described by cognitive scientist Margaret A. Boden (2001, pp. 562–568). It is not the intent of this essay to suggest that memes and genes are equivalents, but rather that their distinctions simply are those that naturally separate biology and culture. Genetics and memetics also differ in matters of degree of precision and regularity. "There is a persisting tension between the biological imperative of our genes on the one hand and the cultural imperatives of our memes on the other," says philosopher Daniel C. Dennett (1995, p. 365), for example. But memes, like genes, do influence who we are and how we behave, however, the chief differences relevant to this essay being in the areas of sources, nature of diversity, mechanisms and means of diffusion, and facility of modification. For his purposes, Dennett elsewhere (2003, p. 176) defines genes as ingeniously designed informational structures that unwittingly exploit thinkers, but they aren't themselves thinkers," which he follows with a similar definition of the meme as "an information-packet with attitude–a recipe or instruction manual for doing something cultural. Memes are thus analogous to genes." There may be many areas of difference, but there also are some fundamental similarities that invite valid analogy in this essay about library function in the evolution of the most fundamental aspects of culture.

Plotkin (2002, p. 107) theorizes that memories "change in time as we reinterpret the events in our lives, partly as a result of our wants and needs, but partly also as a result of the effects of unconscious generic knowledge structures," or complex models of the world, and, of particular significance to this essay, "Knowledge structures are built cumulatively." Sociologist Charles Horton Cooley (1920, p. 351) is more specific in his assessment that "The test of intelligence is the power to act successfully in new situations," with his conclusion on the relation of these features (p. 352) that "Intelligence, then, is based on memories, but makes a free and constructive use of these, as distinguished from a mechanical use." He refers to this as an act of mental synthesis, an inner organizing process of its own. With the benefit of seven more decades of research and theory than Cooley had at his disposal, cognitive psychologist Merlin Donald (1991, p. 313) posits that

> The locus of memory is everywhere or anywhere in the system at any given moment, depending upon the flow of information, access, and priorities. The biologically encapsulated mind might be called a monad, after Giordano Bruno and Liebnitz. Monads may form temporary connections with specific nodes in the external symbolic system, disconnecting and reconnecting at will in various configurations. A node may be defined simply as a particular location within a network; thus a specific scientific paper in a clearly defined area of the ESS ['external symbolic storage system', defined on his p. 306 as "all memory items stored in some relatively permanent external format, whether or not they are immediately available to the user"]

might be considered a node, whereas the entire collection of journal and reference works in the area constitutes an information network.

Whether belonging to the human or some other species, memory is a highly critical factor. Anthropologist André Leroi-Gourhan (1993, p. 220) compares the apparent similarities of a community of ants and a community of human beings, noting the importance of memory in making their activities possible, moreover in continuing the survival of both, because that is where behaviors are stored. But he notes a highly significant difference[2] between the two groups: "In animals the memory is based on a highly complex instinctual apparatus, whereas in anthropoids the memory of each ethnic group rests on the no less complex apparatus of language."

Linguist Wallace L. Chafe (1979, p. 180) surmises that there seem to be certain units of information storage in the mind that he refers to as *foci,* which are the basic units of memory that represent the amount of information to which a person can devote primary attention at any one time. "During the verbalization of something recalled, the speaker's focus of attention moves from one focus to the next, although it is capable of abandoning a focus before it has been completely verbalized, of dwelling on the same focus for several phrases, or of returning to a focus already but perhaps not satisfactorily communicated." Cognitive psychologist Michael Tomasello (1999, p. 124) makes clear the place of memory in knowledge and learning, advising that "Remembering specific objects, conspecifics, events, and all other aspects of personal experience—and in some cases anticipating future experiences based on this recall—is the *sine qua non* of cognition."

As fundamental as memory is in Tomasello's assessment, philosopher Henri Bergson (1920, pp. 7–8) considers memory to be the most characteristic feature of consciousness, even asserting that without memory there is no consciousness. With all its potential for failure and weakness, memory is central for Bergson, who explains a basic connection between consciousness, memory, and contemplation of the future: "A consciousness unable to conserve its past, forgetting itself unceasingly, would be a consciousness perishing and having to be reborn at each moment; and what is this but unconsciousness? All consciousness, then, is memory,—conservation and accumulation of the past in the present. But all consciousness is also anticipation of the future." Subsequently Bergson (pp. 14–15) argues that as consciousness retains the past and anticipates the future, it is because of the need to engage in selection: "In order to choose, we must know what we can do and remember the consequences, advantageous or injurious, of what we have already done; we must foresee and we must remember . . . If consciousness means memory and anticipation, it is because consciousness is synonymous with choice." But memory is able to function in complex human capacities primarily because of the power of language.

Language

Experience, along with the memory of lessons learned from it and learning from others through language, are especially powerful in the evolution of culture, which also shapes language, as psychologist Patrick Meredith (1961, p. 258) summarizes: "Through the forms of language a culture imposes a world-view, a metaphysic, on the individual. A culture is a totality of experiences, concepts, beliefs and their consequences. It provides the determining context in which language finds its meaning." Biologists E. Sue Savage-Rumbaugh and Duane M. Rumbaugh (1992, p. 106) consider "Language as the inevitable outcome of the social interactions of intelligent creatures," because (p. 86) "The biological capacities which *Homo sapiens* bring to language are the anatomical specialization of the speech apparatus, a very large brain, and a species tendency to live in groups where resources are shared." A specific aspect of the influence of culture on language is examined by cell biologist Karl H. Pfenninger and science writer Valerie R. Shubik (2001, p. 220), who indicate, "The increasing ability to recognize cause and consequence and to act accordingly–as opposed to following blind instincts–provided a huge advantage for the evolution of *Homo sapiens.*" And in discussing the basic fact that animals possess learning and abstraction capacities, neurologist Sir Russell Brain (1961, p. 60) adds, "In man, however, all these capacities are, as it were, raised to a higher power. Speech alone makes the leap of symbolic representation whereby it becomes possible not merely to excite reactions or feelings in others, but to convey ideas in a most economical fashion, and this process in itself becomes a tool in the service of conceptual thought." And he makes a comment that will become of special significance to the present book by concluding his thought with, "From this arises a new 'layer' of evolution, which de Chardin in his pregnant phrase calls the noösphere, and which now extends over the whole earth."

But linguist David M. Levy (1979, p. 208) offers the reminder that language does not come about as casually in communication as it may appear. He stresses that "Mental *activity* is the key here, for the speaker is not merely communicating ideas or propositions, but thought *processes.*" Levy explains that a coherent spoken text is one that allows the hearer to connect each of its pieces with what has come before, and that it is a text that leads the hearer down a strategic trail of mental operations. "Underlying these ideas, then, is a conception of language production as a planning process whereby the speaker chooses linguistic expressions from the options provided by his language in order to satisfy a number of (possibly simultaneous) communicative goals. And his aim in selecting expressions is not only to convey those goals to his hearer but also to convey the mental processes that led to the establishment of those goals."

Neurologist Sir W. Russell Brain (1951, p. 23) emphasizes the fundamental fact that humans both speak and listen to speech, which is the receptive side of language or "the understanding of words which we hear and read. This element in speech seems, in fact, to be more closely related to thinking than the means by which we express our thoughts when we have already arrived at them," which is the activation of the appropriate speech apparatus to communicate the words. Behavioral psychologist B. F. Skinner (1969, p. 203) observes that "The human species took a great step forward when its vocal musculature, previously concerned with the production of responses of phylogenic significance, came under operant control, because the social contingencies responsible for verbal behavior could then begin to operate."

Thus, language empowers memory and facilitates the expanded capacity of the memory to be recalled, altered as conditions change, and employed in communication. Of the many human features that have energized the evolution of culture, writes philosopher Daniel Dennett (2003, p. 174), "it is language that opens the floodgates of cultural transmission that set us apart from all other species." But social anthropologist Jack Goody (2000, p. 43) introduces the admonition that "It is dangerous to speak of a collective memory in oral cultures; memory is held by individuals, who may have some elements in common," although in literate cultures the library function becomes the collective memory. Educator Lyman Bryson (1947, p. 163) observes about this process that "experience is brought under control by the symbols that generalize, organize, and communicate the matter that is deposited by sense experience in the mind." And one fact that is known "with empirical certainty" about psychological memory, according to psychobiologist Henry Plotkin (1998, pp. 257–258), is that, "unlike genetic memory, it is a labile, active and constructive thing. There is much room here for 'mutation'. New variants will arise as innovations, new ideas or blends of old ideas, and their selection will occur within the context of other memes, as well as the needs of the social group."

Exactly when and how symbolic, articulate language was introduced remains unknown, but geneticist Theodosius Dobzhansky (1977, p. 452) underlines the prime role of natural selection in evolving the motivation behind the function of language and the genes that make it possible. "The cognitive structures on which both language and tool-making depend are the foundations of the control of the environment by culture. While all organisms adapt to their environments by changing their genes, man alone adapts mainly, though not exclusively, by creating the environments that suit his genes." Surely no one would seriously question the importance of language in the condition of being human, or even the contention of philosopher Raimo Tuomela (2002, p. 159) that "Language can be regarded as the most fundamental, underlying social institution." Social philosopher Malcolm Hollick (2006, p. 26) describes in a few words the process and product of that institution, writing that "We name every creation, discovery, and new idea. And new activities quickly acquire verbs... And the way the language we learn as a child structures reality actually determines how we see the world as we grow up."

Linguist Edward Sapir (1930, p. 79) interprets the limitation of overt behavior brought about through the homogenizing social processes of communication as the primary condition for the consolidation of society, "for in the process of falling in with the ways of society one in effect acquiesces in the meanings that inhere in these ways." This is the social function of epistemology. There are so many variations of meaning attached to so many words that each one can easily lend itself to criticism and refinement. For such variation involves a process of sharpening communication to capture just the right nuances for the receiver to understand the communication in the way the communicator intends it to be understood, thereby making it ever more complex and uniquely personalized.

Microbiologist and science philosopher Ludwik Fleck (1986, p. 85) places this phenomenon of communication in its broader social context, coining the term thought-styles, which refers to the body of socially conditioned knowledge, expertise, and world view held by social units called thought-collectives. Fleck describes the dynamic:

> When passing from one group to another, words change their meaning, the ideas obtain a different style colouring, the sentences receive another meaning, the opinions a new value... Consequently, each formulated thought, which is destined for real use, bears the sign of the producing unit and the address of destination... Only a sentence in its natural relevance, i.e. in its social meaning within the society, possesses a definite meaning; an abstract sentence can be understood in different manner: it can be equivocal or meaningless, depending on the circle of the recipient.

Fleck (p. 88) goes on to say that the idea being exchanged between such groups "undergoes various vicissitudes... It predominantly fertilizes and enriches the alien style, while being altered and assimilated: the content changes sometimes beyond recognition, even if the word has remained unchanged." Literacy researchers Victoria Purcell-Gates, Erik Jacobson, and Sophie Degener (2004, p. 30) find that "Any act of reading or writing, the use of words, cannot escape this sharing and struggle over words. Therefore, the meaning of what is written or read, and the meaning of the act of reading or writing, is necessarily contextual. It is social."

Clinical psychologist Lev S. Vigotsky (1962, p. 125) clarifies the relation between thought and language. He finds that in mastering nature we master ourselves, and that it is through the capacity of the intellect that this is accomplished. The internalization of overt action stimulates thought, and does so particularly through the internalization of external dialogue that brings the powerful tool of language to bear on the stream of thought. Vigotsky interprets the relation of thought to words not as a thing, but a process, a continual reciprocating movement that causes development in a functional sense. This interaction of thought and word is fundamental, especially as he states that thought is not merely expressed in words, but also comes into existence through them. According to Vigotsky, "Every thought tends to connect something with something else, to establish a relationship between things. Every thought moves, grows and develops, fulfills a function, solves a problem. This flow of thought occurs as an inner movement through a series of planes." But there is a feature of humanness that is still more fundamental than thought and memory alone, and that is the contribution of culture to each individual and group, as anthropologist Theodosius Dobzhansky (1968, p. 237) makes clear in his assertion that "The ability to speak is genetically determined, but what a person will actually say is largely independent of genetics."

The great variety of words, thoughts, concepts, expression, experience, and meaning contained through the library experience cannot be overstated, so reference to the phenomenon is encountered in one way or another throughout the present text. That intellectual richness, alone, may be the single most significant contribution of the library to cultural evolution. Neuroscientist Jean-Pierre Changeux (2004, p. 124) finds that the development of a system of neurons specially adapted to the purposes of syntactic communication suggests that propositions and structured speech can be seen as evolutionary phenomena that accompanied expansion of the human brain, advancing cognitive capacities. This anatomical development, as we shall see, represents a critical genetic step forward in the evolution of human cognitive capacities. "The immense diversity of sentences produced by individuals within a social group raises the equally formidable problem of understanding new sentences and of determining their truth value—this in addition to the problem of variability among individuals. The combinatorial explosion that results from the use of syntax requires new modes of perception and of processing if efficient comprehension among members of a social group is to occur." It is argued in the present essay that the library concept emerged to assist at the macro level in coping with the communication complexities that are part of the richness resulting from this combinatorial explosion.

Without language there would be no evolution in human culture, precious little culture at all, and certainly no humans as we have understood them to be for thousands of years. Literary critic George Steiner (1971, p. 60) argues that "man and language are correlate, that they imply and necessitate each other." He emphasizes that the volume of information is vast, that most of it is of extreme subtlety and specificity, that it is exchanged meaningfully at every point in the life process, and that in biological terms all this has taken place within a brief time span. Without mention of the specific capacities, philosopher Henri Bergson (1944, pp. 174–175) places language at the essence of cultural evolution: communication, knowledge, memory, learning, innovation. He writes,

> So a language is required which makes it possible to be always passing from what is known to what is yet to be known . . . Now, this mobility of words, that makes them able to pass from one thing to another, has enabled them to be extended from things to ideas . . . The word, made to pass from one thing to another, is, in fact, by nature transferable and free. It can therefore be extended, not only from one perceived thing to another, but even from a perceived thing to a recollection of that thing, from the precise recollection to a more fleeting image, and finally from an image fleeting, though still pictured, to the picturing of the act by which the image is pictured, that is to say, to the idea.

The consequences of symboling (language), says anthropologist Leslie A. White (1973, p. 8), "are the humanization of individuals and the origin and development of culture." Symboling, he explains (p. 1), is the "ability freely and arbitrarily to originate, determine, and bestow meaning upon things and events in the external world, and the ability to comprehend such meanings. These meanings cannot be grasped and appreciated with the senses." While non-human beings also communicate among themselves and with other species, communication theorist Wilbur Schramm (1971, p. 25) points out that the ability of man to create means of communication that will be portable throughout space and time is one of the characteristics that sets human communication apart from most animal communication. "With relatively few exceptions, even the more intelligent animals are limited to communications signs that are inseparable from the situation in which they are used," whereas geneticist and science philosopher Bentley Glass (1985, p. xv) points to the opposite power of humans through language: "Language itself as the power of universals, is the basic expression of man's ability to transcend his environment and to transmute tragedy into a moral and spiritual triumph." Leslie White (1949, p. 39) contends that the ability to use symbols was created uniquely in the human by the natural processes of biologic evolution from meaningful gestures to articulate speech,[3] while anthropologist David F. Armstrong and linguists William C. Stokoe and Sherman E. Wilcox (1995) have developed the theory that what appears to be a single iconic manual gesture might also have the structure of a prototypical sentence.[4]

Of the various forms of symbolic expression important in cultural evolution, anthropologist Leslie A. White (1949, p. 39) identifies the preeminence of articulate speech. "Articulate speech means communication of ideas; communication means preservation—tradition—and preservation means accumulation and progress." Furthermore, philosopher John Searle (2007, p. 29) contends that "Human language is an extension of more biologically fundamental forms of intentionality such as perception and action, as well as belief and desire, and we need to see language as derivative from these more basic biological forms of intentionality." These are the life-perpetuating activities of humanity and the sustaining elements of cultural evolution.[5] In the final analysis, there is no disagreement over the unparalleled significance of language in the evolution of culture, only in selecting the one best way to describe that significance.

How did this human marvel come about? In their words, "Boldly countering Noam Chomsky the world's best-known linguist, and Stephen Jay Gould, the world's best-known evolutionary theorist," as linguists Steven Pinker and Paul Bloom (1992, p. 452) claim, "we will argue that there is every reason to believe that language has been shaped by natural selection." The authors state further (p. 486) that their conclusion is based on two facts that they believe to be entirely uncontroversial: "Language shows signs of complex design for the communication of propositional structures, and the only explanation for the origin of organs with the complex design is the process of natural selection." Language has accelerated cultural evolution, and the interactive processes of cultural and biological evolution likely produced language in the first place. Language is so significant a cultural tool that in their study of the eight major evolutionary transitions, biochemist Eörs Szathmary and evolutionary biologist and geneticist John Maynard Smith (1995) postulate the development of language as the key factor in the evolution from primate to human societies. Humanity produces culture for humanity, and in part for this reason, argues philosopher John Searle (2007, p. 8) "we need to think of language as a manifestation and extension of more biologically primitive forms of intentionality. It is a mistake to treat language as if it were not part of human biology." Language is that basic, not just to the human condition, but to the meaning of human. More specifically, Searle (p. 9) notes that "The use of language enables us to create desire-independent reasons for action. All sorts of speech acts, for example statement making and promise making, create commitments and obligations of various kinds."

Lev S. Vigotsky (1962, p. 153) closes his influential book on the relation of mind and language with the provocative thought that "A word is a microcosm of human consciousness." With that poignant statement he connects language and the humanness of being, not just in a relation of cause and effect, but in a relation of synonymy. In a more specific analysis, biologists Peter and Jean Medawar (1977, p. 53) contend that whereas organic evolution is mediated through a genetic mechanism, cultural evolution is made possible by the transfer of information from one generation to the next through *non*-genetic channels, the most important of these being language. Language is the "most distinctive of all human possessions," they write, because of its "subtlety, versatility and information-carrying capacity," which render it "a much more rapid and powerful agency of change . . . than ordinary organic evolution." Concepts or ideas are the generalizations and abstractions of the common features of heterogeneous experience, and symbols are devised to represent them. Thus, language has been developed by humans to provide the capacity to work with conceptual knowledge, writes neurologist C. Judson Herrick (1956, p. 301), "which provides the mental tools of all rational thinking at higher levels. These tools are not energies or structural organs or any other physical things. They are patterns of performance which are recognized subjectively as ideas." The need for new words to denote these new concepts, along with new things and new relations, causes the vocabulary to expand, even as the intellectual development of language becomes simpler in form and structure. Cultural progress in this regard, according to anthropologist and sociologist Wilson D. Wallis (1930, p. 203), lies not "in the greater complexity of language but in its more apt and effectual service."

As a representation of human consciousness, language has much to do with effective use of both the memory and its counterpart view to the future, which are essential influences in cultural evolution. In humans, memory is dominated by language, observes anthropologist André Leroi-Gourhan (1993, p. 235). Moreover, it is language that uniquely makes possible the transfer of "our memory to a social organism outside ourselves." The human sense of the past, "not as immediately, innately acquired reflexes," writes literary critic George Steiner (1971, p. 62), "but as a shaped selection of remembrance, is again radically linguistic." Of equal importance to cultural evolution is the capacity to articulate a future tense. The "ability and need to 'dream forward', to hope," is unique. "Such capacity is inseparable from grammar, from the conventional power of language to exist in advance of that which it designates."

Knowledge & Learning

That humankind has an unusual, organically grounded capacity to process information, argues sociologist Talcott Parsons (1978, p. 416), is surely evidenced by the special status of the human brain among central nervous systems. He continues that there are also two other patently significant features of the human organism that are especially relevant to man's instrumental capacities. "The first of these is provided by the human hands and arms, as generalized, all-purpose tools, and the second by the capacity to use brain, vocal chords, lips, tongue, and oral cavity to produce speech, a conveyor of information par excellence, which requires auditory reception of sound-encoded information, of course through a brain. From the point of view of organic evolution, all three of these are closely linked with the achievement by man of the erect posture. As biologist and philosopher Edward O. Wilson says, 'man is the only true biped!'" Many languages, and all Western languages, says semanticist Paul Ziff (1960, p. 3), have a written as well as a spoken manifestation, and he describes the most striking difference between these two forms of expression. The written sentence, he stresses, "unlike the spoken utterance is an enduring element, the parts of which coexist simultaneously for a certain time: the written word is fixed fast, not held loosely in mind. The greater stability and regularity of written as opposed to spoken language may stem from this fact; the existence of algebraic and logistic systems depends on it." Paleoanthropologist Ian Tattersall (2007, p. 16) summarizes the place of language in the workings of the mind:

> Not all thought, of course, is linguistic; but the reverse is certainly the case: that all linguistic manipulations are symbolic. Human thoughts are processed by a brain that bears the marks of numerous and increasingly remote evolutionary precursors, from brain stem structures up through the neocortex. As a result of the complex evolutionarily derived structure, human thought is not entirely composed of symbolic combinations and recombinations. Instead, our thoughts are also intimately tied up with emotion and intuitive reasoning.

The present study addresses all types of record comprising the social transcript, but with a definite emphasis on written language, for reasons that will become evident in the following paragraphs.

Cultural evolution and learning through the culture arguably are synonymous concepts. Robert Boyd and Peter J. Richerson (2005, p. 44), respectively anthropologist and environmental scientist, find that "Culture increases average fitness [adaptability] if it makes the learning processes that generate new knowledge less costly or more accurate," because "social learning allows the individual learning to be selective," and because "social learning allows learned improvements to accumulate from one generation to the next." This is well supported by others. "Man's biopsychology is that of the development of adaptive and survival techniques through the learning of complex social mechanisms, write clinical psychologists Lawrence Zelic Freedman and Anne Roe (1958, p. 461). "The goal is the resolution of the conflict which results from the dislocation between biological needs and social demands." Economic philosopher Kenneth E. Boulding (1985, p. 91), writes that "If there is any single key to the development of societies it is the way in which individuals in them learn their valuation structures, for the capacity to develop realistic images of the future also depends in no small measure on the values that are placed on learning and on testing and adaptability." Because the generation of knowledge from scraps of information requires the individual to perceive meaning in those scraps, sociologist Talcott Parsons (1949, p. 591) contends that "Selection is the necessary logical prerequisite of *knowledge* as distinguished from raw experience." And viewed sociologically, says sociologist Lloyd Vernor Ballard (1936, p. 3), "education is the process by which the individual is prepared for successful participation in social relations, broadly conceived." Selection is central to successful adaptation and thus to cultural evolution. Ballard continues this line of thought (p. 163), advancing his idea that "The essence of this educational process is the discipline of the mind, the emotions and the volition of the individual so that he develops and directs his capacities and activities toward approved ends."

Concepts, discussed in Chapter 3 as among of the most useful tools of the mind, are considered by psychologist Paul Thagard (1992, p. 19) not as "entities but emergent states of neural networks... My own view... is that concepts are mental entities that are largely learned and open." He characterizes the function of concept elsewhere (2005, p. 62), writing that "Concepts organize knowledge in important ways that are not usually found in rule-based systems." Where there is knowledge there is learning, and where there is learning there is knowledge. Archeologist V. Gordon Childe (1956, p. 7) writes that "knowledge, though derived from personal experiences and personally memorized, is communicable and, if communicated, public." And the view of social philosopher Jürgen Habermas on knowledge defines its linkage to humans in very special ways. According to Andrew Edgar's interpretation (2006, p. 11) of Habermas' thought, "there is no such thing as absolutely 'pure' knowledge. What we regard as knowledge is not some perfect, untainted vision of how the world is, but rather a response to that world that is shaped by what we, as human beings, need to know and are capable of understanding. So, there can only be knowledge that is relevant to humans and that humans will find important and be motivated to pursue." And the rate of increase in knowledge increases for that very reason, for as sociologist Morris Ginsberg (1961, p. 123) observes "Knowledge has increasingly to cope with problems which its own development brings about."

Studies of cultural evolution tend to identify major distinctions between human beings and other beings, and do so with the purpose of explaining what it means to be human, such that the notion of need in humans extends beyond its meaning for other beings. In their interpretation of the views of education held by philosopher David Braybrooke, social philosophers Susan Sherwin and Peter Schotch (2007, p. 43) emphasize this point. They write "In the sense at issue here, what people genuinely need is what is necessary to their thriving as human beings; and, conversely, the absence of what is needed undermines their ability to function physically and in the social roles that make us human. This is a thesis of modern natural law theory... It is more important that we retain the capacity to function as human beings than to get exactly what we want."

Humans most often are compared with other primates, for evident reasons, and with ants, owing mostly to their well-organized collaborative efforts. Thus, in the course of his book on the qualities of being human, mathematician Norbert Wiener (1950, p. 84) devotes a full chapter to a contrast of the mental organization of ants and humans. He concludes that, while ants display a fairly complicated social structure, their dependence on a learning process is minimal, while human mental processes depend on an individual and social organization that "centers around the process of learning." The acquisition of knowledge—both practical and theoretical—is a characteristic activity of the human species, writes science philosopher Marx W. Wartofski (1968, p. 29). "Following the lead of the evolutionary biologists, we may consider the broad thesis that epistemological activities, and the special sort which involves reasoning, have evolved from precognitive responses and adaptations to an environment and that they are the product of natural and cultural selection, in the sense that they have survival value for the human species."

More than that, and of very special significance to the function of the library in cultural evolution, Henry Plotkin (1998, p. 243) contends that a "feature of human culture which is quite different from what is seen in any other species is the incessant and cumulative modification of knowledge and practice over generations." Underlining the significance of the vision of human destiny to the definition of culture, biologist Sir Julian S. Huxley (1958, p. 440) observes, "The most important factor in progressive long-term cultural evolution appears to be knowledge or, to use a more general term, awareness. In this, two elements are involved. One is the quantitative amount and accuracy of factual knowledge . . . the second is the way in which knowledge and awareness are organized." In his review of the relevant literature, intellectual historian Charles Van Doren (1967, p. 335) finds that in the judgment of most scholars, "knowledge must *increase* . . . it is in the very nature of knowledge that it should increase." The increase to which he refers is the amount of knowledge that has accumulated at a given point. The idea of knowledge is forward looking; knowledge is an essential component of humanity and therefore of culture and its evolution. And the system of knowledge, according to sociologist Morris Ginsberg (1961, p. 114), "is in process of correlated growth, changes in any one part inducing or being accompanied by changes in others, so that the whole undergoes transformation, while maintaining its identity through modification. The wider and more coherent the system, the stronger are its claims to represent reality."

While knowledge incorporates the diversity and options for cultural evolution, it also constitutes the limitation. But that, too, can be viewed in a positive light: "In a nutshell," writes Henry Plotkin (1998, p. 244), " the argument is that in a world where there is so much that could be known, where the search space and the possible pathways through it are so vast, unless human cognition is innately constrained, we could each of us end up knowing different things with little knowledge in common and scant facility for communicating with one another. A principle of cognitive constraint is an absolutely essential starting-point for understanding a phenomenon which is defined by shared knowledge. Culture *is* shared knowledge." For the most part, knowledge seems to be a positive force in cultural evolution; but, of course, that is not always so, as was discussed in Chapter 3. And sociologist Morris Ginsberg (1972, p. 77) concludes his study of knowledge within the social construct of progress with this solemn reminder that relates the application of knowledge to selection:

> The moral neutrality or indifference of the sciences leaves the path open to progress or regress. The choice is ours. It remains that if knowledge is not a sufficient, it is a necessary condition of progress. It can give no assurance of ultimate success, but it can point to the possibilities open to men and thus help to provide the will with the opportunity to choose among them.

Knowledge fuels learning, which then stimulates the quest for new knowledge, which is defined as knowledge having meaning that is new to both the society and the individual. Psychologist and anthropologist Donald T. Campbell (1974, p. 413) argues that "evolution—even in its biological aspects—is a knowledge process," and that "the natural-selection paradigm for such knowledge increments can be generalized to other epistemic activities, such as learning, thought, and science." And through the power of language, human learning is cumulative. The process of learning is the greatest source of change in social systems, contends Kenneth Boulding (1985, p. 83), referring to "both the development of new knowledge and know-how that the human race never had before and also the spread of old knowledge around to new minds, which is done informally in the family and formally in schools, universities, and other educational agencies." Similar to Campbell, Boulding explains elsewhere (1978, p. 124) that it is the knowledge process that dominates societal evolution, because "It provides the adaptability that expands the niches and that finds substitute forms of energy and materials when an existing form becomes scarce." The potential to make use of knowledge and to acquire new knowledge is located in the power to think, the power to reason and to formulate concepts communicable through language.

Clinical psychologist Lev S. Vigotsky (1978, p. 83) writes that "research shows that the mind is not a complex network of *general* capabilities such as observation, attention, memory, judgment, and so forth, but a set of specific capabilities, each of which is, to some extent, independent of the others and is developed independently." He explains that "Learning is more than the acquisition of the ability to think; it is the acquisition of many specialized abilities for thinking about a variety of things. Learning does not alter our overall ability to focus attention but rather develops various abilities to focus attention on a variety of things . . . habit governs us . . . the development of consciousness is the development of a set of particular, independent capabilities or of a set of particular habits." As the material, mechanical, physical, chemical, and biological means of adjustment and control are improved and extended, knowledge and understanding increase. Also referring to the place of language in learning, psychologist James Deese (1965, p. 166) argues that while learning is socially determined, the structures for any particular individual are only correlated with, not completely determined by, social usage. "Variations in meaning from person to person and from group to group, as well as from time to time within the same individual, are related to and fundamentally determined by the shifts in grouping and contrast as we establish new relations among verbal elements." Learning, summarizes psychologist Herbert A. Simon (1989, p. 107), "is any process that modifies a system so as to improve, more or less irreversibly, its subsequent performance of the same task or of tasks drawn from the same population."

Philosopher Karl Popper (1999, p. 100) finds that the phrase trial and error understates the importance of mistakes and erroneous trial,[6] because in his view "Error correction is the most important method in technology and learning in general. In biological evolution, it appears to be the only means of progress" (1999, p. 100). With his *Objective Knowledge* Popper had demonstrated that progressive error elimination is not only the method by which conscious scientific thought proceeds towards truth, but also, says historian and philosopher Peter Munz (1985, p. 221), "the method by which all evolution of organisms, from the amoeba to Homo Sapiens, progressed." As learning is essential to cultural evolution, so are trial-and-error and other rational means of error correction essential to learning. In that connection, it is useful again to refer to the analogous situation of science as a process and the processes of knowledge and learning in the evolution of culture. Biologist and neurophilosopher Patricia Smith Churchland (2002, p. 108) identifies philosopher Wilfred Sellars as largely the originator of the analogy between scientific theories in particular, and more generally "a scheme to represent conspecifics as other minds." She observes that in our representational framework for understanding minds, several features, "such as the interdependence of categories, the model's use in observation, prediction, intervention, and explanations—are importantly analogous to the role theories play in science."

Furthermore, physicist John Ziman (1978, p. 107) emphasizes that without knowledge one would have little capacity to contemplate future action: "The influence of knowledge over action arises from its power of prediction. To take a decision is to choose between branching paths into the future, in the light of their imagined or calculated end points." Theory is the determining factor. Herbert A. Simon (1996, pp. 193–194), one of the founders of artificial intelligence and a Nobel laureate in economics, primarily for his research on decision making in organizations, concludes that "The more difficult and novel the problem, the greater is likely to be the amount of trial and error required to find a solution. At the same time, the trial and error is not completely random or blind; it is, in fact, highly selective... Problem solving requires *selective* trial and error."

The result of learning, of course, is the acquisition of knowledge, which in turn stimulates further learning. Pierce Butler (1933, p. 93) refers to the substance of the ideas that are passed along from person to person and generation to generation as that individual's and that generation's scholarship: "The total residual effect of an individual's intellectual experience may well be called his scholarship." Knowledge is one of those concepts that at first appear familiar but, in the effort to define them, are found to be elusive. A look at epistemological studies suggests fairly quickly the directions such efforts can take. Bronislaw Malinowski (1930, p. 634) holds knowledge to be an absolute derived necessity of culture, and he defines it in the context of cultural evolution.

> It is more, however, than a means to an end, and it was not classed therefore with the instrumental imperatives. Its place in culture, its function, is slightly different from that of production, of law or of education. Systems of knowledge serve to connect various types of behavior; they carry over the results of past experiences into future enterprise and they bring together elements of human experience and allow man to coordinate and integrate his activities. Knowledge is a mental attitude, a diathesis of the nervous system, which allows man to carry on the work which culture makes him do. Its function is to organize and integrate the indispensable activities of culture . . . By the very forethought and foresight which it gives, the integrative function of knowledge creates new needs, that is, imposes new imperatives. Knowledge gives man the possibility of planning ahead, of embracing vast spaces of time and distance; it allows a wide range to his hopes and desires.

Beyond increasing human understanding of the answers to questions raised by the simple words *when*, *where*, *who*, *what*, *how*, *how to*, and even *why*, the more essential functions of knowledge reside in its powers of integration and organization. Sociologist and philosopher Talcott Parsons (1949, p. 123) points out that while the faculty of reason might be static, the same is not true of its product, scientific knowledge. "On the contrary it is subject to a process of cumulative increase. Action, then, is determined not by reason directly but indirectly through the rational understanding of conditions and the application of this knowledge to the guidance of action. Thus the concrete result will vary according to the state of knowledge."

Learning constitutes half the knowledge process, being complemented by the generation and communication of new knowledge, even if it may not immediately be accepted as knowledge. Talcott Parsons (1949, p. 73) observes that "Knowledge, so long as it is rational, is not random, but is determined by and is a 'reflection' of the things known." The acquisition of knowledge is influenced by the surrounding culture. For example, says Kenneth Boulding (1983, p. 14), "The production of human artifacts is strongly affected by the value structure of the noosphere, which creates niches in the social ecosystem of things that people want and have the power to acquire." But he also describes the complementary process whereby "An important aspect of evolution is the way in which increased know-how pushes back the limiting factors and permits a larger variety of species and larger populations... Increases in human knowledge and know-how have permitted a huge expansion of the human race and its artifacts." Physicist and Nobel laureate Werner Heisenberg (1958, p. 194) describes the spread of scientific ideas, meaning reasoned, demonstrable ideas, finding that "While political ideas may gain a convincing influence among great masses of people just because they correspond or seem to correspond to the prevailing interests of the people, scientific ideas will spread only because they are true. There are objective and final criteria assuring the correctness of a scientific statement."

Knowledge increases in all its possible areas, but its expansion into many areas and into new areas, its differentiation, "is a condition of progress in human society," writes economic theorist Brian J. Loasby (2002, p. 153). It is important to note that this aspect of progress in cultural evolution happens because society makes it happen. It is a need. This is made clear in current funding for science in any industrialized country, as Jerome B. Wiesner (1964, p. 41), electrical engineer and former president of the Massachusetts Institute of Technology, makes clear. "The research scientist is primarily motivated by an urge to explore and understand, but society supports fundamental research primarily, because experience has demonstrated how essential such work is for continuing progress in technology. Halt the flow of new research and the possible scope of technical developments will soon be limited and ultimately reduced to nothing." Knowledge further differentiates, according to anthropologist and sociologist Wilson D. Wallis (1930, p. 434), as it is "transferred [from one sphere] to others and becomes a stimulus in many lines of thought. Enlargement of the culture horizon, therefore, increases the possibilities of progress." The nature of the development of knowledge prompts the suggestion from Raymond Irwin (1949, p. 90) that "Knowledge does not so much advance as *expand* in every direction, like the smoke and noise of an explosion. It is a chastening thought." V. Gordon Childe (1956) achieves three major deductions about the ever growing, changing corpus of knowledge: that "Knowledge is derived from experience" (p. 55); that "every individual's world enormously transcends the limits of his private experience" (p. 57); and that "not only is the object of knowledge, the pattern of the external world, itself incomplete, but also in so far as it has been completed, it is so rich and complicated that twenty-two million generations of men just have not had time fully to discover it" (p. 66). Humans create knowledge, then most often pass it along for use and modification by others. In that regard, says sociologist Lloyd V. Ballard (1936, p. 166), "education is to be regarded not only as means of enlarging or modifying environment but as environment *per se*. This aspect of education takes on increasing importance as social relationships grow more and more complex." According to evolutionary psychologist Robert J. Richards (1987, p. 475), it was William

James who produced the first thoroughgoing Darwinian epistemology. "He proposed that creative ideas were the result of selection of fit thought variations from among the multitude spontaneously generated." Humanity has not necessarily grown more intelligent over the millennia, but has gained from the handing down of knowledge. Educator Lyman Bryson (1947, p. 160) drives this point home with great clarity in this comparison of primitive peoples, whether of the present or distant past:

> The real difference between the drum beater and the astronomer in the presence of the comet is in the difference between their past experiences! The savage is not the victim of habit but of ignorance; he has no sufficient 'relevant knowledge', and he thinks as well as could be expected with what he has. The astronomer is the possessor of specialized knowledge; he has been living in a culture that provides more and better knowledge relevant to the moment. It is not only the personal past of the astronomer that is superior but the whole cultural past of his people.

Writing

Writing is considered an extension of biologically human intellectual capacities for many reasons, even beyond the biological sphere to the extent that neuroscientist Jean-Pierre Changeux, (1986, p. 244) concludes "The invention of a *written* representation for mental objects is incontestably a cultural phenomenon." There are various means by which knowledge is shared with contemporaries, both individuals and societies, and also with subsequent generations. Language, for the most part speech and writing, is the most powerful tool for the accomplishment of this process of communication, about which Kenneth Boulding (1983, p. 11) makes the important point that "It was not until the invention of writing that the noosphere could expand almost indefinitely. While memory is an important part of sharing thought, language in general adds precision, subtlety, and flexibility to the memory as it moves from person to person and from generation to generation." Moreover, says journalist and novelist Régis Debray (2000, p. 56), "Language is the most tenacious of all group memories." Therefore, the commitment of thought to writing makes the communication from one individual or group to another, and especially from one generation to subsequent generations, much more reliable and better suited to criticism because it allows reflection over the entire discourse. Writing is a device intended for sharing thought, but a sharing not limited by considerations of time and space.

Psychologist and cognitive neuroscientist Merlin Donald (2001, p. 262) finds three major divisions or transitions in the evolution of cognition. The third and most recent occurred about forty thousand years ago in the form of innovation in the technology of symbols. Cognition continued to evolve, he writes, "but this time it was mostly driven by technology and culture itself. The main cognitive driving force underlying its transition was the externalization of memory. Whereas earlier humans had to depend entirely on their biology—that is, on their brains—to remember, modern humans can employ a huge number of powerful external symbolic devices to store and retrieve cultural knowledge." Donald (p. 323) also relates this capacity more specifically to theory development, which is so basic to understanding and acting, noting that "External symbolic storage significantly alters the powers of our larger cognitive-cultural system by creating conditions within which formal theoretic systems can emerge." These aspects of Donald's theory of cognitive evolution will resurface in Chapter 5.

A component of knowledge that renders it amenable to being shared and learned is organization into its various parts. Cultural historian Peter Burke (2000, pp. 87–90) refers to an intellectual tripod, composed of curricula, libraries and encyclopedias, as the way in which the classification of academic knowledge entered into everyday practice in European universities following the emergence of the printing press. Moreover, he reasons that its academic classification likely was adopted by "the population in general, or as the French historian Lucien Febvre used to say, their 'intellectual equipment' (outillage mental)." The simple clarity of D. J. Foskett's (1984, p. 61) summary of all this is captured in his thought that "The essence of public knowledge is the consensus, the general agreement that such and such is the case, among the scholars and experts who know the details." The generic medium of writing, for the purpose of discussing the function of the library in cultural evolution, is the book; in this case, and throughout this text unless otherwise specified, the term book refers to any inanimate conveyance of language.

Printing

The many and complex steps leading from the first human effort to convey significance by means other than sound and gesture appear on the surface, and from the comfortable distance of many millennia, to be few and simple. The act of drawing was the first of these steps; then, with the achievement of language writing evolved, which eventually was facilitated immensely by the development of movable-type printing. Cultural historian Raymond Irwin (1949, p. 67) emphasizes that humanity's "early efforts at representation either in art or symbolic language are the foundation on which his libraries of printed books are based." With the development of the printing press in mid fifteenth century, the availability of uniformly printed sources of information and entertainment were made readily accessible to those who could use them on a scale probably undreamed of before.[7] Historian and philosopher John Herman Randall (1940, p. 120) encapsulates the dynamism of those developments:

> Thus by 1500 all the chief countries of Europe were provided with the means for the rapid multiplication of books. The consequences for intellectual life were momentous. The number of those who could share the best knowledge increased a thousand fold; it became worth while to learn to read, and to write for a wide circle of readers. A library could now contain a wide variety of secular works, instead of the few expensive writings of the fathers and doctors. Prices sank to an eighth of the former cost, and judged by our standards, were low indeed. Ideas could now be sure of a wide hearing; and though the Church soon attempted to control the new force by her censorship, the printing-press had made it impossible ever to extirpate a living idea.

One of the more important influences of the printing press, in terms specifically of knowledge and learning, is to be found in the cross-cultural understanding it stimulated. In her monumental study of the introduction of printing, historian Elizabeth Eisenstein (1983, p. 44) attributes the remarkable increase in innovation both in scholarly and scientific fields to the innovations of the printing press, characterized by the interchange between artists and scholars, practitioners, and theorists. "Printing encouraged forms of combinatory activity which were social as well as intellectual. It changed relationships between men of learning as well as between systems of ideas."

Similarly, she concludes (p. 259) that "Changes wrought by printing had a more immediate effect on cerebral activities and on the learned professions than did many other kinds of 'external' events," and that "The printing press laid the basis for both literal fundamentalism and for modern science. It remains indispensable for humanistic scholarship. It is still responsible for our museum without walls" (1983, p. 274; and 1979, p. 704). Of special interest to the influence of printing on the expansion and sharing of scholarship, observes cultural historian Peter Burke (2000, p. 103), has to do with bibliographies, "a form of reference book which became increasingly common in the period have been described as 'libraries without walls' which could travel all over Europe."

In the twenty-first century the function of the printing press increasingly is assumed in the digital format, which is communicated by various information technologies. The purposes of printing remain much the same, however, while the instruments of their realization are made ubiquitous and their end product considerably more flexible and powerful.[8] What continues is the influence of printing on language, thought, and ultimately understanding, by presenting older ideas in a changed context for rethinking in all areas of human endeavor. In that regard, early anthropologist Edward B. Tylor's conclusion (1871, vol. 2, p. 402) that the value of knowledge held in recorded thought increases by always assuming new significance remains valid:

> Were scientific systems the oracular revelations they sometimes all but pretend to be, it might be justifiable to take no note of the condition of mere opinion or fancy that preceded them. But the investigator who turns from his modern text-books to the antiquated dissertations of the great thinkers of the past, gains from the history of his own craft a truer view of the relation of theory to fact, learns from the course of growth in each current hypothesis to appreciate its raison d'etre and full significance, and even finds that a return to older starting-points may enable him to find new paths, where the modern track seems stopped by impassable barriers.

The library performs an essential function in this aspect of cultural evolution by maintaining a history of thought about virtually any topic, which is a function often referred to as redundancy. But it is a redundancy of very great significance in cultural evolution, and more will be said about it in this study.

Reading

Next to the spoken language, the written language is the most common medium of learning and of transmitting knowledge, and for some kinds of knowledge far surpasses speech. Anthropologist and sociologist Robert Redfield (1962, p. 236) compares societies in which only the oral transmission of knowledge prevails with those in which transmission by written word also is a common means:

> Through books the civilized people communicate with the minds of other people and other times, and an aspect of the isolation of the folk society is the absence of books. The folk communicate only by word of mouth; therefore the communication upon which understanding is built is only that which takes place among neighbors, within the little society itself. The folk have no access to the thought and experience of the past, whether of other peoples or of their own ancestors, such as books provide. Therefore, oral tradition has no check or competitor. Knowledge of what has gone before reaches no further back than memory and speech between old and young can make it go; behind 'the time of our grandfathers' all is legendary and vague. With no form of belief established by written record, there can be no historical sense, such as civilized people have, no theology, and no basis for science in recorded experiment. The only form of accumulation of experience, except the tools and other enduring articles of manufacture, is the increase of wisdom which comes as the individual lives longer; therefore the old, knowing more than the young can know until they too have lived that long, have prestige and authority.

The written word, characterized throughout this text as the generic book, obviously holds much greater potential for cultural evolution.[9] Indeed, the power to ponder the past is linked to the power to contemplate the future, thus enabling human behavior to be uniquely purposive. "Human behaviour can be genuinely purposive," write biologists Peter B. and Jean S. Medawar (1977, p. 171), "because only human beings guide their behaviour by a knowledge of what happened before they were born and a preconception of what may happen after they are dead: thus only human beings find their way by a light that illumines more than the patch of ground they stand on." And, very significantly in matters of cultural evolution, literacy increases the potential of questioning established knowledge, accepted beliefs, and even personal experience.[10] In this regard, sociolinguist Michael Stubbs (1980, p. 104) offers the reminder that "it becomes at least much more convenient to examine statements carefully, if they are written or printed." Written communication lends itself to scrutiny in a demanding way that eludes oral communication, so the two traditions offer different paths in the evolution of culture.

Also in connection with cultural evolution, an excellent description of the intellectual content of a book of fiction is provided by Pierce Butler (1953, p. 161). He emphasizes that such a book does not exist in a vacuum, but "as an integral element in a cultural organism. And one of the most significant things about that organism is its historical character." Again, referring to the historical value of the book, and presumably referring to both fiction and non fiction, Butler observes (1933, p. 60) that "Each book was once a man, some of them whole generations. In its pages remains the knowledge that is distilled from human experience." The ideas and their combinations introduced by the author are seldom more, he believes (1933. p. 32) almost hyperbolically, than borrowings from the author's respective social group: "Though the pen is directed by the writer, it may be said in a very real sense, that usually it can write only what society itself has dictated... What memory is to man the graphic record is, in part, to modern society."

British library leader of the mid twentieth century Lionel R. McColvin (1978, p. 34) emphasizes that books are not an end in themselves, but rather a means of communication of one individual's experience, thought and vision for the further use by the book's reader in sharpening that individual's thought and sensitivity. "Their value lies in enabling men to do, think, feel and understand better than they could if they depended solely on their individual experience and that of those with whom they were in immediate contact... Books are the record of man's reactions to his environment in all its phases." Evidently sharing this view, philosopher of education Paolo Freire and education psychologist Donaldo Macedo (1987, p. 29) provide insight into the relation of reading and mind, concluding that "Reading does not consist merely of decoding the written word or language; rather, it is preceded by and intertwined with knowledge of the world. Language and reality are dynamically interconnected. The understanding attained by critical reading of a text implies perceiving the relationship between text and context." And, to similar affect, literary theorist Wolfgang Iser (1974, p. 278) notes that "each intentional sentence correlative opens up a particular horizon, which is modified, if not completely changed, by succeeding sentences."

These observations suggest why the social record contained in books is truly of timeless value. For even though times do change, as they change the record continues to be subject to reinterpretation and, especially, to be the source of stimulation of different perspectives and insights. "In the main," comments Pierce Butler (1933, p. 98), "the permanent elements of any culture can appear actively in the form of a popular scholarship only as each generation has had them expounded by writers of its own period. This is what gives social value to most books when they are first written. It is a fallacy to assume that the ceaseless restatement of established facts, ideas, and opinions are an unnecessary and futile activity."

Literacy

Reading accompanies writing, of course, and their combination, or literacy, has been essential to the evolution of culture since that capacity for human development came about. Raymond Williams (1981, p. 136) explains that "The culture of the book that printing has produced could only be fully possessed in the course of a long apprenticeship in which the mental equipment for reading was slowly acquired—the ability to make connections and associations, familiarity with idiom, facility of expression, skill in following an argument, an understanding of fine distinctions and, in the end, greater confidence and an increased aptitude for acquiring new knowledge."

Prior to the introduction of the printing press, reading was not a widely shared skill, so the written word was viewed with some fascination by those who could not decode it.[11] Social anthropologist Jack Goody (2000, p. 42) finds that literacy also brought new challenges, for "it is really with literacy and schooling that the task of having to exactly recall vast quantities of data (often half uncomprehendingly) is seen as necessary to keep the culture going." Those who could read and write enjoyed a new social power,[12] and the texts were venerated. Looking back at the earliest of civilizations, intellectual historian Charles Van Doren (1967, 24) surmises that literacy very soon led to "a different kind of test of superiority." Literacy did not establish a person's social or political position, but "it was the entrée into a powerful minority that controlled most of the business of the state, both public and private. Literacy conferred control over a society's information systems, and those have always been crucial to a society's life. They are all the more crucial. . . . Information was a burgeoning business in ancient Mesopotamia. It is the biggest business of all in our time."

Sociologist Ellsworth Faris (1937, p. 303) concludes that "Such facts mean that a continuity of tradition, an enlargement of consciousness, is possible to such a degree that it amounts to a difference in kind. A race without letters has no history, merely tales and traditions. A people without history is like a man without memory, who lives from moment to moment. It is possible, therefore, to make one grand division in the evolution of man at the period where writing begins." So communication both accelerated and became more precise, generating what is called the public sphere, which is the realm of social life where opinion is formed. It emerged among the eighteenth-century bourgeoisie, according to philosophers Andrew Edgar and Peter Sedgwick (2002, p. 90), "not least in the development of journals and a free press. The public sphere thus aspires to form a general will and thus inform and control the activities of the state. Conflict is resolved through open and free communication." Their interpretation of twentieth-century social philosopher Jürgen Habermas on this matter concludes that communicative rationality is "therefore this process of problem solving and conflict resolution through open discussion . . . The life-world . . . is the social world as it is constructed and maintained through the take-for-granted social skills and stocks of knowledge of its members."

Vastly increased accessibility to uniform written texts was not the only influence on the spread of literacy, because other forces strongly encouraged the adoption of increasingly appropriate skills among various segments of the populace. It was in the best interests of religion, for example, to foster reading so that the right texts could guide the religious devotion of the people. In a more widely shared and pragmatic sense, however, during the seventeenth and eighteenth centuries, "the main impetus towards literacy came perhaps from the widening field of commerce and communications," says Raymond Irwin (1964, p. 223), "and the interest in the new experimental philosophy which itself derived partly from the desire to apply the results of scientific discovery to the needs of industry and trade." Also, the physical features of the book and the methods of its distribution depend heavily on manifold aspects of contemporary social life, sometimes in a reciprocal mode. Cultural historian Raymond Williams (1981, p. 136) finds the conclusion inevitable "that access to books has contributed to the structuring of a hierarchical social order in modern times." Referring again to the seventeenth and eighteenth centuries, bibliographer Roy Stokes (1981, p. 85) describes the conditions that merged the energies of the book trade and other commerce: "It is arguable, for example, that the coffeehouse and the newspaper/periodical trade created each other, as it were. That the rise of overseas trade and mercantilism increased the need for a pure news element in the newspaper. That the demand for easily and cheaply accessible fiction brought the rise of serialization in journals." Also contributing to the rapid expansion of literacy was the attraction of the entertainment potential it offered, and this is not a negligible aspect of culture.

Entertainment

Entertainment can be considered a special dimension of the mind, an activity that exercises and recreates the mind in ways that differ from the more clearly purposeful activity of gaining knowledge. As is known from personal experience, all reading is not directed by the clear need to acquire knowledge. How many possible reasons, then, do stand behind the decision to read? Pierce Butler (1933, p. 58) provides a "coarse gradation" to distinguish three motivations: information, aesthetic appreciation, and direct pleasure. Surely there are more possible gradations, as Butler himself notes, but how distinct they may be remains a question, as it does even with the three he identifies. For example, D. J. Foskett (1962, p. 6) points out that any motivation for reading is, in fact, a purpose, so that all reading is purposive, "and this would include the reading of works of light entertainment." Elsewhere, Foskett (1984, p. 38) adds that "Even light fiction has been produced by authors who consider that they have a view of the world which they would like to communicate to others in order to enhance their understanding of that particular view."

It is quite clear that scholars in the field of cultural evolution are unanimous in their assessment that writing and its various technological extensions holds a position of great prominence in cultural evolution. But, do all genres of writing, and thus of reading, contribute importantly to cultural evolution? Surely there is purpose in writing, and if so, what is the influence of writing on reading, and what of the influence of reading on writing? If the cumulative effect of writing and reading is to accelerate the evolution of culture in the long term, then there logically is an effect of similar value in the short term. What gets handed down is not only what is written, but also what is read, then acted upon in some way, then passed on orally or by example. The intellect is not limited to learning, to integrating knowledge and creating new knowledge in the formal sense, but encompasses the full potential of thought. "There are pleasures that perish in the using," writes Librarian of Congress (1865–1897) Ainsworth Rand Spofford (1900, p. 188), "but the pleasure which the art of reading carries with it is perennial. He who can feast on the intellectual spoils of centuries need fear neither poverty nor hunger."[13]

While some genres of writing may exert greater apparent influence on the culture than others, just as do some writers compared with others by dint of their individual abilities or the changing tastes of the times, it all contributes in different ways to the total intellectual development of society. For present purposes, we can define entertainment by following sociologist Lloyd Vernor Ballard's (1936, p. 388) definition of recreation as "an activity in which the individual engages because of an interest so absorbing that it carries him into enthusiastic and persistent participation. The individual's attitude toward the activity in which he engages is hence important." But here, again, is that difficult aspect of cognition called intention.

In his account of the evolution of technology, science historian George Basalla (1988, pp. 74–75) includes accounts of the role fantasy plays in technology, the role of technology in fantasy, and the part they both contribute to society. "Fanciful machines generated by the literary or popular imagination do not originate in the minds of inventors and engineers and, therefore, intimate that the drive to envision a wide range of possibilities is not confined exclusively to the denizens of the technical community." And technology stimulates the imagination of most individuals. Basalla (p. 134) notes that there is no broad theory of technological innovation that includes a majority of the factors influencing the emergence of novelty, and writes that "There are good reasons for the absence of such a theory, because it would have to encompass the irrationality of the playful and fantastic, the rationality of the scientific, the materialism of the economic, and the diversity of the social and cultural."

But Basalla (1988) has much to say about the role of technology in advancing entertainment through the stimulation of imagination and creativity, for he traces technological fantasies back to the early seventeenth-century prophecies of Francis Bacon. He writes (p. 76) that "Industrialization in the nineteenth and twentieth centuries nurtured the predilection for fanciful technological predictions and institutionalized it in the popular arts. Of these arts, science fiction became the single most important source of fantastic machines" (p. 77), also clarifying that it was primarily a Western phenomenon. "The reasons for this Western hegemony are by no means clear, but the process and the results are readily documented. Perhaps the occurrence of technological fantasies at all levels of Western societies can be attributed to certain values that gained ascendancy during the Renaissance: secularism, the idea of progress, and the domination of nature."

We close this section on entertainment as a substantial reason for the spread of literacy with a reminder proffered by library educator Carl M. White (1964, p. 3) that "It has been pointed out time and again from Seneca and the humanists down to the present that the many uses which are made of books for purposes other than reading and study are all derivative ones."[14] The uses of books all derive from an intellectual need.

Summary

The significance of this chapter is that there is no culture without communication and, therefore, that stewardship of the social transcript is an essential function of culture. Throughout this book reference is made to the redundancy of the vast accumulation of words the library carries forward from the remote past and from remote places to enrich the possibilities for meaning and expression. It is an important function of the library in cultural evolution.

Related to this phenomenon of thought enrichment, which is external to the individual, is the phenomenon of meaning development that occurs within each individual. As expressed thoughts, words undergo further variation and refinement upon entering the mind of the receiver of the expression. "The relation of thought to word is not a thing but a process," writes psychologist Lev S. Vigotsky (1962, p. 125), "a continual movement back and forth from thought to word and from word to thought. In that process the relation of thought to word undergoes changes which themselves may be regarded as development in the functional sense. Thought is not merely expressed in words; it comes into existence through them." Vital to the dynamism of human life, this is an essential intellectual process called by Vigotsky inner speech. It is, he continues (p. 149), "not the interior aspect of external speech—it is a function in itself. It still remains speech, i.e., thought connected with words. But while in external speech thought is embodied in words, in inner speech words die as they bring forth thought. Inner speech is to a large extent thinking in pure meanings." Vigotsky's description explains how words assume very specific meaning with each thinker, the formulation of meaning "fluttering between word and thought" in a process that causes continuous change. Knowledge acquisition obviously stimulates the process, while language, and for present purposes language in its written form, has had an immense impact on the communication and the refinement of knowledge. "With the development of writing," neuroscientist Jean-Pierre Changeux (1986, p. 281) summarizes, "an extracerebral memory was available to fix images and concepts in a more stable material than neurons and synapses. It could be used to consolidate and complete an already broad range of events and cultural artifacts, of symbols, customs, and traditions, relearned by each generation and perpetuated without genetic influence. Mental images and concepts were thus able to survive much longer than the brain that had produced them in fractions of a second."

The mind keeps pushing back the limits of its possibility through the accumulation of knowledge and its unique utility with language to facilitate reason and communication. "Every language and every well-knit technical sublanguage," writes linguist Benjamin Lee Whorf (1956, p. 247), "incorporates certain points of view and certain patterned resistances to widely divergent points of view." To this he adds (p. 249) that "The idea, entirely unfamiliar to the modern world, that nature and language are inwardly akin, was for ages well known to various high cultures whose historical continuity on the earth has been enormously longer than that of Western European culture." But anthropologists Theodosius Dobzhansky and Ernest Boesiger (1983, p. 65) indicate that the mind is the least bound aspect of the human body: "The potentiality for the transmission of culture is due to genes." They promptly follow this thought with "The realization of this potentiality depends mostly on human symbolic languages."

Chapter 3 of this book examined the concept of progress, along with other cultural considerations, while the present chapter has examined the concepts of knowledge and learning as forces in cultural evolution. To be sure, there is debate about whether culture exhibits progress overall or, perhaps more likely, a murky mixture of progress and regress. Knowledge, generally agreed to be a pivotal force in culture, might also be expected to stimulate cultural evolution and to do so in a mostly progressive sense. But not necessarily, as intellectual historian Charles Van Doren (1967, p. 336) finds in his survey of the literature on the subject: "Most progress authors either assert explicitly or imply that there is no limit to human knowledge, and that mankind will go on learning as long as it inhabits the earth." The knowledge that continues to be brought forward, however, does not continue to be at a level that really is fundamental to the human condition. It has more of a refining value, achieved in large part by a process not unlike the infinite splitting of atoms or any other physical object. This is the likely reason Van Doren also finds in the literature that "At this point, some sort of progress–moral or political–appears still to be going on, but it is not progress in knowledge." Knowledge increases, but it does not necessarily progress. No one denies the essentiality of knowledge to the evolution in cultures present and past, and that any culture works with and communicates what is available. The question is whether this apparent change in the nature of knowledge, that is, moving from what appears to be new knowledge of very fundamental significance in the human condition, to a refinement of existing knowledge, has an effect on the nature of evolution; that is, whether it will tend more toward progress or regress, toward acceleration or deceleration.

Jesse Shera (1970, p. 44) points out that "our educational system has been built upon this whole concept of communication. Again on the assumption that somehow it will influence conduct, that we will be better people because of what we have read, or what we have been told, and the library then is nothing more nor less than an extrapolation of this educational process." The entire enterprise of library, learning, and communication can be summarized as the effort to improve the human condition. Individual academic and national libraries usually contain great stores of accumulated knowledge, much of which seems upon initial consideration not to be in use. For example, physicist John Ziman (2000, p. 285) observes that "Sometimes, especially in the human sciences, new knowledge simply accumulates, without significantly improving on what was known before. In general, however, the knowledge base of every discipline is continually being constructed and reconstructed." In the end, he says, "even the most famous original contributions... sink out of direct scientific use into a purely historical cultural memory. On a broad scene, in addition to the addition of myriads of particular details, there are usually major changes in the conceptual language in which knowledge is represented within a research community simply to accommodate newly revealed regularities." Knowledge thus accumulated is in fact a dynamic mixture brewing in the cauldron, waiting for just the right moment to be infused into the creation of something new and of a linguistic turn that opens new avenues for reasoning. Most likely with that idea in mind, Sir Francis Bacon, according to rare books curator I. R. Willison (1980, p. 6) referred to librarianship as "the administration of learning." Similarly, "If the book is more than a container of information," writes Jesse Shera (1971, pp. 56–57), "the library... is more than an information-disseminating agency." This notion will be explored more fully in Chapter 5.

CHAPTER 5

A Cultural Technology

The key factor in the evolution of science remains the power of the human mind to recognize a comprehensible pattern in a mass of detail.

—John Ziman, 1978

Introduction

As applied in this chapter, the term cultural technology refers to those mechanisms created and maintained cooperatively that are intended to transmit selected cultural elements needed to sustain continuous adaptation within a society. Philosopher John Searle (2007, p. 84) observes that "The capacity for social cooperation is a biologically based capacity shared by humans and many other species. It is the capacity for collective intentionality, and collective intentionality is just the phenomenon of shared forms of intentionality in human or animal cooperation." He adds (pp. 85–86) that what specifically has to be added to collective intentionality to move toward the forms of institutional reality that are characteristic of human beings, are "First, the imposition of function and, second, certain sorts of rules that I call 'constitutive rules.' It is this combination, in addition to collective intentionality, that is the foundation of what we think of as specifically *human* society." And it is this cultural evolutionary concept of selected function, in conjunction with the phenomenon of human cooperation, that has carved out the place of library, a cultural technology, in society. To understand the activities of tool-use and speaking, writes anthropologist Tim Ingold (1993a, p. 433), "they must be seen not as the behavioural products of the operation of higher intellectual faculties, internal to their possessors, but rather as integral to the functioning of an entire system of perception and action constituted by the nexus of relationships set up by virtue of the immersion of the agent in his or her environment." It is at that nexus of relationships that the library concept was created and is maintained. Biologist Sir Julian S. Huxley (1958, p. 454) provides the context for what follows in this chapter about the library as a cultural technology for human evolution:

> There are two points I would like to make. The first is that in man behavior has been largely internalized and subjectivized, in the form of concepts and

> intellectual ideas, memories and imaginative creations. From an evolutionary point of view, human thought and indeed all higher mental processes can be regarded as latent or potential action—internal behavior. My second point is that culture, in the anthropological sense, is an organ of human behavior. A culture consists partly of overt acts of behavior such as rituals, partly of the concrete results of overt behavior in the shape of material artefacts, partly of potential behavior in the shape of assumptions, ideas, values, and other mentifacts, or of various combination of these. Thus in the perspective of evolution culture is seen as an organ of behavior of human groups, and potentially as the organ of behavior of the entire human species. Through human culture, behavior has reached a supraorganismal level.

It is at the supraorganismal level that the library functions as a specific kind of cultural technology. Geneticist Conrad Hal Waddington (1961, p. 72) lays the background for this technology, describing it very appropriately for present purposes as a sociogenetic mechanism. He begins by noting that evolutionary change involves the gradual modification of the store of genetically transmitted information, also emphasizing that "no creature has such faculties for experiencing not merely the elementary processes of the world, but the relations between them." Waddington considers these unusual capacities of human evolution to be "an immensely extended carrying-forward of the main progressive lines of pre-human evolution into radically new realms." He asserts (pp. 72–73) that "Man, alone among animals, has developed this extra-genetic mode of transmission to a state where it rivals and indeed exceeds the genetic mode in importance." He explains (p. 73) by means of his example that the ability to fly was accomplished not by a change in the store of genes available to the human species, but "by the transmission of information through the cumulative mechanism of social teaching and learning," to which he refers as a *sociogenetic* mechanism of evolution, rather than the term psychosocial employed by biologist Julian S. Huxley, because it "emphasizes the importance of the mechanism as a means of transmitting information from one generation to the next."

Waddington (p. 77) acknowledges that more than the mere acceptance of authority is involved in a fully developed system for the social transmission of information and takes this idea still further by adding that education "is really a second-order process. There must first be a reliable system of transmission, which corresponds to biological heredity, before there can be a process of verification, which we might compare to natural selection." The faculty for conceptual thinking and communication, he says (p. 73), has provided humanity "with what amounts to a completely new mechanism for the most fundamental biological process of all, that of evolution." There is extremely little question about the great significance for cultural evolution that this new mechanism has produced through the phenomenon called in this book the social transcript, the most vividly sustaining technology for which is defined in the following pages of this chapter as the library function.

The Social Transcript

The world in which we begin our life today is very different from the world we would have entered several thousand years ago. And at an early point in life our understanding of the world around us, and of ourselves, is very different from our understanding a few decades later; our expectations, fears, and aspirations are altered by experience over time, and our knowledge is expanded and deepened. But we all had a starting point, which presents a challenge in life that in many ways is more complex and diversified than it would have been long ago, even if not usually so fundamental. The central importance of the ability to store information, to maintain a memory, is outlined by social psychologist Sir Frederic C. Bartlett (1958, pp. 87–88) as follows:

> Since thinking is a high-level response, whenever it occurs it must be able to draw upon information already acquired and to make use of responses already established. Consequently, any theoretical consideration of thinking must deal with problems of the storage of information and its recall. The experimental evidence collected shows that in closed [in his terms, numerical, geometrical and formal logical] system thinking there are two broadly different problems about the storage of information. One concerns the environmental information which starts thinking going, and the other the further evidence which may have to be used to bring the thinking to an issue.

Humans have no greater intelligence today than centuries ago. Biologists E. Sue Savage-Rumbaugh and Duane M. Rumbaugh (1992, p. 106) base their work with children and other primates on "the premise that there is no neurological component which is unique to linguistic process and independent of general cognitive function." And no single individual or any single group created this great difference, for it was evolved over a long stretch of time by many previous generations of societies. The importance humanity attaches to this phenomenon is suggested by social anthropologist Jack Goody (2000, p. 139) in his explanation of why those societies that can easily understand the technical advantages offered by an alphabetic writing over their own cumbersome systems hold fast to those systems. He reasons that "only with the retention of the script (and language) can one continue to have access to all those cumulative records, to the classical literature, to the bodies of knowledge built up by one's predecessors—the very things that writing has made possible." We inherit the world that surrounds us and then start from there, but we inherit a world whose knowledge is in constant process of development. "All human beings," economic philosopher Kenneth Boulding (1956, pp. 48–49) writes, "except perhaps the extremely mentally deranged, regard themselves as oriented in some way in a stream of time." In large part, that is because we are part of the cultural process, the process, according to social anthropologist A. R. Radcliffe-Brown (1952, pp. 4–5), "by which a person acquires, from contact with other persons or from such things as books or works of art, knowledge, skill, ideas, beliefs, tastes, sentiments."

The part of this broad acquisition that comes down through the ages by means of contact with other persons and books or works of art is what Boulding refers to as the transcript, and it comprises a concept to which he assigns a central role in social evolution: "The basic bond of any society, culture, subculture, or organization is a 'public image', that is an image the essential characteristics of which are shared by the individuals participating in the group." The most consistently and reliably preserved among these media, he reasons, are books and works of art. Some of the residue of previous knowledge and experience comes forward by means of an oral tradition, but most of it, says Boulding, is transmitted from one generation to subsequent generations by means of what is referred to in the present synthesis as the social transcript, a conceptual function drawn from Boulding's (1956, pp. 64–65) account:

> Indeed, every public image begins in the mind of some single individual and only becomes public as it is transmitted and shared. Nevertheless, an enormous part of the activity of each society is concerned with the transmission and protection of its public image; that set of images regarding space, time, relation, evaluation, etc., which is shared by the mass of its people. A public image almost invariably produces a "transcript"; that is, a record in more or less permanent form which can be handed down from generation to generation. In primitive nonliterate societies the transcript takes the form of verbal rituals, legends, poems, ceremonials, and the like, the transmission of which from generation to generation is always one of the principal activities of the group.

The conceptualization of this cultural function is not original with Kenneth Boulding, but the assignment of the term transcript to it does seem to be, and it is Boulding who related to it the adjective social, although not in juxtaposition.[1] The idea of a social transcript has for a long time seemed to me most appropriate in any consideration of library function.

The social transcript is comprised of both oral and written communications that are passed on to subsequent generations as knowledge of many kinds, and therefore to be critiqued, accepted, or rejected, or even ignored for the time being. As we know from experience, it is not extraordinary for a book, for example, to rest on the shelves for a long time, perhaps even a very long time, without any apparent sign of its having ever been read. But we are reminded by sociolinguist Michael Stubbs (1980, p. 104) that "A book is a book even if never read," meaning that it is nonetheless an entity of potential import held in readiness. The communication, the ideas, are there waiting to be discovered. And so the transcript accumulates as it absorbs contemporary additions and refinements, but it usually does not disappear entirely. This is especially true of the written transcript, because it serves not only as a studied, reasoned, means of communication but also as a nearly permanent memory. "The invention of writing marks the beginning of the 'disassociated transcript'," writes Boulding (1956, p. 65), "a transcript which is in some sense independent of the communicator." The social transcript can be considered culture in transit,[2] while the function of library is the recorded culture in transit.

Philosopher John Searle (2007, p. 87) explains how and why this kind of cultural phenomenon, which is a social institution, comes about:

> Human beings have the capacity to impose functions on objects, which, unlike sticks, levers, boxes and salt water, cannot perform the function solely in virtue of their physical structure, but only in virtue of a certain form of the collective acceptance of the objects as having a certain sort of status. With that status comes a function that can only be performed in virtue of the collective acceptance by the community that the object has that status, and that the status carries the function with it.

It is no doubt in part owing to the cultural assignment of a status function to the cultural function of the library that it has managed to survive the millennia. But the reasons behind such value assignment are in the long run even more significant, as will be seen.

Pierce Butler (1933, p. 93) considers the content of this particular cultural phenomenon, the social transcript, as an "individual or social or popular scholarship." Essentially, this amounts to everything a person learns and makes use of in a lifetime, through both formal and informal means, both actively and passively. "The total residual effect of an individual's intellectual experience may well be called his scholarship." In the aggregate, that which is called here the social transcript and scholarship in Butler's (1944, p. 7) lexicon is "the total intellectual content of a culture." Elsewhere (1943, pp. 6–7), he points out the impossibility of anyone learning in a normal life-span all there is to be known, and the fact that, because each adult generation starts where the preceding one left off, such is not required. Humanity, then, is both conservative and progressive with respect to knowledge. Butler (1933, p. 98) explains the value of the continuous recasting[3] of established facts, ideas, and opinions by observing that "Each generation, even each decade in a civilization that changes as rapidly as our own, must rewrite the record of its inherited culture if the transmission to a multitude of living individuals is to continue."

This transmission of culture is of highly significant importance to humanity because if, indeed, there is progress in human evolution, then the changes involved in cultural evolution are the results of a process which, in the words of library educator Carl M. White (1964, p. 6), "has been spreading. It is the habit, both social and personal, of applying to the business of everyday life the best ideas . . . available from the recorded experience of the race as a whole." Cultural evolution is an ongoing, gradual yet tenacious, movement that continues with each individual on each new day because, as has been shown, the culture and the individual are interactive and mutually dependent. Sociologist Talcott Parsons (1949, p. 404) describes how this works for both self interest and societal interest:

> Thus in every society there is such a body of normative rules of action, the embodiment of ultimate common value. In one main aspect the integration of the society is to be measured in terms of the degrees to which these rules are lived up to from motives of moral obligation. But besides this there is always the motive of 'interest' which, looking upon the rules as essentially conditions of action, acts in terms of the comparative personal advantage of obedience or disobedience and acceptance of the sanctions which will have to be suffered. Once a body of rules is firmly established in authority it can remain intact through a considerable shift in these motives–for there develops an interlocking of interests in the maintenance of the system.

What are these rules? Anthropologist F. Theodore Cloak (1975, p. 166) proceeds to explain them in terms customary in anthropology, writing that "functionally speaking, learning is part of the *ontogeny* of an individual animal. Just as it needs the right enzymes, etc., produced inside its skin and, therefore, the right nutrients available outside it, so also it needs a set of instructions normal for its kind, and, therefore, the right species-specific sensory and motor experiences." Once these rules, or instructions as he calls them, are acquired through the culture they become as much a part of the being as cells and organs. What subsequently came to be called memes, as referring to memory and defined in Chapter 4 as units of cultural transmission, Cloak refers to in his paper as the i-culture (cultural instructions), which is carried in the central nervous system. He also describes a cultural set called the m-culture (p. 168), which refers to more material structures brought about and maintained by the behaviors resulting from the i-culture. "Features of a people's m-culture thus include features of their behavior, their technology, and their social organization (and their ideology when considered as a set of verbal behaviors)."

Cloak's ideas have considerable bearing on the notion advanced here of the library function in evolution as that of a cultural technology, an example of the m-culture that acts on and maintains the i-culture function. Cloak (p. 170) explains clearly and concisely the relation of the i-culture and the m-culture in generating a function that is considered in this book to be the cultural technology function of library:

> The outcomes of the i-culture/m-culture interactions can be summarized thus: An i-culture builds and operates m-culture features whose *ultimate function* is to provide for the maintenance and propagation of the i-culture in a certain environment. And the m-culture features, in turn, environmentally affect the composition of the i-culture so as to maintain or increase their own capabilities for performing that function. As a result, each m-culture feature is shaped for its *particular* functions in that environment. After certain specific kinds of m-culture features become common through repeated performance of their functions, we can begin correctly to say that m-culture features of that kind have their specific shape in order to perform their particular functions, and that they perform them *in order to* accomplish their universal ultimate function. They are *teleonomic* structures. We can assign the term 'ultimate' function to the maintenance and propagation of the i-culture because cultural instructions, through their behaviors, determine the specific *shape* or fine structure both of m-culture features and of their own replicas. In other words, even if all the m-culture features of a certain kind were wiped out, a single set of the appropriate cultural instructions could reconstruct and repropagate them.

In this scenario the concept of library is an m-culture whose ultimate function is the vigilance over and maintenance of the recorded social transcript; it exemplifies the unfortunately labeled selfish quality identified by Dawkins (2006, p. 200) in writing that "a cultural trait may have evolved in the way that it has, simply because it is *advantageous to itself*." This is to say that the cultural technology was created to maintain and transmit the culture, an idea that would help to explain the otherwise mysteriously long survival of the library function.

Cooperation & Social Institutions

By and large, individuals choose to accommodate the surrounding culture so that the individual's needs and desires will be more likely to be accommodated by the respective society. Philosopher David Kaplan (1970, pp. 73–74) sees in this process a trend of "far-reaching implications for the evolutionary process as a whole. Together with the fact that culture is transmitted in space as well as time by non-genetic mechanisms, it accounts for the trend in cultural evolution which is almost totally absent in biological evolution: this is the trend toward a greater convergence and consequent homogeneity of culture type, accompanied by a decrease in the diversity of cultures." This is what anthropologist Bronislaw Malinowski (1930, p. 623) was alluding to in the latter part of his statement that "The understanding of culture is to be found in the process of its production by succeeding generations and in the way in which it reproduces in each new generation the appropriately molded organism." The phrase *appropriately molded organism* provokes further thought. It builds upon the fact that a new generation does not begin from zero upon birth, each individual entering life at a different point in time, for it is molded by the culture to fit the culture. This is another example of the importance of timing in cultural evolution, the importance of cultural readiness or culture's *mutual* accommodation with individuals toward the ultimate end of evolution, which is to make humanity feel safe, comfortable, and valued. Moreover, cooperation, which is a key mechanism in the implementation of cultural change, certainly depends on this condition.

One of the more visible characteristics of culture and its evolution is cooperation among individuals and groups in any particular society. For the most obvious reasons, communication is essential to cooperation, while language facilitates and expedites communication. "Once you have language and social cooperation, you already have the possibility of creating institutional reality," concludes philosopher John Searle (2007, p. 12). Anthropologist Leslie A. White (1959, p. 100) summarizes the influence of language in this connection: "Language opened the door to cooperation to a virtually unlimited extent. Cooperation made life more secure. Consequently, social evolution moved in the direction of more extensive cooperation." And psychologist Paul Bloom (1998, p. 204) theorizes "As our ancestors' abilities to communicate increased, this may have led to selective pressure for increased social and conceptual capacities—which in turn created more pressure for greater communicative abilities, and so on."

Perhaps the most important contributions of cooperation reside in the development of ideas and the advancement of understanding. More specifically, philosopher Karl Popper (1977, p. 452) writes that "two things seem to me decisively important about language. One is that it allows for criticizability; the other is that it gives rise to the need to criticize because of story-telling." Chapter 3 took account of Popper's views on the significance of criticism in the struggle to identify truth, which he calls "that most important value." He contends (1999, p. 73) that "Language makes it possible to consider our theories critically: to look at them as if they were external objects, as if they belonged to the world outside of ourselves which we share with others. Theories become objects of criticism." It is his conviction that both the critical approach in thinking and the pursuit of truth are rendered possible only by means of language.

With extraordinary speed, especially since the Renaissance, societies have developed in which, according to Leslie A. White (1964, p. 4), "the use of letters is inseparable from matters which are essential to keeping people who are now the most advanced from sliding back to a lower state of civilization." Culture is a highly dynamic environmental control, driven in large part by the flexibility and fluidity of language, in both spoken and written form, more about which will follow. Again, language is arguably the most important tool of cultural evolution, for it facilitates and expedites learning, and makes possible the understanding and communication of complex spheres of knowledge. Language is primarily a product of cooperation, which in turn is greatly facilitated by language.

Cooperation among individuals within a society is the phenomenon that stands behind the creation and continuation of social institutions. These institutions represent select aspects of culture that are generally agreed within the society to be the most highly valued, each for its own perceived contribution. The selection of these aspects of culture for special attention is not achieved through instinct. Rather, according to sociologist Ellsworth Faris (1937, p. 17), "it is far truer to say it is the customs and institutions which explain the individual behavior so long called instinctive. Instincts do not create customs. Customs create instincts, for the putative instincts of human beings are always learned and never native." A highly relevant conclusion is reached by biologist Mary E. Clark (2002, p. 316), who asserts that "Our brains are designed to work both cognitively and emotionally in cooperation with others." She finds (p. 102), for example, that at an early stage of hominid evolution "Success at reproduction was no longer a matter of just a mother, or even of two parents (such as many species of birds manage with). It became necessary that there be a whole, collaborating, functional group. Without such cooperating, sharing groups of ancestors, the intellect of modern humans could never have evolved." Social institutions are distinguished from other social forms because they are established by common will, and therefore are something more than social habits. "Nothing else but institutions can define sameness," writes anthropologist Mary Douglas (1986, p. 55). "Similarity is an institution. Elements get assigned to sets where institutions find their own analogies in nature."

Institutions, according to sociologist Lloyd V. Ballard (1936, pp. 3–4), are "meeting points of wills', seeking to realize some social purpose," to be "conceived of as forms or order established within social life," and "have meaning only as expressions of a collective effort to describe collective activity." Thus their purpose is objectified in the external forms the institutions assume. And the dependency of social life on social institutions is described by sociologist Joyce Hertzler (1946, p. 27) in cultural terms as "a large-scale molding-matrix, the patterning of the behavior of men interacting in groups," and elsewhere (1929, p. 25) in anatomical terms as "a sort of skeleton or frame-work." As anthropologist Bronislaw Malinowski (1944, p. 39) stresses, "Culture in general accounts for most of the organized behavior of man." The concept of the social institution as this kind of unit of human organization "implies an agreement on a set of traditional values for which human beings come together." Philosopher Raimo Tuomela (2002, p. 157) emphasizes the strength of an underlying collective reason in his definition of the social institution.

> Basically I take social institutions to be collectively—but not necessarily intentionally—made devices for creating order in a human community, typically society, and helping people to satisfy their basic needs, such as needs related to food and shelter, sexual relations and reproduction, sociality and social power. Whatever the exact list of the underlying needs is and whatever their precise nature is, we have here a strong underlying reason for the coming about of social institutions. As a result, institutions in different areas of social life arise: familial, educational, religious, political, and economic institutions.

Social institutions are created to give special attention to areas of human life that are agreed upon within the culture to be so important that their development does not belong in the hands of random individuals. Or, as anthropologist Mary Douglas (1986, p. 111) puts it, "The individual tends to leave the important decisions to his institutions while busying himself with tactics and details."

But philosopher John Searle (2007, pp. 108–109) finds another, very distinctive layer of significance to the social institution. He says that "Humans are distinct from other animals in that they have a capacity to create not merely a social but an institutional reality. This institutional reality is, above all, a system of deontic powers," the expression of a sense of social conscience. "These deontic powers provide human agents with the fundamental key for organized human society: the capacity to create and act on desire-independent reasons for action." This is a special kind of cooperation for the good of the whole, without which there surely would be precious little cultural evolution. It works this way, according to Searle (p. 101), because "It is a unique characteristic of human beings that they can create and act on desire-independent reasons for action." It is a capacity unique even among primates. And he continues (p. 103), "Thus, in the case of human society, unlike animal societies, reasons can motivate desires, instead of all reasons having to start with desires." Anthropologist Mary Douglas (1986, p. 46) carries this idea a step further: "The conditions for stable conventions to arise are much more stringent than it might seem. Communities do not grow up into little institutions and these do not grow into big ones by any continuous process. For a convention to turn into a legitimate social institution it needs a parallel cognitive convention to sustain it." Nor does this unusual motivation relate to individual intelligence. Having examined a large number of studies and tests of intelligence that emphasize the relationship between intelligence and varieties of altruistic and selfish conduct, sociologist Pitirim A. Sorokin (1948, p. 73) finds that "intelligence as measured by the foregoing techniques does not appear to be a significant factor in making human beings either altruistic or egoistic. Some slight relationship between these two phenomena possibly exists, higher intelligence slightly favoring altruism; but this relationship appears to be neither uniform nor consistent."

Anthropologist Bronoslaw Malinowski (1930, p. 626) contends that institutions are the only cultural units that bear a considerable degree of permanence, universality, and independence, and that "Every institution centers around a fundamental need, permanently unites a group of people in a cooperative task and has its particular body of doctrine and its technique of craft." Sociologist Joyce Hertzler (1946, p. 51) provides a rationale for such status, going directly to the most profound social forces that support the institution:

> Institutions are first and foremost psychic phenomena. The essence of institutions is ideas and other psychic uniformities that, consciously or unconsciously, dominate our social behavior. Any institution is only the embodiment of an idea. In a very real sense, institutions are only in our heads; they are common and reciprocating attitudes; they are our notions of regulation, they are deep-seated mental habits that dominate our reactions in our social and natural environments. But institutions are unavoidably also societal structures; they have an objective existence, a sort of framework in order to operate effectively and integrate the behavior of men.

Hertzler (p. 27) also summarizes, not the specific activities, but the general non-material cultural functions of social institutions and their de facto consequences: They are "organized to conduct various types of disciplinary, regulatory and operative procedures, and to establish imperative, integrated patterns of ordered social life. They are control devices deeply imbedded in all culture—the dynamic, adjusting, or implementing part. Institutions thus may be looked upon as one class or type of the great universal cultural uniformities."

Because the word need is ambiguous, as suggested in Chapter 3, its interpretation in this context is particularly intriguing and essential to an understanding of the role of the social institution in cultural evolution. Need is the motivator of cultural evolution and, as has been shown, need can be of the most basic kind, involving nourishment, security, and similar considerations required for minimal survival of the individual and the species. For these reasons, Malinowski (1944, p. 90) explains that "By need, then, I understand the system of conditions in the human organism, in the cultural setting, and in relation of both to the natural environment, which are sufficient and necessary for the survival of group and organism of facts." But cultural evolution embraces considerations that extend far beyond the physical needs of minimal survival of the species, exerting a like pressure for change, and more so as the complexity of the society increases. "Thus we see that culture in all its aspects," writes Leslie A. White (1959, p. 10) "ideological, sociological, and technological—serves man's inner, spiritual needs as well as his outer, material needs."

According to developmental psychologists Jaan Valsiner and René Van der Veer (2000, p. 383), the clinical psychologist Lev S. Vigotsky wished to show in his work that human beings had somewhere in human history made the dialectical leap from biological necessity to human self-mastery and freedom.[4] They state that "in essence, then, his was a very optimistic theory that emphasized that humans can master their own fate by making use of the instruments of civilization." The motivation for the establishment and the sustaining of a social institution is need, not just the need experienced by any animal, but the full range of need experienced by thinking beings.[5] Social institutions are means to an end, and "that end is social welfare," writes sociologist Lloyd V. Ballard (1936, 15). "Social welfare, however, implies individual well-being." And sociologist Robert MacDougall (1912, p. 19) advises that "The relation between individual and society may therefore be stated by saying that social organization and social service form the logical basis of individual welfare," concluding with the thought that "Society therefore realizes its logical end, not by the suppression of individuality, but by the fullest possible fostering of its development." It is the individual within society that ultimately creates the society that in turn guides the individual.

Historian and philosopher John Herman Randall (1940, p. 255) observes that the two most influential ideas of the eighteenth century, nature and reason, were as significant a development in thinking then as the notion of evolution was at the beginning of the twentieth century. He emphasizes that they "derived their meaning from the natural sciences, and, carried over to man, led to the attempt to discover a social physics. Man and his institutions were included in the order of nature and the scope of the recognized scientific method, and in all things the newly invented social sciences were assimilated to the physical sciences." Again, we see the tremendous influence of science on the way humans view the world, as witnessed also in the following anthropologist's explanation of cultural processes: Leslie White (1949, p. 391) contends that "Social systems are therefore determined by technological systems, and philosophies and the arts express experience as it is defined by technology and refracted by social systems. Cultural systems like those of the biological level are capable of growth. That is, the power to capture any energy is also the ability to harness more and still more of it. Thus cultural systems, like biological organisms, develop, multiply, and extend themselves." Social institutions perform so prominently in cultural evolution that it even has been suggested by historian Elizabeth L. Eisenstein (1968, p. 234) that the idea of societal evolution makes sense "only insofar as there exist some mechanisms for the transmission of various institutional and adaptive techniques and for creating some common, intersocietal, adaptive and integrative capabilities and frameworks."

The social institution is the mechanism selected to foster, nurture, and protect the essential aspects of culture and to ensure its continued viability. These institutions represent a formal organization of conduct which emanates from the forceful urge of fundamental desires and needs. Sociologist Lloyd V. Ballard (1936, p. 9) perceives that "The roots of social institutions penetrate deeply into human nature. Since they arise out of definite, permanent desires which demand satisfaction, social institutions are rooted in the fundamental human interests, economic, sexual and social. These interests or predispositions are passed on from generation to generation as a part of the socio-biological inheritance." On the one hand, the place of the social institution in society and the evolution of its culture is held rather securely in the midst of ongoing turmoil and challenge; on the other hand, they exert considerable influence on the decisions of individuals, groups, and societies—to the extent that they act as a means of social control. Library educator Lowell Martin (1937, p. 552) describes this function:

> From the many tendencies of human conduct, some beneficial to the group and others harmful, institutions select the beneficial reactions and define them in such a manner as to make them the spontaneous reactions. This is done sometimes by a process closely akin to psychologic conditioning, but more often by a process of definition in which the individual comes to recognize rationally the value of a particular response.

But it is important to note that Martin (p. 552) places his assessment in a broader and more significant perspective, by adding that "institutions exist not only to control and repress the person but even more basically to provide him with freedom and opportunity for self-expression and self-fulfillment. Societal processes must produce not mechanical units in a social machine but human personalities in a social organization." Different societies will apply these two cultural forces in different proportions and probably at different times, but clearly both contribute great value to the process of cultural evolution.

The establishment and maintenance of a social institution require at bare minimum a sufficient number of like-minded individuals to diffuse their ideas and to realize them in action. In the field of physics, this is called achievement of critical mass, which is the amount of fissionable material required to create a sustained nuclear chain reaction. The concept and the term are applied widely in other fields, among them sociology, where they describe the availability of sufficient momentum in a social system that the momentum becomes self-sustaining and fuels further growth; it is a threshold value of the number of people needed to trigger a phenomenon by exchange of ideas. Thus, the concept of critical mass is well suited to the processes of cultural evolution, and the creation of the social institution is a fine example.

Looking back through the millennia, the establishment of urban centers constitutes the quantitative part of the formula for creating critical mass. According to sociologist Bartholomeus Landheer (1957, p. 9), "Culture growth shows a positive correlation to the number of people who make up the culture in question and to the rate of their inter-communications. We refer to what sociologist Emile Durkheim called the numerical and social density of a group." For he adds (p. 134) that "The accumulation of people in one place does not diminish but increases the need for communication because this need is a result of greater social complexity." By dint of cooperation, which is a sine qua non of urban dwelling, archeologist V. Gordon Childe (1956, p. 96) contends that the individuals it embraces form the elements of a structure or pattern of a society, which advances the group's collective interests, and elsewhere (1951, p. 170) that it is "the operation of diffusion more than anything else that distinguishes social from organic evolution and explains the curvature of the lines in any graphic representation of the process." Similarly, but with more apparent conviction, sociologist Stuart Chapin (1928, p. 31) argues that "Life in societies is the most powerful weapon in the struggle for existence."

Language, again, is seen as the lubricant for the cogs of cultural machinery and, as discussed in Chapter 4, it stimulates intelligence as intelligence sharpens the linguistic skill. Articulate speech is a form of behavior that requires the exercise of a higher degree of intelligence than is possessed by any animal except the hominid and, while some other animals had learned throughout the ages the advantages of living in groups, humans were able consciously to raise the level of those advantages. Intelligence, writes sociologist F. Stuart Chapin (1928, p. 32), "is generally admitted to be the most powerful aid in the struggle for existence. But intelligence is eminently a social attribute." And Chapin further suggests (p. 33) that intelligence is advanced, in part, through social discourse: "Indeed, the mental differences that mark men off from other creatures are those that are created by social discourse. Speech in particular, an attainment that has given man his preeminence among other animals, is distinctly a social creation" (p. 33).

One can easily conclude that the communication and socialization demanded and made possible by major population centers have exerted a profound influence on cultural evolution throughout the ages. Indeed, neuropsychologist Merlin Donald (1991, p. 10) posits the theory that "it was not instrumental intelligence that drove brain expansion but rather social intelligence. Complex societies make great demands on memory: large numbers of relationships have to be analyzed, understood, stored, and serviced regularly in order to sustain a large group organization."

To his reminder that the relation between civilization and urban life was observed long ago by Aristotle, cultural historian Raymond Irwin (1964, p. 18) adds the corollary of the growth of libraries and urban life, with its specialization of functions, for "Government and administration, trade and industry, social activities and entertainment, all demand literacy; literacy creates letters, documents and books; books create libraries." In a similar vein, Jesse Shera (1970, p. 45) sees the emergence of the library as "evidence of social maturation. The more sophisticated the society, the more complex its social organization, the more it needs libraries."

LIBRARY IN CONCEPT

James Thompson (1977, p. 204), who has studied the history of libraries at considerable length, concludes that "An historical survey of libraries, from their origins to the present time, demonstrates beyond contention that their destiny is always bound up with the destiny of their society." Indeed, the preceding chapters of the present book describe the cultural context for this tight interweaving of society and library. And when referring to the library, sometimes it is necessary to be reminded that what is under discussion is the entire social institution,[6] which includes the people who establish and implement the policies, both formal and informal, those who most directly cause the library to function in all its operations and services everyday and in the long, sweeping term. In Jesse Shera's (1966, p. 175) words, "From the very beginning, libraries have always been an integral part of the 'business' of operating a society, hence a legitimate collective concern. As the culture matured and became more sophisticated, its dependence upon graphic records increased, and changes in the culture were reflected in the librarian's responsibilities." Librarians function in a liaison capacity between society and the social institution called library, and "If you will examine it now," writes philosopher José Ortega y Gasset (1961, p. 139), "you will observe how clearly the duty of the librarian has varied in direct proportion to the significance of the book as a social necessity." The apparent simplicity of this perception belies the deeper and more comprehensive complexity of the challenge that is incorporated in stewardship of the social transcript. Libraries have a long history because they are needed by society, not because the individuals who manage them wield great power and far-reaching influence; the social transcript they manage holds the power and influence. Library function has survived throughout the ages and, arguably, has become ever stronger and more integral to the social fabric. Chapter 3 demonstrated that as population becomes more dense, society increases in complexity. Moreover, first among Jesse Shera's (1972, p. 494) fundamental assumptions is that man's dependence upon and demand for graphic records will increase as society becomes more and more complex." Since the emergence of transcribed communication the library function has evolved with culture, as an integral dimension of the culture. Throughout later centuries there have been fairly consistent efforts to open the library to all, not just to the elite, so the dissemination of these ideas may have been influential in gathering support of the masses, among whom those who may have seen in that institution the potential for support of their own cause. Public libraries, says social anthropologist Jack Goody (2000, pp. 159–160) "represent a socialization of the book, the communal ownership of the means of communication, making its contents available to all who can read and write." The remarkable public library movement of the nineteenth century in the United States and England did not start from scratch in the middle of the nineteenth century, for conditions had long been developing in anticipation of just the right moment to accommodate such energy.

The idea that communication is a complex phenomenon seems hardly to be challengeable; likewise the idea that language and the motivations of both individual humans and their collectives called societies are complex phenomena. Yet these are the human phenomena that constitute the stuff of libraries when organized to perform the library function in its different dimensions. In that realized state, however, they manifest themselves much more familiarly as bureaucracies. They are managed for the purpose of organizing and preserving recorded experience for effective and efficient sharing every day and throughout the generations of humanity, for, as Kenneth Boulding (1985, p. 46) calls to mind, "The knowledge within human heads is what constitutes the genetic structure of human artifacts, and this seems to grow constantly, even at an accelerated pace." Libraries are about people and ideas because the ultimate library function is about people and ideas. In trying to understand so complex a set of phenomena acting in a single entity, an entity that is at once conceptual and real, one cannot help but search first for a simple, but all-embracing, explanation.

A survey of pertinent literature yields one common feature in the midst of the many that apply to the mélange of elements involved, and it is precisely the variety of intellectual content and expression held in the library. It is a variety that continuously diversifies and can lend itself either to cohesion or tension within the society. This constitutes the library's ready potential to stimulate the intellect in any direction. Without this variety it would be highly unlikely and probably impossible for the institution to be able to accommodate needs at once social and individual in an environment that changes for any number of reasons. Philosopher Mark Johnson (2007, p. 265) emphasizes the place such variety has in determining and communicating human meaning, which is essential to values and decision making. He writes that "meaning is a matter of relations and connection grounded in bodily organism-environment coupling, or interaction. The meaning of something is its relations, actual and potential, to other qualities, things, events, and experiences. In pragmatist lingo, the meaning of something is a matter of how it connects to what has gone before and what it entails for present or future experiences and actions." And linguist Benjamin Lee Whorf (1956, p. 258) also makes this clear with his statement that "Sentences, not words, are the essence of speech, just as equations and functions, and not bare numbers, are the real meat of mathematics. We are all mistaken in our common belief that any word has an 'exact meaning.'"

In studying the history of the public library, Jesse Shera (1949, p. 248) finds that "Judged by every standard and measured by every criterion, the public library is revealed as a social agency dependent upon the objectives of society. It followed–it did not create–social change. It was an outward and visible manifestation of the spirit and ideals of the people." But it did accelerate cultural evolution. The present essay argues that the library function was created as an integral force in cultural evolution. It was invented by society through the forces of cultural evolution, and the library, in its daily activity, follows and/or reflects the values of society. But it also will be demonstrated that the library concept leaves a heavy impression on the evolution of culture beyond the acceleration factor.

Social emphases and collective ideas in change are the constants of cultural evolution and are the forces behind it. While this dynamic is continuous and therefore imperceptible, there are periods when, at least in retrospect, the change and the reasons behind the change are identifiable. The emergence of language, as acknowledged repeatedly in these pages, is the most obvious of these, along with the invention of the printing press and the currently used information technologies driven by the computer. Retrospect permits the rare perspective, made clearer by distance in time, that enables the achievement of a depth of understanding that consideration in the moment most often does not. That is in the nature of evolution. For purposes of examining the place of the library in cultural evolution, it is more difficult to perceive the causes and effects of trends in society and ideation since, for example, the fifteenth century, than before that time. Consequently, it is deduced from the "archeology of the book," according to bibliographer Roy Stokes (1981, p. 57), that "Cave paintings and drawings, such as those at Altamira, Lascaux, or on the rocks of Tassili, provide some indication that from a very early period the decorative urge and the desire to communicate have existed side by side," and, from the study of the replacement of the oral tradition in ancient Greece by the written tradition, according to library philosopher H. Curtis Wright (1977) that the social need of information was the same then as it is now. Philosopher José Ortega y Gasset[7] has outlined the development of social awareness that the library function was of such significance that it justified the special attention of society and the assignment of an individual to bear the authority and responsibility for its administration, which is a development he sees as moving from that of a spontaneous social profession to an office of the state bureaucracy.

The level of social awareness is rarely made more evident than when it is backed by personal financial resources in a cooperative movement to support what is believed to be a common good. The establishment of the Boston Public Library in the early 1850s, according to library historian John Y. Cole (1979, p. 365), "is generally considered as the beginning of the public library movement [in the United States] since that institution was the first large tax-supported municipal library in the United States." He points out that while the expansion of the public library idea was motivated by many complex factors, which varied geographically and by type of community, a common factor was a commitment to popular education and the expansion of educational opportunities. He refers to this as "an elitism that often emphasized the search for an acceptable means of social control, a growing belief in the power of reading books—especially 'good books'—and a healthy dose of local pride."

But during the industrial revolution there also was mounting pressure to acquire knowledge of a practical nature as a way of elevating one's station in life through work and the raising of financial status, as well as through upward social reception. Information scientist Robert V. Williams (1984, p. 6) finds that the motivating factors that led to the establishment of public libraries throughout the rest of the United States in the latter half of the nineteenth century were complex, and that they varied considerably among different cities and townships. But it is clear to him that the widespread establishment of libraries shared a common feature: "they included a commitment to popular education and the expansion of educational opportunities." Williams offers three major thematic explanations of public library development in the United States: the social conditions explanation, which argues that a variety of social forces, working in some undetermined combinations, *caused* public library development; the democratic tradition view, wherein the public library is seen as the result of the growth of democracy; and the social control theory. The latter argues that public library development in the United States is the result of both democratic and anti-democratic forces; it may be partially an outgrowth of the popular need of information for purposes of self-government, and it may be that it was orchestrated by elite groups and influential individuals who established libraries in such a way as to ensure that these libraries would be a means for achieving social control over the masses, much as Harris (see chapter 2, note 5) contends.

In this context it is of special importance to acknowledge the abundantly evident fact that, of the total population incorporated in a general culture, only an extremely few among that population are scientists, theorists, or scholars in the formal sense. In spite of that gross numerical consideration, however, the culturally significant ideas of these relatively few, which take the form of discoveries, inventions, theories, or other shared conclusions of their efforts, do become influences—often very strong influences—in the evolution of culture, as discussed especially in Chapter 3, even though their work is not likely to be understood in depth by those who are not scientists and scholars. In Chapter 4 reference was made specifically to the social phenomena of thought-styles and their collectives, which play an important part in communicating new ideas and gaining either their acceptance or rejection within larger communities of expertise. That is because virtually everyone engulfed in the culture is exposed to these forces, even if not consciously aware of them. They need not read of these events to be aware of them. They need not even hear of them. The world around them changes subtly, and for the most part they move along with it, for the most part adapting to the culture; or they rebel against it, in which case they certainly are experiencing cultural influence. So the results of the work of the intellectual leaders changes the lives even of those who may not be literate. For example, many, perhaps most, of those who do read do not have sufficient knowledge of physics to understand how and why atomic energy comes about; but even those who do not read, yet do engage in other forms of communication, come to have some understanding of nuclear energy in the sense of the destructive potential of the atomic bomb, and have been in possession of that understanding since 1945.

The point is that there is a general splash effect of innovations introduced into a culture that extends beyond the few key individuals to saturate the entire culture. All the members of a society do not need to enter the physical library for the conceptual library to exert a major impact on that society, nor, in fact, do all even need to be literate. And for that reason the cultural technology called library constitutes a strong infrastructural component of literate society that influences society's nonliterate dimension as well. Social forces are always present to vet and receive innovation. Communication scientist Everett M. Rogers and social psychologist and communication scientist F. Floyd Shoemaker (1971, p. 106) find that innovations are diffused through society in various ways, but all as the result of communication processes, so that some come about because of need, while others create the need. And, of course (p. 105), "The predispositions of individuals influence their behavior toward communication messages and the effects which such messages are likely to have. Generally, individuals tend to expose themselves to those ideas which are in accord with their interests, needs, or existing attitudes. We consciously or unconsciously avoid messages which are in conflict with our predispositions. This tendency is called *selective exposure*." Rogers and Shoemaker (p. 11) emphasize that "all explanations of human behavior directly stem from an examination of how individuals acquire and modify ideas through communication with others. The learning process, the diffusion process, the change process, and so on all basically involve the communication of new ideas." But the growing importance of leaders in the reception and diffusion of new ideas that often lead to cultural change is addressed by biologist Sir Julian S. Huxley (1958, p. 443):

> Rapid cultural change, especially if also progressive, usually stems from the discoveries or achievements of exceptional individuals, but will not operate effectively except in a group receptive to the notion of change and technically and professionally equipped to apply the new discoveries and ideas . . . It should be stressed, however, that the role of the individual in evolution has increased in importance, not only in the passage from biological to cultural evolution but also in that from stability-promoting to change-promoting cultures.

The emergence of the library concept constitutes the diffusion of a cultural technology. Library historian Sidney H. Ditzion's (1947, p. 192) study of the pertinent role of the spirit of democracy in many ways summarizes the differing views of why the American public library was given support from late nineteenth century to early twentieth. He notes that the nature of the nation had swung in very formal ways toward greater participation of the populace in decision making, a trend that was fueled by the expanding reaches of knowledge, which offered unprecedented challenge to a formerly supreme supernaturalism. "Scientific knowledge and reason were supplanting faith. The attainment of such knowledge meant increasing the individual's ability to control more adequately his own destiny." Knowledge drawn from reason melded fortuitously with an encouraging political system, the fervor for which was that of the newly converted in religious belief.

Ditzion (1947) also underlines the difference between the reception of the public library idea in America and its reception in England. He cites the advanced state of literacy and popular education in the newly established nation as a means to prepare the workingman, and the more compelling need to prepare the artisan and mechanic for duties of a nature different from those in England. Ditzion writes (pp. 2–3) that "Environmental variations such as these were strongly reflected in the speeches and writings which promoted the cause of public libraries after 1850. The British movement met with strong opposition especially from the landowning groups. The American movement met with taxpayers' opposition only infrequently. The privileged in England feared popular education." Looking at the taxation issue in England from a different angle, library historian Alistair Black finds an interesting paradox in the fact that the public library gained support in both utilitarianism and idealism.[8] Idealists were the first to champion the cause of the public library, but their more practical counterparts also took up the cause because in the end, both, Black (1996, p. 143) writes, "pursued reasoned action, state intervention, political pluralism, equality of opportunity, the notion of citizenship, self-betterment, educational improvement and, above all, social stability within a fundamentally unchanged capitalist order."

Both in concept and concrete, the library is a cultural technology. Among the social institutions that have survived the vicissitudes of time, surely the one that most consistently day-by-day, and most attentively generation-by-generation, is the library. And the clearest support for this assertion is found in the fact that the library has been selected to bear responsibility for the social transcript. As social psychologist David Loye (1998, p. 173) asserts, "The analogue for natural selection in this formulation of concepts and principles for evolutionary action theory might logically be called *cultural selection*." He goes on (p. 176) to explain that creativity has led to a "vast spewing forth of possibility" that is rearranged "to fit what are perceived to be the requirements of what can or should exist. Underlying this process, what most centrally has been set in motion, for better or worse, is a change, a going beyond, a moving forward from, or the *creative transcendence* of what presently exists." Following this theory, the library can be considered the technology that the culture has invented to render accessible the best examples of humanity (along with the worst) on a daily basis, and to ensure continuity of that social responsibility into the future. "Typically, and increasingly," observe sociologists Donald A. MacKenzie and Judy Wajcman (1985, p. 12) "technologies come not in the form of separate, isolated devices but as part of a whole, as part of a system." Thus, they add (p. 14) that "the *compelling* nature of much technological change is best explained by seeing technology not as outside of society, as technological determinism would have it, but as inextricably part of society... If they are to survive at all, much less to prosper, they cannot forever stand still. Technical change is made inevitable, and its nature and direction profoundly conditioned, by this." As a successful cultural technology, the library has evolved in the context of other cultural features, such as language, ideas, beliefs, values, norms, and other non-physical properties, that have nourished it. Geographers Donald G. Janelle and David C. Hodge (2000, p. 2) find that the story of technology generally has been unbalanced because "Social scientists have tended to concentrate on the 'effects' of technology, on the 'impact' of technological change on society. This is a perfectly valid concern, but it leaves a prior, and perhaps more important, question unasked and therefore unanswered. What has shaped the technology that is having 'effects'? What has caused and continues to cause the technological changes whose 'impact' we are experiencing?" The library is the technology that attends to the rich mixture of strictly human features that drive the culture. But the greatest value popularly perceived to be held by the library lies in the reasoned belief that it simply is a common good; that the library, on balance and for one reason or another or many, is generally understood to be a force for good.[9] Library historian Alistair Black (1996, p. 266) finds that "The social benefit of institutions like the public library could not be measured scientifically. However, a teleological reckoning in the form of discourse was possible, and was undertaken." The library is born of reason.

The two axioms of the science of culture, according to anthropologist Bronislaw Malinowski (1944, p. 171), state that "every culture must satisfy the biological system of needs" and that "every cultural achievement that implies the use of artifacts and symbolism is an instrumental enhancement of human anatomy, and refers directly or indirectly to the satisfaction of a bodily need." These artifacts and symbols he calls (1930, p. 628) "the instrumental imperatives of culture," since they are essentially means to an end. They are "as indispensable to man's commissariat, to the satisfaction of his nutritive needs as the raw material of food and the processes of its ingestion." The library is one of these instrumental imperatives of culture. It is interactive in the daily services it provides, and throughout the evolution of culture in a more passive state. Library educator J. M. Orr (1977, p. 194) makes the point that "Information from a library is at best second-hand and is not comprehensible to a person without a knowledge of the real world as a referral point; in this sense, second-hand information only adds to real information as it has been directly perceived." While the category of the culture's instrumental imperatives—in this case the transmission of knowledge—remains a constant, its value at any given time and in any given society varies. "The appreciation of the library shifts according to the evaluation which is placed on knowledge," writes sociologist Bartholmeus Landheer (1957, p. 158). "The function of knowledge is defined by the value-system of each society, and in the case of societies at the national level is often a compromise between the values of social sub-groups."

A theme that surfaced repeatedly throughout the 1960s in the United States, as reported by the National Advisory Commission on Library and Information Science (1969), was the growth and development of the library as it adapts to the needs of an evolving society. Commissioners saw this as a reflection of strong social awareness, a service orientation that pervades every existing and conceivable library and information function, and concluded (p. 76) that "A library can be understood only as it enhances a socially valuable function, one of which—and one that all libraries can enhance—is the personal intellectual and ethical development of every individual in our society." The Commission's findings agree with the eleventh principle of librarianship that James Thompson (1977, p. 218) infers from his comprehensive study of the history and theory of libraries: "A librarian's role can only be an important one if it is fully integrated into the prevailing social and political system."

Pressure from the public to initiate formal actions, and not only those that would cause the reallocation of common funds, began to hold sway in places of power when the general population began to make its strength known. It may not be true that no good deed goes unpunished, but it certainly must be true that no social movement for the common good goes forward without considerable debate, effort, and the cost of time, and certainly not in the absence of the leadership required to organize and stimulate the movement. Some of the leaders of the public library movement in England and the United

States held positions of governmental power, some were librarians, others of no real official status beyond the strength of their personal influence.

Whatever formal acts are required to accomplish such ends represent causes that are taken up by extraordinarily strong and persuasive individuals, the trusted cultural leaders. Over the centuries, and even the millennia, there have been many such individuals who spearheaded the development of the library in the evolution of culture by inspiring the pertinent society. Sociologist René Debray (2000, p. 14) is pragmatic in his contention that there could never have been a modern museum without first "a politically motivated creation of the national patrimony, a matter of institutional authority. Likewise, no literature without a library; in France, no *royal* library without a Charles V to promote it or *national* one without the Revolution's Jacobin phase. No edification without the struggle to build the edifice. In other words, no historical record of memory records itself."

But there are also less dramatic initiatives that combined to create the public library as we know it today, an agency, writes sociologist Lloyd Vernor Ballard (1936, p. 230), that meets "a definite social need universally recognized. It is not the product of philanthropic zeal but of basic social causes working toward a fundamental social objective." Much of the work has been and continues to be carried on behind the scenes by those groups and those strong and persuasive individuals; the shadow leaders, for example, whose ideas, as Alistair Black (1996, p. 90) says in describing the efforts of Edward Edwards to market the role that education could play in maintaining social stability through a diffusion of culture in mid-nineteenth century England,[10] "are scattered through many published and unpublished works, rather than presented in a coherent form."

Antonio Panizzi, a librarian in a position of national leadership and evidently in possession of considerable charisma, entered the scene at the critical moment at that time, and, according to biographer Barbara McCrimmon (1994, p. 495), "vigorously promoted his philosophy that such a publicly supported library was obligated to serve the needs of all students and scholars, whatever their financial or social position." Later, as director of the British Museum, Panizzi enforced the provision in the copyright law that required copies of all new publications to be deposited in that library, which was, according to cultural historian Richard D. Altick (1998, p. 215) an action prior to which "relatively little current literature was received." Considered together, such measures were taken with the purpose of making accessible as much of the accumulated and accumulating culture as possible to as large a part of the society as possible. To the extent that these efforts were successful, library historian James Thompson's (1977, p. 205–207) second principle of librarianship, which states that society conserves the library, is demonstrated and has been demonstrated since society's creation of this particular cultural technology. Thompson describes situations throughout history when libraries were threatened, but were protected by leaders of the society and also by the masses. Of course, the sole fact of the library's survival for thousands of tumultuous years bears the strongest testimony to the validity of this principle. People are the constituents of society; ideas are the constituents of culture.

The single greatest power of the library has been and continues to be its capacity to communicate over time and space in a reasoned and relatively well articulated fashion. Since it does constitute, therefore, a cultural technology, the library's history, writes cultural historian Raymond Irwin (1964, p. 15) "is in brief the history of this conquest of space and time." Analogies of the human memory and the computer memory are inescapable, as neuroscientist Merlin Donald (1991, p. 310) makes evident: "Just as the invention of hard storage was an economical and flexible, in fact essential, feature in expanding the powers of computers, external storage was an extremely important and efficient innovation in the history of human cognition." He draws a distinction (pp. 308–309) between biological memory, which resides in the brain, and external memory, which resides in a variety of non-biological media that are a major factor in intellectual endeavor. Like the human brain, it functions as a true network, Donald writes (p. 310), "for the resources of the system are shared, and the system functions as a unit larger than any of its individual components... they transport the very limited capabilities of the individual into realms that would not be remotely reachable by an isolated mind."

But it is useful to remember that culture behaves as a system[11] so that, just as the system must have organized itself at some propitious juncture in time to be able to accept an innovation, once that innovation is introduced there are greater or lesser ripple affects throughout its entirety. Social anthropologist Wilson D. Wallis (1930, p. 432) postulates that "The culture may become more diverse, but the parts remain interdependent; and if gains in one phase of the culture are not to be offset by losses in another, then with every new device, idea, or knowledge, there must be a new integration, a new evaluation, and a new orientation of the culture."

Thus, an understanding begins to emerge of the library as cultural technology, the durable material expression of adaptation to an environment that has enabled societies to live beyond survival toward the full realization of humanity. From this perspective, the library is much like "the buildings, tools, weapons, ornaments, and other surviving constituents that are interrelated as elements in a functioning whole," which archeologist V. Gordon Childe (1951, p. 16) includes as part of "the durable material expression of an adaptation to an environment, human as well as physiographical, that enabled a society to survive and develop." But the library is more than those kinds of technologies. Without identifying the library per se, anthropologist André Leroi-Gourhan (1993, p. 229) is none the less specific about function in his statement that "The creation of the first artificial tool by the first anthropoid put technics [technologies] outside the scope of zoological realities and outside the multimillennial course of evolution, and at the same time made the social memory capable of adding to itself at a rapid rate." The surrounding paragraphs contain the crux of the case to be made about the place of the library in cultural evolution. For it is at this point that the concept of library is advanced not just as a specific set of services that attempts to meet the equally specific needs of society in ways that have been suggested very thoughtfully by many others as, for example, a source of entertainment and education, by library historian and philosopher Ajit Kumar Mukherjee (1966, p. 55), or as "an *instrument* of informative education . . . in fact, a *method* of education," by sociologist Lloyd Vernor Ballard (1936, p. 231), and not just as "an instrument of research," suggested by philosopher Abraham Kaplan (1964, p. 298). The contention set forth here is that library, while being all those things and more, is considerably greater than the sum of all those specific purposes would suggest. As a concept, it is a cultural technology in the fullest sense of a selected evolutionary concept of mechanism and capacity to extend the power of the mind. The reasoning of biologists Peter and Jean Medawar (1977, p. 52) is of significance here: They write that the characterization of such instruments as the microscope, the telescope, the airplane, the amplifier, and other technologies as external organs of mankind "is not merely whimsical, because all sensory instruments report back through our ordinary or endosomatic senses and all motor instruments are programmed by ourselves either in their actual operation or by reason of the design characteristics that have been built into them." The library concept and its actualization are extensions of language, reasoning, and memory. Such extensions of fundamental and distinctively human capacity are akin to extensions of body, for example the arm, the leg, the ear, and the eye, but differ from them because they extend, perhaps even without limitation, not just the capacity and capability of the brain, but the potential of the mind, and not only of individuals, but also of societies and larger cultures.

Those cultural technologies that extend more specifically the powers of the human brain are referred to by Kenneth Boulding (1983, p. 10) as "the 'prosthetic devices' of the mind, which create records and facilitate the transmission of knowledge from one mind to another. The invention of writing, the first great discovery in this regard, enormously accelerated both the growth and the security of the noosphere." He elaborates (p. 11) that it was not until the invention of writing that the noosphere (commonly accepted knowledge) could expand almost indefinitely, and that "The development of specialized institutions for the storing and transmission of knowledge, like libraries and universities, also assisted this process." Similarly, Sir Karl Popper (1972, p. 239) notes that "Instead of growing better memories and brains, we grow paper, pens, pencils, typewriters, dictaphones, the printing press and libraries." How important is this in the general scheme of evolution? Boulding (1978,

p. 124) is far from alone in his reasons for finding that the knowledge process dominates societal evolution, for "It provides the adaptability that expands the niches and that finds substitute forms of energy and materials when an existing form becomes scarce. Energy and materials are very flexible limitations, because they can both be pushed out by the growth of knowledge, though sometimes this fails to happen." But in that case, he adds, "It is the knowledge limitation that tends to be dominant."

The culture is a system highly dependent on knowledge for its energy and renewal to continue and to evolve, and on the technologies it creates to advance and disseminate that knowledge. "All in all," writes sociologist Régis Debray (2000, p. 12) "*just as there can be no cultural transmission without technological means, so is there no purely technological transmission.*" Many decades ago, Lloyd Vernor Ballard (1936, p. 165) summarized a central feature of the knowledge process in cultural evolution:

> At any given moment, of course, the educative process is also limited by the amount of wisdom and experience which a given group has accumulated. Moreover, in any given situation, education is also restricted by the quantity and kind of knowledge which is accessible. The essential difference between primitive and later education appears at this point. In modern institutions it is apparent that the effectiveness of the educative process is conditioned by the learning of those who teach and the library and laboratory facilities with which they function as well as by the maturity of the subject matter which is to be transmitted. Education, then, cannot transcend knowledge.

Psychologist and neuroscientist Merlin Donald (2001, p. 305) describes the power of symbolic technology, which is "the enterprise of manufacturing and crafting external symbolic artifacts and devices." He notes both the vast cultural storehouse such devices as books and museums include in symbolic technology, and the resultant symbolic storage systems they have led to, amounting to a permanent group memory. What distinguishes symbolic technologies from what archeologists call material culture, Donald says, is that "they are designed specifically to help us think, remember, and represent reality." He elaborates (p. 308):

> Minds that use such devices are changed by that intimate process of interaction. Influence flows both ways, from thinker to symbol and from symbol to thinker. The symbol grows on the page or easel and then invades the mind and takes it over. The reciprocal flow can generate amazing changes in direction, and it is an infinitely open-ended process because it can carry on over many generations. It enables human culture to conquer time and space, its intellectual adventures having been permanently preserved for anyone with the codes to decipher them.

Symbolic and external to the mind, individually and culturally, the library function is the prime example, not just another example, of a cultural technology. The library function, to apply Donald's words (p. 309) ensures the "stable, permanent, virtually unlimited memory records that are infinitely reformattable and more easily displayed to awareness."

Summary

The social transcript is essential to cultural evolution and is, in fact, what makes that possible. For many reasons, it is best transmitted in recorded form, a written record in any number of formats that can be shared. The library was created and is maintained as an essential cultural function solely because of the unique intellectual qualities of humanity, and it is an extension that optimizes those qualities.

As discussed earlier, the term 'selection' applies to cultural evolution in ways that differ from its application to biological evolution, yet is an equally influential and equally significant influence. In the past five hundred thousand years of humanity's existence, writes archeologist V. Gordon Childe (1951, p. 177), "an infinity of innovations must have been attempted or suggested. Owing to a rigorous process of selection, only a fraction have survived as being in the long run beneficial." The library function is among those select few. Sociologist F. Stuart Chapin (1928, p. 385) describes an evolutionary scenario that is highly applicable to the library:

> Beginning with pre-literate peoples and gaining headway with the invention of writing culture has accumulated during the last five thousand years at an ever-accelerating rate. The invention of power machinery and the creation of an economic organization designed for quantity production have combined to facilitate the piling-up process of new traits of material culture. Human behavior conditioned to and habituated to these new culture traits has fallen into patterns which have become conventionalized into the varied configurations of non-material culture which characterize our contemporary civilization.

Science historian George Basalla (1988, p. 63) rightly asserts that "If evolutionary change is to occur, then novelty must find a way to assert itself in the midst of the continuous." We have seen that timing is critical in this regard and that selection leading to the cultural adaptation of the selected innovation are requisite to the production of that evolutionary change. The library is at once an external memory, a medium of communication, and a tool for reasoning.

Moreover, language, being "the most tenacious of all group memories," as Régis Debray (2000, p. 56) says, is also by far the most powerful of cultural stabilizers and transmitters, and it is, most obviously, the sine qua non of that social institution called library. One of the powerful influences exerted by the library in the process of cultural evolution is its presentation of the diversity of extant thought and the potential it has to unite society. "It would not be absurd to maintain, in opposition to the clichés, that culture is what splits apart the human species while technology unites them. The one causes them to dig in, with trenches and barricades; the other clears and flattens the way," writes Debray (p. 56). The library protects a very useful creative tension. For facts never exist in isolation, psychobiologist Henry Plotkin (1998, p. 256) concludes, "except, perhaps, right at the beginning of cognitive life for each person. Facts always aggregate into or become attached to higher-order knowledge structures. Down the years various names have been given to such psychological structures, like schemas, frames, scripts and memory organization packets." In this process, culture is evolved by humans for humans, and thus is distinct from anything else. Philosopher Karl Popper's evolutionary epistemology seeks to explain that the knowledge we have, even when it is highly abstract knowledge, is part of or, an extension of, the adaptive evolutionary process, which began many million years ago when living cells first emerged, writes historian Peter Munz (1985, p. 6). "This process began and has continued through random mutations and selective retentions of some mutations. These adaptations never 'represent' the environment; and the selections are not justified but only tolerated by the environment. Evolutionary epistemology treats knowledge as non-representational and unjustified." Knowledge is what humanity makes of it.

Library as function is a cultural artifact, specifically a cultural *technology*, that has evolved along with the rest of culture. It was created, or selected, because at the time it first came along it *could* be created; the timing was right, and it has been sustained for the same reasons. The library concept has met the need because, as a technology, it is an extension of the greatest of human capacities, among which are the thought processes from reasoning to creativity to memory, and therefore it is also an expeditor and facilitator of the most distinctly human societal intentions. Social anthropologist Jack Goody (2000, p. 136) argues that "in no sense is technology nonhuman, since it is developed and used by human minds and hands. Finally, the products of technology are external only in a formal sense, since they are formed by humanity and in turn form humanity." And in concept the library is an extension of the most human of characteristics. Anthropologist Margaret Mead (1958, p. 483) observes that when contemplating the history of human culture from the perspective of evolutionary theory, two differing outcomes of adaptation can be emphasized in describing them: one being a permanent acquisition; the other being an acquisition that is temporally or spatially limited. An emphasis upon permanent acquisition, she writes, "focuses attention upon the extreme flexibility and survival strength of mankind, in that once a form of cultural behavior has been developed its continuance depends not upon the specific genetic capacities of the group who have developed it but upon the general capacities of men as a species to communicate with one another and to learn from experience." This description of the permanent cultural acquisition applies quite well to the library function in cultural evolution.

But even in view of such fundamental considerations librarianship has allowed, or perhaps caused, the *purpose* of the technology to be overshadowed by the *mechanics* of the technology. Educational psychologist Donaldo Macedo draws an analogy that fits this situation. In his Foreword to a book on language and mind by linguist James Paul Gee (1992), Macedo observes that "Gee elegantly demonstrates that to explicate the internal workings of the machine, and not the uses to which the machine is put in the world of value conflicts and political action is to treat each piece of the *clothesline* separately so as to never allow us to reach a level of comprehension of the complex whole of relations among objects."

It is very easy to point to structural analogies between certain biological processes and the processes involved in technological innovation, asserts physicist John Ziman (2002, p. 4). One can immediately think of mechanisms whereby material artifacts, as well as those less tangible cultural entities, such as scientific theories, social customs, laws, commercial firms, and similar conceptual entities "undergo *variation* by *mutation* or *recombination* of characteristic *traits*. Many different variants are put on the market (or published, or practiced, or adjudicated, or invested in, etc. as the case may be). Here they are subjected to severe *selection*, by customers and other users (or competing groups, courts appeal, banks, and so on). The entities that *survive* are *replicated*, *diffuse* through the population and become the predominant type."

The cultural technology called library was created and sustained because it was selected by a culture to assist in its adaptation to the environment and its purposeful modification of the environment, and to fulfill needs that transcend basic survival: needs to understand, to imagine, to create, to communicate, to refine thought, to innovate, and, in short, to enhance existence and realize human potential, the potential of humanity among all the species. Human technology, summarizes anatomist Kathleen Gibson (1993, p. 256), "is inextricably linked with human social structure. The human lifestyle is not only tool-based, but many tools and constructions are used and reused over long periods of time." It is "cooperative and social in nature"

(p. 257). The library concept was selected by the culture to assist in the peculiarly human effort to control nature and improve the human condition in its changing environment. It functions as an extension of mind for individual and society, and while natural to humanity also has become second nature, almost like the common understanding of the dependability of gravitational force. Biologist and neurophilosopher Patricia Smith Churchland (2002, p. 318) brings to this discussion the highly relevant concepts of situated cognition and distributed cognition. Situated cognition is a condition of the brain that does not require a complete representation of any given situation, that the brain can work on the basis of selective representation on a need-to-know basis, relying on "the fact that the world is mostly stable and continues to be there, available for second looks and closer looks." It is a form of security, a cultural security.

Related to this concept, the theory of distributed cognition accounts for the fact that "social animals can divide cognitive labor, and that if a brain can represent which person has which competence, this general knowledge is far more economical than representing all of the detailed knowledge in one head." One need not learn everything from scratch, or perhaps even at all, because of the understanding that knowledge both broad and deep of many phenomena is a part of the intellectual environment. The library is an obvious contributor, in symbol and concrete, of this kind of security that is essential to both advancing culture and just getting on with life. Educator Lyman Bryson (1947, p. 173) finds that the most direct way to assess the success or quality among societies is through "the degree to which they make possible the attainment of the ends which their citizens are taught to pursue. The educational agencies, and all the other more or less self-conscious institutions of a culture, inculcate ideals, and all the institutions of the culture provide opportunities. If the opportunities make fulfillment of the inculcated ideals possible in high degree and for a large proportion of the group, there will be as much good in the lives of the members as the group circumstances can provide." Bryson's reference is not limited to the temporal benefit of individuals but extends to that experienced by humanity through eternity. Anthropologist Tim Ingold (1993b, p. 450) outlines the scenario by which such a broad sweep is made by harnessing the appropriate elements for the advancement of rationality in the human condition: "Thus intelligence is the faculty of reason, language its vehicle, and technology the means by which a rational understanding of the external world is turned to account for human benefit." The place of the library in cultural evolution is as natural as the nose on our face.

The technology of writing enabled preservation of thought in the sense of rendering precise any specific thought easily subject to scrutiny. The cultural technology of library took this advance of this extracerebral memory a step forward. It offered a more durable preservation of thought and placed it in the context of other thoughts, thus reflecting the way culture functions, and rendered those thoughts subject to relatively facile scrutiny and comparison in a manner ordered by reason. The brain is the representation of the world as a particular individual knows it, and, collectively, of the world as a given society knows it; the library functions as a representation of those worlds and their limitless possibilities. It may be useful now to set into relief the characteristics that distinguish the library function from those of other social institutions and commercial enterprises.

PART III

Convergence of Mind, Society, and Evolution in Library Philosophy

CHAPTER 6

The Unique Function of the Library

> There are few things in the world more interesting than the disclosure of facts which throw into fresh perspective a mass of other historic facts.
>
> —John L. Lowes, 1933

Introduction

As does any other social institution, the library functions within a context of time and space as part of the fabric of forces that determine the nature of that time and that space. But the library's connections to the past are carried through to the present in extraordinarily explicit ways, and its connections are self-consciously harnessed in preparation for the future, because the library's purpose of integrating the intellectual past into the present and ensuring its integration into the future is consistent in society and deeply interwoven into the patterns of cultural evolution. "The idea of function," according to geneticist and science philosopher Bentley Glass (1985, p. 37), "is, in fact, a teleological notion [in the sense of metaphysical belief] unless construed in the light of evolutionary adaptation as a product of natural selection." The three chapters comprising Part Two of this book are dedicated to demonstrating that the library is, indeed, the product of natural selection for the purpose of adaptation to environmental change in ways that make it unique among social institutions because they address considerations that are uniquely human.

Nonetheless, the library manifests its function in ways that conceal such an understanding, thus making the function appear upon cursory examination to be more a cacophony than a symphony. That is largely because what comes first into view, as described in Chapter 2, is no more than the great variety of procedures and transactions witnessed in the variety of *types of libraries* that lead to fulfillment of the ultimate *library* function in society. Second, in the words of philosopher I. C. Jarvie (1996, p. 604), it is because "Rarely is there a perfect fit between a subject as defined by academic bureaucracy and what its practitioners actually do," at least upon cursory examination; or it may just be that the practitioners are not guided each day by ponderous theoretical reflection any more than the theoreticians are continuously in touch with clinical practice. Third, library service usually presents itself as a snapshot of the work of many apparently unrelated efforts in a specific place and time rather than as a video of the contribution of the entire corporate enterprise over a greater expanse of space and time.

Psychobiologist Henry Plotkin (1998, p. 245) identifies the important distinction, which is intended in the present study, that the focus is on a concept or process of indefinite duration, not the building or the discrete acts it houses. He writes that it is "the characteristics of the thing we are trying to explain. It isn't the pots and pans, the temples and music, the space ships and the Internet. These are the material products of culture. As a process, what matters is that culture involves shared knowledge and powerful cohesive forces within a social group, and these together give rise to the immaterial products of social constructions like money, justice and science . . . shared knowledge plus cohesion equals social construction." And finally, the full function of the library does not simply include its foundation in the past in both an artifactual sense and an intellectual sense, but rather is immensely dependent upon it for the presentation of intellectual options to the culture, a consideration which is never immediately in view and rarely understood in its entirety. Humans tend not to think on the large scale and in long term, but humanity does, and employs its institutions for that purpose.

All institutions evolve along with society and are at the same time a part of the cultural energy that sustains its continued evolution. Their past is significant in understanding their present, and by dint of that fact they are a part of their past. For most of them, however, the past is no longer important to their present function beyond the contextual understanding of itself that it offers for conceptualization to be used as a tool for understanding and acting in the present and for contemplating the future. There are, of course, historical stages in the development of social institutions, and that is true as well for the library.

But, in the library concept, the recorded past is much more than a stage through which it develops and evolves, because stewardship of the social transcript constitutes the essential function of the library in society and in cultural evolution. The present never really supersedes the past; culture is derivative. This is particularly significant because the social transcript is considerably more than a record of the past, and it is more than the basis for the present and future. The social transcript is a seemingly limitless natural resource for intellectual development of all kinds, and just as passing along the transcript is the essential function of writing it is also the essential function of the library. Again it is useful to stress that the determination of the appropriate theoretical basis from which to examine this function becomes the critical issue in understanding the library and its unique contribution to humanity through cultural evolution.

Theory

Once function is determined, theory becomes the tool for the uncovering of philosophy. While it may often be difficult to establish theory appropriate to the explanation of the physical sciences, it is even more so in other fields of reasoned discourse, the social sciences and human sciences, for example. Librarianship generally is considered a social (behavioral) science, sometimes with a humanities flavor, so theory is not as straightforward as it may at least appear to be in the physical sciences, which, as discussed in Chapter 1, have become the model for most serious investigation. In any case, however, the application of reason, observation, and questioning in the search for understanding follows an ideal relative to the nature of the object in question. Philosopher David-Hillel Ruben (1998, p. 870) describes some of the differences in theory development and application that distinguish the natural sciences from the social sciences.

> In the developed natural sciences, there are controlled experiments and predictions. Neither seem available to the social scientist. Natural scientists attempt to formulate the laws that govern the phenomena they study. Is this a reasonable goal for the social scientist? . . . Finally, in natural science, we distinguish between theory and observation in a relatively sharp way, and we believe that a rational person should accept that theory which is best confirmed by observations. It is not clear that we can make the same distinction in the social sciences, nor that theory is supported by observation in just the same way. Our observations of the social world seem even more coloured by the theory we employ than is the case in the natural sciences.

Literary critic and theorist N. Katherine Hayles (1990, p. 36) adds that "In science, 'theory' generally means a set of interrelated propositions that have predictive power and therefore have the potential to be refuted. In literature, by contrast, 'theory' means a set of speculative statements that serve as guides to reading and interpreting texts." The social sciences and the humanities most certainly are not inferior to the natural sciences, but they are different in the most fundamental ways, as Ruben and Hayles well note. Yet, all serious investigation follows from theory.

In fact, Ruben (1998, p. 870) writes that theory and observation are clearly distinguished in the natural sciences, such that the theory best confirmed by observation is generally the one accepted, but also that "theory is not supported by observation in just the same way. Our observations of the social world seem even more coloured by the theory we employ than is the case in the natural sciences." Science philosopher Mary Midgley (2002, p. 119) finds that, because of centuries of the obvious success experienced by the natural sciences, twenty-first century ideology provides strong encouragement to identify "a single standpoint which is satisfactory because it is scientific—a standpoint so solid and final that it is self-sufficient and will save us the trouble of attending to any others." In a world that sometimes can seem to present an overabundance of choices of information, including highly conflicting information, premium is awarded to a kind of intellectual security, valid or not.

It is quite likely that most who are not physical or other natural scientists learn about the ways of those sciences via scholars who study them from the outside, such as sociologists and philosophers. And one can surmise that scientists are often dissatisfied with the picture that is thus painted for the lay public. Be that as it may, sociologist Stephen Toulmin observes that within science there are variances, in fact, that do not fit the traditionally construed picture of this extraordinary phenomenon that is unlike any other engaged in via serious and reasoned discourse. In comparing physics and natural history, for example, Toulmin casts physics as an explanatory science, and natural history as a descriptive science, saying (1953, p. 44) "physicists do not hunt out regularities in phenomena, but investigate the form of regularities whose existence is already recognized." He also refers (p. 145) to "the fact that natural historians are committed for the most part to the everyday classification of their subject-matter, whereas it is open to physical scientists to reclassify theirs as they go along." He concludes (p. 148) from this that "it is not Nature that is Uniform, but scientific procedure; and it is uniform only in this, that it is methodical and self-correcting." Surely, humanity is a manifestation of nature. Going considerably further in this line of explication, biologist Lewis Wolpert (1993, p. 108) finds that many distinguished philosophers of science "recognize the failure of philosophy to help understand the nature of science. They have not discovered a scientific method that provides a formula or prescriptions for how to make discoveries. But many famous scientists have given advice." And he lists a dozen suggestions leading in all directions, concluding with the advice that "One could do no better than to try them all. No one method, no paradigm, will capture the process of science. There is no such thing as *the* scientific method."

But there is a long history of the influence of supposed scientific method on the social sciences. Philosopher Wilfrid Sellars (1963, p. 106) writes that "The term 'theory', it is generally recognized, covers a wide variety of explanatory frameworks resembling one another by that family resemblance which is easy to discern but most difficult to describe." The theory with which he is concerned is that of the social sciences and the humanities, primarily the latter, which postulates unobserved entities to explain observable phenomena. Sellars (1963, p. 106) stressed almost half a century ago that theory in these areas was "still suffering from the effects of a Procrustean treatment by positivistically oriented philosophies of science," which is to say scientism.

Science philosopher Carl G. Hempel would be in agreement on this, for Hempel (1965, p. 242) strongly asserts that in any field called a science "Only the establishment of specific laws can fill the general thesis with scientific content, make it amenable to empirical tests, and confer upon it an explanatory function. The elaboration of such laws with as much precision as possible seems clearly to be the direction in which progress in scientific explanation and understanding has to be sought." Two decades later, science sociologist Joseph Ben-David (1973, p. 47) sounded the often repeated and similar warnings about research specifically in the social sciences: "Scientific theories, which describe and explain regularities in empirically observed events, are as necessary to the professional practitioner as techniques and technical aids," and (p. 44) that "Unless we can create conditions to effectively control, test and follow up situations in which the findings of social science research are applied to practical purposes, social science research will be misused and exploited." To the extent that the social sciences have been bound to this rigid and sometimes inappropriate model, it would appear that their research is confronted with the impossible choice of adopting inappropriate ends or of slipping into insignificance.

The misleading fascination with science was recounted in Chapter 2 as one of the reasons for a failure to establish an agreed upon philosophy of the library. It is clear also that scientism has had a long and continuing influence on how scholarship is carried out, how its theory is developed, and how its process and product are received by the public. Surely it is a sound model if not applied literally to all phases of work in the social sciences and humanities; but when applied too literally and rigidly to those phenomena, the science model becomes a limiting factor. While those who adhered adamantly to the science model for all areas of scholarship, thereby finding many to fall below the standard, there were voices in opposition. Of those voices, Karl Popper and Jürgen Habermas stand out because they present compelling, influential cases. Popper (1959, pp. 279–280) argues that science has much in common with other fields, being comprised also of considerably more than verifiable elements:

> Science is not a system of certain, or well-established, statements; nor is it a system which steadily advances towards a state of finality . . . *We do not know: we can only guess.* And our guesses are guided by the unscientific . . . faith in laws, in regularities which we can uncover—discover. Like Bacon, we might describe our own contemporary science—"the method of reasoning which men now ordinarily apply to nature"—as consisting of "anticipations, rash and premature" and as "prejudices" . . . The old scientific ideal of *episteme*—of absolutely certain, demonstrable knowledge—has proved to be an idol. The demand for scientific objectivity makes it inevitable that every scientific statement must remain *tentative for ever.* It may indeed be corroborated, but every corroboration is relative to other statements which, again, are tentative.

Thus, Popper attempted to demystify a noble endeavor that really needed no mystique to achieve its success. Taking a different approach to the distinctions between the natural sciences and other areas of inquiry, Habermas focuses his attention on meaning, on the cognitive aspects of language communication, to distinguish the social from the natural sciences. He argues, writes philosopher and Habermas interpreter Andrew Edgar (2006, pp. 12–13) that the natural sciences, studying objects that exist independently of them as observers and that are subject to regular causal laws, are grounded in a refined and disciplined version of the daily practices of work and problem solving, with no regard for motivation or meaning. Quite to the contrary, Edgar explains, the subjective nature of motivation and meaning constitutes the primary interests of the social sciences. The natural and social sciences are not the same except in their shared efforts to achieve understanding as appropriate to their subject matter and to employ the best methods at their disposal. So, there are both significant differences and significant similarities.

Intellectual puzzles addressed by the philosophy of science may be similar to those addressed by the layman, but to some extent often, although not always, they can be supported through the use of laboratories and formal systems that are beyond the layman's reach. Puzzles encountered in the philosophy of the social sciences, however, are more closely akin to those addressed by the layman, albeit more rigidly and comprehensively. Philosopher David-Hillel Ruben (1998, p. 869) suggests, therefore, that "Since so much of the motivation for critical discussion of the problems in this area comes from philosophical reflection on these quite ordinary modes of thought and understanding, the field should perhaps be called 'the philosophy of *society*', to reflect this nonscientific, as well as the scientific, interest in those problems."

There can be little doubt that the far greater degree of access the public has to the social sciences as compared with access to the natural sciences has much to do with the considerably greater trust that is accorded the latter. In turn, this is a trust that stems in part from having precious little direct knowledge of the subject matter itself, since both the object of study and the procedures followed are beyond public view, so trust is placed in the more understandable methodology. Philosopher I. C. Jarvie 1996, p. 606) stresses the simple fact that "the idea that what makes social things social as opposed to inert are the meaning-generating activities of human beings which show themselves in rules of behaviour."

Language, for example, is not random noises but patterns that make sense. Clearly such rules are not natural in the sense understood in the natural sciences; rather they are activities that define and constitute human life together. We cannot then explain human conduct in the way that we offer mechanical causal explanation in science, but only by mastering from the inside the rules in use and their degrees of freedom. People do social things for reasons, not in obedience to laws." On a similar basis, science sociologist Joseph Ben-David (1973, p. 39) suggests that "the social science researcher ought to regard himself as a re-constructor of social structures and processes, working on the borderline of science and literature, as the clinician or engineer works on the borderline of science and art."[1]

A biologist and neurophilosopher who has spent most of her career studying the relation of philosophy and neuroscience, Patricia Smith Churchland (1986, p. 482) concludes that "In any case, it is a mistake to see science as standing in opposition to humanism; rather, it is the political and entrepreneurial *abuses* of scientific knowledge that have displayed a catastrophic disregard for humanistic principles." Elsewhere, Churchland (2002, p. 242) places the situation in a context that makes eminent sense. She traces the foundation for these two competing traditions to fifth century B.C. Greece and the differing epistemological views of Plato and Aristotle, but points out "that the distinction between the Platonic and Aristotelian methodologies is mainly a difference in *emphasis*, since Platonists perfectly well realize that if you want to know whether it is raining, you have to look, and Aristotelians perfectly well realize that imagination and reasoning are important in figuring out how the world really works." It is in large measure the social aspect of scholarship and science that is the cause of the many misunderstandings among the disciplines that then lead to problems of compared values, methods, and results.

Mind at the Center

Several decades ago, existentialist philosopher Maurice Merleau-Ponty stressed the need to keep in mind what he termed a "truth within situations,"[2] which is the idea that there is a primordial dimension of human being below the level of conscious awareness, and hence prior to reflection, judgment formation and explicit calculation. And this is where the chief problem for the social sciences resides, as political philosopher Michael H. Lessnoff (1975, p. 33) identifies it. He observes that "if social science is concerned with people, the empiricist view must somehow deal with the phenomena of the human mind—that is, with people's beliefs, desires, purposes, intentions, moral principles, values, etc.—for these appear to be closely connected with their actions (and interactions), but to lack the sorts of characteristics that empiricists consider the only ones science can take note of." He concludes that the choice for the empiricist is either to ignore mental phenomena altogether or study them "because they correspond to overt phenomena (of behaviour) which are open to empirical observation." There really is no responsible choice but to incorporate into social science theory and research the workings of the mind, rendering the task of the social scientist always very complex and often difficult to justify.

But behavioral psychologist B. F. Skinner (1965, p. 21) asserts that "A vague sense of order emerges from any sustained observation of human behavior," *observation* being the critical issue. In fact, this notion is presented by cultural historian Raymond Williams (1958, p. 301) as a warning to social scientists, who states that "The minds of men are shaped by their whole experience and the most skilful transmission of material which this experience does not confirm will fail to communicate. Communication is not only transmission; it is also reception and response." And there is within each individual tacit knowledge, the structure of which physical chemist Michael Polanyi (1966, p. x) writes, "shows that all thought contains components of which we are subsidiarily aware in the focal content of our thinking, and that all thought dwells in its subsidiaries, as if they were parts of our body. Hence thinking is not only necessarily intentional, as [Franz] Brentano has taught: it is also necessarily fraught with the roots that it embodies." Fundamental to the conditions of mind that are studied by social scientists is the influence of individual and group value systems, which constitute for sociologist Talcott Parsons (1949, pp. 592–593) the most significant single difference between the two areas of scientific study.

> Natural phenomena are, as an object of science, indifferent to human cultural achievements are the embodiments of value toward which we must, in some degree, take a value attitude. Hence our interest in them is directly determined by their relevance to the values which either the scientist himself shares or which are significant to him by agreement with his own values or conflict with them. It is this 'relevance to value' which constitutes the selective organizing principle for the empirical material of the social sciences.

With so broad a range of complex, often unfathomable, phenomena for investigation, it is no wonder that practice within the social sciences, including that of librarianship, should at times appear to diverge from its theory, even to the point perhaps of bearing no genuine relationship,[3] unlike the natural sciences, where the practice and the theory are one; that is, science is the theory and it is also clearly what one does. Sociologist F. Stuart Chapin (1928, p. 402) may have had the answer to this conundrum more than eight decades ago, summarizing that "The real significance of scientific method for social science consists in its logical procedures of symbolic substitution." By this he meant that we can record experience in language symbols, which are "endowed with independent and objective existence," so as to enable others to review them in a trial and error mode. Ultimately, peer review of the theory or experience at question is the critical factor; it is the formalized manifestation of social criticism, of trial and error. The work of Jürgen Habermas offers another perspective on positivist claims that all scientific inquiry should be based upon the model of the natural sciences, citing its limiting factors. Philosopher Andrew Edgar 2006, p. 14) interprets the thought of Habermas to mean that "Such an approach is not only mistaken as a theory of science, it is also politically dangerous, as it reduces human beings to objects that can be manipulated like molecules or light waves. It encourages social engineering, as opposed to a democratic polity that recognizes the importance of public agreement and understanding of government policies."

Within this context of theory, general considerations about library theory do not differ from those that apply to any of the other social sciences. The library, however, brings them to bear in their entirety, manifesting the full range of possibilities, whereas the other social sciences employ parts of social science theory as appropriate to the specific discipline in question. For the library functions on the basis of its totality, rather than on the basis of separate, but related, disciplines as in the case of the cluster called social sciences; it is an amalgamation of form and function, of operations and purposes guided by a holistic philosophy. "Those who consider, as I have considered in these chapters," writes library theorist Ronald C. Benge (1970, p. 246), "that sociological factors represent a fundamental part of the theory of librarianship, must therefore go beyond the five laws [of S. R. Ranganathan] in order to identify or discuss these factors." The focus of library theory is kaleidoscopic because of its relation to thought in all disciplines, mixed together with the variety of a changing humanity by its evolutionary function in time. Two special conditions of the library appear to underpin its philosophy, its theory, and its practice. They are treated next in this chapter as the ideal of intellectual freedom and the concept of library as place.

Intellectual Freedom

At the close of World War II, according to sociologist Craig Calhoun (2002, p. 372), Karl Popper argued that the best state is one that leaves room for the criticism of its own actions and policies—and the adoption, as necessary, of new courses of action. Popper's thought is shared by many others around the globe, of course, for the freedom to inquire, to think, and to express thought, as demonstrated in Chapters 3 and 4, has much to do with general culture and its evolution.

In fact, a conclusion that may be taken for granted in most Western nations today actually was reached over the course of a relatively brief time in history, according to intellectual historian Charles Van Doren (1991, p. 303). He writes that "In 1900 the great majority of the peoples of the earth did not understand what democracy was and consequently did not desire it. And even among those who understood democracy, not all desired it or believed it was possible to put it into practice." Van Doren points out that the situation reversed itself during the following century. Two world wars and the creation of a bomb that suggested the ease with which a livable planet could be made unlivable, surely led to questioning and reasoning about the human condition and the choices that might inhere. "The most profound measure of the comparative 'merits' of different societies," writes Stephen Toulmin (1972, p. 351), "will then be their respective degrees of 'adaptability': i.e. the scope they allow for social or institutional innovation, and the forums and procedures they recognize for the critical reform of current institutions and customs. Such a populational analysis of social change is relevant, with appropriate changes, not merely to complete societies but also to their individual institutions."

Earlier discussion in this text referred to the fact that cultural evolution occurs in society-by-society order as a universal function, but not all taking the same directions, for each society maintains a distinctiveness in the course of change based on the concurrent environmental conditions of each. Thus, according to cultural anthropologist Elman R. Service (1968, p. 222), "Sometimes this adaptive process brings forth striking advances that permit greater dominance, all-round adaptability, and growth." The particular striking advance under investigation in this book is the library concept, which the cultural technology selected to maintain the social transcript for the options it opens to humanity.

One of the foremost thinkers and writers on behalf of the public library movement in nineteenth century England, Edward Edwards (1865, p. 12) describes the discovery of a number of clay tablets dating from about 650 BC, which he says could be called a Public Library in Clay. The tablets had been placed in the palace of Sardanapalus, king of Assyria, expressly for the purpose of public instruction, as "a foundation of government." Edwards quotes the translated inscription as "I have placed it in the midst of my palace for the instruction of my subjects." Although the segment of society the king intended by the term subjects nearly three thousand years ago would not likely convert to the general populace of society today, so large a part of it being literate, the fundamental intention or spirit of his beneficence may correspond fairly well to that of the democratic ideals realized through the development of the public library.

Thus, sociologist Alvin Johnson (1938, pp. 67–68) emphasizes that "Without the book, the thoughtful and scholarly book, written by an author who accepts responsibility and hopes for the permanence of his work, there can be no adult education worthy of the name. The essential role of the public library in our democratic system is therefore cardinal." The library evolved with the culture of the respective society, which was at least the essential idea that the sharing of knowledge, more or less freely depending upon the particular society, is a good thing. "As society attained greater complexity," writes Jesse Shera (1949, p. 248), "as industry developed and increased in diversity, as populations crowded into congested city areas, as labor and economic life, largely because of the impact of the machine, became more and more specialized, the functions of the library reflected a corresponding intricacy and growing importance."

In that connection, cultural historian Richard D. Altick (1998, p. 5) draws attention to an interesting effect the spread of reading had upon the social habits of mid-nineteenth-century England, writing "Above all, the democratizing of reading led to a far-reaching revolution in English culture. No longer were books and periodicals written chiefly for the comfortable few; more and more, as the century progressed, it was the ill-educated mass audience with pennies in its pocket that called the tune to which writers and editors danced." Political and social democratization creates a wider and more flexible market for intellectual experiences of all kinds, which further encourages responsive production and distribution, which further attracts readers to learning and entertainment via the various print media.

The availability of information sources of all kinds is a condition proven to be essential to democracy, and the library has functioned as a key social institution responsible for that condition through time and across space for many centuries. To the extent that Peter L. Berger and Thomas Luckmann (1966, p. 5) are right in their interpretation of ideology as "Ideas serving as weapons for social interests," the library enables consideration of these competing ideas in a framing context. In principle it is the public library more than any other type, that depends upon the prevalence of social democracy to maintain its health, just as democracy depends upon the library to flourish. The concept of democracy in society is fundamental to that of library in cultural evolution, varying only by degree of interpretation from one location to another, or one society to another.

Library educator and historian James H. Wellard (1940, pp. 155–168) discusses in some detail the democratic values that align with all libraries, but in the most general sense with the public library. He observes in particular (p. 160) that the public library is distinct from all other popular print-distributing agencies because it is social and educational in purpose. "It is not concerned solely with the diffusion of knowledge, but with the intellectual improvement of those groups which most need it and have the least opportunity of getting it. The recognition of this principle is what we mean by the philosophy of librarianship; and the practice of it constitutes the sociology of the profession... The political position of the library, its social relationships, its place in the general field of knowledge, technical and professional considerations, can all be brought together for the fulfillment of this objective, which springs from the human values implicit in the democratic creed." The potential of this cultural technology to fulfill its purpose in society is congruent with the degree of freedom in which it functions.

From a more pragmatic vantage point, public librarian and philosopher A. Broadfield (1949, p. 51) stresses the problem-solving potential brought to bear on social situations through the exchange of ideas and the democratic framework that is conducive to that phenomenon. "If these problems cannot be solved by means of ideas they cannot be solved at all, since force does not solve problems but replaces them with new ones. Ideas must remain freely communicable in books, periodicals, microfilms, and the discussion to which these lead." The basic idea behind the library is to bring people and ideas together, whether physically or spiritually, when and as the individual wishes. Chemist Michael Polanyi (1951, p. 34) makes very clear the essentiality of academic freedom to science in his assertion that "If one day all communications were cut between scientists, that day science would practically come to a standstill."[4] And this result applies as well to all personal scholarship, as described earlier, and cultural evolution.

Among the key concepts comprehended in the concept of intellectual freedom are cooperation, sharing, knowledge, ideas, integration, communication, opportunity, and innovation. As described in Chapter 5 they are also key considerations in library function, just as they are fundamental to the human condition. Discussing the major lessons he had learned about science during his experience through World War II, physicist Karl Taylor Compton (1950, pp. 25–26) identifies the following: the cooperative character of scientific process, depending on the stimulating interplay of ideas and the accumulation of facts and skills; the unpredictable and uncontrollable origin of the new ideas and discoveries which produce scientific progress; to the extent that we wish fundamental science to advance, we must maintain the maximum of opportunity for competent scientist to follow their own bent and to communicate freely with each other; teamwork has proved extraordinarily effective in producing results; increasing extent to which a basic advance in theory or technique in one branch of science is likely to provide new concepts, or new tools, which can open up new frontiers for exploration and exploitation in other fields of science or art. The spirit of intellectual freedom does not simply enable the mental activity essential to living as a human being in a human society but also encourages and stimulates the thought processes and related communication.

Science and scholarship, which depend on the communication of ideas for their validation and acceptance, and society, which depends equally on the communication of those ideas for their value to humanity, function most productively in a democratic environment. Karl Popper (1959, p. 279, note 2) does not believe that knowledge just accumulates because experience does. He reasons instead that "the advance of science depends upon the free competition of thought, and thus upon freedom, and that it must come to an end if freedom is destroyed." And surely, where freedom is restricted, the value of the library as a social institution withers even as its concrete façade of strength endures. "Science can only flourish in an atmosphere of freedom and uncoerciveness," says economic philosopher Kenneth Boulding (1956, p. 80). The parallels between science and the general rationality of humanity are striking because the practice of science can be considered rationality institutionalized, the institution being science. For that reason, the library functions in the way that science functions: that is, it functions best to the extent its ideas and thought processes are unfettered. "Academic freedom consists in the right to choose one's own problem for investigation, to conduct research free from any outside control, and to teach one's subject in the light of one's own opinions," writes chemist Michael Polanyi (1951, p. 33), and "Academic freedom is of course never an isolated phenomenon. It can exist only in a free society; for the principles underlying it are the same on which the most essential liberties of society as a whole are founded" (p. 45). In their most pure state, the motives of science and of the library concept are identical and share a heavy dependence upon democratic principles.

In the course of making his pleas for a library philosophy many decades ago. Periam Danton (1934, p. 547) made it clear that such a philosophy could have value only to the extent that it reflected the philosophy of the community in which it functioned. He stated that "The major aims and objectives of librarianship, as of any constituent of human society, must be derived from the predominating ideals of that society. Consequently, before a library philosophy can be formulated, there must be an understanding and recognition of the ideals and purposes of the society into which that philosophy must fit." Virtually everything we know about the place of the library in society confirms his assessment. Where the library specifically is concerned, however, the most fundamental among the possible ideals of any society would have to be the democratic ideal. The manner in which the library could implement any other ideals would be heavily dependent upon the degree of absence or presence of that one fundamental consideration. And it is in that sense, or in that context, that cultural historian Raymond Irwin (1949, p. 124) posits that "Although librarianship, like scholarship, must be free in the true sense of the word, this does not mean that a library loses thereby its individuality. Every library is to some extent coloured by its environment; every library reflects the community it serves, and assimilates itself to its intellectual surroundings. It can and should do this while still remaining free in its scholarship and book selection." So the basis for acting upon any of the values and interests held by the community is found in the extent of influence and acceptance of the ideals of democracy, not necessarily as a political system but as a concept in support of mind. The realization of free will is itself dependent upon open avenues, and the brain is eager to seize the opportunity to pursue them. Philosopher John Searle (2007, p. 58) reasons that "if free will is a genuine feature of the world and not merely an illusion, then it must have a neurobiological reality; there must be some feature of the brain that realizes free will."

Essential to both the daily and the evolutionary function of the library, and of any other intellectual process, is what Richard Altick (1998, p. 374) states about the recognition of the following assessment assigned by the populace to democratic ideals, perhaps most often by the populace in a relatively democratic state. He observes that

> The average human being does not press for cultural advantages as he does for what he deems his political or social rights. But the capacity to find knowledge, inspiration, escape, and sheer delight in reading is latent in far more people than have ever become confirmed booklovers. And that capacity has nothing to do with social or economic status. The memoirs of self-educated men from the nineteenth-century English working class, as well as the experience, both then and now, of teachers, librarians, and publishers of inexpensive series of good books, prove that the desire and the ability to enrich one's life through reading are not contingent on occupation, weekly wage, or family background.

When realized, it is the democratic ideal that optimizes the intellectual potential of individuals and societies, and that also forms the basis for the library to function in its most human capacity, which is to encourage application of the mind[5] through the range of its totality.

Writings about the role of the library in advancing a democratic society are legion, largely reflecting the logical need of a self-governed state to be as well educated as possible, and as free as possible in its communication; but that is not the primary interest behind discussion of democratic ideals in the present study. In writing of the purpose of the library, A. W. McClellan (1973, p. 134), librarian and library educator, presents a different perspective from which to achieve the same conclusions: "Without freedom, the quality of life cannot develop. The freedom which the library stands for thwarts the ever present pressures for conformity," suggesting a proactive stance.

Toward the close of World War II, librarian and recent European émigrée Myra Kolitsch (1945, p. 31) advocated making of democratic ideals the philosophy of librarianship, rather than an enabler of the fullest expression of librarianship, so tightly did she see them entwined: "The philosophy of librarianship is to be arrived at by analyzing the philosophy of democracy and discovering how librarianship can aid in the realization of democratic ideals . . . Librarianship is but one of the social forces which can and must find its own justification, aims, and ideals in an understanding and practice of true democracy." Thus, librarianship would amount to a method of promoting social democracy. More realistic, or at least better balanced, is the assessment offered by library historian and philosopher Ajit Kumar Mukherjee (1966, p. 55) that "The predominant ideals of the modern society are based principally on democratic conventions underlined in the ideas of freedom of thought, freedom of circulation of knowledge and freedom of instruction. It is the library whose function is to uphold the sanctity of such ideas."

Notions of the library's social calling to stimulate the freedom of thought and the freedom of circulation of knowledge through time and across space, in particular, invite further consideration of those unique qualities. If the value of the library to society is congruent with the degree of freedom within its environment, then the stimulation of inquiry and thought can optimize these already significant cultural benefits.

Sense of Place

Library philosophy and intellectual freedom are tightly interwoven, with each influencing the capacity of the other to realize its potential. And the phrase "sanctity of ideas" in the preceding paragraph suggests two related concepts. One is that ideas are to be held apart from and above most other human characteristics, if for no reason other than that they represent the most distinctive of human achievements; they also are of a very special value in and of themselves. Following from that proposition, the other concept suggested by the phrase is that ideas should be nourished and safeguarded. Jesse Shera (1971, p. 175) describes in compelling fashion the critical function of the library in this process:

> A library should be a place in which myriad schools of thought make contributions to knowledge and the intellect may safely range and speculate and find its equal in some worthy antagonist. It is a place where inquiry is pushed forward and the "discoveries" of the individual verified and tested. Thus the library is protecting and encouraging a very special kind of life, the life of the mind. This life is both intellectual and passionate, and a really unique environment for its exercise is provided by the library. Education and learning are the business of the library, and its very existence proclaims the belief that the life of the mind is a part of the good life for everyone. The life of the mind is work, but it is also delight; it is men and women, young and old, coming together in an activity that is intensely human yet also inspired, in an atmosphere that promotes the silent stir of thought.

The function Shera describes so eloquently extends beyond the daily operations of the library, for the function is cumulative as it passes along knowledge and experience through the generations and in a specially conducive environment. Yet these procedures and transactions also constitute the sine qua non of the total library function because they constitute the daily stages of cultural movement, without which there would be no cultural evolution. Referring to the human brain, neurologist Antonio R. Damasio (1999, p. 198) offers a different perspective on the sense of place intended in this chapter. His reference is specifically to the function of brain in body, using the term extended consciousness, which is "the capacity to be aware of a large compass of entities and events, i.e., the ability to generate a sense of individual perspective, ownership, and agency, over a larger compass of knowledge than that surveyed in core consciousness which, by contrast, is an awareness of the moment, of the here and now. The sense of autobiographical self to which this larger compass of knowledge is attributed includes unique biographical information." Extended consciousness in the brain "provides the organism with an elaborate sense of self" (p. 16), just as the library provides the organism called culture, requiring (pp. 197–198) "the gradual buildup of memories of many instances of a special class of objects: the 'objects' of the organism's biography, of our own life experience, as they unfolded in our past illuminated by core consciousness" and holding those many images "active, simultaneously and for a substantial amount of time." Damasio (p. 142) calls this action of the extended consciousness "regulating devices" for life in a world that "changes dramatically, profoundly, and often unpredictably. Moment by moment, the brain has available a dynamic representation of an entity with a limited range of possible states." The sense of stability, of reassurance about who we are and where we as a culture have been, and about what we know and think as a culture is there, whether or not at any given moment we are aware of a need for it. Damasio (p. 196) refers to this as an autobiographical self.

Taking liberties with Damasio's theory for present purposes, it is an autobiographical culture that accounts for the vast collectivity of this phenomenon of individual self-awareness. In his terms, all living creatures have a core consciousness, while humans possess a very high level of extended consciousness of self that goes beyond that and into an awareness of being part of something larger and expanded over time, a much keener and complex image of self. It is a quality that identifies them as human. The social image of itself is what is reflected and carried forward through evolutionary change in the form of the social transcript, the recorded part of which is held by the library function in culture. An important corollary of this function is the social sense of this source of stability. The life of the mind is rarely an object of discussion in the literature of library and information science and may frequently seem to be irrelevant in the give and take of the daily business of getting on with life.[6] Yet, the life of the mind is where ideas germinate and can grow into something larger, effectively of importance to all of us. Ideas and language are synergistic, for ideas are the "sentences of thought," and one idea leads to another. Literary critic George Steiner (1971, p. 80) notes that "The argument is that every human being's world picture and the specific sum of such pictures in his society are a linguistic function." The following paragraphs treat as place those aspects of the library that bear a special relation to the library concept. Such place aspects have to do with ideas, memory, values, imagination and creativity, and intellectual comfort.

Ideas

Just as it would be misleading and altogether foolish to discuss cultural evolution without reference to large groups, such as societies, and to extended periods of time, such as millennia, it would be a mistake of equal proportion to refrain from invoking the individual in a given time and place. Cultural evolution is, after all, the process of individual ideas functioning interactively within the larger group of individuals, each endowed with the power to think. "Let me think for a moment," we say, as cell biologist Karl H. Pfenninger and science writer Valerie R. Shubik (2001, p. 219) recall from personal experience, drawing attention to the pithy phrase most of us have used and heard, and whose use is intended "to shut out distractions so that we can evaluate an idea or go systematically through a sequence of thoughts or deductions." But it is doubtful that most of us consciously seek this important state without the desperation suggested by that common phrase "Let me think for a moment," and it may be useful to bear in mind the view of nineteenth-century Librarian of Congress Ainsworth Rand Spofford's admonition (1900, p. 178) that "It requires almost as much intelligence to appreciate an idea as to conceive one." The library is foremost a place to think and has been for many centuries, because the recorded thoughts of distant generations even in remote lands are there for consultation at any level. Cultural historian Raymond Irwin (1964, p. 34) thus describes the library process in mind and society.

> The principal agent in the production of a book is, of course, its writer, the author of its being. But the author never works *in vacuo*, and, to a greater or lesser degree, his literary offspring are always the result of a marriage between his own mind and the communicated experience of other minds, either contemporary or in past time. And since this communicated experience is, in the main, received through the medium of books, the conception of and birth of the new book commonly take place in the author's library. It is, indeed, the prime function of a library to be the scene of such marriages; and the genealogy of scholarship, or of a particular book, is the tracing of its parentage and offspring.

It is the process of thinking, of course, that leads to selection of an idea, to achievement of understanding, and to adoption of a position from which to act, so the concept of selection in this case implies choices that require a trial-and-error process. This requirement is suggested by sociologist Robert MacDougall (1912, p. 7), who finds that "One must have thought and doubted before the view of another can be accepted with spiritual profit."

Reading and writing are parts of this process and may fulfill one of those psychic needs discussed in Chapter 3, even though it may be a need that can be left unmet until an extreme situation presents itself so strongly that it momentarily overshadows others. It is worth noting again the importance of language, which cannot be overstated in the context of cultural evolution. For there always is an interplay in language, whereby the choice of words to express ideas with the intention of precision invokes anticipation of how the receiver might interpret or misinterpret the idea, thus demanding careful selection. Whether through introspection or discussion, ideas shape words, while words also shape ideas in a never-ending spiral that concurrently maintains stability and change. There are many sources of ideas and many mental capacities that call them forth to action. The following paragraphs address the principal elements collectively as memory, values, imagination, and intellectual comfort.

Memory

The importance of human memory in cultural evolution was discussed in general terms in Chapter 4, where it is characterized as the storehouse of individual knowledge of all kinds. Memory provides the basis for decisions, and owing particularly to the written language through its strengthening of the continuity of tradition, "an enlargement of consciousness is possible to such a degree that it amounts to a difference in kind," writes Ellsworth Faris (1937, p. 303). "A people without history is like a man without memory, who lives from moment to moment. It is possible, therefore, to make one grand division in the evolution of man at the period where writing begins."

Memory is the capacity that facilitates the acquisition of knowledge, makes possible its ultimate accumulation, and suggests the utility of planning. Extending the individual memory to others is the special power of communication afforded by language. Extending communication beyond those in the immediate proximity of time and space, while in a form that is relatively faithful to the original expression and communicable to many others, is the function of the library. Chapter 5 explained that the library is a cultural technology created for the purposes of human communication through cultural evolution. Thus, without mention of the word library, neuroscientist Merlin Donald (1991, p. 312) outlines its function: "External memory is a critical feature of modern human cognition, if we are trying to build an evolutionary bridge from Neolithic to modern cognitive capabilities or a structural bridge from mythic to theoretic culture. The brain may not have changed recently in its genetic makeup, but its link to an accumulating external memory network affords it cognitive powers that would not have been possible in isolation. This is more than a metaphor; each time the brain carries out an operation in concert with the external symbolic storage system, it becomes part of a network. Its memory structure is temporarily altered; and the locus of cognitive control changes."

Throughout this study, especially in Chapter 4, language is shown to be of critical, essential, importance to the quality of human communication and thought, and therefore to cultural evolution. "Language is the mediator of thought in human beings," summarizes psychologist James Deese (1965, p. 4), thus language and memory also are closely integral. Memory implies association with experience just as experience implies knowledge and learning. Therefore, writes psychologist Deese (1965, p. 177), "Associative processes are fundamental to language and thought," and even, "associative relations may be firmly embedded in all linguistic usage" (p. 170).

One of the chief functions of the library, situated in the variety of experience and meanings contained in its great linguistic store from the past, both recent and remote, is its power to evoke associations that might not be set free in any other way, and certainly not so explicitly. These associations come about in differing ways. Deese (p. 20) points out that classical theory in association is based in either contiguity and similarity of associations, or in contiguity by temporal succession, such that in both cases one idea leads logically and linearly to another. It is quite easy to understand how this works in a library, which by nature is full of ideas. But he adds to this set of motivations for association another source, one far more subtle that is based on structural rather than logical considerations. His theory is that associations may never even have occurred together in the experience of the person who yields them, that "they may, instead, be the result of schemata which serve the function of bringing together structurally related elements from diverse experiences . . . the patterns that exist among associations between words as these are given by people." In this view (p. 176), associative structures provide another way of considering "the highly organized group of processes that make up human cognitive activity. Perceptual organization and operational organizations of the grammatical or logical sort are other aspects of that activity."

Library function embraces humanity's collective memory of fact, experience, conjecture and refutation, and meaning, and arguably is humanity's greatest stimulator of association. By serving as the most complete memory of humanity suitable for close scrutiny, it is a cultural technology devised to preserve and to render useful in any way and at any given time the intellectual aspects of culture that have been and continue to be accumulated, critiqued, and modified through many generations.

Values

Chapter 3 contains a discussion of the strong force of social values in the context of defining culture. It is the value system, ultimately, that defines a society; shared values are the influential products of group experience. They identify, writes sociologist Joyce O. Hertzler (1946, p. 310), "the significance of things, acts, and relationships deemed necessary and vital in the satisfaction of individual or social needs in human groups." The values generally agreed upon by the group, she continues, "bear in upon the individual from the first moments of social consciousness and then are reinforced through the process of learning to become lifelong guidelines of behavior and a framework for thought, determining to a great extent the preferences, likes and dislikes of the individual."

In the undisputable words of philosopher David Malet Armstrong (2004, p. 573), "Minds are the most complex and sophisticated systems known to exist," and it may be owing to that fact that values have been until relatively recently given little note in research; the nature of the abstract construct seems to defy the kind of objectivity preferred in science. "Meaning traffics in patterns, images, qualities, feelings, and eventually concepts and propositions," writes philosopher Mark Johnson (2007, p. 9). He elaborates (p. 10) that "Human meaning concerns the character and significance of a person's interactions with their environments. The meaning of a specific aspect or dimension of some ongoing experience is that aspect's connections to other parts of past, present, or future (possible) experiences. Meaning is relational. It is about how one thing relates to or connects with other things."

But values adhered to by a society do in large measure guide the attitude and behavior of the individual which, replicated many times, become the behavior and attitude of the group. Hertzler (1946, p. 311) concludes that "It is obvious that the social institutions, being such important phases of the life of groups, are most intimately bound up with the values of groups. Every institution involves values which the community has reflected upon and approved. In fact, the institutions tend to be as numerous as the values that the particular society recognizes as basic." For the individual to assess the implications of those attitudinal and behavioral ideas in the press of quotidian life, those values belonging to both the individual and the society, the individual requires supplemental encouragement; encouragement but also the right stimulation to engage the potential of one's mind.

On the other hand, according to anthropologist Bernard G. Campbell (1974, pp. 363–364), "The agony of the human condition arises from man's self-consciousness and his knowledge of the price he pays as an individual for his social life." Therefore, he says (p. 363), the question of ethics also arises "when man finds that he has to make conscious choices in a social context." This phenomenon is identified as a fundamentally distinguishing feature of humanity by clinical psychologists Lawrence Zelic Freedman and Anne Roe (1958, p. 461): "Incompatible aims and choices which are desirable but mutually exclusive are inevitable conditions of human development. This discrepancy between possibility and restriction, stimulation and interdiction, range and constriction, underlies that quantitatively unique characteristic of the human being: conflict." Values are reinforced or questioned through the social exchange of discussion and the processes accorded by written forms of communication, the latter of which provides the opportunity for particularly thoughtful introspection; but it is the kind of introspection that is guided by ideas generated externally. The process of reading is widely understood to be an eminently complex phenomenon, for it is considerably more than the conveying of one simple idea via the text to the reader. Careful to eschew the development of a theory in this instance, literary critic and theorist Wolfgang Iser (1974, p. xiii) notes that the central theme of his book on the novel is discovery: "The reader discovers the meaning of the text, taking negation as his starting-point; he discovers a new reality through a fiction which, at least in part, is different from the world he himself is used to; and he discovers the deficiencies inherent in prevalent norms and in his own restricted behavior." By its nature in affecting meaning, reading doubtless is the beginning rather than the end of an involved intellectual process.

Imagination & Creativity

It should be clear from preceding chapters, especially Chapter 3, that imagination and creativity are major contributors to the speed with which culture evolves, resulting in new concepts, words, understandings, and technologies. "The word imagination covers a spectrum of meanings in everyday language," writes psychologist Ilona Roth (2004, p. 443), "from the experiencing of vivid images in different modalities, to states of mind such as daydreaming, characterized by fantasy and fluidity of thought, to the generation of novel ideas and outputs." Imagination is the capacity that permits us to use knowledge, including values, beyond following an instinctive reaction to it. Physicist and Nobel laureate Werner Heisenberg (1958, p. 187) summarizes the role of what sometimes is referred to as serendipity, which the library experience can offer routinely because of the nature of its assemblage of ideas.

> It is probably true quite generally that in the history of human thinking the most fruitful developments frequently take place at those points where two different lines of thought meet. These lines may have their roots in quite different parts of human culture, in different times or different cultural environments or different religious traditions; hence if they actually meet, that is, if they are at least so much related to each other that a real interaction can take place, then one may hope that new and interesting developments will follow.

Once stimulated, imagination enables innovation and creativity, even taking a direction that moves beyond what is understood to be the accepted position and thus to be logical. "The mind is capable of functioning both intuitively and according to the dictates of common sense," writes experimental psychologist Liam Hudson (2004, p. 226). So, "in order to innovate, the scientist, like anyone else, must break the grip on his imagination that our powers of logical-seeming storytelling impose. We must be willing to subvert the conventional wisdom on which our everyday competence depends." This is counterfactual thinking, writes Ilona Roth (2004, p. 443), "the capacity to disengage from reality in order to think about events and experiences which have not actually occurred and might never occur—is a crucial feature of much imaginative thought." Literary theorist Wolfgang Iser (1974, p. 279) discusses what he refers to as the virtual dimension of the text, which is neither the imagination of the reader nor the text itself, but rather the coming together of text and imagination. This is made evident in the simple facts that "completely different readers can be differently affected" by the same text, but at different times in the reader's life a new reading can lead to different interpretations. Iser explains that "The literary text activates our own faculties, enabling us to recreate the world it presents. The product of this creative activity is what we might call the virtual dimension of the text, which endows it with its reality. This virtual dimension is not the text itself, nor is it the imagination of the reader; it is the coming together of text and imagination." Often imagination and thought are contrasted, and many scholars consider imagination lacking in the discipline necessary to genuine thought.

But philosopher Gilbert Ryle (1979, p. 51) finds this assumption to be faulty, even to the point of missing important connections. He writes that

> There are some contexts and situations in which it comes natural to us to treat thought and imagination as diametrical opposites, as work is opposite to play. In other contexts and situations we are inclined to treat them as merely different, as cricket is different from football. But there remain some other contexts and situations in which we regard a person's thinking and imagination as part and parcel of one another—his thinking is imaginative thinking, or his imaginings are coherent considered imaginings.

The summary of his views on imagining and thinking stresses the connections he finds important to the value of imagination. Ryle (p. 63) continues that "imagining is, I am maintaining, not an activity to be contrasted with thinking; nor yet a species of thinking. It is the innovating, inventing, exploring, adventuring risk-taking-if you like, creative, vanguard or scout-patrol-of thinking... The thinker, in any field whatsoever, who knowingly ventures off or beyond the beaten track, is showing some degree of imaginativeness." Thus, creativity is born of thoughtful imagination, and the question becomes how that is initiated; it continues for the time being as a mystery. Literary scholar John L. Lowes (1933, p. 29) offers a metaphor as a provisional answer, however, one that hints at the potential of the library: "There must be two poles to a battery before a spark can flash. Things have meaning only as they associate themselves with other things, and they take on added meaning only as those associations multiply. It is only when one's mind is already a storehouse of impressions that it will possess the focal points on which fresh impressions will converge."

Creativity is a special capacity of imagination, perhaps a special mixture of imagination and reason in action, and it crops up in all aspects of life, from the mundane and routine to the extraordinarily visible and widely influential. Yet little is known about creativity beyond its achievement. Cell biologist Karl H. Pfenninger and science writer Valerie R. Shubik (2001, p. 216) cite and support the statement that "'You could know every bit of neurocircuitry in somebody's head, and you still would not know whether or not that person was creative'." The mind, not the undersea or the universe, must be the last frontier. One evident conclusion from many different contexts is that, as they also state (p. 219), "creativity requires deep submersion in a thought process... Scientists often describe how a great idea may suddenly strike them. However, the scientist does not just walk into the laboratory and conduct the key experiment.... Scientists—like artists—struggle for extended periods of time with the solution of a particular problem or the expression of a particular idea (linguistic or other)." The processes of creativity have long been of interest in many fields and increasingly so in recent decades. But many decades ago, literary scholar John L. Lowes (1933) shed useful light on the phenomenon by identifying it (p. 37) with translation, and defining discovery as "the perception of some clarity or order. For the essence of what I have called discovery is the perception of some clarity or order implicit in the confusion of phenomena; the business of what I have called translation is to impose another clarity and order upon the chaotic mass of observations and impressions through which we have reached our end." He says that imagination is "a power which sees relations where the eye sees only facts; which sees the lines of form that strike through seeming chaos; which sees in phenomena apparently diverse, their underlying unity" (p. 35).

Such a process emanates from within the individual and seems to come forth even when conditions are highly challenging. The library maintains an environment which, partly by design but mostly by the nature of its most fundamental and accumulated responsibilities, encourages the processes of imagination and creativity.

Intellectual Comfort

There is a connection between the constant change of environment and the human capacity to react to it that is real in a physical sense. As do many other psychologists and scholars in other fields, environmental psychologists Harold M. Proshansky, A. K. Fabian, and R. Kaminoff (1983, p. 66) find that

"Like any other cognitive system, place identity influences what each of us sees, thinks, and feels in our situation-to-situation transactions with the physical world. It serves as a cognitive backdrop, or perhaps better said, as a physical environment 'data base' against which every physical setting experience can be 'experienced' and responded to in some way. Broadly speaking, what is at stake is the well-being of the person." The environment can be a stabilizing force[7] and it also can be a source of intellectual stimulation in various areas of high significance to cultural evolution. Neurophilosopher Evan Thompson (2007, p. 9) also situates the general scientific acceptance of environmental influence in cognition, writing that "The connectionist movement of the 1980s emphasized perceptual pattern recognition as the paradigm of intelligence, in contrast to deductive reasoning, emphasized by cognitivism. Whereas cognitivism firmly lodged the mind within the head, connectionism offered a more dynamic conception of the relation between cognitive processes and the environment."

The capacity of a sense of place to encourage self-discovery and self-identity is the most widely agreed upon of its attributes, and arguably is its single greatest power, while self-identity also has assumed increasing importance in contemporary society. In his survey of the concept of global identity crisis, geographer Wilbur Zelinsky (2001, p. 130) finds use of the term 'identity' in the social sciences to have increased about 30-fold from 1965 to 1998, and even concludes (p. 147) that "The scholarly literature treating questions of contemporary personal and group identity has been growing at an alarming rate in recent years." The conceptualization of place and the conceptualization of self are interdependent functions, both being forms of differentiation to which the sense of place provides reference points for the process of identity definition. Psychologist James Campbell (1989, p. 68) argues that "We become ourselves in large part, by a process of differentiation from various groups of others. In addition, we find the examination and fostering of this social place to be a source of self-understanding and stability."

Among the mental faculties that seem to be found only in humans is intellectual curiosity, which is the seeking of knowledge without prospect of immediate gain. It is an exploration of the unknown that is difficult to explain in behavioral theory. Intellectual curiosity reflects a high level of this kind of thinking. "Now things are interesting," writes literary scholar John Livingston Lowes (1933, p. 31), "when they excite our desire to know more, when they stir us from a passive to an active frame of mind; when, in a word, they awaken intellectual curiosity." It probably is a cause and effect relation that is self apparent only because its complexity is so great that it defies available facts. But it is fairly clear that such curiosity is driven by an interest in a better understanding of self and a better understanding of the world at large. The quality of environment has much to do with the pursuit of intellectual curiosity, and particularly with the contemplation and meditation it may require. Such activity is an essential part of advancing thought, understanding, and stimulation of further intellectual interests. Therefore, philosopher Gilbert Ryle (1949, p. 313) reasons that "Thinking things out involves saying things to oneself, or to one's other companions, with an instructive intent. The assertion of each proposition is intended to equip or prepare the recipient to turn what he is told to further accounts, to use it, for example, as a premise, or as a procedure maxim.... We see then that the well-known fact that pondering can be progressive, despite its consisting only in the serial production of seemingly inert sentences, is not inexplicable."

Social anthropologist Ellsworth Faris (1937, pp. 7–8) observes that an individual's consciousness of himself arises within a social situation as a result of the way in which that individual's actions and gestures are defined by the actions and gestures of others. "We not only judge ourselves by others, but we literally judge that we *are* selves as the result of what others do and say. We become human, to ourselves, when we are met and answered, opposed and blamed, praised and encouraged. The process is mediate, not immediate. It is the result of the activity of the constructive imagination, which is still the best term by which to denote the redintegrative behavior in which there is a present symbol with a past reference and a future consequence." In fact, Faris (p. 10) defines human nature as "that quality which we attribute to others as the result of introspective behavior. There is involved a certain revival of our own past, with its hopes, fears, loves, angers, and other subjective experiences which, in an immediate and unreflective way, we read into the behavior of another." Clearly, introspection, that silent effort to glimpse into one's own mind as a means of understanding oneself, is a central part of thought and also of determining social behavior.

Anthropologist W. T. Jones (1972, p. 83) defines the world view of an individual as "a set of very wide-range vectors [which he explains] in that individual's belief space (a) that he learned early in life and that are not readily changed and (b) that have a determinate influence on much of his observable behavior, to the verbal and nonverbal, but (c) that he seldom or never verbalizes in the referential mode, though (d) they are constantly conveyed by him in the expressive mode and latent meanings." Cultural influences on the individual, the knowledge gathered, and the experiences encountered generate that individual's world view, part of which is shared with others in the society, part of which is individual, perhaps even unique. Environment can offer either challenge or encouragement to the forming and re-forming of world view; as a place, the library offers encouragement.

It is generally agreed by scholars in a variety of disciplines that the sense of place has much to do with stimulation of the imagination, which is considered a prime distinguishing feature of humans among all other animals. Imagination has a wide range, relating to self identity, to the surrounding world, and to creations of the mind. According to psychologist David Canter

(1977, p. 153), it even "has been argued that interactions with our surroundings are a major base for the development of conceptual systems in the first place." And psychologist Joachim Wohlwill (1970, p. 304) observes that "Individuals give evidence of more or less strongly defined attitudes, values, beliefs, and affective responses relating to their environment."

The imagination seems to be boundless. "A marvel of economy," notes literary scholar Leonard Lutwack (1984, p. 33), "the imagination may thrive on the most meager materials to make a place meaningful." And he explains (p. 35) that "Places lend themselves readily to symbolical extension because there is so little that is inherently affective in their physical properties." In his inaugural address as president of the American Geographical Society several decades ago, John K. Wright (1947, p. 15) chose as his subject the role of imagination in geography, and concluded with the thought that "the most fascinating *terrae incognitae* of all are those that lie within the minds and hearts of men." Imagination is not drawn entirely from visual images, but can be generated just through the thought process. Psychologist Ilona Roth (2004, p. 443) emphasizes that "Counterfactual imagining is also involved in contemplating potential courses of action, fantasy and pretence, and understanding other people's thoughts, beliefs, and desires (so-called Theory of Mind), all of which are likely to involve verbal as well as non-verbal processes."

The environment, whether a nation, a landscape, a building or a room, influences the imagination and, therefore, an individual's view of self and of the world in which he lives. Perception of place invokes and gives further definition to a world view, it provides a special comfort by enabling the continued definition of self; and it stirs the imagination. Place is an essential and inspiring sense, but one that sometimes needs to be aroused and sustained through the right kinds of nurturing.

The library can be, and for countless generations has been, a place that produces such an environment. Speaking of place in this sense assigns a very special association to the space in question. From one space to another that sense can vary, but it has personal meaning to the individual, an association with values that are expected to be found there, values that are of high significance to the individual. This phenomenon represents an important consideration in most fields, but the concept of place has most fully been developed in the fields of geography and environmental psychology.[8] For present purposes, discussion here is limited to the effect produced by the library, rather than the reasons behind its production. May it suffice to observe that it is an outstanding place for self-discovery, for energizing the imagination, and for seeing the world anew. The inner self can be revealed continuously through the process of identification with the intellectual intersections of one's chosen paths of inquiry leading toward a higher level of understanding and stimulating further intellectual curiosity. This process of discovering oneself also encourages self-expression. The library can thus be a place of great intellectual comfort. Unfortunately, unlike the physical sciences, librarianship would be hard pressed to record for purposes of replication any particular experience, least of all one as subjective as the sensing of place. However, a composite perception can be extracted from a combination of one's own personal experience and those experiences heard and read about over the years.

Accordingly, the library presents a commingling of culture, nature, and humanity through a range of virtually all subjects, tastes, and points of view. And, of particular importance, it does so in a manner that situates the potential of this diverse intellectual experience immediately in evidence to those who may be receptive. It offers the possibility of easy immersion in a vast, complex, and layered web of knowledge, understanding, and expression, whose connections are created only by the individual contemplating them, when and as the individual chooses. For the individual, this setting invites communication with the thoughts, creations, questions, and discoveries of many others, both past and present. These conditions lead to the pursuit of insight and the continuous construction of completeness, thereby raising further questions and, in turn, rekindling the quest for answers. Such pursuits are undirected by anyone else, but the library does provide just enough fundamental order by which to determine one's own way to one's own destination even if that destination is imprecise or unknown. The guiding thoughts and methods during this intellectual voyage are protected to the extent that the individual determines them to be. The library does not create this personalized freestyle process, but rather enables and encourages it. The library sets the stage then steps back to allow the individual to construct, create, and clarify exactly as we may wish, and to take whatever deviations from what might at first have seemed to be the logical course toward what we thought to be the objective, which can change without warning.

The library is neither demanding nor judgmental about reasons and motivation. A unique social institution, the library also creates the locus for a sense of special community among the apparently like-minded. The visitor knows that in large measure, he/she is communing with others of similar world view, with kindred spirits undeclared, even though their exact interests almost surely differ. It is the experience of library that they share, albeit in quite different ways. One feels like a privileged guest in the library place but, at the same time, like its steward. Often it is a sense of context one lacks but seeks in the confidence that it can be discovered it in that place and in ways not necessarily clear even to the seeker. Context makes possible the kind of distancing that provides new perspective and discovery. Contemplation and informed serendipity are the tools that are crafted in the library to achieve this through the stimulation of imagination, curiosity, and creativity. Whether or not one finds the specific piece of information being sought, the experience will have been fulfilling because of other discoveries along the way and within one's self. If one considers the written word a symbolic technology, as does neuropsychologist Merlin Donald, the library function that holds it together physically and stimulates its use environmentally or spiritually is the epitome of that technology. Donald (2001, p. 308) concludes that "When combined, the conscious mind and its symbolic technologies generate a powerful chemistry."

The importance of a unique sense of place has been attached to libraries for as far back in history as we know of them. The great Greek library of Alexandria in ancient Egypt, which flourished several centuries B.C., is reported to have been a magnificent monumental edifice in the royal palace suite, intended to inspire contemplation, learning, and imagination, the most uplifting thoughts and ideals. Of course, not all libraries can be designed in such splendor. But, in spite of that, they can and usually do maintain that metaphysical force called place, partly as a result of conscious efforts to create the appropriate environment, and partly in reflection of the spirit inherently there. Alistair Black (1996, p. 226), writing of the history of English libraries during the nineteenth century, notes that architectural history traditionally has lacked a broader historical perspective, and thus has viewed built form without meaningful reference to the society that conceived it. He concludes, however, that "as with library history there has emerged in architectural history in recent decades a fresh approach—one which integrates the study of the built environment with that of non-design inputs."[9] He points out (p. 233) that "Civic pride and public library architecture went hand in hand," and that design motivations included "civic power, the pursuit of culture, social cohesion, self-help, social control, national economic performance and technical education" (p. 226). Furthermore, Black (p. 242) surmises that "The fact that designs mirrored the quest for culture might easily be construed as an attempt to transmit middle-class values to a resistant working class. Built forms maintain social forms. Buildings can indoctrinate and hence help to maintain power; ideals can be constructed."

The sense of place captures a certain spirit. And, for the library, that constitutes a significant part of its function, because the spirit of freedom to inquire about anything is induced by the relatively unencumbered availability of a vast mixture of ideas and categories of ideas, even in a fairly small public library. This is a function that clearly sets the library apart from other social institutions. Jesse Shera (1971, p. 58) summarizes this synergism of spirit and function:

> By its very nature librarianship is integrative, and its practice founded upon the perception and utilization of relationship: "time-binding," the general semanticists call it, and the term is a particularly happy one. Some years ago, John Ciardi wrote of the library reading room as a place "for the soft rustle of pages and the quiet stir of thought," by which he meant that the library

> was created for contemplative integration as well as the pursuit of truth. This value of the library as a place where man can mentally sort things out is especially important in our increasingly cacophonous world of specialized fragmentation.

Neurologist Liam Hudson (2004, pp. 225–226) offers the even more poignant observation, drawn, as he says, from more detailed studies of thinking, that "The clear implication is that our brains are at their most efficient when allowed to switch from phases of intense concentration to ones in which we exert no conscious control at all." This important change of pace and focus is not just what the library makes possible, but encourages. Sociologist Robert MacDougall (1912, p. 15) describes this experience in connection with social evolution.

> In the thought of each man the world of individual life takes on a form which is independent of communal experience. It is a world within a world, which in its very nature must be differentiated from that larger social existence within which it appears. Every increase in complexity within the system of social relations serves but to add to the qualitative manifoldness of this world of individual experience, and to bring it into sharper opposition to that of public life. The result of social evolution can thus be expressed, from this point of view, as a process of individualization.

In terms of value, neurologist C. Judson Herrick (1956, p. 142) finds that, while much, if not most, of the value system of any individual comes from the ambient society, "The desires of men and the needs of all other creatures arise as expressions of their own inner natures, however much they may be inflected by social and other environmental conditions. This sets the most significant criteria of value within the organism." Values can be molded by society and can be drawn from the inner self. Moreover, Herrick's (p. 141) review of the literature of motivation leads him "to the conclusion that there is a natural hierarchy of values that begins with life itself and culminates in man's finest aspirations for self-culture and social service."

Concluding his explication of the work of twentieth-century sociologist Erving Goffman, sociologist Thomas J. Scheff (2006, p. 197) remarks that Goffman's work "continually suggests the idea that human beings and their societies are much more complex than we usually assume," and are virtually invisible in modern societies, constituting what he called the emotional/relational world. Scheff (p. 198) explains this condition, asserting that "In modern societies, attention is almost entirely riveted on the material world and, with respect to our selves and our fellows, cognition and behavior. Relationships and emotions lead only a shadow life in our scheme of the world." Library administrator and philosopher Joseph Z. Nitecki (1981, p. 119) is rather more descriptive about this condition, writing that "The reality around us can never be fully apprehended, since it consists of constantly changing relationships between things in space, events in time, and concepts in our minds. Each known relationship becomes a seed for a potentially unlimited series of new relationships waiting to be discovered." But it is in that shadow life of the world that the imagination is aroused and permitted to exercise itself, and it is that world to which the library place is the best suited among all other agencies and institutions to encourage self-analysis and imagination.

Similarly, in his analysis of different types of intelligence strength, cognitive psychologist Howard Gardner (1983, pp. 278–279) writes that "at the core of each intelligence, there exists a computational capacity, or information-processing device, which is unique to that particular intelligence, and upon which are based the more complex realizations and embodiments of that intelligence." He emphasizes that the normal human being "is so constituted as to be sensitive to certain informational content: when a particular form of information is presented, various mechanisms in the nervous system are triggered to carry out specific operations upon it. And from the repeated use of, elaboration of, and iteration among these various computational devices, eventually flow forms of knowledge that we would readily term 'intelligent'."

It is not just access to information[10] that the library traditionally has offered humanity. It is perhaps of at least equal significance and importance that the library offers access to a condition, or a set of conditions, that makes possible and even encourages the kinds of processes that evoke deep thought and intellectual curiosity about one's own identity, about the world in which each individual, as well as each society, lives, and that stirs imagination. The library is unique in offering the combination of that special sense of place and the richness of personal choice in the selection of sources to accommodate the most human of natural inclinations.

Summary

The library, in concept and practice, constitutes the most distinctive technology for the conveyance of the many forces behind cultural evolution. It is the cultural technology that melds into a single function both concept and place, introspection and communication, fact and fantasy; it accommodates the motivations of both community and individual. The value and potential of such integration of conceptualizations are made clear in one thought offered by Peter Medawar (cited by Foskett, 1984, p. 60), biologist and Nobel laureate in Medicine, that all advance in scientific understanding "'begins with a speculative adventure, an imaginative preconception of what might be true—a preconception which always, and necessarily, goes a little way (sometimes a long way) beyond anything which we have logical or factual authority to believe in'." Integration of this sort is the uncharted territory of a fruitful intellectual journey.

The library is at once a producer, a medium, and a product of cultural evolution. This variety in forging what may be the most intimate of relations between institution and society, as well as the most public, is at the heart of what educational sociologist William J. Goode (1961, p. 316) meant when he alluded to "The almost unique relations of the librarian to his client."[11] This is more than the one-on-one relation between librarian and client, although it is on an individual basis that most library transactions take place; for it relates to the social function of the library "to maximize the effective social utilization of the graphic records of civilization" as Jesse Shera (1972, p. 359) long contended. "From the relating of the role of the library to its social *milieu*, to an understanding of the social utilization of graphic records, it becomes possible to describe those activities which are peculiar to the library, shared with other groups or agencies only," he writes, "at the margins, and always intimately intertwined with the changing needs of the supporting culture." Shera couches these as social objectives: advancement of the general cultural level and advancement of the 'scholarship', or commonly accepted knowledge, of the society and, further, that these responsibilities are shared only at the margins with other groups or agencies.

Maintaining the social transcript in perpetuity is the most basic of library functions in a society. Maintaining and continuing. But the way in which it executes this responsibility carries further implications. Cultural historian Raymond Williams (1980, p. 71) rightly states that, "the acquisition of more books and other publications, and the building of large, or larger, collections of volumes, is not a library's purpose. This is only a means toward the accomplishment of its real purpose of helping to improve access to information where and when it is needed."[12] And yet it is to even more than the improvement of access to information that he is referring, for in response to this notion it is appropriate to consider first the most basic administrative distinctions between the library and other social institutions.

Analysis of the deeper substance of librarianship provided by library historian and philosopher Ajit Kumar Mukherjee (1966, p. 53) places that institution squarely in its function by observing that throughout the ages libraries have existed as part of the social fabric; they have not been isolated instances of social development, but an integral part of over-all development at most stages. By his account, it has been particularly since the late nineteenth century that the adjective "social" became attached to the library concept. And in this new institution (a very young profession in 1917 when library administrator and scholar William E. Henry presented his paper), Henry (1967, pp. 79–80) argues that "the service is social, the problems vary as the individual tastes and experiences vary and the service must be sufficiently intelligent to diagnose the symptoms and prescribe a treatment." Here, most certainly, lies the big challenge. He points out that any contemporary society requires the intelligence and experience of the past as well as the present, explaining that

> The life of the individual is too short to reflect the perspective of any fair portion of the past so we must have the vicarious experience of others and the book is the agent of the past bringing us this vicarious experience. All the past has lived for us and we must live for all the future for the future's good. Is there, then, a realm, an area, a mission in life that humanity cannot realize without an unrestrained and self-directed access to the past which the individual alone cannot secure for himself? Can this mission be performed by any other institution? The library is the instrument and the librarian is the social agent which bring the past to the present in preparation for the future, and through these the individual is self-educated for social ends.

As the inveterate critic of librarianship educational sociologist William J. Goode (1961, p. 310) makes clear, in such business the librarian has a great advantage, having "no competitors, and indeed librarians themselves have a sense that their occupation is unique." As mentioned in Chapter 2, that sense no longer prevails in its application to librarianship, library science, and information science, although the library as function continues as a unique cultural technology.

Among the many social institutions and agencies the library is rare in the attentiveness of its function to the motivations of society, whether spoken or silent. In fact, it could be that even within that select grouping called social institutions the library is unique. For the library stimulates and nourishes the highly personal function of free-flowing cognitive activity, and indeed, is dedicated to that end, whether it is a matter that is grounded in reason or faith, fantasy or fact, socially representative or socially denounced.

This is the making of a large part of cultural evolution, for the library can be considered an extension of language. Words lead to the sharpening of thought, which leads to a refined distinction of meaning among words; then new ideas are spawned by those words, thus releasing their potential into communication to others to be refashioned by their reasoning and drawn from experience, thereby creating new or variant concepts which again stir the concoction. This entire process relies on the power of memory, which traces back in the mind of the individual and connects with similar tracing through the memory over the ages by predecessors. Jesse Shera (1973, p. 108) aptly summarizes: "The point is that the library as the main repository for record is a major source of vicarious experience."

The meanings of words, which are symbols for ideas, actions, and concepts, change gradually in this process, but their lineage can be tracked through memory of the individual and of the culture, and of many cultures. "Only a small fragment of his own culture is directly visible to any of its adherents," notes Michael Polanyi (1962, p. 375). And he adds a particularly intriguing notion about the content of this reservoir of memory, that "Large parts of it are altogether buried in books, paintings, musical scores, etc., which remain mostly unread, unseen, unperformed. The messages of these records live, even in the minds best informed about them, only in their awareness of having access to them and of being able to evoke their voice and understand them."

But just knowing that the memory exists in that special social institution has its own importance. Philosopher Herbert Keuth (2005, p. 296) paraphrases Karl R. Popper in emphasizing this very idea, noting that "Even a book that is never read contains objective knowledge. But in order to belong to the third world of objective knowledge, it should in principle, or virtually, be capable of being grasped by somebody."

Seeing this phenomenon from a slightly different perspective is electrical engineer and president of the Massachusetts Institute of Technology, Jerome B. Wiesner (1964, pp. 41–42), who supports the idea, arguing that "scientific knowledge need not be exploited immediately once it becomes available. It exists for all to use forever. Thus, acquiring scientific knowledge is a form of capital investment. Unlike most other capital investments, it does not become obsolete nor can it be used up." But far more broadly, and of particular relevance to the present study, the library is recognized conceptually by a large part, perhaps by the vast majority, of the population in an industrial society as a cultural anchor and source of cultural identity, in a sense both symbolic and real. This makes sense especially if one considers that the library was invented by culture for these human purposes, for as anatomist Kathleen Gibson (1993, p. 251) reminds us, of the three major factors that underlie differences in achievement levels between humans and apes, for example, ranks the fact that "human tool use, language and social behavior are mutually interdependent" and reinforcing.

Cultural historian Stephen Bertman (2000, p. 60) points to a harsher lesson in this regard, quoting a contemporary witness of the late twentieth-century war in Bosnia-Herzegovina that the Serb forces "'knew that if they wanted to destroy this multi-ethnic society, they would have to destroy the library... First you destroy the documents, then you quickly destroy the memory that they ever existed'." And this is but one example of the ideological control that too frequently has been witnessed since the emergence of the library, often in the form of libricide. The library functions as a kind of security, a reassurance that may even be sub-conscious, that knowledge greater than one possesses or hears about through normal daily communication is accessible, and that our cultural heritage is proof of identity.

But there are more obviously pragmatic features of the library that distinguish it from most other institutions and organizations. First is the fact that the library almost always belongs to a host organization.[13] Most often, however, the library is merely appended to the host organization, rather than firmly embedded in it. Whether or not this must be the case or should forever remain the case is not argued here. But this situation is a consequence of the fact that the library is a service to the entire host and, as such, is not part of the assembly line of the host's daily production, policy, procedure, goals, and objectives. Instead, the library operates in a consulting or auxiliary or staff capacity to the host organization. Another feature of libraries that distinguishes them in a most fundamental way from business and industrial organizations is the fact, that, as architect Geoffrey T. Freeman (2005, p. 3) describes it, "The library is the only centralized location where new and emerging information technologies can be combined with traditional knowledge resources in a user-focused, service-rich environment that supports today's social and educational patterns of learning, teaching, and research. Whereas the Internet has tended to isolate people, the library, as a physical place, has done just the opposite. Within the [academic] institution, as a reinvigorated, dynamic learning resource, the librarian once again becomes the centerpiece for establishing the intellectual community and scholarly enterprise." Surely, these distinctions alone are far more than cosmetic.

Then, the library is the epitome treasury of words and meanings, the place that contains words—the articulated precision tooling of ideas and sentiment—used throughout the ages by people of many lands in many varying contexts as definitions for one to ponder and to understand. Not just definitions, not just etymological analyses, but actual usage shaded by context. It is through this value afforded by language that can be discovered the susceptibilities at any age in civilization that helped shape a shared world view, and thus perhaps learn more about our own age. This is what historian of ideas Arthur O. Lovejoy (1936, p. 14) refers to in his use of the phrase philosophical semantics, which he defines as "a study of the sacred words and phrases of a period or a movement, with a view to a clearing up of their ambiguities, a listing of their various shades of meaning, and an examination of the way in which confused associations of ideas arising from these ambiguities have influenced the development of doctrines, or accelerated the insensible transformation of one fashion of thought into another, perhaps its very opposite." It is not necessarily in the sense of a science that this spread of philosophy is useful or influential in culture, but rather as a matter for more general consideration and discussion in a less formal sense, in the sense of achieving a better understanding of ourselves, of the world, and of our total context. Thus, Lovejoy (p. 14) finds the ambiguities of mere words are a force in history and, therefore, in culture:

> A term, a phrase, a formula, which gains currency or acceptance because one of its meanings, or of the thoughts which it suggests, is congenial to the prevalent beliefs, the standards of value, the tastes of a certain age, may help to alter beliefs, standards of value, and tastes, because other meanings or suggested implications, not clearly distinguished by those who employ

> it, gradually become the dominant elements of its signification. The word 'nature', it need hardly be said, is the most extraordinary example of this, and the most pregnant subject for the investigations of philosophical semantics.

Repeated revision and refinement of the meanings of words chosen by others of other times and places and in a vast sample of situations sharpens our thinking abilities and clarifies, and can even refocus, our understanding of ourselves, others, our identity, and our world view. That refinement of meaning is what nineteenth-century French novelist Gustave Flaubert referred to famously as selecting *le mot juste*, the precisely right word for the specific occasion. What may at first appear a chance or unnecessary redundancy of words and meanings is actually necessary and not at all produced by chance. It is selection from among many options for the intended purpose.

The library is a great collection of words held in context, conveyed in varied formats and, therefore, an unequalled source of stimulation for imagination, reason, and creativity, which are the manifestations of the highest order of culture. Yi-fu Tuan (1989, p. 69), geographer and philosopher, proffers for consideration his thought that "Culture makes people truly human and distinguishes them from other animals. This is a widely held view. Common sense suggests that if this is true of culture, then *high* culture in complex societies enables people to explore the further reaches of human potential in both an intellectual and a moral-spiritual sense." To ensure the continued advantage to cultural development, societies created and continue to maintain the library. Thus it is what historian and sociologist of science Thomas P. Hughes (2004, p. 173) refers to as a socially constructed technology, in contradistinction to a result of technological determinism,[14] which follows a course seemingly of its own and not necessarily attuned to the holistic conditions of society. The library is the most distinctive manifestation of a technology of cultural evolution because it is a creation of humanity in response to the holistic conditions of society.

Communication is often identified as the single, all-embracing function of the library, and that certainly is true. But there are many other agencies and institutions whose function very clearly is communication. In mid twentieth century, political scientist Robert D. Leigh (1950, p. 26), who directed the U. S. Public Library Inquiry, observed that non-commercial agencies in the communication sphere, including publication and other communication activities of government, universities and noncommercial agencies "are a relatively small part of the whole machinery of public communication in the United States. Mass communication is largely a profit-seeking business as well as a public service." The study concludes (p. 46) its consideration of the role of the library in mass communication with the thought that "In the light of the incompleteness of the task of communication as performed by the commercial agencies we can begin to discern the natural and appropriate role of the public library in our society. Apparently it is not to attempt to compete with the commercial agencies on their terms, but rather to provide the kinds and qualities of service that those agencies are not equipped to give." The functions not addressed by other communication institutions and agencies, the report says (p. 50) are those that are de facto the core of the library responsibility, those having to do with providing a rich array of authoritative intellectual sources in many areas of knowledge while incorporating a balanced view.

These functions are incorporated in the library to the extent that it operates within a society that values democratic ideals. The centrality of democracy as manifested in daily operations, in long-term accrued cultural contribution, and in the maintenance of a sense of library place, all interacting to the benefit of developing the mind of the individual, and thus of society, to its fullest potential. "Inner differentiation is the measure of a society's evolution," writes sociologist Robert MacDougall (1912, p. 20). "That human group or institution, therefore, is highest in the scale which combines the greatest range of free individualities in an essential community." The library place brings together memory and information and, through its sense potential for environment, it can lead to the creation of knowledge through imagination. "The trouble too often is that the people who know the facts don't use their imagination," according to literary scholar John Livingston Lowes (1933, p. 34); "the people who have imagination don't trouble with the facts. It is the combination, in whatever field, which is the rare, the priceless thing." The library is a place where these two elements are brought together, evidently through very long-term cultural design. The library is humanity's collective memory, "and in quantitative terms is clearly supreme," argues library educator J. M. Orr (1977, p. 194). "On its own, its creative ability is nil, but it complements man's mind by feeding it some of the data on which the re-creation of knowledge is nourished." As a cultural technology, the library concept in cultural evolution makes memory function in every way as an extension of the mind, both individual and societal, and certainly an integral, even inseparable, part of literate society.

The literature of cultural evolution makes clear that the individual and the culture are in a constant give-and-take racheting relationship. "In this process of evolution," writes sociologist Robert MacDougall (1912, p. 18), "every advance serves to render clearer the essential relations of individual and society, as well as to define the instrumental significance of organization. Final worth is to be found only in the values of personal experience." But it is above all the individual that is affected most directly by the degree of democracy in which that individual thinks and acts, influencing others. Again, Robert MacDougall (p. 2): "The centrality of self-determination, in individual reflection and action alike, cannot be questioned. It is a fundamental constituent of rational life and ideal striving." And he stresses (p. 4) that "In its primary aspect the self is a force, not a resistance—a form to be impressed, not a material to receive the die. To be subject, to imitate or obey, is slavery. Freedom is to be found only in self-expression, that is, in the unhampered exercise of natural activities. The self is incarnate will, which manifests itself in affirmation."

There is a strong interplay among sense of place (environment), democracy (intellectual freedom), and stimulation of the thought processes (problem solving, self-identification, development of world view, imagination, and creativity) that is found in the library. Especially in the past two decades, although it has long been emerging, the rise of information technology has posed challenges to the significance of this physico-psychic convergence. No one can know how this situation will be resolved, but a number of writers in the library profession have drawn attention to this aspect of library management that perhaps has been taken for granted almost to the point of having been ignored. As an example, linguist David M. Levy (2006, p. 250) suggests that "people want the advantages of the online world, but not at the expense of the physical, the material side of life. People recognize the value of shared, communal spaces where they can meet and greet or where they can work by themselves while surrounded by others. The library may be the only institution currently capable of creating and maintaining trusted, nonpartisan spaces of this kind." This part of his conclusion is highly debatable; but he appends to it a thought that is not, relating it to library as a cultural function: "It may also be that physical libraries serve as symbols of certain shared, sacred values." In his discussion of culture and psychology, psychobiologist Henry Plotkin (1998, p. 250) embraces these concepts with the statement that "No individual is irreplaceable. In this sense at least, the cultural group is more than its individual members, even though no culture can be other than the combined psychology of those members. Extrasomatic storage strengthens this remarkable characteristic of culture because it increases the fidelity and amount of information that can be stored and transmitted, and such storage truly does stand outside and independent of every member of a culture." The library is unique in its realization of the extrasomatic capacities required to function appropriately.

The library is about people and ideas, both the ideas of individuals and the ideas shared by society, through time and across space. This principle is fundamental to its quotidian operations and to its critical function in cultural evolution. Neurobiologist and philosopher Patricia Smith Churchland (2002, p. 107) emphasizes that an understanding of what others feel, sense around themselves, intend, and want is critical to social success, and that such cognition seems to depend on modeling the cognitive states of others. She concludes that "The advantage of such cognitive representation is that it permits the animal to anticipate and manipulate the behavior of these other cognitive creatures, and to navigate the social world that, collectively, they constitute." The library, in both its physical and conceptual states of being surely offers an unmatched selection of these models and an environment that stimulates their contemplation in relation to one's own situation in society. The library function is to humanity as the tool is to the individual human. It is an extension of the most human of capacities, the mind. It is a tool that can be used as needed, set aside when not needed, and reused, usually in a different way. But when set aside, the individual and the culture are reassured of the tool's stand-by presence, as explained in Chapter 5. The function itself is the subject of the next chapter.

CHAPTER 7

Stewardship of the Social Transcript

Ideas are not dead thoughts, even when they are no longer contemporary; for they remain steps in the evolution of contemporary ideas.

—Jacob Bronowski & Bruce Mazlish, 1960

Introduction

There is no convincing evidence that the individual mind or the putative societal mind is controlled by greater intelligence in the twenty-first century than it was two and a half millennia ago or more. For example, neuroscientist Jean-Pierre Changeux (1986, p. 271) reports that "The genetic mechanisms that gave rise to modern man's brain appear to have stopped several tens of thousands of years ago." Yet in many areas there are abundant and highly evident signs of significant cultural advance. The human brain did adapt to its changing environment, however, particularly when language developed and knowledge grew as it was passed along, thereby also rendering the mind more fluid, if not the brain larger. Various other technologies also have emerged to extend the potential of our legs and arms, eyes and ears, and even to further enhance the adaptability of our brain. Yet, as far as is possible to know at this time, these anatomical parts remain pretty much as they have been throughout the record of civilization. Animal behaviorists Kevin N. Laland and Gillian R. Brown (2002, p. 285) underscore powerful forces that work through a strong cultural evolution, differentiating some species from others. "Gene-culture coevolutionary analyses suggest that evolution in species with a dynamic, socially transmitted culture may be different from evolution in other species, for at least three reasons. First, culture is a particularly effective means of modifying natural selection pressures and driving the population's biological evolution . . . Secondly, culture may generate new evolutionary processes, for instance cultural group selection. Thirdly, cultural transmission may strongly affect evolutionary rates." For purposes of the present examination, the most visible contribution of such processes, referred to here as cultural technologies, has been to facilitate and accelerate the processes of daily communication and understanding in the short term, while, in the long term, the more obscure but very durable purpose has been to evolve culture, usually in a sense that much of society labels progress.

At least that has long been the generally accepted result. Cultural evolution occurs only with the generational passing along of values, beliefs, knowledge, experience, wisdom, and accumulated memory. The power of language, primarily, along with other modes of communicating these cultural elements, is aided by technologies designed to record such communication. The contention of this book is that the library function is the most important cultural technology among them, second only to language to which it is an extension. This technology is manifested by varied library types and sizes, emphasis and detail, but the respective function of all these manifestations is to assist in the processes of cultural evolution, both through immediate action and action delayed until such time as it will be of greatest effect. Whereas biological evolution for a long time held a position within science superior to that of cultural evolution, because it was considered natural and therefore readily subject to objective study, as opposed to social[1] and therefore artificial and not subject to the same rigors of research, science philosopher Mary Midgley (2002, p. 126) reasons that "the evolutionary model does us a great service by its insistence that culture itself is part of nature and must be seen as somehow continuing its patterns." Humanity, whether manifested in the individual or in a society, is a creation of nature. Human behaviors are natural.

Library as Communication

If there is one concept that describes library function in all its aspects, it is the concept of communication; in this case it is communication both immediate and longitudinal in the ongoing stewardship of the social transcript. One of the major aims of communication in society is shared knowledge, or in its highest sense the achievement of common understanding, which requires common perspective. Physicist John Ziman (2000, pp. 289–290) explains that "'Understanding' is a complex process, of which we know less about the parts than about the whole... But for communicating individuals to understand each other, they must somehow establish common mental structures into which each newly shared item can be fitted."

Similarly, cultural evolution is about communication shared over space and time, by individuals and societies, which is a widely embracing process that psychobiologist Henry Plotkin (1998, p. 174) renders intelligible in compelling fashion.

> The concept of a collective species wisdom gleaned over immense periods of evolutionary time, which then launches into the world very short-lived individuals with innate predispositions to learn only certain kinds of thing,

> means that individual people are able to share with one another a rich and complex understanding of the world we live in—or rather of that restricted part of the world to which our innate dispositions give us access. This most certainly would not be the case were we at birth *tabula rasa* intelligences, for then we would all of us enter into some individual and probably unique part of the search space and hence have little shared knowledge in common. So there is an interesting contrast between innate, intrinsic, limiting devices that restrict what we can know on the one hand, and on the other hand how these devices give rise to shared knowledge which, in creatures like ourselves with our remarkable communications skills, allows us entry into those most extraordinary of all psychological domains—self-knowledge, the knowledge of other minds, consciousness and culture.

Jesse Shera (1970, pp. 38–39) assigns a special identity to this concept that relates it to the library and to the democratic ideals that support the library and other cultural concepts. "I submit that the end of communication is the achievement of like-mindedness." But he is quick to note that he does not mean that the aim of communication is to persuade or convince, as is the case with propaganda. What Shera means by the term like-mindedness is instead "the achievement of understanding or getting someone to understand what it is you mean, whether he happens to agree with you or not. Thus, like-mindedness is not to be equated with agreement, but only with comprehension." Theories are steps along the way toward understanding. They are, by Henry Plotkin's reckoning (1998, p. 178), "explanatory nets cast to capture the causal structure of the world." Understanding something is knowledge in its fullest sense, because it means knowing how something came to be, what its implications are, and how to use it. Understanding is also basic to human communication in its fullest sense. But to define understanding as grasping a concept in its absolute fullest sense would be a mistake, because understanding is a goal, an ideal. Understanding is a reflection of the social dimension of knowledge,[2] a stage of knowledge on the way to perfection or knowing all there is to be known about the object in question: the concept does not suggest the idea of knowing all that can be known, but of knowing many different parts and seeing their intersections and relations. The concept of understanding is examined more closely below in this chapter.

Throughout this text reference has been made to the rich redundancy of communication maintained by the library in its capacity to accumulate ideas and meanings from generations in the distant past, mix them with those of the present and make them all available to generations of the future. It is through the device of redundancy that cultural evolution resists entropy because the entire store becomes a vast and growing set of options. While the process of communication through speech from one individual to another is cluttered by redundancy, the process of communication through the evolution of culture is rendered more secure by redundancy, which acts as a fail-safe mechanism to resist and reduce entropy. It offers options that enhance the probabilities for ideas and meanings to be considered and either modified or re-used indefinitely. Such redundancy stimulates thought in alternative directions when perceived from within a different environment, under different conditions and in different circumstances. The process is labeled *bricolage* by anthropologist Claude Lévi-Strauss, who, according to anthropologist Mary Douglas (1986, p. 66), in 1962

> invented the image of the thinker as *bricoleur,* the amateur craftsman who turns the broken clock into a pipe rack the broken table into an umbrella stand, the umbrella stand into a lamp, and anything into something else. The *bricoleur* uses everything there is to make transformations within a stock repertoire of furnishings... Though he did not so extend it, his notion of bric-a-brac describes well the recurrent analogies and styles of thought that characterize any civilization.

Ideas are eternal because humanity recycles ideas, and societies can use them precisely as they were intended in their original usage, but tends more often to adjust them to achieve slightly greater precision. Anyone who has deselected books from a library collection is quite familiar with the admonition that "one man's trash is another man's treasure," a proverb that has been converted into the raison d'être of the recycling industry. As function of cultural evolution, the library maintains the most comprehensive intellectual recycling function known in the universe.

Problems of Philosophy

The great variety in manifestation of library function often can appear, both from within the profession and from without, to be simply a reflection of insignificant divergencies; a mass of just doing things; procedures and transactions of a practice without a cohesive underpinning theory, even to the extent that the means, rather than the end, are the focus. Throughout the twentieth century and continuing today, what is done in the library and how it is done seems to many observers to be the driving force behind the library, even to the disregard for why those things are being done. As noted in Chapter 1, there even has been considerable disagreement within the profession about the need or usefulness of a library philosophy. Yet no one can doubt that the profession does need to achieve the ability to explain itself in simple, concise terms—a brief paragraph—in spite of what may appear to be the impossibility of setting a philosophic guideline for the variety of library operations and services that dominate both daily activity and the literature of the field. It certainly is correct, however, as semanticist Paul Ziff (1960, p. 196) advises, that "It is senseless to speak of an adequate theory without considering what the theory is supposed to be adequate to or adequate for." Such a pragmatic approach has been the guiding principle behind the present study. But looking at the library primarily from the inside, rather than from the outside, which has been the tendency of the profession for a very long time, has posed a persistent obstacle to aligning values and practices, establishing priorities, and evaluating operations and services on a solid foundation, following a methodology that is based on purpose. Furthermore, most would likely agree that professional preparation in this or any field should be based on an understanding of library operations that is supported by theory drawn from a consensual philosophy.

Writings about operations of the library go back many centuries, but usually with little reference to a purpose, evidently because the purpose for the betterment of society and the individual reader must have seemed self evident and subject to the belief system described in Chapter 1. For example, the ancient Greek philosophers, especially Plato and Aristotle, had addressed the cultural memory function. This failure to examine or even acknowledge purpose began to change, however, with the public library movement in the United States and England, when broad popular support for the institution was sought. Then, during the twentieth and early twenty-first centuries, as was discussed in Chapter 2, scholars did commit considerable thought to library philosophy, among them: S. R. Ranganathan (perhaps the name most closely associated with library philosophy); Pierce Butler (whose thoughts on the subject are expressed in a number of brief publications); Jesse Shera (who was the first to self-consciously advance the library as a concept); A. Broadfield (staunch defender of, and advocate for, freedom of thought and reading); H. Curtis Wright (who sees the library in terms of people and ideas, and relates it to ancient Greek thought); and John Budd (who relates the library function to formal epistemological systems and further emphasizes attention to the value of an agreed upon philosophy).

Despite the well-formulated aspects of a philosophy advanced by these and other scholars with compelling reason and passion, a philosophy that would be agreed upon generally by the profession and, one would hope, by the public, has not been achieved. Simple neglect and ambivalence on the part of both librarians and society are the ultimate problems here. But, underlying them have been several other obstacles: the development of a belief system (that the library is an obvious public good), which rendered an agreed upon philosophy superfluous; the facile attraction of the pragmatic things-to-do technical side of the profession; the gripping fascination, particularly in more recent decades, with information technologies per se, as they held promise of a new luster for the library profession; the early invocation of the science model (scientism) at a time when the library profession was just beginning, and which still maintains a grip; the emergence of the cognition model, which takes into account the significance of human qualities that may be unique, and in that regard the nature of thought. Consequently and for reasons that stem, ironically, from its own uniqueness, there is no clear model for the library to follow in the establishment of such a philosophy.

Within any profession, the relation of theory and practice is a complex matter that invites multiple interpretations. What is most commonly understood about the library function emerges at its best from one's personal association with a successful transaction experienced in a particular institution and, at its worst, the image, in any sense, that captures a shared stereotype of discordant policy, procedure, transaction, and bureaucracy. The truth resides in neither of these inferences, for it is far more complex. The library is directly and tightly bound with its human past, yet concurrently operates on behalf of its specific societies in the present and in preparation for the future. Its function, in a very formal way that is well understood even though only subconsciously, is the stewardship of the social transcript.

There seems to be no way to prove this conclusion, except by the simple fact of the consistent tenacity with which society has clung to the library through millennia of challenge that has been visited upon society through the greatest variety of trying environmental conditions possible. The library is not a building or an act or even a bundle of acts; it is a cultural technology that extends the potential of articulate language and mind. It is a concept that expresses the most characteristic facet of the nature of humanity and manifests itself in values that inform acts.

The library relates very directly to all disciplines and to all aspects of life in the universe and within the mind. It is doubtful that any other institution can make that claim so clearly. The library manifests its potential most fruitfully in a social environment of total intellectual freedom, while it also is the institution that advances, in subtle and passive ways, individual liberty more comprehensively than any other. Also, more than any other social institution, the library exists to respond to the individual's freedom to think and inquire, and it also encourages those actions. Unlike any other social institution or commercial organization, the library ensures the continuity of culture through change of which it has, itself, contributed to the making. The library is a guarantor of security for individual expression, but in a way that draws toward a subtle commonality of understanding; this apparent contradiction is in fact a tension that is essential to cultural evolution because it stimulates the trial-and-error critical processes of reason. No other social institution has provided a combination of the freedom of thought, the means of pursuing that thought in relation to distant generations and remote places such that an environment conditioned by these possibilities is produced [3] to stir ideas, experiential memory, values, imagination, and creativity. The library is unique among social institutions.

Cultural technology is developed by and functions for society just as technology in a general sense is developed by and functions for the individual.

General technology is an artificial extension of human anatomical capabilities, and cultural technology is a cooperatively devised and maintained extension of intellectual capacities. The technology created by humanity to support the communication processes of cultural evolution is the library, which can be considered a prosthetic device of the mind. The substance of the responsibility assigned to the library has been referred to by various scholars as the golden chain, among them Irwin, the great chain of being, by Lovejoy, personal scholarship, by Butler,[4] and the social transcript, which is the label used in this book,[5] and surely in other terms. Donald T. Campbell (1974, p. 434), alleged founder of evolutionary epistemology, observes that there are many variation and selective retention processes leading to advances or changes in technology and culture, most direct among them being "the selective survival of complete social organizations, differentially as a function of cultural features. More important is selective borrowing, a process which probably leads to increased adaptation as far as easily tested aspects of technology are concerned, but could involve adaptive irrelevance in areas of culture where reality testing is more difficult." It is the important process of criticism, among other mental processes examined in Chapters 2 and 3, that the library facilitates. As a constant reminder in the reading of this text, while the concept of social transcript accounts for all experience that is shared, whether orally or in a recorded form, the reference here is to recorded experience.

The recorded form of experience is the province of the library, which has conserved it as faithfully as possible to the original thought, entirely through the power of language. This has not come about by accident or coincidence, but by intention and design. In its capacity as a social institution, the library was created and is maintained by society through cooperation among individuals and groups as an extension of the memory, for both individuals and societies, both at the point of origination and the point of reception, for the short term and the long term, spanning societies. Even if a particular record in the transcript is not read for hundreds of years, it remains in the memory, waiting to be evoked and functioning as an ever present redundancy to knowledge and experience.

As mentioned earlier, especially in Chapter 4, the library is also an unsurpassed treasury of words and meanings, therefore of ideas, concepts, and understandings, all of which are central to the interpretation of expressed ideas and the refinement of perceptions drawn from experience and based on self and world view. "The etymology of a word is generally (but not invariably) suggestive," semanticist Paul Ziff (1960, p. 190) reminds us. "For this reason and this reason alone, appeals to etymology are of great help in determining what meaning a word has. Words are transformed and change meaning in time but they rarely throw off every trace of their former meaning." From a different perspective, linguist Patrizia Violi (2001,

p. 219) also indicates this enriching feature of the variety of meanings contained in words used for differing purposes in differing contexts and times, observing that "lexical meanings appear in the form of diversified, partially superimposed, structures... It does not seem possible to define a single semantic structure which can be uniformly described by the same system of representation; rather, lexical meanings appear in the form of diversified, partially superimposed, structures." This unusually rich underpinning of culture and cultural evolution is part of the library experience and only the library experience.[6]

The library as cultural technology is again analogous to language precisely because it does incorporate the clarifying examples typical of linguistic redundancy in communication. Communication scientist Wilbur Schramm (1971, p. 39) observes its significance in communication, noting especially that "redundancy is built into all languages... in practical communication, redundancy is cultivated to combat noise and interference. Repetitions and examples are introduced where it may be hard to get a point." The library responds to a fundamental cultural necessity, helping to ensure the culture's continued viability by making possible the optimum use of the ever-growing store of knowledge and experience, best practices and best reasoning, but also the store of trials and errors.[7] Like any other institution created by society for its culture, the library experiences vicissitudes of societal support, but it remains. The library is the result of a cultural selection process for the purpose of adapting to diversity and change, and also for the purpose of optimizing the capacities that are unique to humanity and valued most highly by humanity to modify the environment.

When it is shared, recorded experience and other recorded information becomes knowledge, which is the basis for learning, problem-solving, decision-making, planning, understanding, mentation in general, and action in general. This sharing of knowledge is the fundamental guide to the provision of each of the specific library services and their development through generations. It defines the library function. This book is not about any one of those library services, which form the subject of library science or librarianship, but about the library itself, as concept and as function included among the class of organizations and services referred to as social institutions. The library as concept incorporates primary features of cultural technology, foremost among them communication, for it can be considered to perform dual capacity functions. But the library as concept is different from most other social institutions. For such apparent dual functions as the library performs serve purposes that are symbiotic, related at once to the present and the future, to the individual and society, to information for action and stimulation for the intellect, to unification of society and allowance for non conformity, to the specific and the universal, and to the effects of both the calming and arousal of mental activity. Library as concept is one cultural function, complex but monolithic.

Jesse Shera (1970, p. 60) preferred to think of the library as a social agency, "as an agency rather than as an institution—because, I think there is a real distinction between the great concepts like family, religion, law, and so on, and the agencies that are responsible for implementing their basic underlying bodies of belief." But when understood as a conceptualization essential to cultural evolution in ways that are being suggested especially by research and theory in cognitive science and neuroscience, the library surely is very much more than an agency, yet different from many other organizations designated as social institutions, as will be examined in the following section.

Thus, especially for those in the library and information professions it is essential that the function be seen in its entirety because, as evolutionary psychologist Leda Cosmides and anthropologists John Tooby and Jerome H. Barkow (1992, p. 11) explain, "understanding function makes an important and sometimes pivotal contribution to understanding design in systems that are otherwise bewildering in their complexity." Environmental psychologist Stephen Kaplan (1992, p. 590) observes that the natural human need of information occupies not just profound or formal learning activities but also the minor and major decisions of everyday life:

> Increasingly we have come to see preference as an expression of an intuitive guide to behavior, an inclination to make choices that would lead the individual away from inappropriate environments and toward desirable ones. As we have seen, the centrality of information in these decisions is quite appropriate. If humans are indeed organisms whose survival through the course of evolution required the construction and use of cognitive maps, then being attracted by information would seem thoroughly adaptive. In particular, people should be enticed by new information, by the prospect of updating and extending their cognitive maps.

This metaphor is also the basis of a paper on the philosophy of librarianship by H. Curtis Wright (1982, p. 7), who interprets the role of the profession as intellectual cartography, or, as he defines it, "the human art of orienting people to ideas—a service that constitutes its entire product, the only legitimate contribution it can make to anyone under any circumstances . . . No one knows the proper technique for maximizing a patron's orientation to knowledge. But creating that technique is clearly an *intellectual* problem in which action is subservient to knowledge." It is in library function that mind and society come together in significance to culture.

Theory, Mind, & Society

In the judgment of sociologist Roy Wood Sellars (1926, p. xxxvi), "The history of society is a history of the differentiation of values." A society is considered as such because of its specific culture, which is a socially inherited manner of fitting together, an evolving combination of systems apart from the state or any single individual. Cultural elements include many values, from the most basic need for survival to the more abstract need for either the comfort or the stimulation found in music. Reflecting on his inquiry into the notion of social progress, historian John B. Bury (1932, p. 348) writes, "we note how the history of the idea has been connected with the growth of modern science, with the growth of rationalism, and with the struggle for political and religious liberty." Not coincidently, these are key considerations in understanding the library function in cultural evolution.

Culture evolves much more rapidly than biology because the nature of its elements are more readily adaptable to a changing environment, as they are amenable to the influence of cultural technology. And culture is responsible for both the continuity of any society and its changes through evolution, a process that is so evident in humans that it may be the most distinguishing of the features that set the human species apart from others. While progress is the commonly accepted result of cultural evolution, there seems always to be justifiable reason to question this assessment. Looking through time retrospectively, however, the overall picture of this movement is at least directional, suggesting purpose in cultural evolution. Nonetheless, the nature of that purpose, if there is indeed purpose, remains to be stated, although it sometimes is considered to be a response to what seems to be a quest for truth. Along with the sense of progress as discussed in Chapter 3, which is a notion that humanity seems to embrace, complexity in life and a sense of increased rapidity in the passage of time are accompanying features that result from the diversification of ideas; ideas about one's self and about the world. This encompasses problem solving, criticism, dialectic, creativity, and imagination, all of which are mechanisms for gaining control over nature and helping humans fit into and ultimately even change the surrounding culture. Above all in this mixture, the molding of values within any society may be the most critical single element of cultural evolution because it is so constant a point of reference in cultural selection.

A perplexing idea of historian Arthur O. Lovejoy (1936, p. 5) holds that "The conclusion reached by a process of thought is also not infrequently the conclusion of the process of thought." He explains this idea with the observation that "The more significant factor in the matter may be, not the dogma which certain persons proclaim–be that single or manifold in its meaning–but the motives or reasons which have led them to it. And motives and reasons partly identical may contribute to the production of very diverse conclusions, and the same substantive conclusions may, at different periods or in different minds, be generated by entirely distinct logical or other motives." Broadfield (1949, p. 67) is quite justified in noting that "No one can seriously question the fundamental rightness of the aim to discover non-personal truth: but although it may be desirable to eliminate the personal, it is never possible to eliminate altogether the subjective element in the relation of the mind to its object." Biologist Edward O. Wilson (1978, p. 67) describes in capsule form the interactive processes of mind and society that results in what often is termed human nature.

> So the human mind is not a tabula rasa, a clean slate on which experience draws intricate pictures with lines and dots. It is more accurately described as an autonomous decision-making instrument, an alert scanner of the environment that approaches certain kinds of choices and not others in the first place, then innately leans toward one option as opposed to others and urges the body into action according to a flexible schedule that shifts automatically and gradually from infancy into old age. The accumulation of old choices, the memory of them, the recollection of those to come, the re- experiencing of emotions by which they were engendered, all constitute the mind. Particularities in decision making distinguish one human being from another. But the rules followed are tight enough to produce a broad overlap in the decisions taken by all individuals and hence a convergence powerful enough to be labeled human nature.

From another perspective, according to anthropologist Donald Symons (1992, p. 144), evolutionary psychologists contend with a certain degree of specificity that the network of evolved modules in the human mind are "the brain/mind mechanisms that collectively constitute human nature." Not everyone, however, agrees that there is such a thing as human nature, although most would concur that human behavior is the product of genetics and culture. In either case, in his chapter titled "Is There Progress in Human Nature?" Charles Van Doren (1967, p. 313) concludes from his review of the pertinent literature "that human nature will remain the same and not progress, and such improvements as may occur will be the result only of progress in the conditions of human life." For present purposes, humans are the most complex beings known, and their reasoning, experience, memory, and communication powers are the substance of the library concept.

Thus, although the development of theory for specific parts of the library function, which is to say the accumulation of daily operations and services, may be fairly straightforward, development of theory for the overall function is much less so. For the content of the library constitutes its memory function, while the daily operations and services of the library constitute its preservation and recall mechanisms, and the whole social phenomenon operates through a context that evolves over time. Information scientist Brenda Dervin (1996, pp. 17–20) finds eight relevant themes common in the research and theory of context: knowledge is partial and temporary; reality is continuous, gap filled, changeable across time-space; the knower-and-the-known are inextricably bound; context is not usefully conceptualized as independent entity; context requires a focus on process; focus must be placed on the dialectical relationships between product and process; focus must be placed on multiple interdependencies; context is a necessary source of meaning. The library function is evident only in a humanly social context, because it is no more and no less than a humanly social function.

The long-term function of the library responds to and fosters cultural evolution; the short-term (quotidian) function is stimulated by and responsive to human behavior, which is a phenomenon described by behavioral psychologist B. F. Skinner (1965, pp. 20–21) as "a difficult subject matter, not because it is inaccessible, but because it is extremely complex. Since it is a process, rather than a thing, it cannot easily be held still for observation. It is changing, fluid, and evanescent, and for this reason it makes great technical demands upon the ingenuity and energy of the scientist. But there is nothing essentially insoluble about the problems which arise from this fact."

An understanding of human behavior is fundamental to the services and operations of the library and, ultimately, of the library function,[8] but theory that would integrate the two has proved elusive. Whereas physical chemist Michael Polanyi (1959, p. 20) no doubt is justified in his statement that "Modern science disclaims any intention of understanding the hidden nature of things; its philosophy condemns any such endeavour as vague, misleading and altogether unscientific," it is the nature of people that is the substance of librarianship and, therefore, the proper basis of theory and philosophy. The library is not really different or separate from the mind, but rather an extension of it. If the mind, in relation to this extension, could be analyzed in the manner of, for example, geological analysis, realization of the library function would be much less a challenge. "Ultimately, all information activity is reducible to individual motivations and actions," observes information scientist Norman Roberts (1982, p. 98); "a circumstance which might be thought conducive to the shaping of ascertained information behaviour tendencies into tools of analysis. Obviously, this has not happened."

It is the complexity of the individual mind that poses the greatest challenge to an understanding of society, and especially to an understanding of the human need for nourishment of the mind and its resultant acts, quite simply because that connection informs the function of the library.[9] Talcott Parsons (1949) sheds light on this problematic aspect of theory in his interpretation of the relevant thought of Max Weber, whose strong influence Parsons acknowledges. He says that Weber contends that our interest in natural phenomena is centered in their aspects of abstract generality, not of concrete individuality, and that the aim of the natural sciences is the formulation of a system of universally applicable general laws. However, he writes (p. 592), "For the natural sciences general concepts constitute an end in themselves. With the social sciences, on the other hand, this is not so. Our interest in human beings and their cultural achievements is not that of abstract generality but of individual uniqueness. They are not to us 'cases' of general laws."

Language is central to mental and social process and, therefore, fundamental to cultural evolution, for language is central to focusing thought, branching thought, recording experience, securing memory, and communicating thought with precision, subtlety, and flexibility. Memory and language function together to form an extraordinary potential to process information and, as a consequence, to help mold the identity of each individual and ultimately to motivate cultural evolution. A pioneer in the classification of knowledge and library education, Melvil Dewey (1968, p. 77) is credited with the observation that "the genealogy is this: reading begets reflection, reflection begets motive, motive begets action, and action begets habit, and habit begets that supreme thing—character." The ends of this process are knowledge, learning, and understanding, the potential of which was greatly enhanced and accelerated with the emergence of movable-type printing; literate entertainment was made possible on a very large scale, commensurate with the expansion of literacy. These are the intellectual elements of communication, and therefore the bases for sharing experience, values, and knowledge. The power of articulate language has proved to be a mighty force in culture's evolution, for language is as natural an energy in the human sciences as the formation of ice from water under freezing conditions is in the physical sciences. Thus the social transcript is equally natural to the evolution of culture. It is in the spirit of this idea that Winston Churchill (1950, p. 59) shared a major lesson he had learned about science as a consequence of the struggle of World War II, and which he relates more broadly to human nature:

> Scientists should never underrate the deep-seated qualities of human nature and how, repressed in one direction, they will certainly break out in another. The *genus homo* . . . is a tough creature who has traveled here by a very long road. His nature has been shaped and his virtues ingrained by many millions of years of struggle, fear, and pain, and his spirit has, from the earliest dawn of history, shown itself upon occasion capable of mounting to the sublime, far above material conditions or mortal terrors.

Contributing quite substantively to the durability of human nature is the maintenance of the social transcript. "Human beings and human societies are not structures that are built or machines that are forged," Churchill (p. 61) reminded his audience of scientists on that occasion, but they do manage to retain their knowledge and values.

The social sciences, in general, and librarianship, in particular, have always struggled to develop theory that would not only explain their purpose, but would also be accepted as scientific, thus as conclusive as theory can be. Talcott Parsons (1978, p. 409) explains the most fundamental reason for the need felt among social scientists, as well as biological scientists, to pattern their work on that of the physical scientists, and sets forth concisely the reasons for this problematic departure. He writes that "In the development of modern science, knowledge of the physical world was the first to develop and has in an important sense remained prototypical. We have, however, already stated emphatically that science is not to be confined to the physical sciences but is to be extended to the other two major categories, which Comte called the biological and the social; the latter we are calling the 'sciences of action.'"

In the social sciences, "There is, and always will be, a real shortage of 'two-way laws' (that is, laws that both predict and explain)," writes social philosopher Michael Scriven (1968, p. 88). "This has typically been treated by social scientists as a sign of the immaturity of their subject; but in fact it is simply a sign of its nature and is very like the situation in the 'messier' areas of the physical sciences." And it is widely understood that John Ziman's summary of the situation (1978, p. 31), that "Needless to say, the most impressive way of validating a scientific theory is to confirm its *prediction*" is valid but discouraging to the social sciences. The idea of vision, the perception of the potential in a concept, is one of those human features that may not be common to all individuals, but is admired generally and sought in positions of leadership. Literary scholar John L. Lowes (1933, p. 35) observes that "For vision—which is seeing with what lies behind the eye—is not something independent of knowledge, or somehow superadded upon knowledge when it is acquired. It is a faculty which works *through* knowledge. And knowledge without vision is barren, as vision without knowledge distorts."

Thus, Michael Scriven's characterization of the social sciences as "messier" than the physical sciences certainly is true in some sense, but it carries an unnecessarily negative connotation, and it overlooks some of the similarities to be found among all the sciences. For example, cell geneticist François Jacob (1982, p. 9) posits that "In some respects at least, myths and science fulfill a similar function: they both provide human beings with a representation of the world and of the forces that are supposed to govern it. They both fix the limits of what is considered as possible," while science philosopher Michael Ruse (2005, p. 277) asserts that "Without metaphor, science could never exhibit epistemic virtues." Like art and religion, science is a product of cognitive fluidity, says archeologist Steven J. Mithen (1996, p. 215). "It relies on psychological processes which had originally evolved in specialized cognitive domains and only emerged when these processes could work together. Cognitive fluidity enabled technology to be developed which could solve problems and store information." And prefiguring the comment of Michael Ruse, he adds "Of perhaps even greater significance, it allowed the possibility for the use of powerful metaphors and analogy, without which science could not exist."

A provocative depiction of the way culture and society interact is offered by Talcott Parsons (1978, p. 373). For him, the environment does not merely condition the functioning of living systems in random ways; "the relation is *selective* on *both* sides. Not least important, there is a set of physico-chemical components that is internally part of any given living organism. Life, from this point of view, is a mode of the *organization* of the physical world, and not every set of physical components is equally favorable to different kinds of living organizations."

For the most part, humanity has selected a means to ensure the durability of its social transcript, and that means is realized through the library function. Science sociologist David Bloor (1976, p. 86) observes that social institutions seem to exhibit intimate connections with objectivity. "Indeed the leap may be made to the hypothesis that perhaps that very special, third status between the physical and psychological belongs, and only belongs, to what is social... But the theoretical component of knowledge is precisely the social component." All areas of investigation are not the same in fundamental nature, therefore each area must be investigated on the basis of its own nature. And appropriateness to the nature of the area is the guiding criterion in choice of strategy in investigation, so that quality of investigation and of findings are determined by appropriateness of the strategy and the degree of expertise in executing it.

Although human beings are extraordinary in the extent to which they try to control nature, they remain a part of nature. They are natural beings. Research in one area is neither superior or inferior to another, so it may be worth more to focus on similarities in areas of research rather than on differences. One model of research does not fit all areas. The essential point, writes Parsons (1978, p. 408), is that "nature, by coming to be humanly known, comes to be in a crucial sense part of the system of action rather than only part of the external world 'out there.' Briefly, I should like to suggest that this may be taken to mean that, though nature is indeed out there, *knowledge* of it becomes part of the *internal environment* of action, with all the very important implications of such a status." And he concludes this train of thought (p. 409) with the theory that "the physical and cultural systems are both adaptive subsystems; however, one is outside, the other inside, the system of action. We referred to this phenomenon in speaking of knowledge as included in the action system, as being part of the internal environment of action for human actors." Library educator J. M. Orr (1977, p. 194) suggests how the library fits into this picture:

> The direct relationship between man and his libraries has already been established. The library is his collective memory and in quantitative terms is clearly supreme... On its own, its creative ability is nil, but it complements man's mind by feeding it some of the data on which the re-creation of knowledge is nourished. Data are also received from other sources. Information from a library is at best second-hand and is not comprehensible to a person without a knowledge of the real world as a referral point; in

this sense, second-hand information only adds to real information as it has been directly perceived.

The library is the cultural technology that extends the human potential to transcend many obstacles that otherwise would limit intellectual experience. Neuropsychologist Merlin Donald (1991, p. 311) points out that some cultural artifacts "have produced a collective memory bank as real, in terms of hardware, as any external memory device for a computer. And because they are not bound by time and space they transport the very limited capabilities of the individual into realms that would not be remotely reachable by an isolated mind." Chapter 3 reviewed aspects of diversity, selection, and adaptation that are particularly instrumental in cultural evolution, and found that selection is the obvious function humanity employs to cope with diversity, in the hope of adapting to a changing environment. Selection applies to all aspects of human life, and it is through selection that the cultural tool library has been created and sustained throughout all of civilization. The library, in all its aspects, is maintained through selection, just as mind and society progress through life. Physicist John Ziman (2000, p. 277) relates selection to the importance in science of the function of falsifiability, although with a wider scope, because of its kinship with criticism in optimizing the reliability of scientific knowledge. But he emphasizes that "It is also a 'sociological' model, in that this process of 'selection' is not limited to self-criticism. The prescription that an individual scientist should check her findings exhaustively before making a research claim is secondary to a pervasive social function exercised publicly by a research community." Well over a century ago, art philosopher Paul Souriau (1881, p. 43) described the value of this trial-and-error process commonly shared in science and daily life:

> By a kind of artificial selection, we can in addition substantially perfect our thought and make it more and more logical. Of all the ideas which present themselves to our mind, we note only those which have some value and can be utilized in reasoning. For every single idea of a judicious and reasonable nature which offers itself to us, what hosts of frivolous, bizarre, and absurd ideas cross our mind. Those persons who, upon considering the marvelous results at which knowledge has arrived, cannot imagine that the human mind could achieve this by a simple fumbling, do not bear in mind the great number of scholars working at the same time on the same problem, and how much time even the smallest discovery costs them. Even genius has need of patience. (Cited by Donald T. Campbell, 1974, p. 429)

Science is an evident process of selection. Two essential aspects of scientific investigation, according to neuroscientist Jean-Pierre Changeux (2004, pp. 224–226), are the collection of data through observation and the use of formal rules, or theory, to organize and interpret the data. He points out that "Each of these two approaches assumes a high degree of projective activity on the part of the human brain: on the one hand, exploring the external world, comparing perceptions with one another, noting inconsistencies and detecting patterns; and, on the other, conducting internal "experiments" with a view to comparing memories of prior events, examining representations for internal consistency, and evaluating their logical implications." Over time, he adds in drawing an analogy between the processes of scientific investigation and those of the larger society, the two approaches combined with the selection process of public debate and in due course generated the vast noosphere. The record of this process serves continuously as a building block for the acquisition of further knowledge, while the process itself "resembles to some extent the biological evolution of species by natural selection." And, he writes, "The storing of this orally transmitted knowledge in the form of written texts in which observational evidence and theoretical conjectures were combined in an organized, rational way marked a decisive change . . . The storing of increasingly large numbers of scrolls (*volumen*) in libraries constitutes perhaps the first sign of the institutionalization of scientific learning." Following the earlier analogy drawn by Changeux, it was also the first sign of the institutionalization of the general noosphere. In their discussion of the abilities of humans that are truly outstanding in every way when compared to other beings, Leda Cosmides and John Tooby (2002, p. 172) conclude that the cognitive niche is to be credited. This is an adaptive mode whose distinguishing feature is "the use of contingent information for the regulation of improvised behavior that is successfully tailored to local conditions—an adaptive mode." It is so sophisticated that it will select certain information "even though the information is only applicable temporarily or locally" (p. 180).

Reference was made earlier to the theory of neuroscientist Merlin Donald (2001, p. 202) that human uniqueness resides in a radically improved conscious capacity and, therefore, that the human level of consciousness is a strong influence in adaptation to and control over the environment. What this conscious capacity requires above all, he says (p. 130), is the ability "to focus, or concentrate, resources." This particular adaptative function in cognitive processing is "a very practical one, to provide extra resources when needed" (p. 131). Donald points out that extended conscious capacity is an efficient solution to the challenges, in part because "it is domain-general and can be used in virtually any situation that a species is likely to encounter."

Donald's explanation (p. 313) of the processes at work in this phenomenon sounds very much like the social function of library in evolution, as it is understood in the present essay:

> Natural memory display is poor, lacks definition and detail, and is notoriously unreliable. The external memory field gives us sharper and more durable mental representations. This allows the conscious mind to reflect on thought itself and to evolve longer, more abstract, procedures that serve

> to verify and control the quality of its own actions. These procedures give us the basis for turning thinking into a more formal activity, subject to much stricter standards of revision. This results in a scaffolded cultural process that can accumulate and improve over time. It allows cultures to develop thought habits that can be communicated back to the individual and have a profound impact on how cognitive business is conducted. Given this, societies can absorb the efforts of previous generations at a faster pace, and the shared cognitive processes that result become easier to refine and reproduce. This leads to qualitative changes in what we can achieve with our limited mental resources. Endless repeated reflections on the same core material over successive generations can give a society a more powerful set of conscious procedures to follow; that is, much better ways of thinking.

Theory underlying the present essay perceives library function in the context of evolving mind and society and, in doing so, incorporates theory and methods followed in all areas of inquiry. It embraces society as a living organism just as the individual is, and library function as a cultural technology, or an extracerebral mechanism, as neuroscientist Jean-Pierre Changeux would likely consider it, or as extended conscious capacity, as Merlin Donald describes it, for both the individual and society. Therefore, cognitive processes of many kinds are at the center of theory pertinent to this essay and, that being the case, memory, knowledge, learning, communication (above all through articulate symbolic language), environmental factors, imagination and innovation, and other considerations that have been addressed in the present text as relating to culture and its evolution play key roles in providing theoretical bases. The library function in its stewardship of the social transcript is the focus of theory, so this essay has concentrated on cultural evolution from that unique perspective.

Against that backdrop the primary forces of evolution (diversity, leading to selection, leading to adaptation) are seen to be strengthened and enhanced by library function in activating culture. Adaptation is solely the function of the individual and society, while the functions of diversity and selection belong also in the domain of library function as a cultural technology. Both the individual human being and the society in which that individual dwells are complex organisms. Such organisms, writes neurologist Antonio R. Damasio (1999, p. 139), "placed in complex environments require large repertoires of knowledge, the possibility of choosing among many available responses, the ability to construct novel combinations of response, and the ability to plan ahead so as to avoid disadvantageous situations and instead propitiate favorable ones." Selection is at once the result of reasoned effort, the instrument of action, and the key to understanding.

Understanding

Paraphrasing eighteenth-century philosopher John Locke, intellectual historian Arthur O. Lovejoy (1936, p. 8) emphasizes that "Man must become habitually mindful of the limitations of his mental powers, must be content with that relative and practical understanding which is the only organ of knowledge that he possesses." This is so, he later concludes (p. 333), because "The utility of a belief and its validity are independent variables; and erroneous hypotheses are often avenues to truth." Things too often are not what they seem, we can easily be misled by our thoughts, and most aspects of our thought processes, if not all, offer only partial adequacy to truth and/or utility. The mental state we seek in reaching conclusions and making decisions, but cannot always achieve, is that of understanding.

The function of understanding is described by Michael Polanyi (1959, p. 20), who argues that the functions of articulate logical operations can be transcended by tacit powers of the mind, also observes that "our tacit powers achieve these results by reorganizing our experience so as to gain intellectual control over it. There is one word which covers all these operations. They all consist in comprehending experience, i.e. in making sense of it; the word which covers them all is simply '*understanding*.'" Philosopher Michael Scriven (1968, pp. 89–90) is somewhat more pragmatic in his definition of understanding as the key notion behind that of explanation, and therefore of cause. He writes that "Understanding is integrated, related knowledge; more generally . . . it is the capacity to produce the appropriate response to novel stimuli within a certain range or field . . . Models, from analogies to axiomatizations, are the key to understanding . . . and the possession of understanding is valuable just because it does embody this capacity to handle novelty." The most general, and therefore the least complex, indication of the significance of understanding is perhaps that suggested by psychobiologist Henry Plotkin (1998, p. 177), who finds that "Nothing is more important to our sense of a sensible and stable world than the connection that we make in our minds between the component bits of, or events in, that world. We understand the world, the kind of place it is, by way of these connections."

Explanation, sense making, experience, tacit knowledge, models, connection, interrelation, and integration are the key considerations in the concept of understanding. In addressing the effort to understand spoken utterances, philosopher Paul Ziff (1972, p. 18) concludes that "in effect one performs a morphological analysis of the utterance; the utterance is segmented, decomposed into its morphological constituents. The data processing that can culminate in understanding has a specific character: it is an analytic process. Understanding, not surprisingly, is akin to figuring out, deciphering, decoding, and the like." Understanding recorded communication surely fits this pattern, but with the advantage of a text that can be analyzed repeatedly for the purpose of refining the deciphered meaning.

Theory is not the same as understanding, but it is a tool that leads toward understanding. Sociologist Stephen Toulmin (1961, p. 30) argues that "To discover that events of a certain kind are predictable—even to develop effective techniques for forecasting them—is evidently quite different from having an adequate theory about them, through which they can be understood." Chemist Michael Polanyi (1959, p. 21) acknowledges that the process of understanding leads well beyond what a "strict empiricism regards as the domain of legitimate knowledge; but I reject such an empiricism." He also rejects such empiricism on the basis of another, conflicting, observation, that "Words can convey information, a series of algebraic symbols can constitute a mathematical deduction, a map can set out the topography of a region; but neither words nor symbols nor maps can be said to communicate an understanding of themselves." Library theorist D. J. Foskett (1984, pp. 39–40) reasons that an individual forms concepts and organizes them into a coherent pattern, finding support for this conclusion in a lecture of geneticist and philosopher Bentley Glass (1970). According to Glass, "The data and the facts alone do not constitute knowledge in the sense of understanding. Information is useful, but the observations must be fitted into concepts and conceptual schemes, or paradigms, that determine our outlook and direct our processes of investigation and enquiry... what is necessary is insight, and insight may come through learning, if we study the right things in the right way."

In other words, understanding means seeing an elusive organization in the perceived phenomena. Biologist Colin S. Pittendrigh (1958, p. 394) observes about the question of order in a biological sense, therefore, that "There is no such thing as organization in any absolute sense, pure and simple. Organization is always relative, and relative to an end." It is not difficult to see a cultural parallel in the actions of selection and adaptation. This is highlighted especially in his further comment (p. 395) that "organization is nonrandomness; it is the converse of disorder or randomness... Organization implies, in modern terms, an information content." Selection, adaptation, and the evolution of culture itself depend on the faculty of understanding and stem from the perception of order relative to some end.

The state of understanding involves knowledge, perception, insight, reproduction, explanation, connection, and prediction. It emerges from the analysis, synthesis, and reasoned merging of concepts. Science historian George Basalla (1988, p. 215) points to the historiographic phenomenon whereby "Local disturbances that loom large in conventional historical accounts recede as the historian studies the entire record of humanity," but it is a phenomenon that applies to all aspects of life and is referred to most commonly as the failure-to-see-the-forest-for-the-trees problem. It is a matter of perspective. In describing his theory of knowledge, Michael Polanyi (1959, p. 29) accounts for the psychological observations that underpin it. He notes that one advances from a knowledge of the parts to an understanding of the whole, and not the reverse. Whether this comprehension is effortless or difficult—even to the point of discovery—the process always works this way, and "Once comprehension is achieved, we are not likely to lose sight again of the whole; yet comprehension is not completely irreversible. By looking very closely at the several parts of a whole, we may succeed in diverting our attention from the whole and even lose sight of it altogether."

But understanding can also derive from the mental phenomenon of intuition, which neuropsychologist Richard L. Gregory (2004, pp. 485–486) defines as "essentially, arriving at decisions or conclusions without explicit or conscious processes of reasoned thinking... Psychologists find these important matters for living almost impossible to formulate." Philosopher Malcolm Hollick (2006, p. 34) broadens the scope of definition a bit, writing that "Intuition means gaining knowledge or insight by direct perception without reasoning. It involves looking deeply into something rather than standing back to get an objective overview. It leads to an understanding that is not accessible to the thinking mind, and that often changes our perception of the way things work or are related. And it often brings a new sense of the unity and wholeness of a phenomenon." Intuition, it would seem, is a capacity that is likely to be stirred in the library environment.

Sociologist and philosopher Max Weber (1947) finds the major distinction between the physical and the social sciences in the matter of understanding, specifically in the usual German translation of *Verstehen*. His interpretation of the term, however, takes the word *understanding* to a more precise meaning, and is analogized as a process engaged by the sociologist or anthropologist to interpret the actions of indigenous people on their own terms, from their own perspectives, and following their own motives and values, rather than interpreting them in terms of the observer's own concepts. In short, it is an attempt to know the object from the inside: its walls, floor, and ceiling, as well as its environment. Perfect understanding is an ideal that has its own criteria. Thus, sociologist Stephen Toulmin (1961, pp. 94–95) advises that "The intellectual frame of a man's thought displays itself less in the detailed results he enunciates than in the questions he asks and the assumptions which underlie his theorizing." Of the various contributions of the library to culture, to the individual and society, both now and over great expanses of time, perspective is the one that incorporates all of them. D. J. Foskett (1962, p. 11) casts this idea in pragmatic terms:

> If we can become enthusiastically involved with the programme of a particular reader, and still remain outside the narrow limits of his special interest, we can very often bring to bear a keener sense of perspective than he has

> himself. One of the most useful functions the librarian can perform to-day is that of taking a broad view, of seeing those factors that are common to many fields, of widening the horizon of the reader, and assisting the cross-fertilisation of ideas that is now recognized as a valuable counter to over-specialisation.

Perspective has much to do with selection, which is fundamental to cultural evolution and to all functions of the library. Perspective can both narrow and broaden the pool of diversity; diversity evokes selection; criticism and dialectic guide the way to selection; words and concepts require selection for purposes of communication; selection in the lexical context leads to understanding through communication. "In the evolution of scientific ideas, as in the evolution of species, change results from the selective perpetuation of variants," says Stephen Toulmin (1961, p. 110). Selection in the context of ideas means that "The scientific ideas which survive are the ones which have best proved their validity, while those which have been discarded—for example, the ideas of the alchemists—can be thought of as the pterodactyls of science" (p. 82). But the remains of the pterodactyl carry knowledge that can provide new perspective; and if that leads to theorization, then the standard for identifying the value of that knowledge (p. 61) "must be, not what is familiar, but rather what is intelligible and reasonable in the course of Nature." For, he says (p. 16), "In the evolution of scientific ideas, as in political history, the critical analysis of contemporary developments is quite as illuminating as the post-mortem dissection of completed episodes." There is nothing new under the sun, only new ways of seeing it, for culture is derivative.

Problem Solving & Creativity

The significance of the concept of *creativity* becomes most clear when considered in contrast with the kind of thinking that offers nothing new, or ordinary thinking. Cognitive psychologist Robert W. Weisberg (1993, pp. 10–11) describes what he calls "ordinary thinking" as beginning in continuity with the past, so that "we use the old to generate the new. Ordinary thinking also goes beyond the past, but does so in straightforward ways, through reasoning and the accumulation of new pieces of information. There are no sudden spontaneous leaps beyond what we have experienced, no unconscious illumination, no bolts of lightning from the blue although things sometimes feel that way." But the challenges we always generate or that are generated in aspects of our environment over which we have little control, and most often even their nature "could never have been forecast in detail on the basis of the earlier historical record alone," says Stephen Toulmin (1972, p. 331). "As a result, men demonstrate the 'rationality' of their social and political procedures as much by their capacity to cope with unforeseeable problems as by their capacity to deal with problems that were already 'implicit' in what had gone before."[10] Specific situations can undergo change, but because the respective environments also undergo evolution, the implications of the situation for the environment and the implications of the environment for the situation no longer are quite the same. There is no end to the need for problem solving and creativity.

Thus, according to cognitive scientist Margaret A. Boden (2004, p. 1), creativity affects all aspects of human life and is within the grasp of virtually everyone. It consists in "the ability to come up with ideas or artifacts that are *new*, *surprising* and *valuable*." But she emphasizes that for the idea to be creative in a fundamental sense it cannot just be unusual or new in the sense of a mere novelty or never having happened before. Boden (pp. 41–42) adds that "Fundamentally creative ideas are surprising in a deeper way. Where this type of creativity is concerned, we have to do with expectations not about probabilities, but about possibilities." Creativity does not necessarily imply an extraordinarily high level of intelligence, such as usually is associated with the notion of genius, which Michael Polanyi (1959, p. 19) cleverly defines as consisting "in the power of applying the originality of youth to the experience of maturity," but it does incorporate the synergism of vision and focus in an especially productive manner.[11] "Genius is the ability to see the world in a profoundly new way," writes sociologist Graeme Donald Snooks (2007, p. 212), broadening the definition somewhat. "This requires a high degree of proficiency in strategic thinking—of pattern recognition and inductive generalization. In turn, such proficiency can only be achieved through a high degree of integration of body and mind." Finally, business consultant Sheila J. Henderson (2004, p. 120) concludes that "One recognizes an inventor through his or her problem-finding vision and strong problem-solving focus."

Consequently, as usually is presumed, intelligence and creativity are related in some way, although not in a way that now is amenable to simple formulization. Combining psychology, anthropology, biology, cognitive science, and neuroscience, the field of evolutionary psychology recognizes that the evolutionary process constructed the computational systems present in the minds of organisms primarily through natural selection. Respectively psychologist and anthropologist, Leda Cosmides and John Tooby (2002, p. 146) distinguish two related meanings of intelligence. "We call these *dedicated intelligence* and *improvisational intelligence*. Dedicated intelligence refers to the ability of a computational system to solve a predefined, target set of problems. Improvisational intelligence refers to the ability of a computational system to improvise solutions to novel problems." Cognitive scientist Margaret A. Boden (2004, pp. 3–6) interprets the differences in forms of creativity to styles of thinking, not just intelligence level, but all motivated by consideration of value, and in doing so, finds three forms of creativity: making unfamiliar combinations of familiar ideas; exploring conceptual spaces; and transforming conceptual spaces.

The complex processes that underlie creativity are summarized by cell and developmental biologist Karl H. Pfenninger (2001, p. 92): "Creativity involves the vision or the determination of novel contexts between facts in our external or our internal worlds—contexts that had not been recognized previously. This requires the association in the mind of diverse and apparently unrelated images and, thus, represents a higher level yet of integrative capacity of the nervous system." Creativity is integrative and it does place higher demands on intelligence. Pfenninger and science writer Valerie Shubik (2001, p. 224) employ a classic example of how creativity functions in natural science to describe the laws that connect the different levels of organization and that govern the organization at each level, observing that "The interactions among a particular set of subunits explain many of the properties of the next-higher unit. A creative work of science presents a novel hypothesis regarding such relationships and contains a set of data supporting it. We call a work of science particularly beautiful or elegant when the conclusions are unambiguous and unexpected, and when a simple theory illuminates a broad range of phenomena." Moreover, sociologist F. Stuart Chapin, (1928, p. 408) states that "It can be shown that speculative thought (running to fantasy and day-dreaming) is not an inherently different kind of thought from scientific thinking, but is only relatively different." A spirit of intellectual freedom in the broadest sense best supports the environment most encouraging of creativity as it is described in the preceding paragraphs. Says Lyman Bryson (1947, p. 7), "The conditions of freedom are the conditions in which the creative powers of men, and all the other creative factors of nature that man has access to, can work best." And he elaborates, connecting creativity to action, saying (p. 13) "changes take place within personalities and these changes are followed by changes in physical events. And this is creative action. By conditions of freedom we shall mean, all the way through this essay, those conditions that make the greatest possible opportunity for creativeness to work. Our whole purpose in seeking the conditions of freedom is to give man's creative powers their chance." The first step in this direction is that provided by the environment.

Summary

The more we know about physical science, which has become the *basis* for comparison within all serious investigation and discourse, the more we see similarities to investigation into any other aspect of human life. Indeed, there are differences that distinguish all the sciences, whether physical, social, or human, because the objects of their interest simply are not the same. The concept of library leans on all the possibilities to be found in the various sciences, most heavily perhaps on the social sciences, but on all of them. That has been a problem in coming to grips with a set of theories from which a philosophy might be derived. These seven chapters have addressed what is found in the relevant literature to be of greatest significance in identifying the function of the library as cultural technology in evolution, its institutional uniqueness, its value to both individual and society. This excursion has proved to be an examination of the mind in society as reflected in the concept of library.

Throughout these chapters, it is quite clear that articulate symbolic language has evinced the most significant influence on culture because of its capacity in so many distinctively human aspects of life: to refine thinking and values; to facilitate the generation of new ideas; to gain insight into the future; to contemplate options, causes and effects; to enable the sharing of knowledge and experience over time and space; and, in short, to expand the scope and depth of the knowledge and experience held in culture. Language also has played a significant part in this book because it structures the social transcript, an ever-increasing part of that being the recorded language, which is to say, the library. The library is humanity's unparalleled lexicon and encyclopedia under continuous revision. In that sense, the library is humanity's memory of any thought that can be formulated and recorded and, therefore, is a major influence in intellectual cooperation at any given time and place, and it is the single most important contributor to intellectual cooperation over time and space. "Specifically, the functions of culture are to relate man to his environment," concludes anthropologist Leslie A. White (1959, p. 8), "his terrestrial habitat and the circumambient cosmos—on the one hand, and to relate man to man, on the other. Man is related to his habitat by means of tools, techniques, attitudes, and beliefs." The place of the library in this grand process is quite significant.

Key concepts other than those associated most directly with language, and which repeatedly have appeared in this study, include selection, diversification, understanding, creativity, and order. The library concept is built around language, for which it constitutes the super lexicon by amassing the gamut of meaning and nuance as they have been expressed for millennia, and by steadfastly continuing to expand the mind's potential through the alternatives in shades of thought it offers. Library function provides order but also accommodates refinement, change, and even the potential to challenge that order. In this regard, linguist Benjamin Lee Whorf (1956, p. 252) observes that, for him, the study of language "shows that the forms of a person's thoughts are controlled by inexorable laws of pattern of which he is unconscious. These patterns are the unperceived intricate systematizations of his own language." Whorf continues that "every language is a vast pattern-system, different from others, in which are culturally ordained the forms and categories by which the personality not only communicates, but also analyzes nature, notices or neglects types of relationship and phenomena, channels his reasoning, and builds the house of his consciousness."

The library stimulates, facilitates, and in various ways encourages to their fullest these critical functions in ways and to the extent that no other social institution or commercial enterprise has the capacity or intention to equal. Social anthropologist Jack Goody (2000, p. 144) calls writing a "technology of the intellect," emphasizing that it is "not about the primary level of physical instrumentation but about the way that writing affects cognitive or intellectual operations, which I take in a wide sense as relating to the understanding of the world in which we live, especially the general methods we use for this." His distinction is similar to that made in the present essay between librarianship and library. With regard to memory held in writing he refers to storage of "an infinity of information in a more or less permanent form—not, of course, at the level of the individual but at the level of the archive, the library, and now the computer, all of which hold information in graphic form." Goody (p. 146) adds that "The use of these devices does not inevitably lead to cumulative knowledge, but they are intrinsic to its development." As a cultural technology the library is intrinsic to knowledge and integral to cultural evolution.

Attention to library philosophy has been very rigid and formalized and has failed to lead to acceptable and useful conclusions. Most often this is because the effort has been a quest for a model thought to exist outside the library, as reflected both in the repeated attempts and the varied explanations of their inadequacy. Historian Charles E. Rosenberg (1979, p. 447) describes a situation in cultural historiography that is similar to that encountered in considering the library concept, and therefore may be helpful in adopting a different approach to the establishment of a basis for the field. "Like the ethnological field-worker, historians of knowledge must integrate formal intellectual content with social and institutional organization, systems of economic support, and finally, the values that sanction and reward the career choice of members of a particular intellectual subculture. Like ethnology itself at the beginning of this century, we must free ourselves from the domination of overschematized developmental models and seek to understand the specific forms of particular cultures." While the library is unique as a cultural technology, the difficulty inherent in understanding it as a concept with broad implications is not.

Stewardship of the social transcript is a function that also incorporates careful attention to democratic ideals and the sense of place, as described in Chapter 6, which are closely connected. Freedom to read and think what one chooses is related in the library to the accessibility of ideas that have been expressed in a vast, even unpredictable array of possibilities, as well as to an environment that encourages freedom of intellectual exploration into at least as broad a range of possibilities. The library's stewardship of the social transcript has long worked within the framework of laws and regulations administered through any number of auspices, both formal and informal, doubtless stretching them on occasion, to encourage this human penchant and to do so even through adverse conditions.

Historian Paul Saenger (1997, p. 263) captures a significant early stage in the development of the expected library environment, writing that

> It was in the chained libraries of the late thirteenth century that the reader's need for silence was first professed. In the late antique library and early medieval monastery, where readers had read aloud, each reader's own voice had acted as a neurophysiological screen, blocking out the sounds of the adjacent readers. When readers began to read visually, any oral reading became a source of potential distraction. Even quiet oral reading at the crowded desks of the chained reference collection in the medieval library would have made study difficult.

Saenger also notes (p. 264) that "Psychologically, silent reading emboldened the reader because it placed the source of his curiosity completely under personal control. In the still largely oral world of the ninth century, if one's intellectual speculations were heretical, they were subject to peer correction and control at every moment." Chapter 8 focuses on the total function of the library in the context described thus far, and on the implications of function for library philosophy.

CHAPTER 8

Sounding for the Embedded Philosophy

There is no such thing as the scientific world. There is, rather, just the world, and what we are trying to do is describe how it works and describe our situation in it.

—John R. Searle, 2004

Introduction

Among the many functions essential to both cultural evolution and the library, selection is the ultimate function because it signals the direct point of change. Without selection, there is neither movement nor direction nor pattern, only an aimless chaos, for the concept of selection means very clearly that there are options from among which to select and that there are criteria for making the selection. Guiding this process, then, is purpose, more apparent in cultural than biological evolution. And the foregoing chapters have demonstrated that the process of cultural evolution engages many complex features of humanity that distinguish it from any other classification of being. Sustained analytical thought, enriched by diversification of options and punctuated by selection, is the defining feature of humanity.

Determining library purpose is not as straightforward an exercise as it might at first appear, and the difficulty of achieving this determination probably accounts for the single greatest obstacle in the path toward a generally accepted philosophy. At different times and in different places, differing purposes for the library have been emphasized, with the implication that each contains the germ of applicable theory. Preparatory to a summary statement of library philosophy in the Epilogue of this book is a recasting of these general ideas, primarily as they relate to current times and societies that espouse the democratic ideal of intellectual freedom.

To the extent that these various purposes can be categorized, the first such category addresses the purposes of learning and communication: "The library is a means of education," writes philosopher Abraham Kaplan (1964, p. 297), "an instrumentality by which special groups and classes in the society can take advantage of experiences not directly their own, and so improve their position in society. Library educator J. M. Orr (1977, p. 33) concludes that "the concept of libraries in terms of systems theory must be that they are systems specifically created for the communication of knowledge," while librarian and educator A. W. McClellan (1973, pp. 126–127) says that "all libraries operate with one purpose; they all exist to facilitate the process of communication. Obvious as this may appear, it is not a trivial role for libraries to play." In the course of preparing the mid twentieth-century federal study of the public library in America, its primary researcher, political scientist Robert D. Leigh (1950, p. 48) observed that "It would seem, then, that the public library's natural role as an agency of public communication is to serve the group of adults whose interest, will, and ability lead them to seek personal enrichment and enlightenment." The public library "is not concerned solely with the diffusion of knowledge, but with the intellectual improvement of those groups which most need it and have the least opportunity of getting it," writes library theorist James H. Wellard (1940, p. 160). "The recognition of this principle is what we mean by the philosophy of librarianship; and the practice of it constitutes the sociology of the profession." In this statement, Wellard is one of the very few, if he is not unique, to refer to a bipartite function in terms other than the simple theory and practice bifurcation.

Library historian and philosopher J. G. Meijer (1982, p. 16) contends that "The main purpose of the library is to stimulate people to make optimal use of that part of mankind's cultural heritage preserved in libraries. The aim of this stimulation is *inter alia* to support decision-making and scientific and technical progress... through optimum provision of sources of information... With a view to a definition, the following conclusion is reached: regarding the total collection, all library users, library functions and objectives, librarianship has a universal character. This universality, involving manifold divergencies, should be expressed in a scientifically tenable definition by means of a genus." Meijer goes on to say (p. 19) that "in a scientifically tenable definition, librarianship belongs under the genus *culture* and must, therefore, be indicated as a 'kind of cultural enterprise.'"

The social need that has engendered the library gives rise to the following definition put forth by library educator Lowell Martin (1937, 549): "the library is an institution for the transmission of group culture and knowledge as recorded in printed materials. This idea forms the core of its being." Library philosopher Pierce Butler (1953, p. 246) adds a touch of reality to the concept of library in culture, writing at the end of his career that "The cultural motivation of librarianship is the promotion of wisdom in the individual and in the community. Wisdom, like health, justice, and utility, embraces a whole hierarchy of supporting qualities, such as understanding, judgment, and prudence. Knowledge in itself is meaningless. Unless it is personally assimilated and its implications comprehended, it has no human value. There is such a thing as a learned fool."

Library philosopher Jesse Shera (1975, p. 169) appears ahead of his time with his reference in 1961 to librarianship as a manifestation of knowledge management, in which he proffered, "But librarianship as the management of knowledge is also rooted in epistemology—the knowledge of knowledge itself—and especially social epistemology, the way in which knowledge is disseminated through a society and influences group behavior. The library as a social invention is concerned with the improvement of the individual, but through the improvement of the individual it seeks the advancement of society." Linkage of individual and society is continued by philosopher Abraham Kaplan (1964, p. 297), who reasons that "The library is for society what memory is for the individual, the repository of what has already been learned, including what has been badly learned or mislearned. At any rate it is the repository of past experience which is now available to be drawn upon in a present response." Finally, to return yet again to Jesse Shera (1973, p. 95), "Though the library serves mainly the individual, the ultimate objective is the betterment of society."

A second category of library purpose emphasizes individual freedom. For example, public librarian and library philosopher A. Broadfield (1949, p. 35) posits that "The human being is the most ultimate of ends, his free condition his highest condition, freedom of thought the most fundamental element in his freedom, and the library one of the first essentials in maintaining it." And library historian and philosopher Ajit Kumar Mukherjee (1966, p. 55) contends "the library has two pre-eminent active functions for society, which are *to entertain* and *to educate*. These functions have originated and grown considerably, in response to society's needs, library constituting an integral part of it"; from a more pragmatic perspective, Pierce Butler (1933, p. 106) suggests "a major phase of the library's service to any individual reader will be to assist him to an effective method for achieving his own private purpose, so long as this is not anti-social, and to safeguard him from losing his labor in activities which are futile with reference to his own immediate desire," and elsewhere concludes (1952, p. 91) "Therefore, to realize the true significance of the library, one should not merely observe the effects of its presence but contemplate, in his imagination, the results that would follow from its absence." Library historian James Thompson (1974, p. 95) cautions that "Librarianship does lose itself in irrelevancies when it lacks a proper philosophy, and part of that philosophy must always be an acknowledgement of the need for social action: which in turn will put complacency and conservatism to flight." Cultural historian Adam Arenson (2007, p. 58) summarizes much of what can be said about the role of the library in society, by noting perceptively that it serves "A private need in a public space."

A third emphasis in the literature on library purpose falls on scholarship and the sharing of knowledge: "The library," says Pierce Butler (1952, pp. 89–90), "therefore, serves three major purposes, which, for convenience, may here be distinguished as its scholarly, bibliographical, and economic functions," to which Abraham Kaplan (1964, p. 298) adds the inclusive thought that "There is a third general and basic function of the library: as an instrument of research." Evidently with research or at least systematic study in mind, Broadfield (1949, p. 26) recommends that "Libraries are better conceived as learned than as social institutions." But it is in a broader sense that Butler (1944, p. 33), using his special definition of scholarship introduced in Chapter 5, advises "The librarian must recognize that the promotion of scholarship—not merely of reading activities—is the true objective of the library. Kaplan (1964, p. 297) puts these basic ideas in a cultural context, saying "A library, then, is first of all an archive, a repository in which society can find what it has already learned. This is also the earliest historical function of the institution." As though considering all these views of library purpose, Shera (1972, p. 298) summarizes a principle that many others also have observed in assessing the many generations of library as concept: He concludes that "The basic role of the library is not changing; it is the dynamics of that role, its expression in implementation, that is undergoing alteration." The present synthesis incorporates all these considerations about library purpose in the statement of philosophy that constitutes the Epilogue.

Appearance of Dual Function

But as mentioned briefly in Chapter 7, the library appears to have two different functions that continue concurrently, essential and related. Pierce Butler (1952, p. 83) provides a description of the context for this duality that attempts to be so concise as to be almost cryptic. He writes, "For a culture to exist, its scholarship must be diffused in living minds, and, for the culture to endure, that scholarship must be transmitted from generation to generation. Actually, however, both results are produced by the same operation." And about a decade earlier (1943, p. 7) he had offered this more explicit elaboration:

> In a civilization the acquisition of information is a continuous process. At any particular moment new knowledge is always being added to what previous generations have acquired. This total stock of information, new and old, which a society possesses exists in two forms: some of it is kinetic, at work in the minds of living men, but a much greater part is potential, stored up in books and other records. Thus in a normal civilization two informative processes must always be maintained, and whenever a particular situation arises the necessary specific knowledge must be released from the reservoir. The first is a general and continuous process; the second is special and intermittent. The rising generation must always be receiving an adequate equipment of knowledge to fit it for participation in cultural routines, and

> constantly to meet the occasion adults must be releasing from potential to kinetic for the available special knowledges that they require.

The role of the daily provision of select information sources, along with all the organization, assistance, and public instruction thereby entailed, in combination with the longer term function of accumulating those records of knowledge, experience, and expression, and rendering them accessible may at first appear simple enough[1] to be comprehended in one philosophy. The problem for the library, however, is that the focus of the public and, indeed, of the profession, itself, is cast toward to the daily operations side of the function, placing the other dimension in a dark shadow that is, in effect, an unwitting shadow of competition. This may be unavoidable for the public, and it probably is even unnecessary for the public to consider anything more than just that set of services. But, for the profession of librarianship, it has meant a near disregard of the encompassing dimension of library function. This apparent dual function of the library[2] no doubt is made a problem at least in part by the several different types and sizes of libraries with which the public may have some contact, and by the nature of the profession in which both the practitioners and theoreticians are established. It is the basis for a situation that is confusing, moreover actually misleading, for an understanding of library purpose. What is unfortunately missing in discussion of library function is the mutual, integral relation of the daily activities and the cultural function in which they are incorporated.

Process

Although there are multiple purposes that combined to achieve a function, in the context of library philosophy there really is only a single function of the library in concept, a function that the present text refers to as dual only because so fundamental an analysis makes an otherwise complex situation seem easier to comprehend. A fitting analogy may be that of sociologist Talcott Parsons (1949, p. v) in his prefatory reminder about the sociology of knowledge, that "It is a study in social *theory*, not *theories*. Its interest is not in the separate and discrete propositions to be found in the works of these men, [exponents of the sociology of knowledge] but in a *single* body of systematic theoretical reasoning." In order to achieve a theory of knowledge at some stage of development, it most likely would be efficient and effective to have considered the various theories that have been advanced, but quite definitely not to stop at that. Thus, in this investigation some fairly simple statements about library purpose have been enumerated and the library's most significant responsibilities to society have been analyzed, meanwhile avoiding the quicksand of their many and varied operations. This approach pares away what could be considered in this context distractions from the primary purpose of investigation, thereby placing in sharper focus the truth of the matter, as sociologist Stephen Toulmin (1972, p. 351) advocates:

> Within an institutional organization, the current conduct of affairs conforms—in the terminology of political theorists—to "standard operating procedures" established during the foundation and subsequent history of the organization. Formally speaking, its structure may be representable by a static "organizational tree"; but, functionally speaking, its activities will be related less systematically, and represent the outcome of all those co-existing policies and procedures which have been established, for different purposes, at different times in the past.

All the events that take place on a daily basis in any library contribute to the accumulation of library function throughout the millennia. It is of special importance to bear in mind that these events are not only of the library's making but that considerably more are the making of those individuals who, by conscious choice or by default through ignorance, participate in communication via the social transcript; both those who contributed the thoughts conveyed and those who absorb them. The library facilitates these transactions which, in most cases by far, could not occur without the library function. Ways of producing these events develop over time as new ways of doing things and new ways of contemplating what is done present themselves. It all involves selecting, acquiring, organizing, instructing, advising, preserving, and planning, just as it always has done. These are operations that contribute directly to the culture in the many ways outlined in this essay. The nature of the transcript evolves, but it does always exist in some form, and because it is of value now, it also will be later, but for different reasons and for reasons one cannot today even imagine. The accumulation aspect of the library is easier to see, once attention is called to it, simply because it is, in fact, a physical accumulation, even in digital form, and an integral part of cultural evolution. The function, itself, cumulates through time within the mind of the individual and in subconscious societal expectation as it is carried forward through the more familiar procedures and transactions that occur every day; every day and with every act that falls within the mission of the library; every act intended to lead to discovering, to inventing, to learning, to entertaining, to understanding, to enhancing and expanding experience, and to communicating and cooperating.

The library is at once the mediator in and guarantor of communication between individuals and groups of all ages of every era, and of every society that has a transcript, and concurrently it also constitutes the curatorial function of the accumulated communication that represents cultural evolution. Of particular significance in understanding the library function is attentiveness to this bipartite function of the library, because, as stated repeatedly in this text, involvement in one aspect can overshadow awareness of the other. They are mutually dependent dimensions of one complex function in a cultural system. Jesse Shera (1973, p. 120) alludes to the situation concisely: "To conserve the record of the past while still remaining responsive to change is the peculiar mission of the librarian, for the librarian stands at the junction where past and future meet in the ever-present now." The cultural function of the historical archive for future use in understanding the past and recasting it for the present may be immediately clear to certain individuals and not to others. For example, an electrical engineer is likely to see the engineering library as serving primarily, if not solely, the function of supplying current information just in time to be applied to the solution of an immediate problem; a historian, on the other hand, would likely see the purpose of the library as that of preserving the record of past events that is speculated to be of value to future historians, even if not of special interest to that historian at the time. This is where the type and size of library are manifestations of specific institutional mission. In these instances, however, the functions of both types of libraries are the same in the broader, cultural context, with a difference only in the most apparent way each type achieves it; the daily activity of the engineering library is going to appear to be entirely for the here and now, while the daily activity of the archive will appear to be primarily for the future. Both libraries function on the same continuum, but at opposite ends of it. They exemplify complementary aspects of one function.

Selection is the common feature of the operations involved in this function. As a cultural technology the library is also a survival tool. It is not a survival tool in the sense of extending the innate ability to find food and shelter, which are features common to all animals, but in the sense of meeting the most human needs of the psyche and intellect. Philosopher Abraham Kaplan (1964, p. 297) finds that "what is most fundamentally constitutive of human culture, as distinct from various subhuman societies, however complex, is this: a society has a culture when the members of the society do not begin the process of learning from scratch with each generation, whenever (that is to say) it becomes possible for the society not to make the same mistakes too often." Every library exists for the purpose of preserving such intellectual sources for accessibility, but this responsibility assumes two forms which at first may appear to be quite different. One form is the acquisition of intellectual sources in a place that ensures their accessibility for the present; the other form requires special attention beyond that through special means to ensure future accessibility. But, whether the primary purpose is immediate accessibility for specific reasons or accessibility for speculated future value, preservation is the first consequence of selection because it optimizes the probability of accessibility.

Moreover, one talks about the book as both physical *artifact* and intellectual *content*, principally for the determination of which characteristic needs to be preserved, there being different methods and outcomes depending upon that determination. Both are cultural artifacts, of course, but by far the major part of library preservation is directed at intellectual content. The physical item contains information about the art and craft of the book at a given time and place; the intellectual content conveys something about its context. In order to bring together the intellectual sources and the relevant constituents of society, selection becomes the key to all other library operations, since the purpose of all of them is to bring together society (individual by individual) and the putative information universe in the most efficient and effective ways. Among the implications of this consideration, according to H. Curtis Wright (1982, p. 8), is that it "means negotiating the tricky intellectual interface between (1) *the intellectual structure of knowledge*, and (2) *the librarian's technology of intellectual access* to the intellectual structure of knowledge." Arguably, there is even more to the responsibility than that, given the large dimension of cognition.

Integration

The physical human body and the mind function together and the mind is connected to its outer extensions, its prosthetic devices, foremost among which is the library in its various forms. If the body and mind were not connected, there likely would be little action displayed by the body, and absolutely no recognizable action of cultural consequence, as culture is understood to be a product of mind. Philosopher John Searle (2004, pp. 301–302) argues that "consciousness and other mental phenomena are biological phenomena; they are created by biological processes and are specific to certain sorts of biological organisms. Of course, this is not to deny that our individual minds are shaped by our culture. But culture is not something in opposition to biology; rather culture is the form that biology takes in different communities."[3] And if the mind were not closely associated with the library, the latter simply would not exist, while the former would perform only at the levels of humanity experienced millions of years ago, perhaps at about the time just prior to the emergence of rudimentary language. Without the library, knowledge would advance only at the slowest possible rate, for what the library does for the mind is extend its memory, its reservoir of knowledge, and in doing so also generates intellectual connections in addition to those with the past. This connectivity is essential to cultural evolution, for in its penchant toward integration the library bends humanity, gently and slowly, toward a holistic view. The reasoning of biochemist Lawrence J. Henderson (1917, p. 206) may be applicable to consideration of the connection between mind and library concept: "For the teleology of nature is recognized through a connection, conceivable only as teleological, among nature's laws, i.e. among the general abstract characteristics of nature which may be exactly defined."

In their comprehensive study of concepts, cognitive psychologists Edward E. Smith and Douglas L. Medin (1981, p. 14) observe that "Regardless of whether dimensions or features are used to describe concepts, the goal is the same: to make apparent the relations between concepts." This makes possible the integration of concepts among diverse fields of inquiry. According to evolutionary psychologist Leda Cosmides and anthropologists John Tooby and Jerome H. Barkow (1992, p. 4), "A conceptually integrated theory is one framed so that it is compatible with data and theory from other relevant fields." Principles from one field are used to make sound inferences about processes in others. And more to the point, "A compatibility principle is so taken for granted in the natural sciences that it is rarely articulated, although generally applied; the natural sciences are understood to be continuous." Philosopher of science Michael Ruse (2005, p. 35) contends "Professional science is an attempt to uncover the regularities—the laws—that govern the natural world and to bring them together into a unified system of knowledge. Each branch of science strives to be internally coherent and externally consistent with other areas of science, and above all it values making successful predictions about the future course of natural events, in the real world and in the laboratory." He continues (pp. 275–276): "A theory that binds together various disparate areas of knowledge is thought to have more power and worth than a theory that explains only one separate piece. Coherence within and consistency without is important too." Integration of concepts and ideas is the function of theory as a basis of explanation, and that is exactly what the present synthesis attempts to accomplish.

Integration also is an essential library function that enables the mind to cope with new ideas and concepts encountered constantly in the changing environment, and to assist the mind in fulfilling its potential for innovating and developing world view and self understanding.[4] Library theorist Douglas J. Foskett (1984, p. 41) reminds us that "The Princes of Serendip were so successful in taking in what chance offered that they gave the useful word 'serendipity' to our vocabulary." He explicates the statement by elaborating his view on the significance of the library to society:

> Information gained from reading may be second-hand, but it is none the less valid for that. Percepts derived from experience, and information from records, are integrated into a coherent pattern in the mind by being processed into becoming part of an organized structure of notions. They are transformed from what Vygotsky calls "spontaneous concepts," immediately perceived in isolation, into 'scientific concepts' assimilated into a pre-existing pattern of thought. When Pasteur said that chance favours the prepared mind, he meant that such a pre-existing pattern prepares the way for the entry of new information so that it falls into place appropriately and with significance.

Library experience offers a mildly structured serendipity that still permits surprise. The mind causes changes within the brain and leads to action of the body in which it is housed. By conveying the social transcript in so great an amount and in its unique way as both function and place, the library is to select individuals and, ultimately, to society in general, an extension of, or an engine of, the mind. It is a cultural technology.

Bibliography, observes Pierce Butler (1953, p. 7), "is the systematic process by which civilized man finds his way about in the world of books that he has created." By this, Butler means personal scholarship, as he describes the substance of the social transcript. Contemporary use of the word book, in its generic sense to include all formats of information media, goes back very many centuries, as cultural historian Raymond Irwin (1949, p. 68) reminds us. "The root form 'biblio' was in common use two thousand years before Caxton, and had nothing to do with printing. It is in fact impossible in practice to draw a hard and fast line between manuscript document and printed books, and most good libraries, being interested in the matter rather than the form of their treasures, collect both." Unless the form, which is to say the physical artifact, contains truly extraordinary information about its contemporary culture, it is the intellectual content that is the primary concern of the library. And this, of course, is what makes the library a unique and unusually complex function.

H. Curtis Wright (1982, p. 9) stresses his understanding that "librarianship is totally interdisciplinary. It is not a subject matter: it is a way of relating to subject matter." One often hears reference to the interdisciplinarity of many subjects and to the interdisciplinary nature of the library as though they are manifestations of the same phenomenon, which they are, but only in terms of the practice in daily operations, not in terms of the single function; not in terms of the philosophy behind those operations. Library practitioner and theorist Donald Beagle (1988, p. 43) discusses the library as expression of "an integrative law of underlying order," and Wright (1982, p. 6) considers librarianship to be "idea science, not data science." He reasons that the difference is "because science [physical science] cannot function without objectified concepts... we all know that. The study of ideas by humanistic methods, in which facts/data/phenomena are *utilized* as communicative instruments, has not been (and probably cannot be) systematized like the methods of science, in which facts/data/phenomena are *analyzed* as objects of study."[5] Some values are determined very convincingly through the processes of the physical sciences, while others are determined through cultural evolution. For example, "Science cannot distinguish good and bad as universal human values" (Butler, 1933, p. 51). In writing of librarianship as a social science, library theorist Maurice B. Line (1965, pp. 271–272) pursues the idea that "Librarianship is not a mere technique that can exist in a social or moral vacuum: because it serves society and affects society in various ways, it must constantly be looked at in its social context and judged by social and moral standards." If there is any administrative principle to be drawn from the present synthesis it is, presented in its most abbreviated form by historian James Thompson (1977, p. 218), that "Libraries and librarians can never afford to be inward-looking."[6]

As parcels of knowledge derive from experience of one kind or another, and because they are but constituents of greater knowledge, knowledge is always incomplete, so it is also expandable as it incorporates more of the phenomena to which it is connected. What humanity does is perceive and discover the connections. Completeness, wholeness, and oneness are the ideals of the knowledge toward which humanity strives. Thus, the organization, differentiation, and integration of extant knowledge for use by humanity, now and in the future, constitute the abbreviated single function of the library. This function is the basis for library philosophy.

Essentials of an Appropriate Philosophy

Although the library has existed in various forms for thousands of years, and the simplest logic indicates that principles for its operation had to have existed for an equal duration, it was not until the middle of the nineteenth century, when spurred by the innovation of the public library movement in England and the United States, according to Jesse Shera (1980b, p. 315), that a philosophy based on the library's place in society and on its intellectual foundations was required "for its justification but also for its guidance as an institution." And it was probably not by coincidence, Shera points out, for that was also the time when the library was just beginning to be recognized as a social entity of interest, in part because new developments had begun to occur throughout all of sociological theory. By the 1930s, writes library historian Michael Harris (1973, p. 2514), "For the first time in the history of library literature, librarians were being regularly exposed to articles with the word 'philosophy' prominently displayed in their titles."

A library philosophy, as it is understood in this study, and as it was by Shera, does not relate solely to the practice of librarianship or with any end product; it guides and explains a process in cultural evolution. Philosopher Robert Audi (2006, p. 325) defines philosophy as "a reasoned pursuit of fundamental truths, a quest for understanding, a study of principles of conduct," which fits the need of the present examination. Placing the library in the context of culture and, more specifically, cultural evolution, invites analogy with biological evolution, and so that analogy has been made in Chapter 3 as it seemed reasonable to do so. "The success of biology in helping us to understand human culture," writes psychobiologist Henry Plotkin (2002, p. 109) "can be measured by the extent to which it can explain social constructions."

The analogies do provide helpful insights. Sociologist Talcott Parsons (1978, p. 357) was very much influenced by the thought of biologist Lawrence J. Henderson, concluding from the latter's work that the physical world constitutes an essential component of the environment of man, as both organism and actor. "Indeed, man himself *is* in one principal aspect a physico-chemical system and this aspect is in certain respects continuous with the others." Parsons (p. 357) seems to have been attracted especially by Henderson's presumption of a teleological aspect even of the physical world, which was based on his conception "that one of the principal properties of the physical world is *order*. Another word he used frequently—one nearly synonymous with order—was *organization*."[7] Clearly, the organization of knowledge is not just a coincidental condition of library management, but ranks among its most essential purposes in satisfying a basic human need.

Theory in Its Place

The basis upon which the library phenomenon might find its philosophy, whether that phenomenon falls under social science, human science, natural or physical science, is to be found not only in disciplines bearing its closest theoretical relations, but even more likely within its own activity, its own purpose, its own cultural function in any society. It is the most basic of functions that will yield the best understanding for the same reasons that "functional problems are most readily solved by examining the highest form of a given activity" (Vigotsky, 1962, p. 125). There is no single model that is valid. "Over particular forms of theory," writes sociologist Stephen Toulmin (1961, p. 84), "black-and-white questions of truth and falsity do not arise. The crucial issue is, rather, what types of happening a particular form of theory will help us to understand and where its use will be unhelpful or misleading." For an explanation to be acceptable, "it must demonstrate that the happenings under investigation are special cases or complex combinations of our fundamental intelligible types" (p. 81).

Description is neither explanation, understanding, theory, nor philosophy; but description of the development of libraries or of the techniques employed and the services rendered and the theories behind them do create a structure for the analysis of function.[8] Analysis of function leads to philosophy, which is extracted only from the determined function; and philosophy drawn from function experienced through thousands of years and around much of the globe, as in the case of the library, must be considered in terms of the human characteristics that created it, that benefit from it, and sustain it. "It is a paradox that the words 'human' and 'scientific' carry for us an undertone of opposition," declares anthropologist Jacob Bronowski (1961, p. 83). In agreement would be physical chemist and social philosopher Michael Polanyi

(1964, p. 68), who observes that discounting the very human element of subjectivity, even in the sciences, can not only miss the point but can lead to erroneous conclusion: "In some fields, as we shall find in the theory of evolution, the ideal of strict detachment impairs the very conclusions of science. When applied to psychology this ideal tends to impoverish inquiry, and may obscure its results. A sociology which must ignore the power of our ideals in society must ignore what is most essential in society or deal with it only obliquely by a breach of its principles." This assessment holds its greatest validity for the study of humanity.

A philosophy of some activity, rather than of philosophy as a discipline, can be defined as the totality of its principles, theories, and purpose, comprehended in a coherent intellectual unity that functions as a system.[9] In his classic book on the philosophy of education, which reflects an effort not totally unlike that of identifying library philosophy, sociologist Ross L. Finney (1928, pp. 6–7) explains the nature of the task in a context broader than that of simple comparison with the hard sciences.

> The public can never wait for strictly scientific solutions, but is compelled by the very nature of life itself to proceed upon the basis of tentative conclusions. Such is ever the tyranny of human circumstance. Always it has been so in the past; and it will continue to be so as long as human knowledge remains incomplete. If philosophical method means the most careful search for the most probable guess, there will always remain good work for the philosopher.

Again, it is not so much a matter of cutting some slack for a field that in appearance may be less rigorous in its standards and their application as it is of recognizing the nature of the field in a wholly human environment. Anthropologist Mary Douglas (1986, p. 56) clarifies the context for scientific theory, for example, as "the result of a struggle between the classifications being developed for professional purposes by a group of scientists and the classifications being operated in a wider social environment." She emphasizes (p. 45) the social dimension of science in this regarding, noting that "The entrenching of an idea is a social process. This is compatible with the prevailing notion in the philosophy of science that a theory is entrenched by its coherence with other theories." It is that matter of sameness that characterizes culture and social institutions discussed above, for science is a social institution, and therefore is not unlike others. Douglas analogizes (p. 59) the emergence of such institutions within culture and the emergence of theory within disciplines: "We would add that institutions perform the same task as theory. They also confer sameness. Once a theoretical scheme has been developed, elements that in the pre-theoretical stage were of dubious standing lose their ambiguity. They acquire definition when their regular functioning within the system is demonstrated."

Jesse Shera (1973, p. 262), not at all unique in his assessment of librarianship in his time, pointed out that "Librarians know very well how to do what they do, but they never concern themselves to any great extent with why they do it... Their discipline is a vast accumulation of technical details rather than a body of organized abstract principles that can be applied in concrete situations." And he wrote (1979, p. 315) strongly about the negative effects this situation brought to research of a scientific nature in the field: "The conduct of inquiry is as much an art as it is a science... But subjective skill that derives from the humanities is required, as well, in interpreting the results of such statistical operations. Despite all of our investigatory experience in the social science disciplines, we still have not established the basic principles of human behavior that would make research more of a science and less an art than it is today." And, as observed in Chapter 2, the latter idea about the lack of basic principles of human behavior, has been the major source of difficulty for the library profession in establishing a philosophy.

Despite the many "use and user studies" that have accumulated over recent decades in library and information science, along with the constant and eminently justifiable surveys and discussions about community, the profession does not seem to have come close to knowing much at all about motivations, methods, and outcomes, except that use and the clientele are fundamental to what is to be done. As much falls to conjecture as it did three quarters of a century ago, when J. Periam Danton[10] described the situation. Danton found that librarianship was operating in a state of flux that eluded science and factual knowledge and, as a relatively new branch of formalized learning, was wholly lacking in scientific data. He reasoned that the greater the degree of social change surrounding practice, and the greater rate at which it takes place, the more imperative it is that both the philosophy and objectives of the field be revised to accommodate societal evolution, and the more likely it will be that science and factual knowledge would be of assistance in solving problems. To some extent prefiguring H. Curtis Wright, he even asked (1934, p. 550), "Does the library have a *Wesen* of its own and does it have metaphysical implications? That is, is the library an institution merely or does it contain within itself the germs of a philosophical relation to epistemological progress?" Danton (1934, p. 539) also wrote that the most important benefit of a library philosophy would be "the achievement of a definite and recognized place for the library in the social order."

Conversely, the present study attempts to find library philosophy embedded in cultural evolution. Economic theorist Brian Loasby (1999, p. 35) finds that even sensory perception within the cognitive process relies on a classification system that interprets phenomena according to selected characteristics, while many different classifications may in principle be constructed by varying the basis of selection. "Consciously or unconsciously, some basis must be chosen; when we think it inappropriate we may try to revise it; but we cannot escape the constraint that *all* we know about the world is of the nature of theories and all experience can do is to change these theories."

What is abundantly clear about both cultural evolution and the function of library is that they are energized by language and given direction by the mind—the individual mind and the social mind. Individuals compete within a social framework of cooperation, and psychologist Denise Dellarosa Cummins (1998, p. 30) even argues that the pressure to compete and cooperate successfully constitutes "a major force behind the evolution of reasoning capacity." It sharpens and demands more of the mind. This particular kind of struggle for survival in a human sense, she reasons (pp. 45–46), "is as old as life itself. If the data on social norm and theory of mind reasoning show us anything it is that the winners are most likely to be those with the capacity to exploit or route the constraints of the dominance hierarchy." Neurons, which are the basic structural-functional units of the brain, writes neurophilosopher Patricia Smith Churchland (1986, p. 14), "are evolution's solution to the problem of adaptative movement."

Biologist and psychologist J. A. Scott Kelso and psychologist David A. Engstrom (2006, p. 143) critique a scientific debate about the human brain they describe as hinging on whether information is represented in the brain in a "modular, category-specific way or in a distributed fashion in which many distinct areas of the brain are engaged, each one representing different kinds of information." They ask, "why couldn't the brain be both: Instead of viewing global integration and local segregatons as conflicting processes and theories, why not vie them a s complementary?" Their response to this is 'coordination dynamics', which is a theory of the way human beings and human brains are coordinated in a blend of integration and segregation. As explained in various parts of the present essay that address imagination and mind, the library performs an analogous function of blending knowledge and experience. It is a cultural technology, a human invention. Psychologist Paul Bloom (1998, p. 204) draws attention to a debate about the genesis of language, observing that "The dominant theory in the social sciences is that language is a human invention," rather than a result of natural selection, for which he argues. Applying these terms to the present discussion, then, my inference is that language is not an invention; that it is a result of natural selection for desirable adaptation, while the emergence of the library concept—very different from language—is indeed a human invention to extend the critical powers of language and mind. This is the theory that underlies the present essay.

Practice in Its Place

Before examining what might be called a library philosophy, it will be useful first to examine aspects of theory that have been advanced with less difficulty for the practice of librarianship or, if one prefers, library science. Going directly to the heart of the matter, Pierce Butler (1944, p. 33) declares that the librarian's "working philosophy may be called 'culturalism.'" In this statement he clearly sees the total function to be considerably more than the array of daily procedures and transactions that are, from the perspective of most citizens, the most visible and immediately apparent function of the library. And this, of course, has posed a problem not only for how the library is viewed by society, but more so for the way it tends to be considered, for the most part, by the library profession itself.

But the elementary fact is that the accumulating cultural dimension of the library function, which in the long term is the more profound or significant dimension of library function, can be no better than the daily services and operations that result in it through evolution. The library contribution to culture, which is the most human dimension of the whole evolution phenomenon, occurs each day, never vanishing through time but ever amassing greater potential for humanity. "If librarianship is concerned with the act of mediation between man, either individually or collectively, and his graphic records," Shera advocates (1965, pp. 162–163), "then the paradigm of librarianship as a science is to be sought in the total communication process in society and in its epistemological, sociological, psychological, and institutional ramifications." He could well have included evolution in that itemization, since one way or another it consistently figured among his considerations about the library, whether explicitly or implicitly. As is to be expected, Shera was not alone in his advocacy of extending considerations about theory of librarianship and library philosophy well beyond the practical matters[11] that were agreed to be necessary, but that ultimately have become more obfuscating.

In the course of daily procedures and transactions in the library, theory is employed to explain those routines and their purposes. But that can best be done by placing them in the context of library mission, goals, objectives, strategies, priorities, and even the respective job descriptions. The organization and its constituent individuals can thus understand better what they are doing, explain it to others, and generally justify the activity in terms of service to the host institution. These activities in turn are subject to research that evaluates their effectiveness and their efficiency; and it points the way toward further investigation, all of which informs management decisions at all levels of organization. There should be no doubt that these activities are essential to the provision of good service, to the maintenance of a good library, and to the maintenance of library concept as described in this essay. Arnold K. Borden (1931, p. 176) is probably right, however, in writing "The mere doing of the research may yield something in the way of training and technique but the conclusions will sound hollow without a philosophy to back them up." There is a context beyond even the theory inferred from mission and goals of any particular library that provides more substance to those daily routines; it is the philosophy of library in concept.

Unity of the Profession

To the extent that the library and information profession sees libraries organized only as an assortment of school, public, academic, and special libraries, all of differing size and each performing its varied services and operations within communities of differing composition, a philosophy very likely cannot be identified. Examined in this essay, however, is the synthesis of the library function in cultural evolution and in contemporary society, where it is described as a unified cultural process rather than as disparate clusters of procedures, operations, types of libraries, or locations, or on the basis of differences related to size of the collection or of the specific community served. This synthesis discusses the library as inclusive of all that, but as more than all that. It is about a cultural technology, a system created to be greater than the sum of its very many parts, a system transcendent of time and space. Pierce Butler (1953, p. 9) advocated a similar conceptualization more than half a century ago when he wrote that "Librarianship is a typical segment of human activity in its highest cultural development. Therefore, anyone who studies librarianship systematically must discover principles that prevail in every other reach of civilization. Accordingly a thorough-going philosophy of librarianship would be a philosophy of universal application." It comes down to a matter of understanding the unity of the library concept and its implications for the information professions.

Intellectual freedom, which was discussed as an environmental ideal in Chapter 6, constitutes an underlying spirit that unifies the profession. A paper on that subject by Myra Kolitsch (1945) following her personal experience during World War II, while a political statement, also conveys a philosophy. She writes that "A philosophy of librarianship must, therefore, be of such a character that it not only 1) is satisfactory to librarians but 2) will also be consistent with the social philosophy of the nation or group of people within which it is but one of many interests. Other necessary attributes of a democratic philosophy of librarianship are: 3) it must be able to exist and have its ends and ideals pursued in a world of many conflicting social philosophies, ends, and ideals; 4) it must promote rather than retard or obstruct the fullest development of the highest potentialities of the individual, society, and the library itself; 5) it must be forward-looking, and, as a corollary, it must continually submit to self-criticism, both in its theoretical formulations and in its practical applications; and, finally, 6) its ideals must be capable of progressive realization and application" (p. 25). Adopted in many societies as a democratic ideal, intellectual freedom also reflects an ideal of librarianship as a calling, and serves as a fundamental unifying factor, even though its potential, which forever and anywhere is under attack, may be challenged more in some parts of the world than in others.

Looking beyond the many questions about how specifically to engage in library and information practice, considerations that bind them all together can be found in society and cultural evolution to indicate what they are trying to do and why. If so, then there is sound reason to think that there are, indeed, unifying forces called into play when it comes to those daily transactions and procedures; they are based on something. But, as discussed in Chapter 2, these unifying features have not been identified to the satisfaction of the profession. In his survey of research judged to convey the potential to contribute to a unified theory, library educator William E. McGrath (2002, p. 357) finds "There is much literature on the philosophy of LIS containing provocative and stimulating ideas that always seem on the verge of offering testable theories or of challenging empirical researchers to operationalize abstract themes." That may be so, yet they have not borne fruit. The present essay suggests that the need is not so much for a unifying theory or for a way to unify existing theory but, instead, for a fundamental philosophy that would serve to unify the focus of operational theories. There are essential characteristics that relate the library and the human condition and, therefore, those who carry the library forward that need to be considered, because they are the unifying elements.

Nature of the Profession

Apparently in the spirit of intellectual freedom, Norbert Wiener (1950, p. 135), the mathematical logician who founded cybernetics, declares that "to be alive is to participate in a continuous stream of influences from the outer world and acts on the outer world, in which we are merely the transitional stage. To be alive in the figurative sense to what is happening in the world, means to participate in a continual development of knowledge and its unhampered exchange." His statement suggests that there is something almost metaphysical in this evolutionary process of sharing knowledge and experience through time and across space. Wiener is quite far from alone in this sensing of the nature of the process; but while many have experienced it, few have analyzed it with the intention of communicating an understanding of it. In his 1949 essay on library philosophy, Broadfield (p. 66) had argued that "The theory is that when the human being and the library are brought into relation things happen, just as things happen when two substances capable of chemical interaction are brought together... Librarianship is regarded as being presented to us like a slice of the natural world."

In a similar vein, sociologist Lloyd V. Ballard (1936, p. 230), who has studied the library in the course of his work, argues that "books must be regarded as spiritual forces, not merely as physical materials. Indeed educators now admit that their chief duty is to arouse the curiosity of students with respect to social interactions and social values and to train them to satisfy that curiosity through the use of such intellectual tools as books, libraries and laboratories." And Jesse Shera (1976, p. 68) tells about poet Archibald MacLeish, who also was the Librarian of Congress from 1929 to 1944, raising the question of whether a book changes its character by being associated with other books in a library collection, thereby broadening the scope of inquiry into the nature of a book.

> He was not, of course, suggesting that the book itself underwent some mystical metamorphosis respecting its physical form or intellectual content. Rather, he believed that a book in concert with related books could evoke in the mind of the library patron concepts, relationships, and avenues of reflective thought that a book alone could not induce. Thus, a true library is not merely an agglomeration of books brought together by a series of fortuitous circumstances, but a meaningful creation designed to stimulate in the user purposeful cerebration. Two books, like two heads, may be better than one. The addition of a book to a collection, or the withdrawal of one from it, alters the character of the whole, and the importance of the book determines the magnitude of the change. Thus the building of a library collection is itself an act of scholarly creation, and if the librarian is to be the architect of his 'house of intellect,' he must know both books and men, and the uses to which the former is put by the latter.

Like any concept, the library experience and its place in cultural evolution, in both its quotidian and millennial dimensions, is much greater than the library as a service organization or even as a social institution.[12] Thus, library philosopher Broadfield (1949, pp. 5–6) was right on target with his admonition that "The philosophy of librarianship does not *contain* the solutions to the problems of librarianship; it is the sort of knowledge that the man has who can solve them."

The present study has been occupied for the most part with the definition of the library as a function in society and as an integral force in cultural evolution. A library philosophy can be formulated only upon an understanding of the ideals and purposes of the society into which that philosophy is to fit. Many decades ago, J. Periam Danton (1934) made this the essence of his essay on the need for a library philosophy, and he posed the question (p. 550) "is the library an institution merely or does it contain within itself the germs of a philosophical relation to epistemological progress?" This is surely a provocative question that has not, of course, escaped notice by others interested in a philosophy. Jesse Shera (1965, p. 176) concludes a great deal of thought on the subject of library philosophy with the following equally provocative idea: He writes, "I submit, then, that librarianship is the management of human knowledge—the most inter-disciplinary of all the disciplines—and because it is concerned with the philosophy of knowledge it is potentially the most deeply philosophical of all the professions."

In several of his writings, H. Curtis Wright has been probably the most adamant in his parallels between librarianship and philosophy, observing (1978, p. 256), for example, that "Both are concerned with how the human mind operates rather than the sense data of experience."[13] Elsewhere, Wright (1976, p. 302) reasons that "Whereas librarianship can be studied scientifically as an existential object, or as a social phenomenon, its nature can be studied, perhaps, as an integral part of the larger study of the nature of man which contains it. It is essentially the philosophical study of human information processes, not the scientific study of data. The natures of man and information are probably the same thing, just as librarianship and philosophy may turn out to be, not merely similar, but identical." Philosopher Luciano Floridi (2003, p. 531) places this development of thought into historical perspective, calling it a rebirth (renaissance) and writing that the upsurge of interest in epistemology was fueled by developments in mathematical, natural, and social sciences that "transformed epistemology from a theory of ideas and judgment into a theory of propositional attitudes, sentences, and meanings," prompting "a reconsideration of the role of philosophy as a critical exercise of analysis, rather than as an autonomous and superior form of knowledge." A philosophy is a guideline for practice while also an approach to critical analysis and, for the library in its total meaning, philosophy guides at a level even more essential than the particular institutional mission.[14]

Library as Concept

The philosophy this study seeks is of library as a concept in culture and cultural evolution, which certainly is closely related to, but not congruent with librarianship, library science or information science. Library function in culture transcends time. It is not a philosophy of how to engage a practice but a philosophy of the purpose behind the practice, an understanding of why the practice is performed. Librarianship, library science, and information science employ theories in order to explain and evaluate the things that are done in the immediate interests of efficiency and effectiveness. Thus they are the things that are done toward the fulfillment of a larger purpose in fulfillment of an institutional mission that can be understood, supported, and guided by philosophy.

Early in the twenty-first century, library historian Wayne Wiegand (2003, p. v) urged that scholarship in the library and information profession broaden its scope and otherwise change focus. "To move beyond our tunnel vision and blind spots," he writes, "we need to expand our perspectives beyond current professional discourse and shift them from the user in the life of the library to the library in the life of the user." His stated intention in arguing this point is not to identify a philosophy per se, but to advance issues and questions whose broader deliberation could lead to a more useful foundation on which to construct a holistic philosophy. While it is important to the LIS professions to understand how society affects the library, it is of at least equal significance to understand how the library affects society, and at present, according to Wiegand and surely to anyone else who examines the literature, there exists a problematic imbalance that has been mentioned throughout this text and discussed at some length in Chapter 2. Philosopher and information scientist Rafael Capurro (1992, pp. 90–91) analogizes the potential of these problematic implications for the field's formal communication in his challenging statement that "An information economy that seeks to reduce 'information' to an exchange value without taking into account the different 'forms of life' in which it is grounded is no less dangerous than a blind exploitation of nature." Poorly adjusted focus and too narrow a scope offer little guidance and understanding, for they are most likely to result only in misguided direction and distorted vision.

Whether reference is to librarianship, library science, information science or library and information science, or even to knowledge or wisdom management, the fundamental interest of the present essay is in the essence of library, the function that has survived and even flourished for millennia. The essence located in that function is not about how to do what we do; it is not specifically about practice, teaching or research in the field, and it is not about whether or not the organized activity comprising the function actually is a profession, or about relative competence. It is about fathoming prime purpose; it is about understanding library function as the basis for knowing where the relevant practice, teaching, and research fit in the grand scheme of the human condition and about finding fundamental guidance.

The library is deeply embedded in society and in the evolution of its culture. It was invented by the culture for the purpose of the stability and transmission capacity it provides and for the quality of adaptation it will support for the culture's continued survival in the fullest sense intended in the concept of humanity. All the procedures and transactions of librarianship are mounted for the purpose of creating an environment conducive to what can be expressed only as the library experience. That is to say that such operations and services are set in place to facilitate participation in the concept of library, which is comprised of the diversity it manifests, the discovery, the freedom, the mentation, the serendipity, the imagination, and the sharing of experience, all without limitation or judgment. It is a social experience, grounded in the thought of countless others through time and across space, that have been selected by and sifted through many minds. In underlining his point that "The social life implies ever richer and richer series of initiations," social philosopher Célestin Bouglé (1926, p. 36) observes in the most specific sense that "'We should remember what we owe to the book and the tool,' said Léon Bourgeois, not long since, hoping through the idea of what the individual owes to society, to revivify the sentiment of social duty."

Yet, in the face of this truth, which is recognized as such by most thinkers outside the library profession, Douglas J. Foskett (1962, p. 4), a librarian who has studied the profession for decades, seems quite justified in concluding that "Of all the librarian's lack of philosophy perhaps the most striking is the profound absence of a sense of continuity." Yet, continuity is in fact the essence of the library's being. Perspective can be broadened in scholarship and research, and in thinking and teaching, and can otherwise be benefited through contemplation of the longer span of the function because it does bear strong significance. Psychobiologist Henry Plotkin (1998, p. 222) offers a comment on the field of psychology that analogizes well with the library profession, because it emphasizes people and ideas: "while one may often reasonably choose to understand something in psychology solely in terms of the proximate causes of brains and minds, the importance and sheer magnitude of culture as a phenomenon provides compelling reason for wanting to understand it in as large a context as possible, and that must include evolution if a complete understanding is what one wants." It is within the brain, an organ of the physical body, that biological and cultural evolution intersect, and therefore in those areas of serious inquiry, particularly in the evolution of culture, that library function and philosophy are to be found.

Within cultural evolution, the closest affiliation of the library function is with the human's unique endowment of articulate language, which is a symbolizing system of communication that is conducive to constant refinement, nuance, and expansion in order to optimize both the reflection and the advancement of thought. The library as concept contains all of this potential. Language is the more-or-less tangible evidentiary entity for an understanding of library in culture. Comprehended in its full actuality and potential, it is the basis for analysis of the library function and the consideration that comes closest to the tangible phenomena of physical scientific analysis. "Science concerns itself directly with concrete phenomena," J. Periam Danton recalls to mind (1934, p. 536). "A philosophy, on the other hand, is interested in aims and function, in purpose and meaning." But, as discussed earlier, the theory and method of the physical sciences are different from the range of possibilities for the examination of the social sciences, which can, to some extent and in some instances, model themselves on theories and methods common to the physical sciences.

Such transfer has not proved to be fully effective, however. Jesse Shera (1980, p. 315) adds to the discussion that "The librarians talk glibly of library science, and indeed strive to endow it with scientific principles, but neglect the fact that librarianship has emerged from a humanistic tradition." While there has been much written about the library field as a social science and about the social sciences having methods in addition to those of the physical sciences, relatively little has ever been said about the humanity of librarianship. Yet, that is most likely where the concept of library, that is of library function, would fall. More time and effort than truly is necessary may be spent trying to determine just the right category to which the library field properly belongs,[15] with the resulting cost of attention to understanding essential function, and therefore philosophy. "Information is made of metaphysical subsistents, not of physical existents," reasons H. Curtis Wright (1979, p. 73). "It must therefore be studied philosophically as a formal object composed of structural relationships: it cannot be studied scientifically as a material object."

Language, as explained in Chapter 4, is the basis for understanding oneself and other concepts, for establishing a world view, for expressing oneself, for reasoning, and therefore for determining actions to adopt from among the many options. Human nature and the human condition, which belong as much to nature as an apple falling from a tree and as the parents' characteristics being inherited by the child, constitute the subject matter of both philosophy and library. Very similar in potential to language, although secondary to it, library creates diversification and holds it; moreover, it enables and even stimulates diversification in those who select to benefit from its full potential.

Library as concept is the principal cultural technology devised to convey the social transcript, whose foundation and structure draw upon the potential of language to the extent permitted by its surrounding environment, and the degree of freedom in which it functions. "Democracy is primarily an increase of consciousness and personal choice in the social system," explains sociologist Charles Horton Cooley (1920, p. 365) "which cannot take place except through the growth of diversity." He also calls this to mind in his judgment that society begins and ends with the individual, stating (p. 29) that "liberty can exist in the individual only as he is part of a whole which is also free... it is false to regard him as separate from or antithetical to the larger unity." Choice and freedom are the two sides of a coin we understand most fully as ultimate balance in the human condition, the furtherance of which library philosopher A. Broadfield (1949, p. 18) ascribes to the library, saying that "Books are far the strongest safeguards of freedom of individual thought." Few would likely disagree with the notion that individual knowledge yields choice, but that within a society such knowledge does not automatically yield the freedom to choose. However, science philosopher Marx W. Wartofski (1968, pp. 29–30) makes an interesting connection between knowledge and freedom, and individual and society, that commands attention. He finds that

> rational knowledge (and scientific knowledge, in particular) is a major instrument of human adaptation, and hence, of survival. The hope is that scientific knowledge, as the mode of adaptation and of human control over nature, may also be a major instrument of human self-control, by means of rational intelligence. Such rational self-control, such clear knowledge of our own nature is that ideal of human self-knowledge, the fulfillment of the imperative, "Know thyself," which the Athenian philosophers spoke of. It is, as they already knew, the condition of human freedom.

Ultimately, there is the consideration raised by geneticist and science philosopher Bentley Glass (1985, p. 163) that calls the concept of library to mind, which is, "To paraphrase Lyman Bryson: Man is not free to choose what he has never heard of or what doesn't exist" (Bryson, 1947, p. 5). Knowledge and intellectual freedom go hand in hand, and are intended through cultural selection to unite in the library.

The introductory comments of this book refer to the complication of determining whether library philosophy should be about a discipline, a profession, or a function. Resolution of this problem is fundamental to proceeding with the establishment of an appropriate philosophy, for any guiding statement is likely to encourage disagreement if it is not at least formulated to fit the needs of the total respective constituency while remaining within the bounds of reason drawn from solid evidence. The Epilogue to this book is a philosophy of library as a cultural function. It is intended to guide the related responsibilities of the LIS professions in fulfillment of the intentions inherent in the concept efficiently and effectively. If all the interests and questions are not addressed under one philosophy, then that philosophy will by definition be inadequate. The philosophy must be inclusive, yet understandable throughout the responsibilities and operations it incorporates. This suggests that the most direct approach to library philosophy is through the social transcript, much as Karl Popper alludes to it in his notion of objective knowledge. Popper proposes that reality comprises three ontologically distinct worlds. World 1 denotes the world of physical objects and states; it is the sphere of physics, of rocks, and trees and physical fields of forces. World 2 refers to subjective psychological consciousness, which is the sphere of feelings of fear and of hope, of dispositions to act , and of all kinds of subjective experiences. World 3 describes the sphere of the products of the human mind, ideas, both in the broad cultural sense and the logical or intellectual sense, including ethical and social values. Philosopher Geoffrey Stokes (1998, p. 115), whose interpretation is paraphrased , observes that "Popper regards world 3 as real, if not more *real* than 'a social institution, such as a university or a police force'". In the present study, library as concept belongs to World 3. It is more than an agency, more even than a social institution.[16]

Since one certainly must define the word philosophy as it is used in a given context, we will follow the lead provided by Danton (1934) in adopting for similar purposes the definition supplied six years earlier by sociologist Ross L. Finney (1928, p. 3). Finney's use of the word intends the "careful, critical, systematic work of the intellect in the formulation of beliefs, with the aim of making them represent the highest degree of probability, in face of the fact that adequate data are not obtainable for strictly demonstrable conclusions." His definition further includes the idea that "such beliefs shall have to do with aims, functions, and general objectives, that these last shall be intelligently related—with an eye to the future—to the social order, and that the beliefs, taken together, shall comprise a systematic body of general concepts." In the twentieth century, such a systematic body of general concepts was comprehended in the idea of social epistemology. This philosophical system examines the social dimensions of knowledge, so it has a history that can be traced to the classical philosophers. But as a concept with the specific label, social epistemology, studied as a cognitive mode for its own value rather than just as part of the dynamism of individual knowledge, was born in the field of librarianship. The sociology of knowledge, for example, and especially its application to science, had become a defined field of philosophy well in advance of use and acceptance of the phrase social epistemology, whose history has special significance for library philosophy.

As recounted in Chapter 1, Jesse Shera and his collaborator Margaret Egan introduced their concept of social epistemology, which was an innovative term at the time defined by them (1952, p. 132) as "the study of those processes by which society *as a whole* seeks to achieve a perceptive or understanding relation to the total environment." By the 1990s, the idea of social epistemology had become a field within the epistemology division of philosophy, independent of the work of Shera and Egan, with the variations of interpretation and definition that inheres in the intellectual effort to determine truth through reason.[17] Along the way, however, in a 1967 lecture series, Shera (1970, pp. 107–109) related social epistemology to the sociology of knowledge. He declared it to be the reverse of the sociology of knowledge, seeing it as the impact of knowledge upon society, and believed (p. 108) "that social epistemology can give librarianship its intellectual foundation for which we have been searching for so long." Shera's statement (p. 109) on the significance of social epistemology for the library warrants citing more fully:

> The librarian's responsibility is the efficient and effective management of the transcript, to use Boulding's phrase, the graphic records of all that society knows about itself and the world in which the self lives. His responsibility includes that which the social organism has learnt, its values as well as its facts, its imagery as well as its reality. The librarian is at once historical, contemporary, and anticipatory. Thus he can carry out his social responsibilities with maximum effectiveness only when he understands the cognitive process in society as well as in the individual, and can translate

that understanding into service. I submit that this is the real intellectual foundation of librarianship.

His statement connects the role of librarianship, which is an administrative technique, as library historian and theorist D. J. Foskett (1949, p. 27) has noted, to library, which is a concept; it joins the many *operations* of *the library* with the *function* of *library*. Social epistemology approaches more closely than any other single concept the congruence of librarianship and philosophy.

Among the relatively few who have shown an interest in library philosophy, John M. Budd and Gary P. Radford have continued to steer thinking in a direction away from a nineteenth-century positivist interpretation of library function. Budd (1995) revises Shera's social epistemology to bring into relief the library as the essence of its relevant phenomena, rather than in the context of its internal activities, somewhat as referred to in these pages as library as concept. His idea in this matter (p. 301), which he credits in part to John Searle (1983), stresses the role of intention, which sets the social apart from the physical. "Inherent in the mental character of social actors (human beings) is intention, which underlies action." Radford considers the subjectivity of the library user and user group to be evolving integral parts of a process that begins not with the discovery of objective, a priori knowledge, but rather with the social creation of knowledge. He argues that it is through the social processes of discourse, iteration, and dialectic that information is produced, given context, and validated as accepted knowledge with potential for continued interpretation and further relation to other pieces of knowledge. Interpreting the library experience in this way, it is a microcosm of dynamic social processes and "The library becomes an instrument of possibility." (p. 420). As discussed in Chapter 6, I understand this interpretation to emanate from the sense of library as place, and to be characterized by intellectual diversity in an environment of freedom. The percentage of any community that benefits directly from the library, as acknowledged earlier, certainly is small; but the fact remains that ideas are held in place through the library function, to be selected advantageously and the results passed along in society such that the greater numbers eventually reap the benefits of those selections.[18] Choice means possibility for the individual and the society.

During his address to the International Congress of Bibliographers and Librarians, held in Paris in 1934, philosopher José Ortega y Gasset (1961, p. 135) observed that every human life has a mission, which he defines as "the consciousness that every man has of his most authentic being, of that which he is called upon to realize. The idea of mission is, therefore, a constitutive ingredient of the human condition; and as I said a while ago, without man there is no mission. We may now add that without mission there is no man." Thus, Ortega directly connects the mission of humanity with the function of library, which, when understood in the context of cultural evolution, could justly be interpreted as the realization of the potential expressed in Shera and Egan's depiction of social epistemology.

Summary

To uncover library philosophy, the library function must be understood in its full dimension. This means the accommodation of both its evolutionary role in molding, adapting, and reflecting culture and its more immediate role exemplified by the many activities demanded daily as interests and needs emerge. Such activities are found in the intellectual exchange between the individual and the current society in which that individual functions; the cultural things that daily alter any society and cause it to question and reaffirm or reject as belonging together at any given point in time; not just how humanity came together over the generations, but the more or less concurrent activity that consists of steps taken in smaller segments of time and causes society to identify and re-identify itself, its culture in all the rich variety described in Chapter 3. The process called into play is found in the daily activity of the library vis-à-vis the public: the daily selection, organization, preservation, consultation, and instruction that comprise the social awareness of library. Each of these activities constitutes an aspect of the barest management fundamentals of *libraries.* But *library* conceived as a function in culture is the complex of communication phenomena involved in thought and the articulation of thought, that continuously is formed and reformed to suit the evolving need of humanity for both learning and expressing, ever available for those purposes. The research and theory synthesized throughout this book lend support to the fundamental belief in the value of the library to both the individual and society. Although it has not been among the purposes of this essay to validate the belief system described in Chapter 1, that probably has been accomplished just through the demonstration of how library function is central to the evolution of culture, every day and for all time as a technology necessary to culture, to society, to the individual.

As we have seen in various sections of this essay, throughout library history many expressions have been applied used to characterize it as both agency and institution. The library exists as an agency of society in meeting certain kinds of contemporary ephemeral needs, and as a social institution, as it is described in Chapter 5, in meeting cultural needs of indefinite implication. But both these classifications—agency and institution—as well as the traditional characterizations are inadequate to capture the concept of library function in its totality, as intended in this essay. In the latter decades of the twentieth century, however, scholarly and scientific attention in numerous fields with emerging interest cultural evolution began to be drawn toward consideration of *ultimate function*, rather than *definition*. In such instances, however, this has not been toward function of the library per se, but rather of a somewhat mysterious function that links mind purposefully to culture. As a consequence, there now are new perspectives on mind in society that attempt to identify and understand an as yet unclear function in cultural phenomena. To me, these various perspectives provide insight into library function in a holistic sense. It may be useful at this point in this presentation to collect for review some of these concepts, because they all have great potential for application to library as function in cultural evolution. And, in fact, they lend further legitimacy to the idea of library function as cultural technology in human evolution.

Economic philosopher Kenneth Boulding (1983, p. 10) describes the function as a prosthetic device of the mind; neuropsychologist Merlin Donald (2001, p. 305) refers to it variously as symbolic technology (2001, p. 305), whose power to create an external memory field (2001, pp. 308–309) extends conscious capacity and thus cognition; evolutionary psychologist Leda Cosmides and anthropologist John Tooby (2002, p. 172) refer to the function as the cognitive niche, or an adaptive mode; social anthropologist Jack Goody (2000, p. 132) finds writing to be a technology of the intellect; neuroscientist Jean-Pierre Changeux (1986, p. 281) discusses the function at issue in terms of an 'extracerebral memory'; in process very much like that used to define library function in this book, anthropologist F. Theodore Cloak (1975, p. 170) describes the M-culture, a concept adopted by Richard Dawkins (1999, p. 109) to define the extended phenotypic meme; anthropologist Leslie A White, (1949, p. 122) refers to relevant phenomena as extra-somatic, "in the sense that they have an existence independent of any individual organism and act upon it from the outside just as meteorologic forces do," very much in the manner of biologists Peter and Jean Medawar (1977, p. 55) in their reference to such phenomena as exosomatic; neurologist Antonio R. Damasio (1999, pp. 196–198) refers to it as extended consciousness; and geneticist Conrad Hal Waddington (1961, pp. 72–73) writes of both an "extra-genetic mode of transmission" and a sociogenetic mechanism. Most of these terms may seem at first to be somewhat mysterious.

But none of this is mysterious when placed in the context of library understood as function, as a cultural technology. That function is *stewardship of the social transcript.* It is a power of mind that acts outside the mind and extends to all of humanity through the powers inherent in cultural evolution. It is something more than a physical organ, in the sense of a feature added to mind, for it operates through culture for all the purposes held in culture. Any of the characterizations used in the preceding paragraph accommodates this function, of course, because the function each of the cited scholars describes acts accordingly.

What these writers seem to hold in common in their descriptions of this extraordinary feature of mind stems from the innovative tool of writing. Writing has been so obviously a critical force in cultural evolution since its emergence that this is easily understandable. But so are all the other components of the scenario, namely, mind, culture, and spoken language, which had to precede writing. There arguably has been a progression in the function of language leading to ever greater complexity. To be sure, what the library function offers humanity depends almost entirely upon the writing function. But whereas writing serves to extend the power of the individual, library in concept extends the power of the culture; in an evolutionary sense, library is the function that converts individual intellectual powers to cultural power. The oral tradition in cultural transmission, which occupies one dimension of the social transcript, ends with its recording, in any form, at which time it enters the dimension of the library's stewardship. Throughout this essay, allusions to the synergistic energies of redundancy, the treasury of words and meanings, the rich mixture of accumulation through time and juxtaposition of ideas, the unconscious reassurance of intellectual stability, the stirring of imagination, the extension of consciousness, and the maintenance of cultural memory describe an enhancement and extension of thought, which, as philosopher Bertrand Russell (1917, p. 178) once wrote, "is great and swift and free, the light of the world, and the chief glory of man." These phenomena combine to constitute library function in cultural evolution, and it all amounts to stewardship of the social transcript.

In considering a philosophy, library function does not present an either/or position. Neither the long-term accumulation of culture to be drawn upon, alone, nor the daily manifestation of snapshot society in action, alone, constitutes the function of library. It is both. The function is at once the result of the vast accumulation of culture and the incremental accumulation of culture in the making. Neither half of the equation exists without the other, for in this case the daily and the evolutionary are one. Evolutionary psychologist Leda Cosmides and anthropologist John Tooby (2002, p. 173) describe the larger, contextual process:

> This contrast—between transient, local, contingent facts and relationships that hold over the species range—is at the heart of what makes humans so different... If information only needs to be true temporarily, locally, and situationally to be useful, then a vastly enlarged universe of context-dependent information becomes potentially available to be employed in the successful regulation of behavior. This tremendously enlarged universe of information can be used to fuel the identification of an immensely more varied set of advantageous behaviors than other species employ, giving human life its distinctive complexity, variety, and relative success. Hominids entered the cognitive niche, with all its attendant benefits and dangers, by evolving a new suite of cognitive adaptations that are evolutionarily designed to exploit this broadened universe of information, as well as the older universe species-extensive true relationships.

The primary human cognitive adaptation, most scholars would agree, is that of articulate speech, a code that can be recorded for purposes of sharing knowledge and experience and for the many reasons that anything is committed to record. Linguist Patrizia Violi (2001, p. 241) emphasizes that although there may be intrinsic limitations in the production of language, that very characteristic is compensated by the almost limitless flexibility of the adaptive capacity, writing that "The number of words at our disposition will always be limited and woefully inadequate to describe the multiplicity of the real: the world contains more things than we will ever be able to name, and our experience is constantly confronted with the limits of our words. But at the same time our language always seems able to transgress its own limits, and also our own." And this is where the library, both in concrete and in concept, enters the picture. For the library is the technology created and sustained by culture to pass on, in an efficient and effective manner, the many and varied advantages the transcript has to offer humanity.

But the library accomplishes even more than the passing along of the social transcript. Epistemologist and science philosopher C. D. Dunbar (1927, p. 16) gets right to the heart of the matter, observing that "the most fundamental task of philosophy is to take the concepts that we daily use in common life and science, to analyse them, and thus to determine their precise meanings and their mutual relations." Language, above all its vocabulary, changes from writer to writer and reader to reader because words are intended to express the concepts, ideas, and feelings with the countless possibilities that increase with each writer and reader over time, not only as the culture evolves, but also as it does so in ever more complex and diverse ways. Subtleties, nuances, shades of meaning, all emerge to help the mind adjust to the ever-changing environment and, in time, to change the culture. Meanwhile, however, words may also retain their meanings of many earlier generations. The meanings of these symbols are as many, in potential, as there may be objects of thought, whether now, in the past, or in the future. These are captured in the library for consideration and use by others in the effort to understand or to express or to explain. This phenomenon is at least in part responsible for the variety of interpretation and meaning of the text in fiction, which olds an extraordinary power to open the mind to imagination. In his book on the relation of the reader to the novel, Wolfgang Iser (1974, p. 280) reminds us that "With all literary texts, then, we may say that the reading process is selective, and the potential text is infinitely richer than any of its individual realizations. This is borne out by the fact that a second reading of a piece of literature often produces a different impression from the first."[19] In summary, the library supplies unparalleled variety in substance joined with degree of precision in articulated expression to stimulate thought and imagination that enable humanity to evolve and to extend its cooperative and individually creative efforts.

Of particular interest in considering the concept of library as a cultural technology is John Ziman's (2000, p. 8) conclusion that the general concept of technology "is not restricted to material objects. It also includes a whole variety of systematic technical procedures, such as farming routines or medical therapies, where the material instruments are not the centre of attention." Selection generates complex designs that are organized by function to solve adaptive problems, and the design feature spreads if it solves problems and fits the environment, say Leda Cosmides, John Tooby, and Jerome H. Barkow (1992, p. 9). And they conclude that" Evolution by natural selection is the only presently validated explanation for the accumulation of functional design features across generations."

Evolution, both biological and cultural, is a process that goes on indefinitely. Therefore, predicting future trajectories based on best information available about past directions is not yet productive, because it hinges in large part on the vicissitudes of environment. That is, after all, what evolution is about. Moreover, as Bentley Glass (1985, p. 63) points out, the process delimits the possible situations existing in the next period of time, "Like the flow of human history, which also contains a similar element of uniqueness of events, with the past limiting the character of the present and the future, there is limited usefulness of the evolutionary past for prediction." With a bit of tongue-in-cheek wisdom, economic philosopher Kenneth Boulding (1985, p. 65) concurs that "we cannot predict what we are going to know twenty-five years from now, or we would know it now and not have to wait."

If we cannot foresee the future, at least we can better understand how we got where we are and, therefore, something about who we are, and these are no small matters. Moreover, we can also understand the potential of the library as concept and its realization in daily and cumulated services; in summary its significant place in cultural evolution as a continuing life process. Precisely in the middle of the twentieth century, Norbert Wiener (1950, p. 144) noted "We have seen that communication is the cement of society, and that those who have made the clear maintenance of channels of communication their business are those who have most to do with the continued existence or fall of our civilization."

In the course of the foregoing chapters, direction has been step by step toward the identification of the most likely site in which to locate a library philosophy. It has proved difficult to identify the site, because the philosophy in question long ago came into being quietly, evolved with increasing quiet strength, and continues to evolve through the dependence of human experience and reason, even though ever concealed from the full light of common awareness. To those who would say that the library profession has not succeeded in establishing its purpose, I would respond that they may be right, but that the culture, itself, created library philosophy long ago. What remains for the profession to do, however, is to uncover the philosophy that has been at work, under low profile and quietly, for several thousand years, and present it for discussion. Kenneth Boulding (1985, p. 139) summarizes the unique function of the library accordingly: "The written record of the human race, as we find it in the great libraries, is a precious heritage of communication and profoundly affects the content of what we have to communicate about. Indeed, we stand on the shoulders of the past through its records." To some extent, the present essay is an elaboration of this very rich statement.

With the ultimate purpose to define a library philosophy, this book has proceeded to describe library function in society, reasoning that philosophy flows most naturally from function, rather than from the actions involved in fulfilling that function. Owing to the longevity of the library, which has existed since the earliest stages of written language and, in concept, even before that in the oral tradition, its function is determined to be related closely to cultural evolution. Given that premise, this essay has examined the research and theory advanced by a large number of scholars who represent the perspective of many disciplines in the physical, social, and human sciences. This exercise produces a rich variety of perspectives, resulting in a synthesis that offers a solid foundation from which to consider the nature and implications of library function. When understood from the library perspective, this synthesis of research and theory relative to cultural evolution sheds much light on the basic function of the library and leads to the conclusion that the library is sufficiently integrated into cultural evolution, in fact, for it to be considered a cultural technology and, therefore, a manifestation of the nature of humanity.

Consequently, library philosophy is especially well situated within this function, rather than within the context of direction provided primarily by the practice that follows from it, or by the mold of an established philosophical system that is attuned only partially to the total symbiosis of function and practice.

Epilogue: Library Philosophy Uncovered

Theories do not get selected because they fit or are right, but because they are not incompatible with a niche in the environment.

—Peter Munz, 1985

SIX OF THE EIGHT CHAPTERS OF THIS BOOK have been directed at an understanding of why the library function has been sustained throughout the millennia of its existence, steadily growing stronger and more ubiquitous despite specific setbacks described in the records of history. Guided by a theory that the answer to this question must be located in some deeply embedded and tightly integral relation between the library and the human condition, research has been focused on cultural evolution as the appropriate context. Associated with this hypothesis has been the thought that whatever is the answer to its guiding question, that answer must also hold, and even constitute, library philosophy, which for nearly a century has proved to be frustratingly elusive.

Theory applied every day to librarianship, library science, and information science gives direction to the administration of daily practice in any type of library. But, ultimately, it is philosophy that guides these aggregated theories and practices in a single direction. The critical concepts from which library philosophy is constructed are those that are inherent in those of culture, function, reason, language, selection, knowledge, cooperation, transcript, and evolution. All are concepts of process which, together through time, have interacted to mold a coherent library philosophy that optimizes for humanity the potential of mind in all its aspects and manifestations. More than a specific place, the library is a force that contributes substantively to human adaptation to the environment. More than an outcome of cultural phenomena it is a cultural technology.

Within its cultural environment the library functions in cyclical fashion: It collects to preserve and communicate humanity's transcript of knowledge and experience, as considered in their broadest interpretation; it continuously builds and restructures the foundation for the generation of new knowledge, which then enters the ever-accumulating store of social capital to be passed along in a continuing movement toward the human ideal of understanding, whether individual understanding or social understanding. Thus, knowledge is both the significance of anything held in an individual's mind at any given time and a process of culture. The cycles assume a linear direction, but the function is layered, or scaffolded, because it integrates countless seemingly unrelated cycles that have been amassing and evolving for ages.

Throughout the millennia, humanity selects from among ubiquitous sources those it will ultimately use in the effort either to adapt to the environment or to change the environment, depending on need relative to readiness. This it accomplishes by synthesizing what previously were divergent parcels of information and allusions of knowledge into a basis upon which a society can analyze, test, understand, explore further, and present to others, even without attention to considerations of time and space. This process is engaged both at the level of the individual and at the level of society through vast expanses of time. As the social mind is formed and re-formed, so the individual mind is formed and re-formed through the layering, with very little left to go astray in the process; culture has selected a means both to construct the social transcript that conveys it and to ensure its dependable continuation.

Mention of the relation between biological and cultural evolution has been made frequently throughout this text. The chart incorporated below depicts the biological and cultural concepts whose mutual influence proves to be of greatest significance to an understanding of library function within cultural evolution and, thereby, to the identification of library philosophy. Specifically, the chart depicts three critical spheres of human life: Body, Mind, and Culture. Each is accompanied in the chart by the respective technology that lends itself to the transmission of a corresponding agent in evolution. In summary, the human body selects *genetics* as the technology for transmission of the agent genes; mind selects *memory* as the technology for transmission of agent memes; culture selects *library* function as the technology for transmission of agent social transcript.

Library as Cultural Technology in Evolution

Sphere	Technology	Agent
Body	Genetics	Genes
Mind	Memory	Memes
Culture	Library	Transcript

Also conveyed in this chart is the broadly encompassing idea that body, mind, and society constitute the essence of humanity. Mind and society, working together, are molded in large measure by culture, which in turn is carried forward and structured in many ways by the social transcript. As body and mind function together so do mind and culture, and for literate societies it is above all the social transcript in its recorded form that energizes and channels this evolutionary process of culture. The integrity of the concepts displayed in this chart constitutes, to borrow the thoughtful language of sixteenth-century French humanist and humorist François Rabelais, the *substantifique moelle*, or the nourishing marrow, of the research and theory in many fields that has been focused on cultural evolution and is synthesized from the library perspective represented in the present study.

From this unique perspective, library philosophy is seen to be embedded deep within thousands of generations of cultural evolution in response to humanity's extraordinarily broad spectrum of physical, intellectual, and psychic needs. The philosophy certainly was not first established and then followed by humanity in due course; rather, it emerged imperceptibly over time as it evolved from within, to lend dependable guidance to the culture that had created it, as though in an instinctive mode. Stewardship of the social transcript is entirely natural to humanity, and may very well amount to the epitome of humanity's most distinctive features. Library philosophy is to be found in the great accumulation of all the acts associated uniquely with the social transcript. It is in the composite of daily transactions and decisions demanded of service to the contemporary respective society and to the greater evolutionary culture. These transactions and decisions, amassing through generation after generation, reflect the various needs of culture as it diversifies and expands, only to diversify and expand ever more. Preservation of the human record for the purposes of both stability and re-formation of the culture through continuous stimulation and fulfillment of the intellect are the responsibilities of the cultural technology that is contained in the concept of library. For these are the human phenomena that lead to questions, to answers, to learning, to understanding, to communication, to new knowledge, to higher levels of understanding, to innovation in technology, and, essentially and ultimately, to survival; but it is foremost the survival of human beings as distinct among all living beings.

The concept of philosophy inheres in culture. Philosophy reflects upon, expresses, and explains cultural phenomena, among which is the intellectual dimension of culture referred to in this synthesis as the social transcript. The social transcript is the central force that enables the reassuring continuity and at the same time the rational evolution of any literate society in ways that are unique among social institutions and commercial enterprises alike. And, while the social transcript in its entirety is a purposeful and direct extension of the mind, its recorded dimension is also a great facilitator of communication among minds for the same purposes. But, more than that, because of its relative clarity, uniformity, and shareablility, the recorded social transcript is extraordinarily conducive to thoughtful scrutiny and reflection. Knowledge and experience are its substance. Intellectual freedom, diversity, reason, skepticism, understanding, organization, integration, imagination, and preservation are its fundamental principles. Therefore, the greatest potential of humanity is realized in very large measure through the capacity of the social transcript. It is above all the recorded social transcript that tells the story of literate culture and defines its status at any point in time. Since inception of the transcribed social record, the library function has realized the potential of this capacity. It continues every day in many ways to ensure this extraordinary ongoing reflection of humanity through an aggregated complex of accumulated actions, transactions, and processes.

Stewardship of the recorded social transcript defines library philosophy. It is a responsibility that is assigned in varying degrees through culture from one society to another. Not simply a matter of locking away this dynamic intellectual treasure for the use of some unidentified posterity in the indefinite future, the philosophy is acted upon through the selection of the extant records of thought and experience to be preserved in whatever form its contemporary culture designates. This means organizing those records for the relative ease of consultation in the broadest interpretation, assisting in consultation, and fostering a social environment that will optimize an intellectual spirit appropriate to the vast range of possibilities afforded by the experience. It all comes together as library function, a function created by culture for culture and managed by the evolving expressions of library and information science.

The book in its varied manifestations of physical design and structure, including its attendant electronic devices, and all those means of recording communication that are fitted together to achieve library purpose through services and operations, is an artifact. Even when multiplied by great accumulation, books do not constitute a library. They are the extant vehicles of any given society that are intended for convenient conveyance of the record from individual to individual, society to society, generation to generation, and anywhere on this planet and beyond. Books contain the record. They are not the record; they are not the content of recorded experience and knowledge. Briefly, all these many physical manifestations do not constitute the library because library is a concept of experience that is realized through a cultural process in fulfillment of a fundamental need that is singularly human. The library experience has been sustained by humanity throughout the millennia because it is integral to cultural evolution as a reliable source of its energy. The phenomenal complex of intellectual processes that are constructed uniquely by library experience constitutes the larger and more profoundly human condition that is held in evolving culture by the joining of people and ideas through time and across space. Thus, library philosophy is uncovered, and its rich substance can be abstracted: The library is about people and ideas.

Notes

Chapter 1

1. Also substantiating Danton's assessment, Shera (1971, p. 151) points out that "During the years between Butler [1931] and Foskett [1962] a handful of librarians have insisted that there was a serious need for a structured philosophy of librarianship that would provide a setting to which practice could be related and against which the effectiveness of that practice might be measured." Similar statements are scattered throughout this text.

2. Sociologist William J. Goode (1961, p. 311) provides an interpretation of this phenomenon, writing that "The repeated calls which librarians have made for 'a philosophy of librarianship' essentially express the need to define what *is* the intellectual problem of the occupation." He also points out (p. 314) the effect on the future of librarianship: "The failure to define adequately the nature of the intellectual problem means that practitioners themselves often fail to see the challenge of developing the field," which is a thought that another commentator, Myra Kolitsch (1945, p. 30) finds to be an essential benefit that could be offered by a philosophy, saying that it ought to be forward looking. "By 'forward looking' I mean that it must recognize the values, opportunities, and problems of the present and be alert and ready to adjust to the values, opportunities, and problems of the future." And in that connection, Jesse Shera (1971) blames the failure of librarians to accept new information technologies as they were being introduced on the absence of a philosophical foundation. In the same vein, thirty years earlier Pierce Butler (1933, p. 103) had argued that "A professional philosophy would give to librarianship that directness of action which can spring only from a complete consciousness of purpose." Library administrator and theorist James Wellard (1940, p. 100) finds sarcastic humor in the notion that "It is not unlikely, indeed, that many library techniques give more satisfaction to librarians than to readers." Library theorist Ronald C. Benge (1970, p. 257) brings up a fundamental issue that conjures a haunting sensation: "It has often been remarked (notably by the American Public Library Inquiry) that official professional statements about library ideals are too far removed from what actually happens in libraries. In the same way the 'idealism' of library schools leaves students unprepared for what they eventually face in work situations." Finally, in this context one cannot help thinking about the findings of early missionaries in primitive areas of the globe, as described by anthropologist Lucien Lévy-Bruhl (1923, p. 30): "the primitives whom they have studied never thought, and never wanted to think, of more than a very few things—those necessary to their subsistence, their flocks and herds, their game, fish, etc. The mental

habits they would thus acquire would become so pronounced that all other things, especially if abstract in their nature, would be powerless to arrest their attention. 'They only believe what they see; their ideas go no further than the regions of sense; what is not directly perceived is not thought,' and so on."

3. For more on this issue see especially the articles by Jonathan Furner (2004) and John M. Budd (2002).

4. A revealing "Check List of Statements on Selection Principles" is provided in the 4th edition of the book by library educators Mary Duncan Carter, Wallace J. Bonk, and Rose Mary Magrill (1974, pp. 25–46).

5. "Libraries may be taken for granted simply because they constitute no social problem," is a conclusion reached by J. Periam Danton (1934, p. 541). Of course libraries are not taken for granted when one society determines to eradicate the culture of another in achieving its purpose of dominating that society. From a completely different perspective, perhaps contrarily, Broadfield (1949, p. 78) points out a feature of the library which, while very interesting and probably true, is not very often recognized: "Libraries create one of the major problems of our society, for they develop immense efficiency in the diffusion and communication of ideas, without engendering any corresponding increase in the power to discriminate and to think fundamentally."

6. But Pierce Butler (1942, p. 6) adds a different perspective on the situation, asserting that "Librarians, without being fully aware of their attitude, hold a strong conviction that somehow reading for information is nobler than reading for emotional experience . . . this quaint prejudice among librarians is of more than passing academic interest." Barry Totterdell (1978, p. 13) offers a more pragmatic slant on the issue: "Certainly from the earliest days of public libraries, users have remained largely unaware of attempts to impose some 'grand design' of purpose on the service. It is significant that all the evidence from surveys suggests users have 'voted with their feet' for a largely recreational service, the one aspect of library purpose most consistently ignored by the theoreticians." And historian Charles E. Rosenberg (1979, p. 449) discusses this kind of situation more generally in the social sciences, which "were shaped to a large extent in the half-century before 1920 by conflicting tendencies toward social intervention and reform, on the one had, and a value-free, neutral stance on the other. Though some of the most prominent leaders in the formative decades of American social science were imbued with an almost evangelical desire to intervene righteously in society, it soon became clear that such intervention could be dangerous, not only to the individuals involved but to the disciplinary needs of the nascent social sciences. Certainly one of the characteristic themes in all of the social sciences in the last quarter of the nineteenth century and first quarter of the twentieth was this very conflict between social consciousness and academic cautiousness."

7. Concluding his book on library power, James Thompson (1974, p. 110) contends that "libraries are the storehouses of knowledge and the repositories of the records of mankind's achievements and discoveries. They conserve and transmit our culture. They underpin education, both individual and formal. They feature significantly in our economic welfare; they are crucially related to all other intellectual, artistic and creative activities. They are instruments of social and political change. And as the guardians of the freedom of thought, they are bastions of liberty. It follows therefore that any philosophy of librarianship must be firmly based on a full appreciation of

this power of libraries; but it is only too apparent that the library profession as it presently exists does not have such an appreciation, and expends the greater part of its energies on techniques and clerical routines." In fact, Jesse Shera (1980, p. 315) argues that "Not until the advent of the Great Depression in the 1930s did librarians suddenly awaken to the realization, and its implications, that they really were a part of the public sector, that they were created by society, and that what affected the social fabric of which they were a part also had serious implications for them."

8. Garceau (1949, p. 148) casts this in a more salubrious context, finding that "Disillusionment comes to librarians when they apply their library faith too exactingly and more particularly when they use it as a measure for concrete library programs and apply it to particular political situations. That faith is essential in the strategy of their politics, but it must be used strategically and as a social myth, not as a measuring rod. When the political forces of a community and the political moves open to the library are examined, the library faith, classical and modernized, retains a persistent validity. A few people use the library and feel that they benefit greatly; society assumes that they are important and that their intellectual enlightenment is socially valuable, for in some inscrutable way knowledge is virtue and information power."

9. The problem evidently has not been limited to library science, for Carl G. Hempel (1942, p. 47) also ridicules the emphasis in psychology and the social sciences on 'operational definitions', to the more powerful and fruitful of concept. "But concept formation in science cannot be separated from theoretical considerations; indeed, it is precisely the discovery of concept systems with theoretical import which advances scientific understanding; and such discovery requires scientific inventiveness and cannot be replaced by the—certainly indispensable, but also definitely insufficient—operationist or empiricist requirement of empirical import alone." The lack of conceptualization and therefore of a comprehensive philosophy, of course, has an effect on the formal preparation of librarians.

10. For a full accounting of the excitement, both positive and negative, surrounding the development of the Graduate Library School of the University of Chicago, see John V. Richardson (1982).

11. While there is a very substantial number of published comments in opposition to the adoption of the science model in librarianship, they often are more emotional than reasoned. An early exception is provided by library theorist C. Seymour Thompson (1931), who provides balance to the controversy.

12. For example, long-time Librarian of Congress Ainsworth Rand Spofford (1900, pp. 174–175) deduced more than a century ago that "It is unhappily true that books do not teach the use of books. The art of extracting what is important or instructive in any book, from the mass of verbiage that commonly overlays it, cannot be learned by theory. Invaluable as the art of reading is, as a means of enlightenment, its highest uses can only be obtained by a certain method of reading, which will separate the wheat from the chaff. Different readers will, of course, possess different capacities for doing this."

13. Otherwise we in the profession will simply continue to pretend we know what we're talking about. The profession makes a pretense at communication and understanding, when its exponents fall prey to the thoughtless ease of invoking concepts of such significance. The LIS professions are not alone in this regard. In the course of

his explanation of the importance and difficulty of concepts when used in communication, journalist and philosopher John Wilson (1971, pp. 44–45) offers a glimpse into their potential to become a misleading magic. As an example, he shows how the apparently simple statement about gravity making the stone fall downwards can be thought of as meaning gravity is an abstract thing or force, that the stone therefore was compelled to fall; in short that things have the human capacity to obey the laws of nature. This is what Wilson calls magic, about which he says further that "This tendency to magic, deeply inbred into our thinking, used to cause endless trouble in the early days of science: and it now causes just as much trouble when we face problems connected with people—problems of morality, psychology and so on." Libraries are connected with people, and we sometimes revert to magic to smooth over the problems incurred in this relation. A doctoral dissertation analyzing the concept of use as it appears in LIS discourse was completed in 2008 by Rachel Fleming-May, University of Alabama.

14. Sociologist Thomas J. Scheff (2006, p. 198) writes that Erving Goffman, sociologist of the "microworld of emotions and relationships," was devoted to the development of a new lexicon for the hitherto shadowy world of social interaction. "He somehow sensed that, in the English language at least, it is virtually impossible to describe the structure/process of interaction in ways that don't merely confirm and justify it. The way that each of us is socialized leads us to that impression, and our relationships, emotions, and the very language we use continually reaffirm it."

Chapter 2

1. Examples used throughout this text are drawn very heavily from the Anglo-American library world. Consideration of location, however, is made moot by the focus of the essay, which is on library as a function of cultural evolution rather than as a topographic or temporal situation.

2. Arthur E. Bostwick (1920) edits a collection of nineteenth- and early twentieth-century assessments of the place of the library that extends the sampling mentioned here. Debate about purpose has long been engaged in the public library sector. Yet it is a debate that strikes (in varying degrees) at the heart of most issues relating to the purpose of all types of libraries. Anyone whose responsibility it is to select information sources to be made accessible via the library in any setting deals with the principles. Consequently, much of the library-oriented literature on this issue addresses the public library sector. But that sector simply is the clearest exemplar of library purpose, as can best be seen in the function of the national library.

3. This is a situation Jesse Shera (1980, p. 317) synthesizes and explains: "Though the library is the creature of society, it does not reach the individual as do the mass media. Each must seek the library and its resources out for himself, and it is through the individual that the library achieves its social goals. Therefore, for the library, 'the proper study of mankind is man'."

4. Redundancy is a concept that will recur frequently in this book for it is a function of the long-term storage aspect of library function. The concept lends to library function an element of reliability so that ideas are not lost in time. Social psychologist

Sir Frederic C. Bartlett (1958, p. 90) explains the workings of the human memory as long-term storage in a manner that easily can be applied to the library function in cultural evolution: "Thus 'long-term' may mean anything from a second or less, to not far short of the full span of individual life. There can be no fixed interval of measured time, after which long-term storage begins, for in any given instance the actual interval depends in part on the nature and complexity of the evidence that must be dealt with. Once information goes into 'long-term store', subject to the changes which it may subsequently undergo, it may be drawn upon to meet a lot of different requirements. It may be remembered; made the basis and justification of belief, and of doubt; it may be utilized in a great variety of learning acquirements; it may be called upon to bolster up prejudice and bias; it may issue in thinking. Each one of these distinguishable psychological processes has to be able to use the stored information in ways peculiar to itself, and at least in part different from those of the others." From a different perspective, Jesse Shera (1972, p. 360) writes that "Librarianship is, in the final analysis, a cluster of specializations united by certain bonds of knowledge that are common to all bibliothecal activity." But, to be sure, it is a purposeful cluster of specializations, as J.G. Meijer (1982, p. 15)contends in his assessment that "the unproven statement that the library is a conglomerate of heterogeneous components is untenable, and the conclusion is therefore reached that, for the purposes of definition, the functions of librarianship should be regarded as properties of a homogeneous entity."

5. This positive interpretation has been challenged by other scholars. For example, Michael H. Harris (1991) interprets social engineering negatively in several venues. He and his associate Masaru Itoga (p. 352) conclude that "the library is an institution embedded in a stratified ensemble of institutions functioning in the high cultural region, an ensemble of institutions dedicated to the creation, transmission, and reproduction of the hegemonic ideology. Such a conclusion challenges the 'apolitical' conception of the library so commonly held by library professionals, and strips the library of the ethical and political innocence attributed to it by library apologists." See also Harris (1973 and 1986). Following is a useful description of the motivation in Victorian England, offered by literary and cultural historian scholar Richard Altick (1998, p. 85), who writes that "as literacy and interest in reading spread, the 'superior orders of society'—a term much in favor in the period—reacted to the phenomenon in terms of their special interests. Once they conceded it was impossible to prevent the lower ranks from reading, they embarked on a long campaign to insure that through the press the masses of people would be induced to help preserve the status quo and bulwark the security and prosperity of the particular sort of national life that they, its upper- and middle-class rulers, cherished. This campaign took many forms." Library historian Alistair Black (1996, p. 257) places this issue of control in a larger context: "Control was certainly a facet of the early public library's history. However, the notion of the public library as nothing more than an agency of dominant ideology has been rejected in this study. Control (power indeed) is a feature of any social circumstance, from the family to the operations of multinational capital. It was also integral to the ethos of the early public library; but it does not follow that social control engineered through the mechanism of the municipal library was conspiratorial or, more pertinently, successful. It is not feasible to apply to the early public library, in any wholesale fashion, theories of bourgeois-directed, conspiratorial

domination. Hegemony was to a degree attempted, but was generally unsuccessful." Library administrator and theorist Joseph Z. Nitecki (1964, p. 277) gives the social engineering interpretation of library purpose a more positive spin, concluding that it is "to contribute towards the unification of society by re-directing and re-interpreting group interests in terms of the ultimate interests of a society." Library historian James Thompson (1974, pp. 62–63) acknowledges the liabilities of social engineering and adds balance to his caveat: "Society, through education, seeks to condition and process its members, supposedly for their own good. Libraries, so long as they can avoid becoming agencies of the state, provide a corrective: they are a constant subversion, a perpetual guerrilla movement for freedom." Library theorist Bryan Luckham (1971, p. 119) also acknowledges a negative potential of the library function: "The manifest function of public libraries may be to encourage the reading habit and diffuse literary culture more widely. On the other hand, book selection policies, administrative regulations, the ethos of the public library service itself might instead serve a latent function of preserving social differentials and advantages." Historian Ann Robson (1976, p. 187), however, contributes to the debate her understanding of the intellectual background of the British public library movement: "It is essential to keep in mind that a widespread faith in factual knowledge as the alkahest for utopia was behind the founding of free libraries and that their purpose was to provide for all men the knowledge necessary for the improvement of their own lot and of all mankind. It is the nineteenth-century vision of the ideal society which provides the key to an understanding of their objectives."

Chapter 3

1. Sociologist Ellsworth Faris (1937, p. 17) clarifies, observing that "Instead of the instincts of individuals being the cause of our customs and institutions, it is far truer to say it is the customs and institutions which explain the individual behavior so long called instinctive. Instincts do not create customs. Customs create instincts, for the putative instincts of human beings are always learned and never native." Geneticist Bentley Glass (1943, p. 2) summarizes the essentials of contributions by nature and nurture, writing that "The physical basis of our heredity is, indeed, determined from our life's beginning, but from that moment on our surroundings continuously exert their influence, sometimes strongly, sometimes with little effect. The interplay of these contrasting factors is evident at every stage in the emergence of a man or a woman." Adding to the complexity of social order, as is known simply from observation of everyday life, the individual and society frequently are at odds. But, according to philosopher Henri Bergson (1944, p. 282), "among the dissociated individuals, one life goes on moving: everywhere the tendency to individualize is opposed and at the same time completed by an antagonistic and complementary tendency to associate, as if the manifold unity of life, drawn in the direction of multiplicity, made so much the more effort to withdraw itself on to itself. A part is no sooner detached than it ends to reunite itself, if not to all the rest, at least to what is nearest to it. Hence, throughout the whole realm of life, a balancing between individuation and association. Individuals join together into a society; but the society, as soon as formed, tends to melt the

associated individuals into a new organism, so as to become itself an individual, able in its turn to be part and parcel of a new association."

2. Singer (1968, p. 527) explains this idea further: "His [Tylor's] definition does not distinguish social organization and social institutions from a general concept of culture." Also according to Singer, "this led to rival anthropological theories of culture—the theory of culture patterns . . . and the theory of 'social structure'" He also says (p. 532) that "The parallels between the theory of culture patterns and the theory of social structure are numerous and striking. Both theories have explanatory aims, although each finds different factors to be primary." It is near impossible to explain the distinction between a 'society' and a 'culture', except that the society is a population group within a culture, because the distinction will vary according to the subject in question. Therefore, social anthropologist A. R. Radcliffe-Brown (1948, p. 60) posits this description of the process in place of an explanation: "In all sciences the scientist attempts to separate conceptually what he is studying from its environment. To some extent, as I have said, such abstractions are arbitrary, but some abstractions are expedient and some are not. The art of science is to know where to make the abstraction. The art of the scientist lies in his ability to distinguish between the expedient and the inexpedient, thus assuring that his investigation will have positive results. This distinguishes a good scientist from a bad. It involves a certain amount of intuition."

3. Anthropologist Leslie A White (1968, p. 549) is more specific: "To consider culture—languages, institutions, ideologies, and technological systems—as distinct orders of phenomena, explainable in terms of themselves, is not to reify them. They are real, observable things and events in the external world, just as atoms, cells, and stars are." Social psychologist Sir Frederic C. Bartlett (1932, p. 296) connects memory and social context in his statement "Social organisation gives a persistent framework into which all detailed recall must fit, and it very powerfully influences both the manner and matter of recall. Moreover, this persistent framework helps to provide those 'schemata' which are a basis for the imaginative reconstruction called memory."

4. Cultural anthropologists Alfred L. Kroeber and Clyde Kluckhohn (1952) summarize 164 definitions of the concept of culture in the scholarly literature up to their publication date. The work is divided in three parts, plus a summary: General History of the Word Culture; Definitions; and Some Statements about Culture. Anthropologist Adam Kuper (2002) tersely summarizes competing theories of cultural evolution.

5. White (1973, p. 13) writes that "When we say that man has psychological needs, spiritual needs, we are expressing an inference drawn from our observations of his behavior. One of the tremendously important functions of culture is to satisfy these needs, to give man courage, confidence, morale, comfort, consolation." Anthropologist Ralph Linton (1947, p. 4) characterizes these as psychic needs, writing that "It may be assumed that it is the needs of the individual which provide the motivations for his behaviour and which are, through this, responsible for the operation of society and culture. The needs of human beings appear to be more numerous and more varied than those of any other species. In addition to those which can be traced directly to physiological tensions, as the needs for food, for sleep, for escape from pain and for sexual satisfaction, man has a whole series of other needs whose connection with such tensions cannot be clearly demonstrated. These, for lack of a better term,

we may call the *psychic needs.*" Evolutionary psychologist Robert J. Richards (1987, p. 557) also emphasizes psychic needs, contending that "There is no justification for historians to assume a priori that only social forces (i.e., political and ideological interests) finally determine ideas. Historians must rather empirically analyze both the conceptual system in question and its intellectual environment to discriminate the several kinds of force that are cooperative and to estimate their respective strengths."

6. Pierce Butler (1952, p. 81) describes the interactive quality of the process: "Man evokes culture out of the latent possibilities of nature, and culture evokes humanity out of the latent possibilities of man."

7. Plotkin (2004, p. 64) cites a key passage that did not appear prior to the 1871 edition of Darwin's 1859 classic that "important as the struggle for existence has been and even still is, yet as far as the highest parts of man's nature is concerned there are other agencies more important. For the moral qualities are advanced, either directly or indirectly, much more through the effects of habit, the reasoning powers, instruction, religion, etc., than through natural selection; though to this latter agency may be safely attributed the social instincts, which afforded the basis for the development of the moral sense." Social psychologist David Loye (1998, p. 168) offers another reminder of Darwin's thought: "Darwin's other major theory was of the development of the 'moral sense'. Though long ignored as a 19th-century peculiarity, it has received striking confirmation from modern brain research. The picture that now emerges from both Darwin's original theory and this brain research is of a capacity for moral sensitivity that enters organic evolution with the emergence of sex over 1 billion years ago." In this regard, Loye (p. 171) also refers to biologist Julian Huxley's assessment that "Counter-poised to natural selection at the human level is '*psychosocial* selection', which also acts as an ordering principle. It is a goal-selecting mechanism, and the goals that it selects will change with the picture of the world and of human nature provided by [our] increasing knowledge."

8. White (1949, p. 366) is adamant about this: "The technological system is basic and primary. Social systems are functions of technologies; and philosophies express technological forces and reflect social systems. The technological factor is therefore the determinant of a cultural system as a whole." Journalist and novelist Régis Debray (2000, pp. 51–54) separates technology and culture with some interesting distinctions. These include, but are not limited to, the ideas that culture is inherited, technology received; culture has an intimate function of self identification, technology does not; technology directs only one way—to the future, culture opens in both directions; technology is never a message, only culture can be addressed to someone; there are technological lineages but only cultural legacies. This set of distinctions does not argue with White's conclusions, but provides a different perspective. Anthropologist André Leroi-Gourhan (1993, p. 147) proffers yet another perspective on the influence of various cultural forces "We can prove that the way in which material, technical, and economic factors are balanced influences social forms and therefore a society's thinking, but we cannot establish the principle that philosophical or religious thought coincides with a society's material development."

9. The timely development of the printing press, whose significance in the evolution of culture can hardly be overstated, serves as an example. According to historian

Elizabeth Eisenstein (1979, pp. 702–703), "The early presses which were first established between 1460 and 1480 were powered by many different forces which had been incubating in the age of scribes. In a different cultural context, the same technology might have been used for different ends (as was the case in China and Korea) or might have been unwelcome and not been used at all (as was the case in many regions outside Europe where Western missionary presses were the first to be installed). In this light one may agree with authorities who hold that the duplicating process which was developed in fifteenth-century Mainz, was *in itself* of no more consequence than any other inanimate tool. Unless it had been deemed useful to human agents it would never have been put into operation in fifteenth-century European towns. Under different circumstances, moreover, it might have been welcomed and put to entirely different uses—monopolized by priests and rulers, for example, and withheld from free-wheeling urban entrepreneurs." Also related to the matter of such timing, anthropologist Mary Douglas (1986, p. 77) concludes thus: "Scientific precursors disappear from view because they never had an earthly chance of making their way to the surface of public memory... Most rediscovered theories turn out not to have built originally on the current cognitive infrastructure and so to have missed savings in energy. Often when a new scientific discovery has been rejected and left to lie inert until later, it is precisely an idea which lacked formulaic interlocking with normal procedures of validation." Basing their theory on that of psychologist and neurologist Pierre Janet (1928, p. 321), developmental psychologists Jaan Valsiner and René Van der Veer (2000, p. 61) offer another perspective: "We have often remarked that fashion exists in scientific research as it does in the creation of ladies' dresses and hats. For no apparent reason a particular, sometimes very tiny study becomes the order of the day in a certain epoch. Everybody feels obliged to write an article on this problem. Works, books, publications accumulate during ten or fifteen years. Then, for no apparent reason, the wind turns, and this problem, which seemed exciting, rather quickly becomes uninteresting. In reality it has not been solved, but that does not matter. One loses interest, because in that epoch everything has been said that could be said with the existing methods and points of view. This does not mean that the problem is completely and definitively suppressed. It generally comes again into fashion twenty or twenty-five years later. This is the way scientific progress is made" Archeologist V. Gordon Childe (1951, p. 172) approaches the issue from the more general perspective of cultural diffusion: "Diffusion is not an automatic process, like infection with a disease. One society can borrow an idea—a technical invention, a political institution, a superstitious rite, or an artistic motive—only when it fits into the general pattern of the society's culture—in other words, when that society has evolved to a stage which allows of the acceptance of the idea." Timing and readiness are also significant for considerations that run even deeper than technology and innovative ideas. For example, success of the fundamental units of cultural memory units takes a similar course, as ethologist and evolutionary biologist Richard Dawkins (1999, p. 11) writes: "It is true that the relative survival success of a meme will depend critically on the social and biological climate in which it finds itself, and this climate will certainly be influenced by the genetic make-up of the population. But it will also depend on the memes that are already numerous in the meme-pool."

10. As might be expected, there is disagreement among the experts as to the nature of cultural evolution, especially in the context of concepts of selection and adaptation. Biologist Colin S. Pittendrigh (1958, pp. 391–392) examines four meanings attached to the concept of adaptation in biological evolution, which have in common a purpose or end-directedness. He emphasizes (p. 393) that "The concepts of adaptation and natural selection are so interwoven that it is impossible to misunderstand one without doing violence to the other." Social theorist Stephen K. Sanderson (2001, pp. 143–157) unravels the key threads of the debate about the nature of evolution in his chapter 9, "Darwinian Conflict Theory: A Unified Evolutionary Theory of Human Society." His position (p. 149) in this debate is that "Adaptation is a process pertaining to individuals and not to units larger than the individual. Social groups and societies in and of themselves cannot be adaptational—i.e., cannot be the units on which selection operates—because they cannot and do not exist apart from concrete flesh-and-blood individuals and because groups cannot have a critical trait of individuals, viz., consciousness and a brain. Although social groups may be said to have needs and wants, the needs and wants are ultimately only the needs and wants of their constituent members. Any social form that is said to be adaptive for any group or society as a whole is so only because it is adaptive for all (or nearly all) of that group's or society's constituent members. Any so-called adaptation at the level of a group or society is but a statistical aggregate of individual adaptations." This is a rather rigorous definition, given its application to energies that are social in nature. The conclusions to his entire study include a position less rigorous, however: "Society is the creation of individuals acting in accordance with preferences and aims" (p. 331). These would be the cultural preferences and aims. Sociologist W. G. Runciman (2002, pp. 22–23) takes a much stronger stand, observing that "Sceptics about the relevance of neo-Darwinian theory to human social behaviour are apt to claim that its application to sociocultural as opposed to natural selection is 'merely' metaphorical. But quite apart from the point that much of the language of science is metaphorical and none the worse for it, in what sense is it metaphorical to say that a heritable information affecting phenotype [the visible properties of an organism that are produced by the interaction of the genotype and the environment] is replicated in a number of different ways down and across human populations? The idea is straightforward enough." Henry Plotkin (1998, p. 230) is very specific about the application of selection and adaptation to groups: "In summary, the group *can* be considered a unitary vehicle on which selection acts . . . Human evolution, therefore, will have favoured behavioural traits that enhance the fitness of individuals, but some of these will do so because they operate at the group level. Since culture only has meaning within the context of a social group, developments in contemporary evolutionary theory that sanction the idea of group selection gives us the conceptual firepower that allows us to think of the human capacity culture as being a product of evolutionary forces." John Ziman (2002, p. 6) invokes sociobiology, which argues that human behavior, including mental faculties and language, has biological correlates with which it co-evolved. "That is to say, the cognitive and perceptive capabilities of the human brain were shaped bio-organically over millions of years by selection and adaptation to social existence—and vice versa. Evolutionary reasoning is thus basic to an understanding of *epistemology*." Very explicitly, Ziman (p. 3) writes that "*Selectionist reasoning* applies to the changing membership of a

population, rather than to changes that might be occurring in any particular member of that population." In his book *Sociobiology*, biologist E. O. Wilson (1975) made what were at the time radical assertions, according to social historian Robert J. Richards (1987, p. 542): "Our various cultural institutions—marriage, trade, religion, esthetics, habits of labor, and ethics—he argued, all carried an evolutionary legacy. He proclaimed, with undoubted intention to unplug the emotional reservoirs, that our religious aspirations were an artifact of 'conformer genes', of the same variety that also prompted obedience to Hitler. He cited IQ theorists to suggest that individuals were pushed by an 'upward-mobile gene' into higher socioeconomic classes. . . . From that vantage he fought the Darwinian fight. That is, he attempted to explain the very defining traits of human nature in evolutionary terms." Wilson (1978), in his sustained and convincing effort to make the clear analogy between biology and sociology, examines (p. x) "the reciprocal impact that a truly evolutionary explanation of human behavior must have on the social sciences and humanities." Cell geneticist François Jacob (1982, p. 59) reasons that "The old epistemological tradition . . . was based mainly on introspection. It considered mental events to be of a different nature than physical events. Yet it seems very hard to imagine how an immaterial mind could have arisen from a process of evolution by natural selection. Endowing the elementary particles that constitute matter with some kind of a psyche does not help much, and the conclusion is inescapable that mind is a product of brain organization in the same way that life is a product of molecular organization." Selection clearly is the triggering event in evolution, both biological and cultural. We have come to think of selection as essentially the only source of order in the biological world, writes theoretical biologist Stuart A. Kauffman (1993, p. 26). "If 'only' is an overstatement, then surely it is accurate to state that selection is viewed as the overwhelming source of order in the biological world. It follows that, in our current view, organisms are largely ad hoc solutions to design problems cobbled together by selection. It follows that most properties which are widespread in organisms are widespread by virtue of common descent from a tinkered-together ancestor, with selective maintenance of the useful tinkerings." The phenomenon of tinkering in biological evolution to which he refers is analogous to the phenomenon of bricolage in cultural evolution described by anthropologist Claude Lévy-Strauss, who is quoted below in Chapter 7. Of course, the whole notion of order in evolutionary science, whether biological or cultural, can be refuted on the basis of not knowing what will happen next, as anthropologist Jacob Bronowski (1961, p. 88) suggests: "The order which science finds in nature is *derived* from our experience; it makes our experience comprehensible, but it cannot itself be directly experienced. Therefore we can have no assurance that the order we find at any one time is final."

11. From another perspective, Kaplan (1970, pp. 75–76) says that "the law states that a cultural system will tend to be found precisely in those environments in which it yields a higher energy return per unit of human labor than any alternative system available." More specifically in science, developmental psychologists Jaan Valsiner and RenéVan der Veer (2000, p. 423) observe that "Development of any science on a worldwide basis is a heterogeneous affair. Some sciences move ahead in some countries very vigorously, only to become relatively stagnant in a subsequent period. The same ideas may be taken up by scientists in another country during a different decade, and developed in new directions. The latter may still be intellectually interdependent

with the former, even if our tendencies to view progress in science as monotonically progressing would hide the actual ups and downs of the progress of basic ideas."

12. Anthropologist Marshall D. Sahlins (1970, p. 35) concludes "It seems to us that progress is the total transformation of energy involved in the creation and perpetuation of a cultural organization. A culture harnesses and delivers energy; it extracts energy from nature and transforms it into people, material goods, and work into political systems and the generation of ideas, into social customs and into adherence to them. The total energy so transformed from the free to the cultural state, in combination perhaps with the degree to which it is raised in the transformation . . . , may represent a culture's general standing, a measure of its achievement." However, a caveat on the matter of purpose is offered from the perspective of an historian of ideas, as Arthur O. Lovejoy (1936, p. 329) posits that "A world of time and change—this, at least, our history has shown—is a world which can neither be deduced from nor reconciled with the postulate that existence is the expression and consequence of a system of 'eternal' and 'necessary' truths inherent in the very logic of being." Sociologist Morris Ginsberg (1972, p. 45) summarizes caveats about the notion of progress in evolution: "It is clear that progress in the sense defined is not a universal law of evolution and, if it were, it is difficult to see how ethical problems could arise at all. As biologists tell us again and again, the history of life provides examples not only of 'progress' but of retrogression, degeneration and decay. Clearly this is equally true of human history. In social change as in biological change many trends, often of long range, can be traced." Literary theorist Reinhart Koselleck (2002, p. 235) throws at least the matter of progress during the past century and a half up to question, writing "Hence, the following conclusion is unavoidable. The progress of modernity, despite its universal claim, reflects only a partial, self-consistent experience and, instead, masks or obscures other modes of experience for understandable reasons. Obviously, there are long-term structures that persist across human history without being affected by technologically and industrially determined progress at all." In his review of the literature on human progress, intellectual historian Charles Van Doren (1967, p. 56) finds that "All of the authors discussed in this section conclude in accepting the Pascalian analogy between the race as a whole and an individual man, with its attendant notion that progress occurs through the transmission of knowledge and other intellectual assets from one generation to the next." Biologist Sir Julian S. Huxley (1958, p. 444) adds, "From a slightly different angle, we may say that cultural evolution, i.e. evolution in the psychosocial phase, can now be seen as an extension of biological evolution, but with its own peculiarities of method and results, and 'progress' and 'advance' can be profitably redefined as processes leading to greater realization of desirable possibilities."

13. Because Henderson's fundamental theories (1917) on the subject of evolutionary purpose continue to be influential, it may be useful to look more closely into some of his findings, particularly in his chapter 10 on "The Teleological Order" (pp. 180–211), where he states "Thus we reach the conclusion that the properties of hydrogen, carbon, and oxygen make up a unique ensemble of properties each one of which is itself unique . . . We may therefore conclude that there is here revealed an order or pattern in the properties of the elements. This new order is, so to speak, hidden, when one considers the properties of matter abstractly and statically, for it is recognizable

and intelligible *only* through its effects. It becomes evident only when time is taken into consideration" (p. 184). And further (p. 192), that "This complex connection is almost infinitely improbable as a chance occurrence." It cannot be contingent. "And yet this original peculiarity of things is the chief cause of diversity in the stage of the evolutionary process which is fully within the grasp of natural science" (p. 198). "Thus we say that adaptation is teleological, but do not say that it is the result of design or purpose. I shall therefore... assert that the connection between the properties of the three elements and the evolutionary process is teleological and non-mechanical" (p. 204). In the final paragraph of the chapter, Henderson (p. 211) concludes that "According to the theory of probabilities this connection between the properties of matter and the process of evolution cannot be due to mere contingency. Therefore, since the physico-chemical functional relationship is not in question, there must be admitted a functional relationship of another kind, somewhat like that known to physiology. This functional relationship can only be described as teleological." Based on more recent research and theory, neurophilosopher Evan Thompson (2007, pp. 148–149) places his conclusion about purpose in life in the context of biological adaptation and cognition, concluding that "living beings embody an immanent purposiveness and this purposiveness manifests itself in the two complementary modes of autopoiesis (the intrinsic teleology of self-production) and sense-making (the projective teleology of adaptivity and cognition). Minimal autopoiesis is necessary but not sufficient for sense-making (or cognition), but an enlarged conception of autopoiesis that includes adaptivity is necessary and sufficient."

14. In the total context of life and the influence of human decisions, it sometimes is difficult to understand purpose that is directional. Discussing change in other species, specifically in pest and disease organisms, biologist Stephen R. Palumbi (2004, p. 422) contends that "Human impact on the global biosphere now controls many major facets of ecosystem function... Accelerated evolutionary changes are easy to understand—they derive from strong natural selection exerted by human technology. However, technological impact has increased so markedly over the past few decades that humans may be the world's dominant evolutionary force."

15. Anthropologist Adam Kuper (2002, p. 94) refers to Claude Lévi-Strauss's contention that all cultures are the result of a mishmash, borrowings, mixtures that have occurred, though at different rates, ever since the beginning of time. Kuper says that we all depend on difference, for "new ideas will usually come from outside. Advances, better adaptations, come about normally through the collaboration of cultures. However, Lévi-Strauss's conclusion was somber. Since the sixteenth century a Western, industrial, scientific civilization has spread through the world, imposing, or buying, uniformity. The consequence has been the progressive elimination of variety, and the end result will be stagnation or entropy."

16. Popper (1994, p. 203) comments further in connecting dialectic and the search for truth and noting that Plato, Bacon, and Descartes believed "that error is to be explained by our personal shortcomings. We err because we stubbornly cling to our prejudices instead of opening our physical or mental eyes to the manifest truth.... Bacon's method, therefore, consists in cleansing our minds of prejudices. It is the unbiased mind, the pure mind, the mind cleansed of prejudice, that cannot fail to recognize the truth. With this theory I have reached a final formulation of radical epistemological

optimism. The theory is of great importance. It became the cornerstone of modern science. It made the scientist a priest of truth, and the worship of truth a sort of divine service." Psychobiologist Henry Plotkin (2004, p. 7) connects method to truth: "Now, claims upon truth are always precarious if not plain foolhardy. But the prevailing view amongst most scientists is that science does gradually move towards some kind of truth about the world. The astonishing success of science and its application, which ranges from placing humans on the moon and soon enough on Mars too, to linking human nervous systems to computers, and on to cloning, is some sort of measure of truth. Thus most scientists writing history would incline to an intellectual perspective, believing that insofar as science is truth-seeking, it does so under the harsh disciplines of accuracy of observations, the adequacy of theory to explain them, and the ingenuity of their application. Yet no scientist is immune to the effects of their lives outside of science on their thinking within their science. And when their science sails close to the ideological winds of what it means to be human, which is what both human evolution and psychology do, then some degree of awareness of a social perspective must be allowed to enter the picture." Cultural anthropologist Wilson D. Wallis (1930, p. 432) was perhaps a bit more candid in his assessment of the value of science in noting that "more precisely it is science which enables man to attain a finer paradise or to create a fiercer hell than was possible in a prescientific age." A matter of human choice.

17. In a subsequent work, Polanyi (1966, pp. 3–25) explains more fully the concept of tacit knowing (not to be equated with, although loosely related to, the management strategy of drawing upon tacit knowledge).

18. Philosopher Andrew Edgar (2006, p. 10) summarizes the thought of Jürgen Habermas about the relation of thinking and survival. Cognitive interests, he writes, "are the preconditions that make knowledge possible. Cognitive (or knowledge-constitutive) interests are the conditions for survival of the human species that stimulate human beings to generate knowledge about the physical world, about the social world and about the exercise of political power. In order to flourish, it is in the interest of human beings to be able to control and reshape their physical environment, to communicate with each other and thereby to maintain society, and to live free of political oppression. In the pursuit of each of these interests, humans will inquire into, and thus generate knowledge about, the natural world, society and politics. This knowledge will in turn be linked to certain forms of action."

19. Archeologist Steven J. Mithen (1996, p. 209) asserts that "As soon as language acted as a vehicle for delivering information into the mind (whether one's own or that of another person), carrying with it snippets of non-social information, a transformation in the nature of the mind began . . . language switched from a social to a general-purpose function, consciousness from a means to predict other individuals' behaviour to managing a mental database of information relating to all domains of behaviour. A cognitive fluidity arose within the mind, reflecting new connections rather than new processing power. And consequently this mental transformation occurred with no increase in brain size. It was, in essence, the origins of the symbolic capacity that is unique to the human mind with the manifold consequences for hunter-gatherer behaviour." Recounting research in the connection between brain size and intellect, to which they refer as a nineteenth-century idea, paleontologist Juan Luis Arsuaga and paleoanthropologist Ignacio Martinez (2006, p. 128) state that "it is not overall brain

size which determines the size of the intellect, but the proportion of brain size to body size, or the degree of encephalization." The major areas of research on intelligence are surveyed by systems scientist Anna T. Cianciolo and psychologist Robert J. Sternberg (2004, especially in chapter one, "The Nature of Intelligence," pp. 1–29). Closely related is the work of social anthropologist Nicholas Humphrey (1992).

Chapter 4

1. Physical chemist and social philosopher Michael Polanyi (1959, pp. 13–14) offers an interesting analogy of humans and other animals related to language: "Animals have no speech, and all the towering superiority of man over the animals is due almost entirely to man's gift of speech. Babies and infants up to the age of eighteen months or so are mentally not much superior to chimpanzees of the same age; only when they start learning to speak do they rapidly out-distance and leave far behind their simian contemporaries. Even adults show no distinctly greater intelligence than animals so long as their minds work unaided by language. In the absence of linguistic clues man sees things, hears things, feels things, moves about, explores his surroundings and gets to know his way about, very much as animals do."

2. Two differing perspectives summarize the place of language in cultural evolution: Psychologist Paul Bloom (1998, p. 215) writes "Without language, most of human culture—everything from scientific inquiry to professional football—would not exist," while literary critic George Steiner (1971, p. 66) says about language that "Man becomes man as he enters on a linguistic stage... when we ask when or how language began, we are in fact asking 'What are the origins of man's humanity'?"

3. White (1949, p. 33) elaborates further on the significance of language: "All culture (civilization) depends upon the symbol. It was the exercise of the symbolic faculty that brought culture into existence and it is the use of symbols that makes the perpetuation of culture possible. Without the symbol there would be no culture, and man would be merely an animal, not a human being. Articulate speech is the most important form of symbolic expression. Remove speech from culture and what would remain?" Pierce Butler (1942, P. 3) surely was wrong in declaring that "There can be no language unless its speakers have a common intellectual background to which their words refer."

4. In that connection, sociologist Bartholomeus Landheer (1957, pp. 6–7) assesses the significance of language from the opposite perspective, noting that "Although cultures have varied in their appreciation of the written word, there has been none which has claimed to be able to exist without it."

5. All human beings, however, are not created with equal brain power, whether that means cranial capacity or cognitive fluidity or what we summarily call intelligence. And given the disparity some individuals no doubt fare better in this than others, contributing more or less to society in the long term. We know this simply from daily experience. We also are provided some degree of insight into this mysterious area through the testing of the putative intelligence quotient. But neurologist Liam Hudson (2004, p. 225) observes about such tests that "above a surprisingly low level, there is little or no relationship between IQ and achievement in any sphere of adult endeavour yet studied," and he provides an example: "In the American context the

budding scientist of high renown seems typically to be a 'B+' student: one who works hard when a topic captures his or her imagination, but otherwise does the bare minimum. Science springs to life for such individuals when they discover that instead of assimilating knowledge created by others, they can create knowledge for themselves—and are hooked from that moment onwards." Average human intelligence, and perhaps considerably less than that, is quite adequate to evolve the culture, even if not at the same rate of speed.

6. A collection of essays by Popper (1963) is based on the thesis that we can learn from our mistakes. He revised the preface to its second edition (1965, p. ix) to emphasize that "It is part of my thesis that all our knowledge grows only through the correcting of our mistakes." More recently, economic theorist Brian J. Loasby (2002, p. 157) observes that "Knowledge itself is organization, produced by trial and error, and always subject to challenge including changes in its form and relationships to other bodies of knowledge." Loasby (p. 152) also offers a more sophisticated interpretation of trial and error, writing that "invented principles, however widely accepted, are not proven truth, they are liable eventually to be confronted with unexpected phenomena which they cannot be adapted to explain. This disjunction between evidence and established means of explanation defines a pressing problem; when satisfactory adaptation is despaired of, a new search for connecting principles begins." This constitutes a resurgence of the evolutionary process. A slightly different perspective is provided by evolutionary psychologist David J. Buller (2006, p. 201), in his conclusion "Consequently, the specialized structures in an adult human's brain are not the product of hundreds of thousands of years of cumulative selection for incremental, genetically-induced modifications to the human brain; they are, instead, the product of that individual's history of interaction with the local environment."

7. For example, historian Elizabeth L. Eisenstein (1979) presents a comprehensive view of the dramatic influence of the printing press on cultural change.

8. Library philosopher H. Curtis Wright (1977, p. 34) describes the period in Greek history when a written tradition was beginning to replace the oral tradition. He points out that the social need of information was the same then as now, only the means of recording and passing it on have changed. Thirty years later, his assessment remains valid.

9. Pierce Butler (1953, p. 159) extols the power of the book as follows: "In the book man does not merely improve upon nature; he transcends it . . . Indeed, it is probably the most remarkable achievement of culture. In general terms it may be described as a graphic reduction of a mental reduction, of a linguistic reduction, of a specific stream of human consciousness. All these reductions are man-wrought miracles and as such deserve more notice than we ordinarily give them." Anthropologist Tim Ingold (1993b, 458) offers a somewhat different twist to Butler's idea: "For writing is not simply the equivalent of speech in an alternative medium. It is rather a kind of reconstructed, *as if* speech: as if the verbal utterance were fully amenable to systematic analysis in terms of syntactical rules; as if the tone of voice and pronunciation were entirely dispensable to meaning; as if the utterance had an existence in its own right, independently of the context of its production." Archeologist V. Gordon Childe (1948, p. 186) observes about the pragmatic power of writing that "By its means a man can immortalize his experience and transmit it directly to contemporaries living far off and to generations

yet unborn. It is the first step to raising science above the limits of space and time." And economic philosopher Kenneth Boulding (1983, p. 10) describes how knowledge expands more readily and can be shared more expansively with the written word: "The noosphere, however, is continually able to expand because the knowledge structure that exists in one brain can be transmitted into another and also can be put into records, which can be transmitted to another brain even after a considerable interval of time. The invention of writing meant that knowledge could be transferred from the dead to the living."

10. According to social anthropologist Jack Goody and literary critic and historian Ian Watt (1988, p. 16), "not long after the widespread diffusion of writing throughout the Greek world, and the recording of the previously oral cultural tradition, there arose an attitude to the past very different from that common in non-literate societies. Instead of the unobtrusive adaptation of past tradition to present needs, a great many individuals found in the written records, where much of their traditional cultural repertoire had been given permanent form, so many inconsistencies in the beliefs and categories of understanding handed down to them that they were impelled to a much more conscious, comparative and critical attitude to the accepted world picture, and notably to the notions of God, the universe, and the past. Many individual solutions to these problems were themselves written down, and these versions formed the basis for further investigations."

11. "Inevitably, too," writes archeologist V. Gordon Childe (1948, p. 189) "words written with such difficulty and deciphered so laboriously must seem to possess an authority of their own. The immortalization of a word in writing must have seemed a supernatural process; it was surely magical that a man long vanished from the land of the living could still speak from a clay tablet or a papyrus roll." Cultural historian Roger Chartier (1989, p. 6) describes the powers or supposed powers of the drawn image, which preceded printing and thus set the stage for the reception of the printed text: "The printed image, like other images, was thought of and used as an important aid to knowledge and as if it were capable of adequate representation of reality. It was considered to engage the unfailing adherence of the beholder and, even more than or better than the text that it accompanied, to induce persuasion or belief."

12. Literacy, write literacy researchers Victoria Purcell-Gates, Erik Jacobson, and Sophie Degener is "ideological in that it recognizes, given the multiplicity of literacies, that literacy practices are always associated with issues of power; they are never neutral technologies." According to social anthropologist Jack Goody and literary critic and historian Ian Watt (1988, p. 24), the greater individualization of personal experience in literate societies is explained in large part by the adoption of techniques of reading and writing. They conclude that "There is, first of all the formal distinction which alphabetic culture has emphasized between the divine, the natural, and the human orders; secondly, there is the social differentiation to which the institutions of literate culture give rise; third, there is the effect of professional intellectual specialization on an unprecedented scale; lastly, there is the immense variety of choice offered by the whole corpus of recorded literature; and from these four factors there ensues, in any individual case, the highly complex totality deriving from the selection of these literate orientations and from the series of primary groups in which the individual has also been involved."

13. Science historian George Basalla (1988, p. 77) finds that "the technological imagination is very rich. Hardly constrained by biological or economic necessity it often exceeds the boundaries of rationality as it contemplates the improbable and the impossible. The fertile technological imaginations create a superfluity of novel artifacts from which society makes selections," and that "the technological imagination is very rich. Hardly constrained by biological or economic necessity it often exceeds the boundaries of rationality as it contemplates the improbable and the impossible. The fertile technological imaginations create a superfluity of novel artifacts from which society makes selections."

14. Long-time nineteenth-century Librarian of Congress Ainsworth Rand Spofford (1900, pp. 183–184) elaborates on this idea: "But the formative power of books can never be overrated: their subtle mastery to stimulate all the germs of intellectual and moral life that lie enfolded in the mind... They furnish us the means, and the only means, whereby we may hold communion with the master-spirits of all ages. They bring us acquainted with the best thoughts which the human mind has produced, expressed in the noblest language. Books create for us the many-sided world, carry us abroad, out of our narrow provincial horizons, and reveal to us new scenery, new men, new languages, and new modes of life. As we read, the mind expands with the horizon, and becomes broad as the blue heaven above us."

Chapter 5

1. As far as I can tell, Jesse Shera (1975) was the first to refer in this exact expression to this function in the library literature, describing it in an article in the *Louisiana Library Association Bulletin* 24, Fall 1961, pp. 117–118, and subsequently reprinted (Shera, 1975). His description amounts to a verbatim restatement of that by Boulding (1956, pp. 64–65), to which this note refers, even though Boulding is not mentioned. For comparison to the block quotation that accompanies this note, here follows Shera's statement: "A culture, almost by definition, produces a 'transcript', a record in more or less permanent form that can be transmitted from generation to generation. In primitive non-literate societies this record takes the form of verbal ritual, legends, poems and ceremonials. The communication of this transcript is one of the most important activities of primitive groups. The invention of writing marked the beginning of the dissociated transcript, a form of communication independent of the communicator. The growth of this social transcript, in recent years, has proceeded at an increasingly accelerated rate, and the problem of the efficient social utilization of this transcript has become correspondingly more difficult." In this article, Shera uses the term social transcript only once and the term 'cultural transcript' also just once and synonymously. Many others have referred to this phenomenon, and following are just a few statements about the function under discussion, but which label it differently or do not label it at all: Sociologist F. Stuart Chapin (1928, p. 52) calls it 'the sinuous thread of written language' in his summary of the accumulation of culture. "And always, woven in and out, back and forth, throughout the whole growing fabric of culture traits, there is the sinuous thread of written language, externally stored mental patterns and ideas, reinforcing, strengthening, stiffening, and yet flexing the stream of culture."

Cultural anthropologists Clyde Kluckhohn and ethnographer William H. Kelly (1945, p. 105) say that "Every human being is born into a world defined by already existing cultural patterns. Just as an individual who has lost his memory is no longer 'normal', so the idea that at any point in its history a society can become completely emancipated from its past culture is inconceivable." Popper (1972) refers to the kind of knowledge maintained by libraries and universities as objective knowledge. Cultural historian Raymond Irwin (1964, p. 26) refers to the written dimension of this function as the golden chain. "This golden chain of written record is indeed the conquest of time and space of which we have spoken. By its magic (and it is not extravagant to use the word 'magic') its links have been forged." Library theorist Ronald C. Benge (1970, p. 223) concludes that "The history of libraries indicates how each culture maintained itself by the preservation of records, and how libraries were an indispensable agency in bridging the gaps in time between different civilizations. The library is thus an active medium of communication, because without the libraries the books would not have survived. This is what Professor [Raymond] Irwin called 'the golden chain', and this is how the intellectual content of the cultures of ancient Greece and Rome was preserved." An analogy between the effect of the social transcript and the effect of the mass media as imagined by communication scientist Wilbur Schramm (1971, pp. 52–53) can be drawn, but in compressed time and space: "Among the long-term effects, [of the mass media] the most potent may well turn out to be the less dramatic ones—not the gross anti-social effects, but the gradual building up of pictures of the world from what the mass media choose to report of it; the gradual homogenization of images and behaviors over large populations, as a result of the universality of the mass media; the granting of status to persons who have access to the media. I once described this effect as resembling the gradual building up of a stalagmite in a cave, from the constant drip-drip of calcareous water upon it, each drop leaving a residue so small as to be invisible until the dripping had continued for years. And not until hundreds of years later could visitors see that the stalagmite had grown and altered its shape. This kind of effect, rather than quick and dramatic change, may be the chief impact of the mass media on human society." Information scientist Kevin McGarry (1993, pp. 60–61) emphasizes that "Permanence and conservation are essential for the continuity of a culture. To enable human beings to benefit from the knowledge and skills of others we must have some kind of storage system to transmit these benefits over time. We need the societal equivalent of our own memories, in fact a social memory or cultural memory... This storage system appears under many names. Some scholars call it the 'cultural memory', others the 'social transcript', some even use the term 'cultural book', which suggests comparison with the storage function of the library." This is in part why psychologist Leda Cosmides and anthropologist John H. Tooby (2002, pp. 165–166) conclude that many dedicated intelligences "are equipped with design features that function as crib sheets. They come to a problem already 'knowing' a great deal about it. This allows them to be far more intelligent than they otherwise would be if they embodied no equivalent to innate knowledge." In a sense, the library exists to give current and future humanity a head start. With reference specifically to science, scholar of scientific rhetoric Charles Bazerman (1988, p. 128), describes what he calls the linguistic technology, saying that "the technology and the genre are no simple, rule-determined set of inflexible procedures and forms. They rather represent continuing realizations of social activity within socially structured situations. Industrial, social, and linguistic inventions, such as the inventions of the printing press, the scientific society, and the scientific journal, helped shape the situations out of which the technology emerged and in which the new technology provided the means of social action. The linguistic inventions of this new communication technology, because they themselves embodied social actions, in turn set in motion changes within the structured social situation. Humanly made solutions addressed the immediately perceived problems and provided an environment influencing the perceived structure of future problems." This scenario seems to be quite applicable to culture in general.

2. Printer John Lewis von Hoelle (2001, p. ix) offers his perspective on the library function in culture: "The basic function of the library has changed little in the past five millennia. They still serve to collect and preserve the memories of man's endeavor. The history of the library is also the celebration of the immortality of the written word. Libraries make available to all, the thoughts of famous philosophers, pharaohs and prophets. They also preserve the precious wisdom of countless scholars, poets and teachers. They serve us by sharing the experiences of remarkable people who have made us proud to be human; and made us wiser by recording the dark deeds of madmen—lest we forget."

3. Kenneth Boulding (1978, p. 136) relates the value of this kind of restatement more specifically to science: "Observational science is concerned with the records of the past and with improving the records in the present so that, when they become records of the past, they will be better and we will then have a better chance of perceiving the patterns and regularities in them. The improvement of the record of the past . . . is one of the major and most important activities of the scientific community and it has a cumulative effect, because the better our records of the past are, the more accurate our images of it will be, and the better our chance will be of perceiving regularities and projecting them into the future." Elsewhere, Boulding (1964, p. 39) emphasizes the accelerating and sustaining powers of record in the formal establishment of knowledge, "With the development of writing we get the subculture of scholarship in which books created by minds long dead can have as powerful an influence as the words of the living. The scholar lives and moves within a network of communication that extends many centuries into the past." Anthropologist Mary Douglas (1986, p. 70) has the last word on this. Referring to sociologist Robert Merton's 1965 book *On the Shoulders of Giants,* in which, she says, "he elaborates on the pointlessness of asking who said a thing first," Douglas concludes that "The best ideas and most famous quotations seem to have been around forever."

4. Valsiner and Van der Veer (2000, pp. 382–383) elaborate on their conclusion about Vigotsky's work: "He wished to show that humans share emotions with animals but that they, in addition, have higher emotions. He acknowledged that animals have a memory but added that humans can master their memory by making use of instruments. He accepted that animals make use of tools but argued that humans dispose of the very special tool of speech which fundamentally alters their mind. He wished to show that humans have consciousness but emphasized its biological function and wanted this phenomenon to be causally explicable." Science historian George Basalla (1988, p. 14) analyzes the cultural concept of need in a similar way, but related specifically to technology: "We cultivate technology to meet our perceived needs not

a set of universal ones legislated by nature. According to French philosopher Gaston Bachelard the conquest of the superfluous gives us a greater spiritual stimulus than the conquest of the necessary because humans are creations of desire, not need . . . The artifacts that constitute the made world are not a series of narrow solutions to problems generated in satisfying basic needs but are material manifestations of the various ways men and women throughout time have chosen to define and pursue existence. Seen in this light, the history of technology is a part of the much broader history of human aspirations, and the plethora of made things are a product of human aspirations, and the plethora of made things are a product of human minds replete with fantasies, longings, wants, and desires. The artifactual world would exhibit far less diversity if it operated primarily under the constraints imposed by fundamental needs."

5. Anthropologists Sherwood L. Washburn and Virginia Avis (1958, 434–435) trace an evolutionary scenario of the relation of mind and body against the background of evolving technology: "If one views the first stage in human evolution . . . all subsequent human change is increasingly dominated by the use of tools. Increase in brain size resulted from the new selection pressures stemming from tool use. Speech, made possible by the larger brain, was correlated with a complicated technological tradition; and the larger and more complicated society was made possible by the larger food supply . . . Increase in brain size was associated with a slowing of the growth rate and a much greater period of dependency. This changed the social life, establishing long-term social relations. Thus the hunting life changed man's psychology and the way of life of the human group . . . As one looks back over the complex and multiple adaptive radiations of the primates, one can see the succession of ways of life which made possible lemurs, monkeys, apes and, finally, a biped. After this adaptation came the use of tools, the hunting habit, increase in intelligence and, finally, the animal we know as man." Anthropologist Leslie A White (1959, p. 12) advances the idea that the somatic needs of a human exert a force of similar strength as those of the exosomatic needs. "We mean that although culture is produced and perpetuated only by the human species and therefore has its origin and basis in the biological make-up of man, in its relation to human beings after it has come into existence and become established as a tradition, culture exists and behaves and is related to man as if it were *nonbiological in character.*" White (p. 15) finds support in the words of Emile Durkheim, who contended that "'the first and most fundamental rule [for the observation of social facts] is: *Consider social facts as things*'." Biologist Larry Arnhart (1998, pp. 29–36) provides a list of twenty 'natural and universal desires', which is summarized by sociologist Stephen K. Sanderson (2001, pp. 130–132), and to which he contributes two additions.

6. Library theorist Bryan Luckham (1971, p. 3) begins his study of the library's complex role in society with the idea that the library is "a social institution operating in a dynamic environment of aspirations, expectations and ideologies, manned and controlled by personnel who can modify the character of the service offered in significant, even subtle ways. Furthermore, it is an environment which can change considerably in relatively short periods of time."

7. Sociologist John T. Graham (2001, pp. 24–25) interprets Ortega's understanding of the social dimension of the historical milieu of the library. "Discounting ancient types and medieval monasteries, Ortega attributed the historical beginning of this

social process to the fifteenth century, to the Renaissance, when the collection and printing of books allowed sufficient princely and secular libraries to be founded. Then the social 'need' was perceived by 'others' [outside librarianship] for the regular, permanent services of librarians as a profession of keeper, or guardians, and catalogers of books. Then also arose the 'faith in books', secularized and transferred from biblical revelation to 'reason alone'. After three centuries of development, after 1800 and in consequence of 'faith in books' shifting to the new democracy rising out of the French Revolution, the profession had reached maturity with the great multiplication of books, new disciplines and sciences, libraries, and librarians. By 1850 quantitative aspects had so increased that librarianship ceased to be 'a spontaneous social profession' of diffuse 'uses customs, public opinion, language, free market, etc.', and was made a state function and 'office'—turned into part of the 'State bureaucracy'."

8. Black (1996, p. 143) writes that "It is paradoxical that utilitarianism and idealism stood shoulder to shoulder in the fight for books on the rates, in that the two philosophies were, at a fundamental level, divergent. Utilitarians argued that reality and sense-experience determined ideas and character: knowledge developed *a posteriori*. They believed that individuals were like the atoms of Newtonian theory, each atom being exposed to exterior forces, thereby moulding humans into essentially asocial, isolated and mechanistic beings. Whereas utilitarians attempted to subordinate the mental to the physical, idealists taught the reverse of this relationship; prominence was given to ideas, to the ideal and to the inwardly creative human spirit." And he concludes (pp. 265–266) that "The utilitarian and idealist philosophies which underpinned the early public library movement were not exclusive monoliths . . . The public library, to be sure, incorporated, and still does, the deontological language of natural rights—witness its debt to romanticism, social criticism and aesthetic learning. But the institution's worth was conceived, for the most part, in a teleological fashion. Its greatest worth was seen to be the positive social utility it could generate, and the contribution it could make to social stability. While public library promoters might have viewed the right of the individual to self-fulfillment as 'natural', their overwhelming motivation was the belief that individualism in this regard was directed towards collective prosperity, and was recognized as such by individuals knowingly engaging in the civilizing process. The triumph of teleology was also manifest in the unquestioning acceptance of the public library as a 'public good'. Utilitarians and idealists had a broad understanding of what constituted a public good."

9. This is the library faith discussed in Chapter 2. Cultural historian Raymond Irwin (1964, p. 41) describes one of the ramifications of this faith, which in its extreme form can become a compulsion: "The over-riding belief that we must at all costs preserve our heritage for posterity has arisen with the establishment of national libraries to house the national and international collections of the world, and strangely enough it is grounded not on any scarcity of books or their threatened destruction, but rather on their abundance; the mass-production of printed material is piling up the volumes almost beyond counting. The belief has however resulted in the concept of the sanctity of literary and archival records, comparable almost to the sanctity of human life: nothing must be destroyed. This concept is not supported by any sanction except that of expediency."

10. According to library historian Alistair Black (1996, p. 94), Edwards was a leader among those who believed that education had a key role to play in the preservation of social order. "Education as means of control was preferable, in his opinion, to the alternative of coercion: 'Truly the masses need guidance... more than they need repression'." And according to Victorian scholar Richard Altick (1998, p. 224), Edwards also stooped to the lower, politically more powerful, level of persuasion in an 1848 address he gave, subsequently published as *Remarks on the Paucity of Libraries Freely Open to the Public,* wherein Edwards "revealed the appalling lack of public library facilities in Great Britain as contrasted with those in western Europe and the United States."

11. Anthropologist André Leroi-Gourhan (1993, p. 147) writes that "The close interdependence between social institutions and the technical and economic apparatus is borne out by countless facts. Although the nature of moral problems remains essentially unchanged, each society molds its behavior using such implements as the material world will offer."

Chapter 6

1. Ben-David (1973, p. 48) summarizes his understanding of this situation, stating that "The argument of this paper is that social scientists have done a disservice to their own work by trying to mold it according to the model of basic natural science. This should not be interpreted as agreement with certain current trends which deny the relevance of scientific logic to the social sciences, or which cast doubt on the validity of scientific logic altogether. However, although the logic of science is generally valid, its proper application differs according to the nature of the problem under investigation." And science historian George Basalla (1988, p. 25) explains his relevant theory of technological evolution: "As I have already shown, the made world contains a far greater variety of things than are required to meet fundamental human needs. This *diversity* can be explained as the result of technological evolution because artifactual *continuity* exists; *novelty* is an integral part of the made world; and a *selection* process operates to choose novel artifacts for replication and addition to the stock of made things."

2. I owe this allusion to physicists Ilya Prigione and Isabelle Stengers (1984, p. 300), who observe that "Today we believe that the epoch of certainties and absolute oppositions is over. Physicists have no privilege whatsoever to any kind of extraterritoriality. As scientists they belong to their culture, to which, in their turn, they make an essential contribution. We have reached a situation close to the one recognized long ago in sociology: Merleau-Ponty had already stressed the need to keep in mind what he termed a 'truth within situations.' Introducing his paper on social science research, sociologist of science Joseph Ben-David (1973, p. 39) cautions that "Writing about the organization of research assumes, as a rule, the knowledge of what research is, and what research is about. Such knowledge cannot be taken for granted in the social sciences. In this field there is usually a gap, and often a very considerable gap between the theoretical description of what is being done and what is actually being done, and there is widespread feeling that neither is very satisfactory."

3. This introduces a new way of perceiving both social and natural sciences from a more holistic vantage point. In his Foreword to the work of Prigogine and Stengers (1984), science fiction writer Alvin Toffler summarizes their chaos theory, saying (p. xxiii) that "they hold that while some parts of the universe may operate like machines, these are closed systems, and closed systems, at best, form only a small part of the physical universe. Most phenomena of interest to us are, in fact, open systems, exchanging energy or matter (and, one might add, information) with their environment. Surely biological and social systems are open, which means that the attempt to understand them in mechanistic terms is doomed to failure" (p. xv). And further (p. xxiii) that "They not only demonstrate that both determinism and chance operate . . . , they also attempt to show how the two fit together." Literary critic and novelist N. Katherine Hayles (1991, p. 1) observes that "In both contemporary literature and science, chaos has been conceptualized as extremely complex information rather than an absence of order," and further (p. 7) that both the "literary and scientific manifestations of chaotics are involved in feedback loops with the culture. They help to create the context that energizes the questions they ask; at the same time, they also ask questions energized by the context . . . The impact of chaotics derives less from specific theories than from the general awareness it fosters of nonlinear processes and forms. To some extent, we see what we are taught to see." Hayles sees in chaos theory (pp. 10–11) "a new way to think about order, conceptualizing it not as a totalized condition but as the replication of symmetries that also allows for asymmetries and unpredictabilities. In her new conceptualization, (p. 3) "chaos may either lead to order, as it does with self-organizing systems, or in yin/yang fashion it may have deep structures of order encoded within it. In either case, its relation to order is more complex than traditional Western oppositions have allowed." Contrary to popular assumption about science, chemist and science philosopher Michael Polanyi (1951, p. 31) suggests rather subjective limits to theory, saying that "Science or scholarship can never be more than an affirmation of the things we believe in . . . To all further critical scruples we must at some point finally reply: 'For I believe so'."

4. Anyone writing about science refers to communication as an essential aspect of the phenomenon; and it is certainly the most social aspect. The classic example of the explanation of the role of communication in science is elaborated in a book-length study by science sociologist William D. Garvey (1979). It is largely the communication aspect of science that accounts for its social dimension.

5. Lionel R. McColvin was the leading public librarian during the mid twentieth century in England and internationally. His public library philosophy, summarized here by Philip Whiteman (1986, p. 7), succinctly captures much of what is written about the place of the library in ensuring successful democracy: "Because of the power of enlightenment enshrined in books, their contribution to effective participation in a democratic society was vital, for 'no other equalities can avail if access to so important a means of individual development is not full and universal'." And it may be useful to note that Whiteman (p. 4) adds that "By books, he meant 'all printed, manuscript, graphic and related records by which knowledge, ideas and imagination can be conserved and disseminated'." Democratic principles may be so fundamental or essential in the thinking of librarians in some societies, however, that they tend to be taken for granted. The conclusion reached following a review of the LIS literature,

analyzed by library theorist John E. Buschman (2007, p. 1492), is that the place of democracy is not given the attention that it warrants. "If LIS makes any claim in terms of social and normative values or if LIS stakes any normative claim to the substantial public investments in libraries and information systems, then a democratic theory of LIS linked to the principles of the regime would go some ways to ground the field beyond an instrumental or relativistic basis."

6. In the course of his work on defining information science, Norman Roberts (1976, p. 255) reasons that "A major defect of the regularity interpretation of action-explanations is its failure to do justice to the individuality of agents' responses to their situations, a criticism which has special relevance for information work because the ultimate explanation of information actions resides in the motives and attitudes of individuals. [Bertram C.] Brookes advocates the concentration upon objective knowledge, and its interaction with society; an interesting and significant form of words implying the deification of knowledge as a thing apart from the individuals possessing it. In reality it is not knowledge interacts with society but individuals with individuals within a social framework which we call society—a quite different situation which suggests that explanations of information activities and interactions, as distinct from generalized descriptions, are possible only in terms derived from the study of individuals."

7. Biologist Nicholas Petrunkevitch (1924, pp. 76–77) found this phenomenon in all animals: "'Normal' development and 'normal' morphological structure can not be therefore attributed to the structure of the germ plasm alone. To be sure, there must be a certain chemo-physical structure to start with; and this structure must be very much alike in the case of all animals belonging to the same species. Nevertheless, its further fate, its mode of development and its ultimate characters, whatever their hereditary value, are dependent upon, and in a way are a function of, the environment." Anthropologist Bernard G. Campbell (1974, p. 333) argues that in humans memory extends perceptions are produced by the environment, so that "the memory component of perception is of fundamental importance and must almost inevitably come to include not merely an experiential record of events but some generalizations about spatial relationships These generalizations are immeasurably expanded and deepened by the information obtained about the environment as a result of the manipulation of objects. By manipulation, the higher primate can extract an object from the environment, free it, as it were, from spatial implication, and build up a perception of it as a discrete object, not merely as part of a pattern. In time, the primate will come to perceive the environment not only as a three-dimensional pattern but also as an assemblage of objects."

8. The applications of place sense are described in many sources, very succinctly by Relf (1976 and 1996). Pertinent scholarship in a number of fields is applied explicitly to place sense of the library by Osburn (2007), who includes extensive bibliography.

9. Black (1996) has much more to say about library architecture in his chapter 10, "Architecture: The Social Causes of Design," pp. 225–255, in which he discusses the dominance of aesthetic consideration over functional.

10. The words access and accessibility tend to be used commonly in their simplest sense, which constricts the concept far beyond library intentions. Among recent writings that embrace this view, geographers Donald G. Janelle and David C. Hodge

(2000, p. 4) state that "In the most general sense, accessibility relates to the ease by which people and institutions gain use of what they need to survive and to share in the opportunities of a society. As such, accessibility is a function of several factors. These include physical proximity to opportunities, the technical capability to overcome distance (e.g., automobile ownership), and the ability to surmount barriers to entry (e.g., income to pay for theatre tickets, laws to prohibit discrimination, or knowledge to use effectively a computer)." They do raise questions about the future quality of accessibility (p. 6), however: "The roles of places as repositories and conveyors of social capital are central to any consideration of accessibility." And further (p. 7) "It remains to be seen if networks in cyberspace alter our identities with grounded locations in physical space... At issue is whether or not Internet usage results in a bonding of people and institutions within the local region that is as strong (or stronger) as any bonding that may occur with distant opportunities through cyberspace." This mindset of limiting the concept of access to finding information for survival, much as a raccoon forages the garbage cans in a residential neighborhood, can even be applied to the concept of 'browsing', long considered an access activity of special importance in the library. Lucy A. Tedd and Andrew Large (2005) discuss browsing as a level of searching, and write (p. 163) that "The objective of any search is to encapsulate a user's information need in one or several words-the query-and display the resulting matched items." In particular, they address browsing techniques in the digital library on pages 171–172 of the chapter on "Searching and Browsing" (pp. 163–187). But this forces the question of whether there really can be *techniques* for browsing in the manner it usually is interpreted to its fullest sense in the library context.

11. According to management theorists Peter M. Blau and W. Richard Scott (2003, pp. 40–41) "The crucial difference between the two resulting types—production and service organizations—is that only the latter are confronted with problems of establishing social relations with the 'objects' of their endeavors and of having to motivate them in various ways."

12. Jesse Shera (1970, p. 30) went a bit further in stating that "the social function, or role of the library, is to maximize the effective social utilization of the graphic records of civilization... I am convinced that the role of the librarian in society... is to maximize the utilization of graphic records for the benefit of society. In other words, his function is to serve as the mediator between man and graphic records."

13. "Those who write books about communication problems rarely mention libraries," acknowledges library theorist Ronald C. Benge (1970, p. 251), "and it is not difficult to discover why. Libraries are largely dependent on other cultural agencies: they do not originate communications, but transmit them."

14. Hughes (2004, p. 173) also finds that "In recent years, historians and sociologists have provided many examples of socially constructed technology, the opposite of technological determinism. By socially constructed, they mean that the public, through organizations and as individuals, can make choices about the characteristics of the technology they use and the effects that it will have upon them." He also provides (pp. 175–203) a "Bibliographic Essay."

Chapter 7

1. Science journalist James Gleick (1988, p. 308) summarizes the relevant fundamentals of nature: "Nature forms patterns. Some are orderly in space but disorderly in time, others orderly in time but disorderly in space. Some patterns are fractal, exhibiting structures self-similar in scale. Others give rise to steady states or oscillating ones."

2. The possibilities for understanding and expression that can be generated by mere words are deep and extensive, as linguist Patrizia Violi (2001, p. 221) suggests in her substantial explanation that "Perception is undoubtedly one of the most significant possible parameters of variation in the structuring of the semantic system, as was already implicitly recognized in certain categories of traditional analysis such as the opposition between concrete and abstract. We can imagine that the role of perceptual experience in semantic classification lies along a continuum; at one extreme are terms for whose semantics the perceptual dimension is an essential component, and at the other extreme terms which relate to abstract schemata." Semanticist Paul Ziff (1960, p. 42) stresses the importance and extent of the possibilities of meaning in words based on context and linguistic environment: "I am inclined to suppose that meaning is essentially a matter of nonsyntactic semantic regularities. This is not to say that meaning is simply a matter of such regularities but it does seem reasonable to suppose that an element's having meaning in the language can be explicated primarily in terms of the nonsyntactic semantic regularities to be found pertaining (directly or indirectly) to the element." Science philosopher Carl G. Hempel (1952, p. 11) describes the process of explaining phenomena in any science, which appears to be similar, if not identical, to the rational process attempted in daily communication: "Explication is concerned with expressions whose meaning in conversational language or even in scientific discourse is more or less vague... and aims at giving those expressions a new and precisely determined meaning, so as to render them more suitable for clear and rigorous discourse on the subject matter at hand... The definitions proposed in [outstanding examples of explication] are not arrived at simply by an analysis of customary meanings. To be sure, the considerations leading to the precise definitions are guided initially by reference to customary scientific or conversational usage; but eventually the issues which call for clarification become so subtle that a study of prevailing usage can no longer shed any light upon them. Hence, the assignment of precise meanings to the terms under explication becomes a matter of judicious synthesis, or rational reconstruction, rather than of merely descriptive analysis: An explication sentence does not simply exhibit the commonly accepted meaning of the expression under study but rather proposes a specified new and precise meaning for it."

3. Psychologists Robert J. Sternberg and Elena L. Grigorenko (2001, p. vii) place this idea in a context, writing that "We can control environment, at least to some extent. Whereas we can do relatively little about genes, we can do a great deal about the environment. Thus, to the extent that we wish to maximize the cognitive development both of children and adults, we need to understand environmental effects on cognitive abilities so as to have a basis for constructing optimal environments."

4. Butler (1942, pp. 6–7) defines his term: "No one, starting from nothing and compelled to find out everything for himself, could become very learned during a normal life-span. But humanity is able to cumulate its experience and accomplishments so that each adult generation may start where the last one left off. This implies that, to attain civilization, man must be both conservative and progressive. He must preserve the culture which he has inherited, but he must also extend and improve it in the light of his own experience. This principle holds true for the intellectual no less than for the material content of culture... Among the basic processes of civilization are therefore included not only the discovery but also the preservation and transmission of knowledge." Butler (1953, p. 240) sheds further light on the concept: "Any scholarship, general or special, is a system of ideas—facts, theories, and opinions that a people has accumulated and uses in the routine of living. It therefore represents the intellectual element in its culture and consists of rationalization of its past experience. Hence any scholarship, to be complete, must embrace the whole ambit of the experience to which it is related... Therefore, culture, the routine of exploitation dominant in any period, is necessarily an organic integration of a scholarship, a physical equipment, and a social organization. In other words, scholarship is the intellectual content of culture, and its pattern conforms to the pattern of the cultural activities to which it is related." It is in the context he describes above that Butler (1944, p. 31) also states that "The ruling purpose of the library is the promotion of scholarship." It is important to know that Butler (1933, pp. 92–93) uses a broad definition of scholarship in his philosophy: "One person may remember a great deal of what he once learned in his lessons and yet make but little use of it in his mental life. Another, though perhaps he possesses far less as the effect of academic discipline, may weave what he has into the fabric of his intellectual activities. But even more than this much of the content of every adult mind has been acquired outside of the classroom. All sorts of direct personal contacts as well as the indirect process of learning by reading have left a deposit."

5. But there is no shortage of library metaphors, and physicist John Ziman (1968, p. 102), writing about science information, notes that "A scientific laboratory without a library is like a decorticated cat: the motor activities continue to function, but lack coordination of memory and purpose. Ultimately, all our elaborate apparatus and skilled technicians exist only to add a few more pages to the books on the shelves."

6. "If a definition, therefore, states that libraries 'hold coded thoughts in readiness for use'," writes information scientist and philosopher J. G. Meijer (1982, p. 24), "then they have been fundamentally distinguished from the mass communication media... On the basis of the above, it is justifiable to conclude that through the defining terms *coded thoughts* and *hold in readiness for use*, libraries are functionally and essentially different from museums and other cultural institutions, publishing companies, bookstores, educational institutions, and the mass communication media."

7. Thus, according to library theorist Gerald W. Johnson (1978, p. 67), the library is "the function of an open door. The public library is a way of escape from the narrow area of our individual lives into the field, finite, no doubt, but unbounded, of the wisdom and experience of all mankind. It is not the only way of escape, but for the majority of us it is by far the widest and the easiest to pass through, thus the one that we should be most careful to keep open and free from impediments."

8. Jesse Shera (1966, p. 177) translates this condition to questions the librarian needs to ask: "What happens within that psycho-physiological process that takes place when a human mind confronts a library store or the bibliographic tools that are intended to be the key to it? How does the knowledge that the individual assimilates become a part of the collective intelligence of a culture: How is social behaviour influenced by the knowledge that society absorbs? These are the basic problems that confront the librarian and should guide his professional practice." Similarly, Pierce Butler (1942, p. 7) describes the context in which the librarian works: "In a civilization the acquisition of information is a continuous process. At any particular moment new knowledge is always being added to what previous generations have acquired. This total stock of information, new and old, which a society possesses exists in two forms: some of it is kinetic, at work in the minds of living men, but a much greater part is potential, stored up in books and other records. Thus in a normal civilization two informative processes must always be maintained, and whenever a particular situation arises the necessary specific knowledge must be released from the reservoir. The first is a general and continuous process; the second is special and intermittent. The rising generation must always be receiving an adequate equipment of knowledge to fit it for participation in cultural routines, and constantly to meet the occasion adults must be releasing from potential to kinetic for the available special knowledges that they require. In both of the processes four methods for the transmission of knowledge may be distinguished." Butler (pp. 9–10) explores these methods, being education, research, social communication, and consultation.

9. Jesse Shera (1966, p. 27) provides a modest historical framework for this situation: "Such library pioneers as Edwards and Panizzi in Britain and Jewett, Winsor, Cutter, and Poole in the United States had seen, in the provision of the bibliographic machinery necessary to provide both physical and subject access to printed records, the real social purpose of the library. It remained for their successors to reject a considerable part of this primary responsibility and to take up, in a futile attempt to rehabilitate their professional prestige, aims and objectives which were quite incompatible with the very nature of the library." He finds two reasons for this (pp. 26–27): first, the determination that both physical and content access would be provided on a purely local basis; and second, the rapid development of the journal, which did not fit the mechanism of the catalogue, since it had been developed for the book format, so the journal part became the focus of the field of documentation, which then could clearly differentiate itself from librarianship.

10. Toulmin (1972, p. 330) elaborates. "The confidence we have in our retrospective appraisals imposes no retroactive 'compulsion' on the processes of social and conceptual change themselves. In social and political history, as in the history of scientific thought, the 'dialectic' lies primarily in our writing of history, rather than in the historical events about which we write. We can properly speak of social and political institutions evolving in a more or less 'rational' manner, only if we consider the detailed ways in which such institutions develop—or fail to develop—in response to the specific requirements of changing historical situations. As for the specific forms these 'ecological demands' will take, in future situations, we can no more forecast these with confidence in the intellectual and social field than we can do in the field of organic evolution. Just because all the changing conditions that will in fact face future organic

populations cannot be predicted, or even guessed at, the characteristics of later organic species cannot be said, in any real sense, to have been 'wholly implied in' those of the earlier species."

11. Psychologists Robert J. Sternberg and Todd I. Lubart (1999, p. 3) identify levels of daily life at which creativity functions: "Creativity is the ability to produce work that is both novel (i.e., original, unexpected) and appropriate (i.e., useful, adaptive concerning task constraints) . . . At an individual level, creativity is relevant, for example, when one is solving problems on the job and in daily life. At a societal level, creativity can lead to new scientific findings, new movements in art, new inventions, and new social programs. The economic importance of creativity is clear because new products or services create jobs. Furthermore, individuals, organizations, and societies must adapt existing resources to changing task demands to remain competitive."

Chapter 8

1. Most closely resembling this dual function of the generic library is that of the academic research library, which library administrator and theorist Herman Fussler (1967, pp. 129–130) describes as follows: "This enormous diversity and unpredictable character of university research have forced the university library into something of a dual function: first, the library builds and maintains a 'working' library, oriented around the reasonably clear needs of students and faculty members and the materials most likely to be used in support of current research and teaching; and secondly, the library acquires, keeps, and services a collection of 'permanent record' in which many future needs are anticipated as far as good judgment and available resources permit, and in which the relatively inactive acquisitions of the past are retained for possible future uses. These future uses, it is recognized, are often entirely different from the original purposes of the publications." Michael Polanyi (1964, p. 67) describes a situation in the natural sciences, between the physical and the biological sciences, that can be analogized to the situation of the concept of library and the operations of a library: "The distinction is important and yet fairly simple. The laws of physics and chemistry determine the processes and structures of inanimate nature. We inquire into these processes and structures without asking what they are for, because we assume that they achieve nothing. Thus do we discover the laws of physics and chemistry. Take by contrast the study of physiology. It consists in observing the structures of living beings and the processes occurring in them, with a bearing on the question of what these things are for. For the task of physiology is to explain the achievements of living beings. It usually explains them in terms of a mechanism which functions in the way a machine works. Physiological mechanisms are based, like machines, on the laws of physics and chemistry, but they are not accounted for by these laws. They are determined by rules which, as in machines, may be called *operational principles.* Operational principles describe the parts composing a mechanism and define the way they function in making the mechanism work . . . the physical sciences expressly leave open certain conditions of a system that are usually described as its *boundary conditions,* and . . . the operational principles of a mechanism take effect by controlling these boundary conditions. As a result, physical and chemical laws *are made to serve*

the physiological mechanism of living beings." Function and operating principles constitute the library, not just the operating principles.

2. Akin to this apparent duality are the ideas expressed by geneticist and science philosopher Bentley Glass (1970) about the timely, which is the empirical knowledge used in everyday relations with society, and the timeless, which is the whole range of human values that have become ideals as a result of our long evolutionary development. From a different perspective, the news media fairly recently carried a review of a television series retelling classical literature. The author of the review, culture writer Malcom Jones (2007, p. 66) captures very succinctly this dual function: "From epic poem to television series, the stories don't really change. The only thing that changes is how we tell the stories." This strikes me as analogous to the library situation, where the story is the evolution of culture (knowledge, belief, values, etc.) and the way it is told is the set of everyday operations, amounting to the way the service is continued.

3. Philosopher John Searle (1995, p. 227) had earlier elaborated on the same conclusion: "On my view the traditional opposition that we tend to make between biology and culture is as misguided as the traditional opposition between body and mind. Just as mental states are higher-level features of our nervous system, and consequently there is not opposition between the mental and the physical, the mental is simply a set of physical features of the brain at a higher level of description than that of neurons; so there is no opposition between culture and biology; culture is the form that biology takes." Others take issue with this view, among them philosopher David-Hillel Ruben (1998, p. 869), who asserts that "Many philosophers, in the grip of the ideal of the unity of science, have held out the prospect that social science can be derived from, and is therefore reducible to, psychology (the latter eventually being reducible to chemistry and physics). For such thinkers, the world is ultimately a simple place, with only many different ways in which to speak about it. Other thinkers have been struck by the reality and integrity of the social world, and how it seems to impress itself on the individual willy-nilly." I fail to see the incompatibility of the two theories, precisely if the social world is one of reality and integrity. Physicist John Ziman (1978, p. 101) seems to disregard this issue, writing "Even the scientific observer is not a camera. In due course, he must communicate his experience to other scientists; but between the pattern of excitations on his retina and the uttered message there occur many stages of internal neural manipulation. To these *mental processes* we have no direct access, except by introspection and highly circumstantial experimental inference. Yet they play an essential role in science, not simply by the extra-logicality that they introduce in the most elementary acts of perception but as the primary elements of individual human cognition. The concept of 'knowledge' is entirely meaningless in the absence of some mental acts in the mind of some knower."

4. Evolutionary psychologist Leda Cosmides and anthropologist John Tooby (2002, p. 191) describe a scenario for this process: "Because contingent information can change its status at any time with any new change in the world, it is important to have tools available that can take architecturally true information and scrutinize it." They add (p. 193) "In general, our minds are full of conclusions without our having maintained the grounds or evidence that led us to think of them as true. For a massively inferential architecture like the human mind, each item can serve as input to many other inferential processes, whose outputs are inputs to others. To the extent that

the information is sourced, or its grounds and derivation are preserved in association with the data, then new data about its evidential basis can be used to correct or update its inferential descendants." And they conclude (p. 167) "The structure of a dedicated intelligence reflects the long-enduring structure of the adaptive problem it solves. Natural selection coordinates the structure of a recurrent adaptive problem (including the features of the environment in which it occurs) with the structure of an adaptive problem solver such that the interaction of the two produces the solution to the problem. If selection has created a well-engineered adaptation, then elements that are necessary to solve the problem but lacking from the world are supplied by the structure of the problem-solving device."

5. Sociologist Roy Wood Sellars (1926, p. xx) essentially advises that each area of reasoned investigation must proceed according to the nature of the areas being investigated: "*The sciences must correspond to the nature of their fields or objects.* And if these fields are diverse, the sciences must also be diverse in many ways. A certain logical discontinuity or diversity of the sciences must exist to reflect the actual diversity of things, a diversity which has come about genetically i.e., by accumulative growth." The common ground of all sciences, it seems, is a conscious effort to be rational and to be guided by an ideal of truth and objectivity. Science philosopher Marx W. Wartofski, 1968, p. 413) concludes that, "In the broadest sense we may characterize science as rational action; and whereas the sources of this action may be need, intellectual adventure, or personal satisfaction, its guide and judge in all things is critical and reflective intelligence. Such intelligence judges not only intentions but results, and not only immediate success and failure but the qualities of vision and insight." Here he links science and ethics.

6. Library theorist Maurice Line (1965, p. 275) advocates this principle, writing "To sum up: Librarianship is ultimately social in its purpose and the librarian should have a clear conception of his role in society, both his own immediate group and society as a whole. Librarianship should be viewed as a means of communication between knowledge and people, and our techniques, our tools, our buildings and ourselves should be examined in this light."

7. Parsons (1978, p. 381) clarifies and further supports Henderson's conceptualization: "We should not forget that for Henderson 'organization', which for him was closely related to the concept 'system', was an essential feature of the order of nature generally, including its physical aspect... Indeed, it may be appropriate to close this phase of the discussion by recalling the famous statement of Einstein that the most incomprehensible thing about nature is its comprehensibility for human understanding. Einstein was thinking mainly of physical nature, and if the category of information has strictly nothing to do with the 'nature of nature', it would be difficult to make sense of Einstein's dictum."

8. "Whether or not theory formation is the most important and distinctive scientific activity," writes philosopher Abraham Kaplan (1964, p. 294), "in one sense of the term 'theory' this activity might well be regarded as the most important and instinctive for human beings.. In this sense it stands for the symbolic dimension of experience, as opposed to the apprehension of brute fact. The content of our experience is not a succession of mere happenings, but a sequence of more or less meaningful events, meaningful both in themselves and in the patterns of their occurrence. They are

consequential, that is—significant in their bearings on one another." Science philosopher and theorist Carl G. Hempel (1965, p. 241) provides a useful elaboration of the explanatory role of theory that is sufficiently terse that I must quote it in entirety. "In the historical explanation of some social institutions great emphasis is laid upon an analysis of the *development* of the institution up to the stage under consideration. Critics of this approach have objected that a mere description of this kind is not a genuine explanation. This argument may be given a slightly different form in terms of the preceding reflections: An account of the development of an institution is obviously not simply a description of *all* the events which temporally preceded it; only those events are meant to be included which are *'relevant'* to the formation of institution. And whether an event is relevant to that development is not a matter of evaluative opinion, but an objective question depending upon what is sometimes called a causal analysis of the rise of that institution. Now, the causal analysis of an event establishes an explanation for it, and since this requires reference to general hypotheses, so do assumptions about relevance, and, consequently, so does the adequate analysis of the historical development of an institution."

9. Cultural historian Raymond Irwin (1949, p. 50) follows a similar guideline for defining a theory of librarianship, writing that theory comprises "the governing principles of the subject, or the subject itself, considered as a unity. There is no significance in the term unless the principles are applied, or capable of being applied, in practice, nor can there be anything coherent and systematic about the practice unless it is based on a reasoned theory." This again calls to mind the category-mistake described by philosopher Gilbert Ryle (1949).

10. Most frequently mentioned in this regard is J. Periam Danton, but there are still more, such as Pierce Butler, who reportedly stated that "The final challenge, as Butler suggests (noted by Richardson, 1992, p. 140), is that we need to balance our science (the facts of librarianship), our technology (the skill to manipulate these facts), and our humanity (the study of the abstract principles of librarianship)." Library theorist Ronald C. Benge (1970, p. 246) argues "Those who consider . . . that sociological factors represent a fundamental part of the theory of librarianship, must therefore go beyond the five laws [of Ranganathan] in order to identify or discuss these factors." And library theorist D. J. Foskett (1962, pp. 3–4) states more generally that what the profession needs to do is engage in "a quest for normative principles by whose light we can illuminate our practice," and to identify (p. 4) "some normative principles which would stimulate thought and illuminate action." This is but a small sampling of those who have seen the need not just to establish a theory of librarianship and a philosophy of larger scope in which to place it, and a few others have been cited in the course of this text.

11. Pierce Butler did so throughout his entire career, writing thirty years earlier (1933, p. 26) for example, that if librarians adopt a more appropriate outlook, they "will transfer their attention from process to function. They will come to strive for accurate understanding just as ardently as they now do for practical efficiency. They will temper their ideals with realistic considerations and discover standards in the nature of their elements rather than assume them as *a priori* values. They will seek for knowledge in typical phenomena instead of in particular occurrences. They will study librarianship rather than single libraries. Their enthusiasm for vocational unanimity

will give way to a recognition of real differences in operative levels, but their quest they will still regard as a cooperative enterprise of the whole profession." Not long after Butler's remarks, library theorist James Wellard (1940, pp. 147-148) described what he believed to be lacking in librarianship: "What is required is a recognition of the whole field of librarianship—not only of techniques, routines, special phases, and research projects—but of books, readers, and society as a whole. This is a philosophy of librarianship which has as its basis the whole field of knowledge in its particular relation to the organisation and dissemination of literature."

12. Cultural historian Raymond Irwin (1949, p. 107) couches similar sentiments in a matter of his own faith: "Knowledge has absolute value. This is the faith of all scholarship. And if knowledge is thus precious for its own sake, we must struggle daily and hourly with its arrangement, however hard the task. For knowledge unarranged and unrelated is knowledge lost."

13. Jesse Shera, in his Foreword to one of Wright's works (1977, pp. x-xi), finds that "Of particular interest to the author of the foreword are Wright's hints at the isomorphism of philosophy and librarianship. The physical realities of librarianship and philosophy are not alike, but their basic forms may well be the same. Such a thesis, if it can be established, will surprise both librarians and philosophers. Yet it would be harmonious with my own thinking about the philosophical character of the librarian's social role." I do not believe the isomorphism at issue is properly of philosophy and librarianship, but rather of philosophy and the concept of library. It is not so much a matter of an administrative approach to responsibility as a functional approach to culture.

14. Library administrator and theorist Lewis F. Stieg (1978, p. 354) also tried to look beyond the confines of social science, hinting at the larger context of cultural evolution: "If librarianship's scientific manifestation is legitimately classified as a social science, it seems axiomatic that any search for the kind of theory that it may be able to achieve must at some point include analysis of its relationship to the social forces that brought it into being and continue to chart its course."

15. Information scientist Norman Roberts (1976, p. 256) finds a similar situation in his field that is prompted by considerations of its inevitable involvement in the more social dimension of life: "Associated with this broader social view is the acceptance that, as with other social sciences, the separation of theory from practice, as something peculiarly scientific, is not crucial to a definition of science. The complementary activities of theory and practice have only one aim, the improvement of the presentation, transfer and use of information."

16. In answer to his own question, "What is a book?" philosopher José Ortega y Gasset responded with ideas that parallel those of Popper in describing his World 3. According to sociologist John T. Graham (2001, pp. 12-13) "The answer he gave them then came out of Plato, as perhaps the oldest of surviving definitions: a book is 'written sayings' that are meant thus to have 'permanence'. From Ortega's *social* perspective, a book is—besides something someone 'says'—something one 'does', makes, or creates '*for* something' that is deemed useful for human, *social* 'living'. A book not only may preserve *words* recording someone's historic sayings, acts, or happenings but also may convey his *thought* and 'theory, or science.' Like the library, the book has had an origin and a *history*, for neither has existed always, and they would probably not do so forever

in the future by the same mode and techniques. Just as bound books had succeeded clay tablets and scrolls, 'virtual' books may succeed bound ones."

17. For example, published eleven years after the Fuller (1988) book, that of Goldman (1999) refers to Fuller's work only by way of a bare-bones footnote. The development of social epistemology is traced through librarianship and into philosophy by Tarcisio Zandonade (2004). It is worth noting here that the earliest influential books in English on social epistemology were written by philosophers (Steve Fuller, 1988; and Alvin I. Goldman, 1999). In neither of these works is there mention of Jesse Shera or of Margaret F. Egan, whose collaborative work on "Foundations of a Theory of Bibliography" in 1952 is a very early, perhaps the earliest, use of the phrase. Much is known about Shera, who is cited throughout the pages of the present book, but much less about Egan (Furner, 2004). John M. Budd (2004, p. 362), however, does point out that in publications subsequent to their initial works on social epistemology, both Fuller and Goldman do give Shera credit for his pioneering work. Budd (2002) also provides an examination of Shera's thoughts in the context of more recent work on social epistemology.

18. Microbiologist and science philosopher Ludwik Fleck (1986, pp. 101–102) explains how this process works: "Not all of the members of the thought-collective [those in a culture, whether large or small, who may be affected directly or indirectly] have the same attitude towards its products: a smaller part play the role of *sui generis* intermediaries with respect to the—larger—remainder. In this way there arises, round every product of collective life, a smaller *esoteric circle*, composed of members having a more direct relationship to this product, and a larger *exoteric circle* composed of members who participate in it through the intermediation of the other ones... Every scientific idea, every artistic or any other thought possesses its few 'initiates' and its more numerous 'adherents' who adopt this thought through trust in the initiated ones: without such a division of roles and work any coexistence within the collective would be impossible. It is precisely this division that results in the collective being not the simple sum of individuals, in the fact that the circulation of thought in it has creative capabilities whose result is not an individual work, but precisely a collective one. The collective consists of many such mutually intersecting esoteric and exoteric circles, an individual belongs to many exoteric circles and to few—or no—esoteric circles. There are various *degrees* of initiation and numerous links between them, just as there exist paths and links which unite different circles."

19. Iser (1974, p. 277) also argues that "the statements made or information conveyed in the sentence are already in a certain sense qualified: the sentence does not consist solely of a statement... but aims at something beyond what it actually says. This is true of all sentences in literary works, and it is through the interaction of these sentences that their common aim is fulfilled."

References

Abbott, Andrew. 1998. "Professionalism and the Future of Librarianship." *Library Trends* 46: 430-443.

Altick, Richard D. 1998. *The English Common Reader. A Social History of the Mass Reading Public, 1800–1900.* Second edition. Columbus: Ohio State University Press.

Apter, David E., ed. 1964. *Ideology and Discontent.* Glencoe: Free Press.

Arenson, Adam. 2007. "Libraries in Public before the Age of Public Libraries: Interpreting the Furnishings and Design of Athenaeums and Other 'Social Libraries', 1800-1860." In *The Library as Place. History, Community, and Culture.* Eds. John E. Buschman and Gloria J. Leckie. Westport: Libraries Unlimited, pp. 41-60.

Armstrong, David F., William C. Stokoe, and Sherman E. Wilcox. 1995. *Gesture and the Nature of Knowledge.* Cambridge: Cambridge University Press.

Armstrong, David Malet. 2004 a. "Mental Concepts: Causal Analysis." *The Oxford Companion to the Mind.* Second edition. Ed. Richard L. Gregory. Oxford: Oxford University Press, pp. 572-574.

Armstrong, David Malet. 2004 b. "Mind-Body Problems: Philosophical Theories." *The Oxford Companion to the Mind.* Second edition. Ed. Richard L. Gregory. Oxford: Oxford University Press, pp. 604-605.

Arnhart, Larry. 1998. *Darwinian Natural Right. The Biological Ethics of Human Nature.* Albany: State University of New York Press.

Arsuaga, Juan Luis and Ignacio Martínez. 2006. *The Chosen Species. The Long March of Human Evolution.* London: Blackwell. (Orig. Spanish 1998)

Audi, Robert. 2006. "Philosophy." *Encyclopedia of Philosophy.* Second edition. 10 vols. Ed. Donald M. Borchert. Detroit: Thomson Gale, vol. 7, pp. 325-337.

Bakewell, Kenneth G. B. 1980. "Ranganathan." *ALA World Encyclopedia of Library* and *Information Services.* Chicago: American Library Association, pp. 467-468.

Ballard, Lloyd V. 1936. *Social Institutions.* New York: Appleton Century. (Contains a chapter on "The Public Library," pp. 227-251, which was published separately by the American Library Association, 1937)

Barrett, Louise, Robin Dunbar, and John Lycett. 2002. *Human Evolutionary Psychology.* Princeton: Princeton University Press.

Bartlett, Sir Frederic C. 1932. *Remembering. A Study in Experimental and Social Psychology.* Cambridge: Cambridge University Press.

Bartlett, Sir Frederic C. 1958. *Thinking. An Experimental and Social Study.* New York: Basic Books.

Basalla, George. 1988. *The Evolution of Technology.* Cambridge: Cambridge University Press.

Bazerman, Charles. 1988. *Shaping Written Knowledge. The Genre and Activity of the Experimental Article in Science*. Madison: University of Wisconsin Press.

Beagle, Donald. 1988. "Libraries and the 'Implicate Order': A Contextual Approach to Theory." *Libri* 38: 26–44.

Beard, Charles A. 1932. "Introduction." *The Idea of Progress. An Inquiry into Its Origin and Growth,* by John B. Bury. New York: Macmillan, pp. ix–xl.

Belkin, Nicholas J. 1978. "Progress in Documentation: Information Concepts for Information Science." *Journal of Documentation* 34 (March): 55–85.

Ben-David, Joseph. 1973. "How to Organize Research in the Social Sciences." *Daedalus* 102 (Spring): 39–51.

Benge, Ronald C. 1970. "Philosophies of Librarianship." *Libraries and Cultural Change*. London: Clive Bingley, pp. 244–257.

Berger, Peter L. and Thomas Luckmann. 1966. *The Social Construction of Reality*. Garden City: Doubleday.

Bergson, Henri. 1944. *Creative Evolution*. New York: Modern Library. (Orig. French 1907)

Bergson, Henri. 1920. *Mind-Energy. Lectures and Essays*. New York: Holt. (Orig. French 1919)

Bertman, Stephen. 2000. *Cultural Amnesia. America's Future and the Crisis of Memory*. Westport: Praeger.

Binford, Lewis R. 1989. "Isolating the Transition to Cultural Adaptations: An Organizational Approach." *The Emergence of Modern Humans*. New York: Cambridge University Press, pp. 18–41.

Bjorklund, David F. and Anthony D. Pellegrini. 2002. *The Origins of Human Nature. Evolutionary Developmental Psychology*. Washington, D.C.: American Psychological Association.

Black, Alistair. 1996. *A New History of the English Public Library. Social and Intellectual Contexts, 1850–1914*. London: Leicester University Press.

Blau, Peter M. and W. Richard Scott. 2003. *Formal Organizations: A Comparative Approach*. Stanford: Stanford University Press. (Orig. London: Routledge & Kegan Paul, 1963)

Bliss, Henry Evelyn. 1935. "As to a Philosophy for Librarianship." *Library Quarterly* 5: 232–235.

Bloom, Paul. 1998. "Some Issues in the Evolution of Language and Thought." *The Evolution of Mind*. Eds. Denise Dellarosa Cummins and Colin Allen. New York: Oxford University Press, pp. 204–223.

Bloor, David. 1976. *Knowledge and Social Imagery*. London: Routledge & Kegan Paul.

Boden, Margaret A. 2004. *The Creative Mind. Myths and Mechanisms*. Second edition. London: Routledge.

Boden, Margaret A. 2006. Mind as Machine. A History of Cognitive Science. 2 vols. Oxford: Oxford University Press.

Borden, Arnold K. 1931. "We Need a Philosophy." *Libraries* 36 (April): 175–176.

Borko, Harold. 1968. "Information Science: What Is It?" *American Documentation* 19 (January): 3–5.

Bouglé, Célestin. 1926. *The Evolution of Values*. New York: Henry Holt. (Orig. French ed. Paris: Colin, 1922)

Boulding, Kenneth E. 1978. *Ecodynamics. A New Theory of Societal Evolution*. Beverly Hills: Sage.
Boulding, Kenneth E. 1985. *Human Betterment*. Beverly Hills: Sage.
Boulding, Kenneth E. 1985. *The World as a Total System*. Beverly Hills: Sage.
Boulding, Kenneth E. 1983. "The Optimum Utilization of Knowledge: Some Central Concepts." *The Optimum Utilization of Knowledge: Making Knowledge Serve Human Betterment*. Eds. Kenneth E. Boulding and Lawrence Senesh. Boulder: Westview Press, pp. 1-19.
Bowler, Peter J. 1989. *The Invention of Progress. The Victorians and the Past*. Oxford: Blackwell.
Boyd, Robert and Peter J. Richerson. 1985. *Culture and the Evolutionary Process*. Chicago: University of Chicago Press.
Boyd, Robert and Peter J. Richerson. 2005. *The Origin and Evolution of Cultures*. New York: Oxford University Press.
Brain, Sir W. Russell. 1961. "Body, Brain, Mind and Soul." *The Humanist Frame*. Ed. Julian Huxley. New York: Harper, pp. 51-63.
Brain, Sir W. Russell. 1951. *Mind, Perception and Science*. Oxford: Blackwell.
Broad, C. D. 1927. *Scientific Thought*. New York: Harcourt Brace.
Broadfield, A. 1949. *A Philosophy of Librarianship*. London: Grafton.
Bronowski, Jacob. 1961. "Science Is Human." *The Humanist Frame*. Ed. Julian Huxley. New York: Harper, pp. 83-94.
Bronowski, Jacob and Bruce Mazlish. 1960. *The Western Intellectual Tradition. From Leonardo to Hegel*. New York: Harper & Row.
Brookes, Bertram C. 1980. "The Foundations of Information Science. Part I. Philosophical Aspects." *Journal of Information Science* 2: 125-133.
Brophy, Peter. 2001. *The Library in the Twenty-First Century*. London: Library Association.
Bryson, Lyman. 1947. *Science and Freedom*. New York: Columbia University Press.
Budd, John M. 2004. "Academic Libraries and Knowledge: A Social Epistemology Framework." *Journal of Academic Librarianship* 30: 361-367.
Budd, John M. 1995. "An Epistemological Foundation for Library and Information Science." *Library Quarterly* 65: 295-318.
Budd, John M. 2001. "Instances of Ideology in Discursive Practices: Implications for Library and Information Science." *Library Quarterly* 71 (October): 498-517.
Budd, John M. 2001. *Knowledge and Knowing in Library and Information Science. A Philosophical Framework*. Lanham: Scarecrow Press.
Budd, John M. 2003. "The Library, Praxis, and Symbolic Power." *Library Quarterly* 73: 19-32.
Budd, John M. 2002. "Jesse Shera, Social Epistemology and Praxis." *Social Epistemology* 16: 93-98.
Budd, John M. 2002. "Jesse Shera, Sociologist of Knowledge?" *Library Quarterly* 72: 423-440.
Budd, John M. 2008. *Self-Examination. The Present and Future of Librarianship*. Westport: Libraries Unlimited.
Buller, David J. 2005. *Adapting Minds. Evolutionary Psychology and the Persistent Quest for Human Nature*. Cambridge: MIT Press.

Buller, David J. 2006. "Evolutionary Psychology: A Critique." *Conceptual Issues in Evolutionary Biology*. Third edition. Ed. Elliott Sober. Cambridge: MIT Press, pp. 197–214.

Burke, Peter. 2000. *A Social History of Knowledge. From Gutenberg to Diderot*. Cambridge: Polity Press.

Bury, John B. 1932. *The Idea of Progress. An Inquiry into Its Origin and Growth*. New York: Macmillan.

Buschman, John E. 2007. "Democratic Theory in Library Information Science: Toward an Emendation." *Journal of the American Society for Information Science and Technology* 58: 1483–1496.

Buschman, John E. 2006. "'The Integrity and Obstinacy of Intellectual Creations': Jürgen Habermas and Librarianship's Theoretical Literature." *Library Quarterly* 76: 270–299.

Buschman, John E. and Gloria J. Leckie, eds. 2007. *The Library as Place. History, Community, and Culture*. Westport: Libraries Unlimited.

Bush, Vannevar. 1950. "Men Against Nature." *Mid-Century Implications of Scientific Progress*. Ed. John Ely Burchard. Cambridge: The Technology Press of the Massachusetts Institute of Technology.

Butler, Pierce. 1953. "The Bibliographical Function of the Library." *Journal of Cataloging and Classification* 9: 3–11.

Butler, Pierce. 1933. *An Introduction to Library Science*. Chicago: University of Chicago Press.

Butler, Pierce. 1953. "The Life of the Book." *Library Quarterly* 23: 157–163.

Butler, Pierce. 1942. "Survey of the Reference Field." *The Reference Function of the Library*. Ed. Pierce Butler. Chicago: University of Chicago Press.

Butler, Pierce. 1945. "The Intellectual Content of Librarianship." *Library Quarterly* 15: 347–351.

Butler, Pierce. 1952. "The Cultural Function of the Library." *Library Quarterly* 22: 79–91.

Butler, Pierce. 1944. *Scholarship and Civilization*. Chicago: University of Chicago, Graduate Library School.

Calhoun, Craig, ed. 2002. *Dictionary of the Social Sciences*. Oxford: Oxford University Press.

Campbell, Bernard G. 1974. *Human Evolution. An Introduction to Man's Adaptations*. Second edition. Chicago: Aldine.

Campbell, Donald T. 1975. "On the Conflicts between Biological and Social Evolution and Between Psychology and Moral Tradition." *American Psychologist* 30: 1103–1126.

Campbell, Donald T. 1974. "Evolutionary Epistemology." *The Philosophy of Karl Popper*. Ed. P. A. Schilpp. Lasalle, IL: Open Court, pp. 413–463.

Campbell, James. 1989. "Place as Social and Geographical." *Commonplaces. Essays on the Nature of Place*. Eds. D. W. Black, D. Kunze, and J. Pickles. Lanham: University Press of America.

Canter, David. 1977. *The Psychology of Place*. London: Architectural Press.

Capurro, Rafael. 1992. "What Is Information Science for?" *Conceptions of Library and Information Science*. Eds. Pertti Vakkari and Blaise Cronin. London: Taylor Graham, pp. 82–96.

Carter, Mary Duncan, Wallace J. Bonk, and Rose Mary Magrill. 1974. *Building Library Collections*. Fourth edition. Metuchen: Scarecrow Press.

Chafe, Wallace L. 1979. "The Flow of Thought and the Flow of Language." *Syntax and Semantics: Discourse and Syntax*. Ed. Talmy Givon. New York: Academic Press, pp. 159–181.

Changeux, Jean-Pierre. 1986. *Neuronal Man. The Biology of Mind*. Oxford: Oxford University Press. (Orig. French 1983)

Changeux, Jean-Pierre. 2004. *The Physiology of Truth. Neuroscience and Human Knowledge*. Cambridge: Harvard University Press.

Chapin, F. Stuart. 1928. *Cultural Change*. New York: Century.

Chartier, Roger. 1989. "General Introduction: Print Culture." *The Culture of Print. Power and the Uses of Print in Early Modern Europe*. Ed. Roger Chartier. Princeton: Princeton University Press, pp. 1–10. (Orig. French 1987)

Childe, V. Gordon. 1948. *Man Makes Himself*. London: Watts.

Childe, V. Gordon. 1951. *Social Evolution*. London: Watts.

Childe, V. Gordon. 1956. *Society and Knowledge*. New York: Harper.

Christ, John M. 1972. "The Crisis of Theory and Philosophy in Library Science." *Toward a Philosophy of Educational Librarianship*. Littleton: Libraries Unlimited, pp. 14–37.

Christ, John M. 1969. "Functional Analysis and Library Science." *College and Research Libraries* 30 (May): 242–246.

Churchill, Winston Spencer. 1950. "The Twentieth Century-Its Promise and Its Realization." *Mid-Century Implications of Scientific Progress*. Ed. John Ely Burchard. Cambridge: The Technology Press of the Massachusetts Institute of Technology, pp. 34–76.

Churchland, Patricia Smith. 2002. *Brain-Wise. Studies in Neurophilosophy*. Cambridge: MIT Press.

Churchland, Patricia Smith. 1986. *Neurophilosophy. Toward a Unified Science of the Mind-Brain*. Cambridge: MIT Press.

Cianciolo, Anna T. and Robert J. Sternberg. 2004. *Intelligence: A Brief History*. Oxford: Blackwell.

Clark, Mary E. 2002. *In Search of Human Nature*. London: Routledge.

Clarke, Jack A. 1970. *Gabriel Naudé, 1600–1653*. Hamden: Archon Books.

Cloak, F. Theodore. 1975. "Is Cultural Ethology Possible?" *Human Ecology* 3 (no. 3): 161–182.

Cole, John Y. 1979. "Storehouses and Workshops: American Libraries and the Uses of Knowledge." *The Organization of Knowledge in Modern America, 1860–1920*. Eds. Alexandra Oleson and John Voss. Baltimore: Johns Hopkins University Press, pp. 364–385.

Collingwood, R. G. 1999. *The Principles of History*. Eds. W. H. Dray and W. J. van der Dussen. Oxford: Oxford University Press.

Compton, Karl Taylor. 1950. "The State of Science." *Mid-Century Implications of Scientific Progress*. Ed. John Ely Burchard. Cambridge: The Technology Press of the Massachusetts Institute of Technology.

Converse, Philip E. 1964. "The Nature of Belief Systems in Mass Publics." *Ideology and Discontent*. Ed. David E. Apter. New York: Free Press, pp. 206–261.

Cooley, Charles Horton. 1920. *Social Process*. New York: Charles Scribner's Sons.

Corfield, Penelope J. 2007. *Time and the Shape of History*. New Haven: Yale University Press.

Cosmides, Leda and John Tooby. 2002. "Unraveling the Enigma of Human Intelligence: Evolutionary Psychology and the Multimodular Mind." *The Evolution of Intelligence*. Eds. Robert J. Sternberg and James C. Kaufman. Mahwah: Erlbaum, pp. 145-198.

Cosmides, Leda, John Tooby, and Jerome H. Barkow. 1992. "Introduction: Evolutionary Psychology and Conceptual Integration." *The Adapted Mind. Evolutionary Psychology and the Generation of Culture*. Eds. Jerome H. Barkow, Leda Cosmides, and John Tooby. New York: Oxford University Press, pp. 3-15.

Cummins, Denise Dellarosa. 1998. "Social Norms and Other Minds. The Evolutionary Roots of Higher Cognition." *The Evolution of Mind*. Ed. Denise Dellarosa Cummins and Colin Allen. New York: Oxford University Press, pp. 30-50.

Damasio, Antonio R. 1999. *The Feeling of What Happens. Body and Emotion in the Making of Consciousness*. New York: Harcourt Brace.

Damasio, Antonio R. 2002. "How the Brain Creates the Mind." *Scientific American. Special Edition* 12 (1): 4-9.

Dance, Frank E. X. 1985. "The Functions of Human Communication." *Information and Behavior* 1: 62-75.

Danton, J. Periam. 1934. "Plea for a Philosophy of Librarianship." *Library Quarterly* 4 (1934): 527-551.

Darwin, Charles Robert. 1859. *On the Origin of Species by Natural Selection*. London: Murray.

Davidson, Iain and William Noble. 1993. "Tools and Language in Human Evolution." *Tools, Language and Cognition in Human Evolution*. Eds. Kathleen R. Gibson and Tim Ingold. Cambridge: Cambridge University Press, pp. 363-388.

Dawkins, Richard. (1999). *The Extended Phenotype. The Long Reach of the Gene*. Revised edition. Oxford: Oxford University Press.

Dawkins, Richard. 1976. *The Selfish Gene*. Oxford: Oxford University Press.

Debray, Régis. 2000. *Transmitting Culture*. New York: Columbia University Press. (Orig. French 1997)

Deese, James. 1965. *The Structure of Associations in Language and Thought*. Baltimore: Johns Hopkins Press.

Dennett, Daniel C. 1995. *Darwin's Dangerous Idea. Evolution and the Meanings of Life*. New York: Simon & Schuster.

Dennett, Daniel C. 2003. *Freedom Evolves*. New York: Viking.

Dervin, Brenda. 1996. "Given a Context by any Other Name: Methodological Tools for Taming the Unruly Beast." *Information Seeking in Context*. Eds. Pertti Vakkari, Reijo Savolainen, and Brenda Dervin. London: Taylor Graham.

Dewey, Melvil. 1968. "What a Library Can Be and What It Should Do." *The Library and Society*. Ed. Arthur E. Bostwick. Freeport: Books for Libraries, pp. 75-78. (Orig. in *Public Libraries*, 1899)

Ditzion, Sidney H. 1947. *Arsenals of a Democratic Culture*. Chicago: American Library Association.

Dobzhansky, Theodosius. 1968. "Evolution and Behavior." *International Encyclopedia of the Social Sciences*. 19 vols. Ed. David L Sills. New York: Macmillan and Free Press, vol. 5, pp. 235-238.

Dobzhansky, Theodosius. 1962. *Mankind Evolving: The Evolution of the Human Species.* New Haven: Yale University Press.

Dobzhansky, Theodosius. 1964. *Heredity and the Nature of Man.* New Haven: Yale University Press.

Dobzhansky, Theodosius. 1973. "Nothing in Biology Makes Sense Except in the Light of Evolution." *American Biology Teacher* 35: 125–129.

Dobzhansky, Theodosius and Ernest Boisiger. 1983. *Human Culture. A Moment in Evolution.* Ed. Bruce Wallace. New York: Columbia University Press.

Dobzhansky, Theodosius, Francisco J. Ayala, G. Ledyard Stebbins, and James W. Valentine. 1977. *Evolution.* San Francisco: W. H. Freeman.

Donald, Merlin. 2001. *A Mind So Rare. The Evolution of Human Consciousness.* New York: Norton.

Donald, Merlin. 1991. *Origins of the Modern Mind. Three Stages in the Evolution of Culture and Cognition.* Cambridge: Cambridge University Press.

Douglas, Mary. 1986. *How Institutions Think.* Syracuse: Syracuse University Press.

Durkheim, Emile. 1950. *The Rules of Sociological Method.* Chicago: Free Press.

Edgar, Andrew. 2006. *Habermas. The Key Concepts.* London: Routledge.

Edgar, Andrew and Peter Sedgwick. 2002. *Cultural Theory. The Key Thinkers.* London: Routledge.

Edwards, Edward. 1865. *Libraries and Founders of Libraries.* London: Trubner.

Egan, Margaret E. 1951. "Synthesis and Summary." *Bibliographic Organization.* Eds. Jesse H. Shera and Margaret F. Egan. Chicago: University of Chicago Press, pp. 253–265.

Egan, Margaret E. and Jesse H. Shera. 1952. "Foundations of a Theory of Bibliography." *Library Quarterly* 22: 125–137.

Eisenstadt, Shmuel N. 1968. "Social Evolution." *International Encyclopedia of the Social Sciences.* 19 vols. Ed. David L. Sills. New York: Macmillan and Free Press, vol. 5, pp. 228–234.

Eisenstein, Elizabeth L. 1979. *The Printing Press as an Agent of Change. Communications and Cultural Transformations in Early Modern Europe.* 2 vols. Cambridge: Cambridge University Press.

Eisenstein, Elizabeth L. 1983. *The Printing Revolution in Early Modern Europe.* Cambridge: Cambridge University Press.

Faris, Ellsworth. 1937. *The Nature of Human Nature.* New York: McGraw-Hill.

Fernandez de Zamora, Rosa María. 1997. "Mexican Library History: A Survey of the Literature of the Last Fifteen years." *Libraries & Culture* 32: 227–244.

Finney, Ross L. 1928. *A Sociological Philosophy of Education.* New York: Macmillan.

Fleck, Ludwik. 1986. "Crisis in Science." *Cognition and Fact. Materials on Ludwik Fleck.* Eds. Robert S. Cohen and Thomas Schnelle. Dordrecht: D. Reidel, pp. 153–158. (Orig. Polish 1960)

Fleck, Ludwik. 1986. "The Problem of Epistemology." *Cognition and Fact. Materials on Ludwik Fleck.* Eds. Robert S. Cohen and Thomas Schnelle. Dordrecht: D. Reidel, pp. 79–112. (Orig. Polish 1936)

Fleck, Ludwik. 1986. "Problems of the Science of Science." *Cognition and Fact. Materials on Ludwik Fleck.* Eds. Robert S. Cohen and Thomas Schnelle. Dordrecht: D. Reidel, pp. 113–127. (Orig. Polish 1946)

Fleck, Ludwik. 1986. "To Look, to See, to Know." *Cognition and Fact. Materials on Ludwik Fleck*. Eds. Robert S. Cohen and Thomas Schnelle. Dordrecht: D. Reidel, pp. 129–151. (Orig. Polish 1947)

Fleming-May, Rachel Anne. 2008. "Use" in the Literature of Library and Information Science: A Concept Analysis and Typology. PhD diss., University of Alabama.

Floridi, Luciano. 2003. "The Renaissance of Epistemology." *The Cambridge History of Philosophy: 1870–1945*. Ed. T. Baldwin. Cambridge: Cambridge University Press, pp. 531–541.

Foskett, D. J. 1964. *Science, Humanism and Libraries*. New York: Hafner.

Foskett, D. J. 1962. *The Creed of a Librarian-No politics, No Religion, No Morals*. London: Library Association.

Foskett, D. J. 1984. *Pathways for Communication. Books and Libraries in the Information Age*. London: Clive Bingley.

Freedman, Lawrence Zelic and Anne Roe. 1958. "Evolution and Human Behavior." *Behavior and Evolution*. Eds. Anne Roe and George Gaylord Simpson. New Haven: Yale University Press, pp. 455–479.

Freeman, Geoffrey T. 2005. "The Library as Place: Changes in Learning Patterns, Collections, Technology, and Use." *Library as Place: Rethinking Roles, Rethinking Space*. Ed. K. Smith. Washington, D.C.: Council on Library and Information Resources, pp. 1–9.

Freire, Paulo and Donaldo Macedo. 1987. *Literacy. Reading the Word & the World*. South Hadley: Bergin & Garvey.

Frohmann, Bernd. 2004. *Deflating Information. From Science Studies to Documentation*. Toronto: University of Toronto Press.

Fuller, Steve. 1988. *Social Epistemology*. Bloomington: Indiana University Press.

Furner, Jonathan. 2004. "'A Brilliant Mind': Margaret Egan and Social Epistemology." *Library Trends* 52: 792–809.

Fussler, Herman H. 1967. "The Research Library in Transition" *The Library in the University*. Ed. William H. Jesse. Hamden: Shoe String Press, pp. 120–148.

Garceau, Oliver. 1949. *The Public Library in the Political Process*. New York: Columbia University Press. (A Report of the Public Library Inquiry)

Gardner, Howard. 1983. *Frames of Mind. The Theory of Multiple Intelligences*. New York: Basic Books.

Gardner, Howard. 1985. *The Mind's New Science. A History of the Cognitive Revolution*. New York: Basic Books.

Garvey, William D. 1979. *Communication, the Essence of Science*. New York: Pergamon Press.

Gee, James Paul. 1992. *The Social Mind. Language, Ideology, and Social Practice*. New York: Bergin & Garvey.

Gibson Kathleen R. 1993. "Tool Use, Language and Social Behavior in Relationship to Information Processing Capacities." *Tools, Language and Cognition in Human Evolution*. Eds. Kathleen R. Gibson and Tim Ingold. Cambridge: Cambridge University Press, pp. 251–269.

Giddings, F. H. 1924. *The Scientific Study of Human Society*. Chapel Hill: University of North Carolina Press.

Ginsberg, Morris. 1961. "A Humanist view of Progress." *The Humanist Frame*. Ed. Julian Huxley. New York: Harper, pp. 113–128.

Ginsberg, Morris. 1972. *The Idea of Progress. A Revaluation*. Westport: Greenwood Press.

Glass, Bentley. 1943. *Genes and the Man*. New York: Teachers College, Columbia University.

Glass, Bentley. 1985. *Progress or Catastrophe. The Nature of Biological Science and Its Impact on Human Society*. New York: Praeger.

Glass, Bentley. 1970. *The Timely and the Timeless: The Interrelationships of Science, Education and Society*. New York: Basic Books.

Gleick, James. 1988. *Chaos. Making a New Science*. New York: Penguin.

Goldenweiser, Alexander. 1931. "Evolution, Social." *Encyclopedia of the Social Sciences*. 15 vols. Eds. Edwin R. Seligman and Alvin Johnson. New York: Macmillan, vol. 15, pp. 656–662.

Goldman, Alvin I. 1999. *Knowledge in a Social World*. Oxford: Clarendon Press.

Goode, William J. 1961. "The Librarian: From Occupation to Profession?" *Library Quarterly* 31 (1961): 306–320.

Goody, Jack. 2000. *The Power of the Written Tradition*. Washington, D.C.: Smithsonian Institution Press.

Goody, Jack and Ian Watt. 1988. "The Consequences of Literacy." *Perspectives on Literacy*. Eds. Eugene R. Kintgen, Barry M. Kroll, and Mike Rose. Carbondale: Southern Illinois University Press. (Orig. 1968)

Gopinath, M. A. 2003. "Ranganathan, Shiyali Ramamrita." *Encyclopedia of Library and Information Science*. Second edition. Ed. Miriam A Drake. New York: Marcel Dekker, vol. 4, pp. 2419–2437. (Orig. 1978 ed., vol. 25)

Graham, John T. 2001. *The Social Thought of Ortega y Gasset*. Columbia: University of Missouri Press.

Halbwachs, Maurice. 1980. *Collective Memory*. New York: Harper & Row. (Orig. French, 1950)

Harris, Michael H. 1973. "The Purpose of the American Public Library: A Revisionist Interpretation." *Library Journal* 98: 2509–2514.

Harris, Michael H. 1986. "State, Class and Cultural Reproduction: Toward a Theory of Library Service in the United States." *Advances in Librarianship* 14: 211–252.

Harris, Michael H. and Masaru Itoga. 1991. "Becoming Critical: For a Theory of Purpose and Necessity in American Librarianship." *Library and Information Science Research: Perspectives and Strategies for Improvement*. Eds. Charles R. McClure and Peter Hernon. Norwood: Ablex Publishing, pp. 347–357.

Hart, Donna and Robert W. Sussman. 2005. *Man the Hunted. Primates, Predators, and Human Evolution*. New York: Westview Press.

Hayles, N. Katherine. 1990. *Chaos Bound: Orderly Disorder in Contemporary Literature and Science*. Ithaca: Cornell University Press.

Hayles, N. Katherine. 1991. "Introduction: Complex Dynamics in Literature and Science." *Chaos and Order. Complex Dynamics in Literature and Science*. Ed. N. Katherine Hayles. Chicago: University of Chicago Press, pp. 1–33.

Heisenberg, Werner. 1958. *Physics and Philosophy. The Revolution in Modern Science*. New York: Harper.

Hempel, Carl G. 1965. *Aspects of Scientific Explanation and Other Essays in the Philosophy of Science*. New York: Free Press, pp. 231–243. (This chapter is an altered version of "The Function of General Laws in History." *Journal of Philosophy* 39 (1942): 35–48)
Henderson, Lawrence J. 1924. *The Fitness of the Environment. An Inquiry into the Biological Significance of the Properties of Matter*. New York: Macmillan.
Henderson, Lawrence J. 1917. *The Order of Nature: An Essay*. Cambridge: Harvard University Press.
Henderson, Sheila J. 2004. "Inventors: the Ordinary Genius Next Door." *Creativity. From Potential to Realization*. Eds. Robert J. Sternberg, Elena L. Grigorenko, and Jerome L. Singer. Washington, D.C.: American Psychological Association, pp. 103–125.
Henry, William E. 1967. *My Own Opinions upon Libraries and Librarianship*. Freeport: Books for Libraries, pp. 75–89. (A lecture given in 1916 and first published in 1931)
Herrick, C. Judson. 1956. *The Evolution of Human Nature*. Austin: University of Texas Press.
Hertzler, Joyce O. 1946. *Social Institutions*. Lincoln: University of Nebraska Press.
Hobsbawm, Eric. 1983. "Introduction: Inventing Traditions." *The Invention of Tradition*. Eds. Eric Hobsbawm and Terence Ranger. Cambridge: Cambridge University Press, pp. 1–14.
Hoelle, John Lewis von. 2001. "Preface." *The Memory of Mankind*. Don Heinrich Tolzmann, Alfred Hessel and Reuben Peiss. Wilmington: Oak Knoll Press.
Hollick, Malcolm. 2006. *The Science of Oneness. A Worldview for the Twenty-first Century*. New York: O Books.
Hudson, Liam. 2004. "Creativity." *Oxford Companion to the Mind*. Second edition. Ed. Richard L. Gregory. Oxford: Oxford University Press, pp. 225–226.
Hughes, Thomas P. 2004. *Human-Built World. How to Think about Technology and Culture*. Chicago: University of Chicago Press.
Hume, David. 2007. *An Enquiry Concerning Human Understanding*. Ed. Peter Millican. Oxford: Oxford University Press.
Humphrey, Nicholas. 1992. *A History of the Mind. Evolution and the Birth of Consciousness*. London: Chatto & Windus.
Huxley, Julian S. 1958. "Cultural Process and Evolution." *Behavior and Evolution*. Eds. Anne Roe and George Gaylord Simpson. New Haven: Yale University Press, pp. 437–454.
Ingold, Tim. 2002. "Between Evolution and History: Biology, Culture, and the Myth of Human Origins." *The Evolution of Cultural Entities*. Eds. Michael Wheeler, John Ziman, and Margaret A. Boden. Oxford: Oxford University Press, pp. 43–66.
Ingold, Tim. 1993a. "Tool-Use, Sociality and Intelligence." *Tools, Language and Cognition in Human Evolution*. Eds. Kathleen R. Gibson and Tim Ingold. Cambridge: Cambridge University Press, pp. 429–445.
Ingold, Tim. 1993b. "Epilogue: Technology, Language, Intelligence: A Reconsideration of Basic Concepts." *Tools, Language and Cognition in Human Evolution*. Eds. Kathleen R. Gibson and Tim Ingold. Cambridge: Cambridge University Press, pp. 449–472.
Irwin, Raymond. 1949. *Librarianship. Essays in Applied Bibliography*. London: Grafton.
Irwin, Raymond. 1964. *The Heritage of the English Library*. London: Allen & Unwin.
Iser, Wolfgang. 1974. *The Implied Reader*. Baltimore: Johns Hopkins University Press.

Jacob, François. 1982. *The Possible and the Actual*. Seattle: University of Washington Press.

Janelle, Donald G. and David C. Hodge. 2000. "Information, Place, Cyberspace, and Accessibility." *Information, Place, and Cyberspace. Issues in Accessibility*. Eds. Donald G. Janelle and David C. Hodge. Berlin: Springer, pp. 3–11.

Janet, Pierre. 1928. *L'Evolution de la mémoire et de la notion du temps*. Paris: Chahine.

Jarvie, I. C. 1996. "Philosophy of the Social Sciences." *The Social Science Encyclopedia*. Second edition. Eds. Adam Kuper and Jessica Kuper. London: Routledge, pp. 604–609.

Johnson, Alvin. 1938. *The Public Library: A People's University*. New York: American Association for Adult Education.

Johnson, Gerald W. 1978. "The Role of the Public Library." *Public Library Purpose. A Reader*. Ed. Barry Totterdell. London: Clive Bingley, pp. 65–70.

Johnson, Mark. 2007. *The Meaning of the Body. Aesthetics of Human Understanding*. Chicago: University of Chicago Press.

Jones, K. H. 1978. "Towards a Re-interpretation of Public Library Purpose." *Public Library Purpose. A Reader*. Ed. Barry Totterdell. London: Clive Bingley, pp. 122–135.

Jones, Malcolm. 2007. "No Place Like Rome. Virgil's Aeneid and HBO's Lurid series about the Caesars Couldn't Be More Different—and More Alike." *Newsweek* (January 22): 66.

Jones, W. T. 1972. "World Views: Their Nature and their Function." *Current Anthropology* 13 (February): 79–109.

Kaltenbach, Margaret. 1980. "Shera, Jesse H." *World Encyclopedia of Library and Information Services*. Chicago: American Library Association, pp. 524–526.

Kaplan, Abraham. 1964. "The Age of the Symbol—A Philosophy of Library Education." *Library Quarterly* 34 (October): 295–304.

Kaplan, Abraham. 1964. *The Conduct of Inquiry*. San Francisco: Chandler.

Kaplan, David. 1970. "The Law of Cultural Dominance." *Evolution and Culture*. Eds. Marshall D. Sahlins and Elman R. Service. Ann Arbor: University of Michigan Press, pp. 69–92.

Kaplan, Stephen. 1992. "Environmental Preference in a Knowledge-Seeking, Knowledge-Using Organism." *The Adapted Mind. Evolutionary Psychology and the Generation of Culture*. Eds. Jerome H. Barkow, Leda Cosmides, and John Tooby. New York: Oxford University Press, pp. 581–598.

Kauffman, Stuart A. 1993. *The Origins of Order. Self-Organization and Selection in Evolution*. New York: Oxford University Press.

Kelso, J. A. Scott and David A. Engstrom. 2006. *The Complementary Nature*. Cambridge: MIT Press.

Keuth, Herbert. 2005. *The Philosophy of Karl Popper*. Cambridge: Cambridge University Press. (Orig. German 2000)

Kluckhohn, Clyde. 1953. "Universal Categories of Culture." *Anthropology Today*. Ed. A. L. Kroeber. Chicago: University of Chicago Press, pp. 507–523.

Kluckhohn, Clyde and William H. Kelly. 1945. "The Concept of Culture." *The Science of Man in the World Crisis*. Ed. Ralph Linton. New York: Columbia University Press, pp. 78–106.

Kolitsch, Myra. 1945. "Toward a Philosophy of Librarianship." *Library Quarterly* 15 (January): 25–31.

Koselleck, Reinhart. 2002. *The Practice of Conceptual History: Timing History, Spacing Concepts.* Stanford: Stanford University Press.

Kothari, D. S. 1975. *Some Thoughts on Truth.* New Delhi: Anniversary Address, Indian National Science Academy.

Kroeber, A. L. and Clyde Kluckhohn. 1952. *Culture. A Critical Review of Concepts and Definitions.* Cambridge, MA: Peabody Museum.

Kunda, Ziva. 1999. *Social Cognition. Making Sense of People.* Cambridge: MIT Press, p. 16.

Kuper, Adam. 2002. "Culture." *The Evolution of Cultural Entities.* Eds. Michael Wheeler, John Ziman, and Margaret A. Boden. Oxford: Oxford University Press, pp. 87–102.

Kuper, Adam. 1994. *The Chosen Primate. Human Nature and Cultural Diversity.* Cambridge: Harvard University Press.

Laland, Kevin N. and Gillian R. Brown. 2002. *Sense and Nonsense. Evolutionary Perspectives on Human Behaviour.* Oxford: Oxford University Press.

Landheer, Bartholomeus. 1952. *Mind and Society: Epistemological Essays on Sociology.* The Hague: Nijhoff.

Landheer, Bartholomeus. 1973. "The Library in Different Culture-Stages." *Reader in Library and Information Services.* Ed. Michael M. Reynolds. Englewood: Microcard Editions Books, pp. 59–78. (Orig. chapter 9 of his *Social Functions of Libraries.* New York: Scarecrow, 1957, pp. 152–170)

Laudan, Rachel. 2003. "Philosophy and Science." *The Oxford Companion to the History of Modern Science.* Ed. J. L. Heilbron. Oxford: Oxford University Press, pp. 632–634.

Learned, William S. 1924. *The American Public Library and the Diffusion of Knowledge.* New York: Harcourt, Brace.

Leigh, Robert D. 1950. *The Public Library in the United States.* New York: Columbia University Press.

Leigh, Robert D. 1957. "Changing Concepts of the Public Library's Role." *Library Quarterly* 17: 223–234.

Leroi-Gourhan, André. 1993. *Gesture and Speech.* Cambridge: MIT Press. (Orig. French 1964).

Lessnoff, Michael H. 1975. *The Structure of Social Science. A Philosophical Introduction.* New York: International Publications Service.

Levy, David M. 1979. "Communicative Goals and Strategies: Between Discourse and Syntax." *Syntax and Semantics: Discourse and Syntax.* Ed. Talmy Givon. New York: Academic Press, pp. 183–210.

Levy, David M. 2006. "The Place of Libraries in a Digital Age." *Digital Library Development.* Eds. Deanna B. Marcum and G. George. Westport: Libraries Unlimited, pp. 243–252.

Lévy-Bruhl, Lucien. 1923. *Primitive Mentality.* London: Allen & Unwin. (Orig. French 1922)

Line, Maurice B. 1965. "Ends and Means: Librarianship as a Social Science." *Library World* 66 (May): 270–275.

Linton, Ralph. 1947. *The Cultural Background of Personality.* London: Routledge & Kegan Paul.

Loasby, Brian J. 2002. "The Evolution of Technological Knowledge: Reflections on *Technological Innovation as an Evolutionary Process.*" *The Evolution of Cultural Entities.*

Eds. Michael Wheeler, John Ziman, and Margaret A. Boden. Oxford: Oxford University Press, pp. 145–159.

Lovejoy, Arthur O. 1936. *The Great Chain of Being. A Study of the History of an Idea.* Cambridge: Harvard University Press.

Lowes, John Livingston. 1933. "Teaching and the Spirit of Research." *American Scholar* 2: 28–38.

Loye, David. 1998. "Evolutionary Action Theory: a Brief Outline." *The Evolutionary Outrider. The Impact of the Human Agent on Evolution. Essays Honouring Ervin Laszlo.* Ed. David Loye. Westport: Praeger, pp. 167–189.

Luckham, Bryan. 1971. *The Library in Society.* London: Library Association.

Lutwack, Leonard. 1984. *The Role of Place in Literature.* Syracuse: Syracuse University Press.

MacDougall, Robert. 1912. "The Social Basis of Individuality." *American Journal of Sociology* 18 (July): 1–20.

MacKenzie, Donald A. and Judy Wajcman. 1985. "Introductory Essay: The Social Shaping of Technology." *The Social Shaping of Technology. How the Refrigerator Got its Hum.* Eds. Donald MacKenzie and Judy Wajcman. Philadelphia: Open University Press, pp. 2–25.

Malinowski, Bronislaw. 1930–1935. "Culture." *Encyclopedia of the Social Sciences.* 15 vols. Eds. Edwin R. Seligman and Alvin Johnson. New York: Macmillan, vol. 4, pp. 621–646.

Malinowski, Bronislaw. 1944. *A Scientific Theory of Culture.* Chapel Hill: University of North Carolina Press.

Martin, Lowell. 1937. "The American Public Library as a Social Institution." *Library Quarterly* 7: 546–563.

Mayhew, Leon H. 1968–1979. "Society." *International Encyclopedia of the Social Sciences.* 18 vols. Ed. David L. Sills. New York: Macmillan, vol. 14, pp. 577–586.

McClellan, A. W. 1973. "The Purpose of Libraries." *The Reader, the Library and the Book.* London: Clive Bingley, pp. 124–135.

McColvin, Lionel R. 1978. "The Purposes and Values of a Library Service." *Public Library Purpose. A Reader.* Ed. Barry Totterdell. London: Clive Bingley, pp. 33–37.

McCook, K. P. 2001. "Social Justice, Personalism and the Practice of Librarianship." *Catholic Library World* 72: 80–84.

McCrimmon, Barbara. 1994. "Philosophies of Librarianship." *Encyclopedia of Library History.* Eds. Wayne A. Wiegand and Donald G. Davis, Jr. New York: Garland, pp. 494–498.

McCrimmon, Barbara. 1975. *American Library Philosophy: An Anthology.* Hamden: Shoestring Press.

McGarry, Kevin. 1993. *The Changing Context of Information.* Second edition. London: Library Association.

McGrath, William E. 2002. "Explanation and Prediction: Building a Unified Theory of Librarianship, Concept and Review." *Library Trends* 50: 350–370.

Mead, Margaret. 1949. "Character Formation and Diachronic Theory." *Social Structure. Studies Presented to A. R. Radcliffe-Brown.* Ed. Meyer Fortes. Oxford: Clarendon Press, pp. 18–34.

Mead, Margaret. 1928. *Coming of Age in Samoa. A Psychological Study of Primitive Youth for Western Civilization.* New York: Morrow.

Mead, Margaret. 1958. "Cultural Determinants of Behavior." *Behavior and Evolution*. Eds. Anne Roe and George Gaylord Simpson. New Haven: Yale University Press, pp. 480–503.

Medawar, Peter B. 1969. *Induction and Intuition in Scientific Thought*. Philadelphia: American Philosophical Society.

Medawar, Peter B. and Jean S. Medawar. 1977. *The Life Science. Current Ideas of Biology*. New York: Harper & Row.

Meijer, J. G. 1982. *Librarianship: A Definition*. Urbana: University of Illinois, Graduate School of Library and Information Science Occasional Papers No. 155 (September).

Meredith, Patrick. 1961. "The Frame of Humanist Communication." *The Humanist Frame*. Ed. Julian Huxley. New York: Harper, pp. 253–265.

Midgley, Mary. 2002. "Choosing the Selectors." *The Evolution of Cultural Entities*. Eds. Michael Wheeler, John Ziman, and Margaret A. Boden. Oxford: Oxford University Press, pp. 119–133.

Mithen, Steven. 1996. *The Prehistory of the Mind. The Cognitive Origins of Art, Religion and Science*. London: Thames and Hudson.

Mukherjee, Ajit Kumar. 1966. *Librarianship: Its Philosophy and History*. New York: Asia Publishing House.

Munford, W. A. 1963. *Edward Edwards 1812–1886: Portrait of a Librarian*. London: Library Association.

Munz, Peter. 1985. *Our Knowledge of the Growth of Knowledge. Popper or Wittgenstein?* London: Routledge & Kegan Paul.

Murdock, George P. 1945. "The Common Denominator of Cultures." *The Science of Man in the World Crisis*. Ed. Ralph Linton. New York: Columbia University Press, pp. 123–142.

National Advisory Commission on Libraries. 1969. "Library Services for the Nation's Needs: Toward Fulfillment of a National Policy." *ALA Bulletin* 63 (January): 67–94.

Naudé, Gabriel. 1950. *Advice on Establishing a Library. With an Introduction by Archer Taylor*. Berkeley: University of California Press. (Orig. French 1627)

Nisbet, Robert. 1980. *History of the Idea of Progress*. New York: Basic Books.

Nisbet, Robert. 1969. *Social Change and History. Aspects of the Western Theory of Development*. New York: Oxford University Press.

Nitecki, Joseph Z. 1998. "Conceptual Aspects of Bibliothecal Communication: Philosophical legacy of Twentieth Century American Librarianship." *Public Library Quarterly* 17: 27–36.

Nitecki, Joseph Z. 1981. "Idea of Librarianship: An Outline for a Root-Metaphor Theory in Library Science." *Journal of Library History, Philosophy, and Comparative Librarianship* 16 (Winter): 106–120.

Nitecki, Joseph Z. 1995. *Philosophical Aspects of Library Information Science in Retrospect*. (ERIC, ED 381 162, IR 055 446)

Nitecki, Joseph Z. 1964. "Public Interest and the Theory of Librarianship." *College and Research Libraries* 25: 269–278, 325.

Orr, J. M. 1977. *Libraries as Communication Systems*. Westport: Greenwood.

Ortega y Gasset, José. 1961. "The Mission of the Librarian." *Antioch Review* 21: 133–154. (Lecture given in Paris, 1934)

Osburn, Charles B. 2007. "Regaining Place." *Advances in Library Administration and Organization* 24: 55–93.

Palumbi, Sephen R. 2004. "Humans as the World's Greatest Evolutionary Force." *Evolution*. Second edition. Ed. Mark Ridley. Oxford: Oxford University Press, pp. 421-433.

Parsons, Talcott. 1978. *Action Theory and the Human Condition*. New York: Free Press.

Parsons, Talcott. 1949. *The Structure of Social Action*. Second edition. Glencoe: Free Press. (First edition 1937)

Petrunkevitch, Alexander. 1924. "Environment as a Stabilizing Factor." *Organic Adaptation to Environment*. Ed. M. R. Thorpe. New Haven: Yale University Press, pp. 76-77.

Pfenninger, Karl H. 2001. "The Evolving Brain." *The Origins of Creativity*. Eds. Karl H. Pfenninger and Valerie R. Shubik. Oxford: Oxford University Press, pp. 89-97.

Pfenninger, Karl H. and Valerie R. Shubik. 2001. "Insights into the Foundations of Creativity: A Synthesis." *The Origins of Creativity*. Eds. Karl H. Pfenninger and Valerie R. Shubik. Oxford: Oxford University Press, pp. 213-236.

Pinker, Steven and Paul Bloom. 1992. "Natural Language and Natural Selection." *The Adapted Mind. Evolutionary Psychology and the Generation of Culture*. New York: Oxford University Press, pp. 451-493.

Pittendrigh, Colin S. 1958. "Adaptation, Natural Selection, and Behavior." *Behavior and Evolution*. Eds. Anne Roe and George Gaylord Simpson. New Haven: Yale University Press, pp. 390-419.

Plotkin, Henry. 2004. *Evolutionary Thought in Psychology. A Brief History*. Oxford: Blackwell.

Plotkin, Henry. 2002. "Learning from Culture." *The Evolution of Cultural Entities*. Eds. Michael Wheeler, John Ziman, and Margaret A. Boden. Oxford: Oxford University Press, pp. 103-118.

Plotkin, Henry. 1998. *Evolution in Mind. An Introduction to Evolutionary Psychology*. Cambridge: Harvard University Press.

Polanyi, Michael. 1951. *The Logic of Liberty. Reflections and Rejoinders*. Chicago: University of Chicago Press.

Polanyi, Michael. 1958. *Personal Knowledge. Towards a Post-Critical Philosophy*. Chicago: University of Chicago Press.

Polanyi, Michael. 1964. "Science and Man's Place in the Universe." *Science as a Cultural Force*. Ed. Harry Woolf. Baltimore: The Johns Hopkins Press, pp. 54-76.

Polanyi, Michael. 1959. *The Study of Man*. Chicago: University of Chicago Press.

Polanyi, Michael. 1966. *The Tacit Dimension*. Garden City: Doubleday.

Popper, Karl R. 1999. *All Life is Problem Solving*. London: Routledge.

Popper, Karl R. 1963. *Conjectures and Refutations: The Growth of Scientific Knowledge*. New York: Harper & Row.

Popper, Karl R. 1959. *The Logic of Scientific Discovery*. New York: Basic Books. (Original German 1935)

Popper, Karl R. 1972. *Objective Knowledge. An Evolutionary Approach*. Oxford: Clarendon Press.

Popper, Karl R. and John C. Eccles. 1977. *The Self and Its Brain*. Berlin: Springer.

Prigogine, Ilya and Isabelle Stengers. 1984. *Order Out of Chaos. Man's New Dialogue with Nature*. New York: Bantam. (Original French, *La nouvelle alliance*, 1979)

Proshansky, H. M., A. K. Fabian, and R. Kaminoff. 1983. "Place Identity: Physical World Socialization of the Self." *Journal of Environmental Psychology* 3: 57-83.

Purcell-Gates, Victoria, Erik Jacobson, and Sophie Degener. 2004. *Print Literacy Development. Uniting Cognitive and Social Practice Theories*. Cambridge: Harvard University Press.

Radcliffe-Brown, Alfred Reginald. 1948. *A Natural Science of Society*. Chicago: University of Chicago Press.

Randall, John Herman, Jr. 1940. *The Making of the Modern Mind*. Revised edition. Cambridge: Houghton Mifflin.

Ranganathan, Shiyali Ramamrita. 1931. *The Five Laws of Library Science*. Madras: Madras Library Association.

Redfield, Robert. 1962. *Human Nature and the Study of Society*. Chicago: University of Chicago Press.

Relf, Edward. C. 1976. *Place and Placelessness*. London: Pion.

Richards, Robert J. 1987. *Darwin and the Emergence of Evolutionary Theories of Mind and Behavior*. Chicago: University of Chicago Press.

Richardson, John V., Jr. 1992. *The Gospel of Scholarship: Pierce Butler and a Critique of American Librarianship*. Metuchen: Scarecrow Press.

Roberts, Norman. 1982. "A Search for Information Man." *Social Science Information Studies* 2: 93–104.

Roberts, Norman. 1976. "Social Considerations towards a Definition of Information Science." *Journal of Documentation* 32: 249–257.

Robson, Ann. 1976. "The Intellectual Background of the Public Library Movement in Britain." *Journal of Library History* 11: 187–205.

Rogers, A. Robert. 1984. "An Introduction to Philosophies of Librarianship." *The Library in Society*. Eds. A. Robert Rogers and Kathryn McChesney. Littleton: Libraries Unlimited, pp. 17–32.

Rogers, Everett M. and F. Floyd Shoemaker. 1971. *Communication of Innovations. A Cross-Cultural Approach*. Second edition. New York: Free Press.

Rosenberg, Charles. 1979. "Toward an Ecology of Knowledge: On Discipline, Context, and History." *The Organization of Knowledge in Modern America, 1860–1920*. Eds. Alexandra Oleson and John Voss. Baltimore: Johns Hopkins University Press, pp. 440–455.

Roth, Ilona. 2004. "Imagination." *Oxford Companion to the Mind*. Second edition. Ed. Richard L. Gregory. Oxford: Oxford University Press, pp. 443–447.

Rousseau, Jérôme. 2006. *Rethinking Social Evolution. The Perspective from Middle-Range Societies*. Montreal: McGill-Queen's University Press.

Ruben, David-Hillel. 1998. "Social Sciences, Philosophy of." *Routledge Encyclopedia of Philosophy*. London: Routledge, vol. 8, pp. 868–871.

Runciman, Walter G. 2002. "Heritable Variation and Competitive Selection as the Mechanism of Sociocultural Evolution." *The Evolution of Cultural Entities*. Eds. Michael Wheeler, John Ziman, and Margaret A. Boden. Oxford: Oxford University Press, pp. 9–25.

Ruse, Michael. 2005. *The Evolution-Creation Struggle*. Cambridge: Harvard University Press.

Russell, Bertrand. 1917. Why Men Fight. A Method of Abolishing the International Duel. New York: The Century Co.

Ryle, Gilbert. 1949. *The Concept of Mind*. Chicago: University of Chicago Press.

Ryle, Gilbert. 1979. *On Thinking*. Totowa: Rowman and Littlefield.

Saenger, Paul. 1997. *Space Between Words. The Origins of Silent Reading.* Stanford: Stanford University Press.
Sahlins, Marshall D. 1970. "Evolution: Specific and General." *Evolution and Culture.* Eds. Marshall D. Sahlins and Elman R. Service. Ann Arbor: University of Michigan Press, pp. 12–44.
Sanderson, Stephen K. 2001. *The Evolution of Human Sociality. A Darwinian Conflict Perspective.* Boston: Rowman & Littlefield.
Sapir, Edward. 1931. "Communication." *Encyclopedia of the Social Sciences.* 15 vols. Eds. Edwin R. A. Seligman and Alvin Johnson. New York: Macmillan, vol. 4, pp. 78–81.
Sapir, Edward. 1921. *Language.* New York: Harcourt, Brace.
Satija, Mohinder Partap. 1986. "Five Laws: The Theory and Philosophy of Library and Information Science." *Ranganathan's Philosophy. Assessment, Impact and Relevance.* Ed. T.S. Rajagopalan. New Delhi: Vikas Publishing House, pp. 85–94.
Savage-Rumbaugh, E. Sue and Duane M. Rumbaugh. 1993. "The Emergence of Language." *Tools, Language and Cognition in Human Evolution.* Eds. by Kathleen R. Gibson and Tim Ingold. Cambridge: Cambridge University Press, pp. 86–108.
Scheff, Thomas J. 2006. *Goffman Unbound! A New Paradigm for Social Science.* Boulder: Paradigm.
Schramm, Wilbur. 1971. "The Nature of Communication between Humans." *The Process and Effects of Mass Communication.* Revised edition. Eds. Wilbur Schramm and Donald F. Roberts. Urbana: University of Illinois Press, pp. 3–53.
Schulte-Albert, Hans G. 1971. "Gottfried Wilhelm Leibniz and Library Classification." *Journal of Library History* 6: 133–152.
Scriven, Michael. 1968. "The Philosophy of Science." *International Encyclopedia of the Social Sciences.* 18 vols. Ed. David L. Sills. New York: Macmillan and Free Press, vol. 14, pp. 83–92.
Searle, John R. 2007. *Freedom and Neurobiology. Reflections on Free Will, Language, and Political Power.* New York: Columbia University Press. (Orig. French 2004)
Searle, John R. 1983. *Intentionality. An Essay in the Philosophy of Mind.* Cambridge: Cambridge University Press.
Searle, John R. 1995. *The Construction of Social Reality.* New York: Free Press.
Searle, John R. 2004. *Mind. A Brief Introduction.* New York: Oxford University Press.
Sellars, Roy Wood. 1926. "Introduction." *The Evolution of Values.* By Célestin Bouglé. Eds. Helen Stalker Sellars and Roy Wood Sellars. New York: Holt, pp. v–xxxvii.
Sellars, Wilfrid. 1963. *Science, Perception and Reality.* New York: Humanities Press.
Service, Elman R. 1968–1979. "Cultural Evolution." *International Encyclopedia of the Social Sciences.* 18 vols. Ed. David L. Sills. New York: Macmillan, vol. 5, pp. 221–228.
Shennan, Stephen. 2002. *Genes, Memes and Human History. Darwinian Archaeology and Cultural Evolution.* London: Thames & Hudson.
Shera, Jesse H. 1980a. "Butler, Pierce." *ALA World Encyclopedia of Library and Information Services.* Chicago: American Library Association, pp. 105–106.
Shera, Jesse H. 1980b. "Librarianship, Philosophy of." *ALA World Encyclopedia of Library and Information Services.* Chicago: American Library Association, pp. 314–317.
Shera, Jesse H. 1973. "Foundations of a Theory of Reference Service." *Knowing Books and Men; Knowing Computers, Too.* Littleton: Libraries Unlimited, pp. 196–206. (Orig. *Texas Library Journal*, 1966)

Shera, Jesse H. 1972. *The Foundations of Education for Librarianship*. New York: Becker and Hayes.

Shera, Jesse H. 1976. *Introduction to Library Science*. Littleton: Libraries Unlimited.

Shera, Jesse H. 1973. "Librarians against Machines." *Knowing Books and Men; Knowing Computer, Too*. Littleton: Libraries Unlimited, pp. 257–268. (Orig. *Wilson Library Bulletin*, 1967)

Shera, Jesse H. 1963. "Diagnosis: Formulate a Professional Philosophy." *Library Journal* 88 (January 1): 50.

Shera, Jesse H. 1979. "Education for Librarianship—An Assessment and a Perspective: A Review Article." *Library Quarterly* 49: 310–316.

Shera, Jesse H. 1970. *Sociological Foundations of Librarianship*. Bombay: Asia Publishing House.

Shera, Jesse H. 1965. *Libraries and the Organization of Knowledge*. Hamden: Archon Books.

Shera, Jesse H. 1973. "Toward a Theory of Librarianship and Information Science." *Knowing Books and Men: Knowing Computers, Too*. Littleton: Libraries Unlimited, pp. 93–110.

Shera, Jesse H. 1972. "The Neglected Search for a Philosophy." *The Foundations of Education for Librarianship*. New York: Wiley-Becker and Hayes, pp. 348–358.

Shera, Jesse H. 1949. *Foundations of the Public Library*. Chicago: University of Chicago Press.

Shera, Jesse H. 1971. "On the Importance of Theory." *The Compleat Librarian and Other Essays*. Cleveland: The Press of Case Western University, pp. 151–153. (Orig. *Wilson Library Bulletin*, Oct. 1968)

Shera, Jesse H. 1966. *Documentation and the Organization of Knowledge*. Hamden: Archon Books.

Shera, Jesse H. 1975. "What Is Librarianship?" *American Library Philosophy. An Anthology*. Ed. Barbara McCrimmon. Hamden: Shoe String Press, pp. 165–171. (Orig. 1961)

Shera, Jesse H. 1971. "The Compleat Librarian." *The Compleat Librarian*. Cleveland: Case Western University, pp. 56–59. (Orig. *Wilson Library Bulletin*, June, 1964)

Shera, Jesse H. 1971. "The Quiet Stir of Thought." *The Compleat Librarian*. Cleveland: Case Western Reserve University, pp. 167–183. (Orig. *Library Journal* Sept 1, 1969)

Sherman, Clarence E. 1939. "The Definition of Library Objectives." *Current Issues in Library Administration*. Ed. Carleton B. Joeckel. Chicago: University of Chicago Press, pp. 22–46.

Sherwin, Susan and Peter Schotch, eds. 2007. *Engaged Philosophy. Essays in Honour of David Braybrooke*. Toronto: University of Toronto Press.

Shotter, John. 1990. "The Social Construction of Remembering and Forgetting." *Collective Remembering*. Eds. David Middleton and Derek Edwards. London: Sage, pp. 120–138.

Simon, Herbert A. and Pat Langley. 1989. "The Central Role of Learning in Cognition." *Models of Thought*. New Haven: Yale University Press, vol. 2, pp. 102–115. (Orig. 1981)

Simon, Herbert A. 1996. *The Sciences of the Artificial*. Third edition. Cambridge: MIT Press.

Singer, Milton. 1968. "The Concept of Culture." *International Encyclopedia of the Social Sciences*. 18 vols. Ed. David L. Sills. New York: Macmillan, vol. 3, pp. 527–543.

Skinner, B. F. 1969. *Contingencies of Reinforcement. A Theoretical Analysis*. Englewood Cliffs: Prentice-Hall.

Skinner, B. F. 1965. "Is a Science of Human Behavior Possible"? *Philosophical Problems of the Social Sciences*. Ed. David Braybrooke. New York: Macmillan, pp. 19–26.

Smith, Edward E. and Douglas L. Medin. 1981. *Categories and Concepts*. Cambridge: Harvard University Press.

Snooks, Graeme Donald. 2007. *The Selfcreating Mind*. Lanham: University Press of America.

Sorokin, Pitirim A. 1948. *The Reconstruction of Humanity*. Boston: Beacon Press.

Sorokin, Pitirum A. 1927. "A Survey of the Cyclical Conceptions of Social and Historical Process." *Social Forces* 6 (September): 28–40.

Souriau, Paul. 1881. *Théorie de l'invention*. Paris: Hachette.

Spofford, Ainsworth Rand. 1900. "The Art of Reading." *A Book for all Readers*. Second edition. New York: Putnam's, pp. 171–189.

Steiner, George. 1971. *Extra-Territorial*. New York: Atheneum.

Sternberg, Robert J. and Todd I. Lubart. 1999. "The Concept of Creativity: Prospects and Paradigms." *Handbook of Creativity*. Ed. Robert J. Sternberg. Cambridge: Cambridge University Press, pp. 3–15.

Sternberg, Robert J. and Elena L. Grigorenko, eds. 2001. *Environmental Effects on Cognitive Abilities*. Mahwah: Erlbaum.

Stieg, Lewis F. 1978. "The Library and American Education: the Search for Theory in Academic Librarianship." *Library Trends* 27 (Winter): 353-365.

Stieg, Margaret F. 1992. *Change and Challenge in Library and Information Science Education*. Chicago: American Library Association.

Stokes, Geoffrey. 1998. *Popper. Philosophy, Politics and Scientific Method*. Cambridge: Polity Press.

Stokes, Roy. 1981. *Esdaile's Manual of Bibliography*. Fifth revised edition. Metuchen: Scarecrow Press.

Stubbs, Michael. 1980. *Language and Literacy. The Sociolinguistics of Reading and Writing*. London: Routledge & Kegan Paul.

Sykes, Paul. 1979. *The Public Library in Perspective. An Examination of its Origins and Modern Role*. London: Clive Bingley.

Symons, Donald. 1992. "On the Use and Misuse of Darwinism in the Study of Human Behavior." *The Adapted Mind. Evolutionary Psychology and the Generation of Culture*. Eds. Jerome H. Barkow, Leda Cosmides, and John Tooby. New York: Oxford University Press, pp. 137–162.

Szathmary, Eörs and John Maynard Smith. 1995. "The Major Evolutionary Transitions." *Nature* 374 (16 March): 227–232.

Tattersall, Ian. 2007. "How Did Modern Human Cognition Evolve?" *Consciousness and Cognition. Fragments of Mind and Brain*. Eds. Henri Cohen and Brigitte Stemmer. London: Academic Press, pp. 3–17.

Tedd, Lucy A. and Andrew Large. 2005. *Digital Libraries: Principles and Practice in a Global Environment*. Munich: Saur.

Thagard, Paul. 1992. *Conceptual Revolutions*. Princeton: Princeton University Press.

Thompson, C. Seymour. 1931. "Do We Want a Library Science?" *Library Journal* 56 (July): 581–587.

Thompson, Evan. 2007. *Mind in Life. Biology, Phenomenology, and the Sciences of Mind.* Cambridge: Harvard University Press.

Thompson, James. 1974. *Library Power: A New Philosophy of Librarianship.* London: Clive Bingley.

Thompson, James. 1977. *A History of the Principles of Librarianship.* London: Clive Bingley.

Thompson, William R. 1958. "Social Behavior." *Behavior and Evolution.* Eds. Anne Roe and George Gaylord Simpson. New Haven: Yale University Press, pp. 291–310.

Tolman, Edward C. 1932. *Purposive Behavior in Animals and Man.* New York: Appleton Century.

Tooby, John and Leda Cosmides. 1992. "The Psychological Foundations of Culture." *The Adapted Mind. Evolutionary Psychology and the Generation of Culture.* New York: Oxford University Press, pp. 19–136.

Tomasello, Michael. 1999. *The Cultural Origins of Human Cognition.* Cambridge: Harvard University Press.

Toulmin, Stephen. 1961. *Foresight and Understanding. An Enquiry into the Aims of Science.* Bloomington: Indiana University Press.

Toulmin, Stephen. 1972. *Human Understanding.* Princeton: Princeton University Press, vol 1.

Toulmin, Stephen. 1953. *The Philosophy of Science.* London: Hutchinson House.

Tuan, Yi-fu. 1989. *Morality and Imagination. Paradoxes of Progress.* Madison: University of Wisconsin Press.

Tuomela, Raimo. 2002. *The Philosophy of Social Practices. A Collective Acceptance View.* Cambridge: Cambridge University Press.

Tylor, Edward B. 1871. *Primitive Culture: Researches into the Development of Mythology, Philosophy, Religion, Art, and Custom.* 2 vols. London: Murray.

Valsiner, Jaan and René Van der Veer. 2000. *The Social Mind. Construction of the Idea.* Cambridge: Cambridge University Press.

Van Doren, Charles. 1991. *A History of Knowledge. Past, Present, and Future.* New York: Carol Publishing.

Van Doren, Charles. 1967. *The Idea of Progress.* New York: Praeger.

Vigotsky, Lev Semenovich. 1978. *Mind in Society: the Development of Higher Psychological Processes.* Cambridge: Harvard University Press.

Vigotsky, Lev Semenovich. 1962. *Thought and Language.* Cambridge: MIT Press. (Original Russian 1934)

Violi, Patrizia. 2001. *Meaning and Experience.* Bloomington: Indiana University Press. (Original Italian 1997)

Waddington, Conrad Hal. 1961. "The Human Animal." *The Humanist Frame.* Ed. Julian Huxley. New York: Harper, pp. 67–80.

Wallis, Wilson D. 1930. *Culture and Progress.* New York: Whittlesey House.

Waples, Douglas, Bernard Berelson, and Franklyn R. Bradshaw. 1940. *What Reading Does to People.* Chicago: University of Chicago Press.

Wartofski, Marx W. 1968. *Conceptual Foundations of Scientific Thought.* New York: Macmillan.

Washburn, Sherwood L. and Virginia Avis. 1958. "Evolution of Human Behavior." *Behavior and Evolution.* Eds. Anne Roe and George Gaylord Simpson. New Haven: Yale University Press, pp. 421–436.

Weber, Max. 1947. *The Theory of Social and Economic Organization*. New York: Oxford University Press.

Weiner, Norbert. 1950. *The Human Use of Human Beings*. Boston: Houghton Mifflin.

Weisberg, Robert W. 1993. *Creativity. Beyond the Myth of Genius*. New York: W. H. Freeman.

Wellard, James H. 1940. *The Public Library Comes of Age*. London: Grafton.

White, Carl M. 1964. *Bases of Modern Librarianship*. New York: Macmillan.

White, Leslie A. 1968. "Culturology." *International Encyclopedia of the Social Sciences*. Ed. David L. Sills. New York: Macmillan, 1968–1979, vol. 3, pp. 547–551.

White, Leslie A. 1973. *The Concept of Culture*. Minneapolis: Burgess.

White, Leslie A. 1975. *The Concept of Cultural Systems*. New York: Columbia University Press.

White, Leslie A. 1959. *The Evolution of Culture*. New York: McGraw-Hill.

White, Leslie A. 1949. *The Science of Culture*. New York: Farrar, Straus.

Whiteman, Philip. 1986. "Lionel McColvin: Librarian and Library Philosopher." *Public Libraries since 1945*. London: Clive Bingley, pp. 1–7.

Whorf, Benjamin Lee. 1956. *Language, Thought, and Reality. Selected Writing of Benjamin Lee Whorf*. Ed. John B. Carroll. Cambridge: MIT Press.

Wiegand, Wayne A. 1988. "The Role of the Library in American History." *Bowker Annual* 33: 69–75.

Wiegand, Wayne A. 2003. "Broadening Our Perspectives." *Library Quarterly* 73: v–x.

Wiesner, Jerome B. 1964. "Technology and Society." *Science as a Cultural Force*. Ed. Harry Woolf. Baltimore: Johns Hopkins Press.

Williams, Patrick. 1988. *The American Public Library and the Problem of Purpose*. New York: Greenwood.

Williams, Raymond. 1958. *Culture and Society, 1780–1950*. London: Chatto and Windus.

Williams, Raymond. 1981. *Contact: Human Communication and Its History*. London: Thames and Hudson.

Williams, Robert V. 1984. "Theoretical Issues and Constructs Underlying the Study of Library Development." *Libri* 34: 1–16.

Willison, I. R. 1980. *On the History of Libraries and Scholarship*. A Paper Presented before the Library History Round Table of the American Library Association. Washington, D.C.: Library of Congress.

Wilson, Edward O. 1998. *Consilience. The Unity of Knowledge*. New York: Knopf.

Wilson, Edward O. 1978. *On Human Nature*. Cambridge: Harvard University Press.

Wilson, Edward O. 1975. *Sociobiology: The New Synthesis*. Cambridge: Harvard University Press.

Wilson, John. 1971. *Thinking with Concepts*. Cambridge: Cambridge University Press.

Wohlwill, Joachim F. 1970. "The Emerging Discipline of Environmental Psychology." *American Psychologist* 25 (April): 303–312.

Wolpert, Lewis. 1993. *The Unnatural Nature of Science*. Cambridge: Harvard University Press.

Wright, H. Curtis. 1982. "An Interdisciplinary Philosophy of Librarianship." *Annual Conference of the Society of Educators and Scholars*. Union, N.J.: Sept. 29–Oct. 2. (ERIC ED 227 864)

Wright, H. Curtis. 1979. "The Wrong Way to Go." *Journal of the American Society for Information Science* 30: 67–76.

Wright, H. Curtis. 1976. "The Immateriality of Information." *Journal of Library History* 11: 297–315.

Wright, H. Curtis. 1977. *The Oral Antecedents of Greek Librarianship*. Provo: Brigham Young University Press.

Wright, John K. 1947. "Terrae Incognitae: The Place of the Imagination in Geography." *Annals of the Association of American Geographers* 37 (March): 1–15.

Zandonade, Tarcisio. 2004. "Social Epistemology from Jesse Shera to Steve Fuller." *Library Trends* 52 (Spring): 810-832.

Zelinsky, Wilbur. 2001. "The World and Its Identity Crisis." *Textures of Place. Exploring Humanist Geographies*. Eds. P. C. Adams, S. Hoelscher, and K. E. Till. Minneapolis: University of Minnesota Press, pp. 129–149.

Ziff, Paul. 1960. *Semantic Analysis*. Ithaca: Cornell University Press.

Ziff, Paul. 1972. *Understanding Understanding*. Ithaca: Cornell University Press.

Ziman, John. 2002. "Introduction: Selectionist Reasoning as a Tool of Thought." *The Evolution of Cultural Entities*. Eds. Michael Wheeler, John Ziman, and Margaret A. Boden. Oxford: Oxford University Press, pp. 1–8.

Ziman, John. 1968. *Public Knowledge. An Essay Concerning the Social Dimension of Science*. Cambridge: Cambridge University Press.

Ziman, John. 2000. *Real Science. What It Is and What It Means*. Cambridge: Cambridge University Press.

Ziman, John. 1978. *Reliable Knowledge. An Exploration of the Grounds for Belief in Science*. Cambridge: Cambridge University Press.

Zins, Chaim. 2006. "Redefining Information Science: from 'Information Science' to 'Knowledge Science'" *Journal of Documentation* 62: 447–461.

Zwadlo, Jim. 1997. "We Don't Need A Philosophy of Library and Information Science—We're Confused Enough Already." *Library Quarterly* 67: 103–121.

Index

About the Author

CHARLES B. OSBURN is Dean and Professor Emeritus, University Libraries, University of Alabama, and since retirement is adjunct professor in the School of Library and Information Studies.

Recent Titles in the
Beta Phi Mu Monograph Series

"An Active Instrument for Propaganda": The American Library During World War I
Wayne A. Wiegand

Libraries and Scholarly Communication in the United States: The Historical Dimension
Phyllis Dain and John Y. Cole, editors

Carnegie Denied: Communities Rejecting Carnegie Library Construction Grants, 1898–1925
Robert Sidney Martin, editor

Publishing and Readership in Revolutionary France and America: A Symposium at the Library of Congress, Sponsored by the Center for the Book and the European Division
Carol Armbruster, editor

Daring to Find Our Names: The Search for Lesbigay Library History
James V. Carmichael, Jr., editor

American Libraries before 1876
Haynes McMullen

Defining Print Culture for Youth: The Cultural Work of Children's Literature
Anne Lundin and Wayne A. Wiegand, editors

Self-Examination: The Present and Future of Librianship
John M. Budd

Renewing Professional Librarianship: A Fundamental Rethinking
Bill Crowley